MW01127657

THE POLITICS OF
WORLD FEDERATION

THE POLITICS OF WORLD FEDERATION

UNITED NATIONS, UN REFORM,
ATOMIC CONTROL

JOSEPH PRESTON BARATTA

Westport, Connecticut
London

Library of Congress Cataloging-in-Publication Data

Baratta, Joseph Preston.
 The politics of world federation / Joseph Preston Baratta.
   p. cm.
 Includes bibliographical references and index.
 Contents: v. 1. United Nations, UN reform, atomic control—v. 2. From world
federalism to global governance.
 ISBN 0–275–98066–9 (set: alk. paper)—0–275–98067–7 (v. 1: alk. paper)—
0–275–98068–5 (v. 2: alk. paper)
   1. International organization.   I. Title.
 JZ5566.B37 2004
 341.2—dc21   2003046304

British Library Cataloguing in Publication Data is available.

Copyright © 2004 by Joseph Preston Baratta

All rights reserved. No portion of this book may be
reproduced, by any process or technique, without the
express written consent of the publisher.

Library of Congress Catalog Card Number: 2003046304
ISBN: 0–275–98066–9 (Set)
       0–275–98067–7 [Vol. I]
       0–275–98068–5 [Vol. II]

First published in 2004

Praeger Publishers, 88 Post Road West, Westport, CT 06881
An imprint of Greenwood Publishing Group, Inc.
www.praeger.com

Printed in the United States of America

The paper used in this book complies with the
Permanent Paper Standard issued by the National
Information Standards Organization (Z39.48–1984).

10 9 8 7 6 5 4 3 2 1

Copyright Acknowledgments

The author and publisher gratefully acknowledge use excerpts from:
Imagine. Words and Music by John Lennon. © 1971 (Renewed 1999)
LENONO.MUSIC. All rights controlled and administered by EMI BLACKWOOD
MUSIC INC. All rights reserved. International copyright secured. Used by
permission.
The People, Yes, by Carl Sandburg, copyright 1936 by Harcourt, Inc. and renewed
1964 by Carl Sandburg, reprinted by permission of the publisher.

In memory of my sister,
Mary Florence Baratta (1944–1978),
educator, environmentalist, friend

Epigraph

There are a great many more believers in the one-world ideal in the West to-day than there were Bolsheviks in Russia at the time of the October [1917] revolution, or Christians in the Roman empire at the time of Constantine's conversion. Something holds them back. Is it the Mid-Western isolationists in the United States? The surviving nationalism of Europe? Stalin? The iron curtain? Then what about the darkness of the pre-revolutionary Russian *muzjik*, what about Nero, what about the lions?

Clearly, what holds us back, what prevents our idealisms from being effective, is that we do not have the personalities of Bolsheviks or of early Christians. ... The trouble is that we do not believe in soul-force in the modern West. Instead we believe in the magic power of ideas, which is considerably less scientific than believing in soul–force.... We believe it is leadership to tell other nations that we will disarm if they do, that we will stop calling names if they stop, that if all other nations want to do away with the veto they will not find us blocking the way. We believe that we can order one world by mail and have it come wrapped in cellophane.

That is why our peace personalities are less developed than our intellects, or our war personalities. That is why we cannot convert a Soviet commissar and why we find it so difficult to convert a Kansas farmer. That is why reason and right seem so unavailing against the powers of darkness.

—Edmund Taylor, 1947
Richer by Asia (1947), pp. 408, 417, 418.
Common Cause, 4 (August 1950).

Contents

Vol. 1:

The United Nations, U.N. Reform, Atomic Control

Contents

Vol. 2:

From World Federalism to Global Governance

Preface

When I was a young man, I volunteered to serve a tour of duty in the U.S. Marine Corps. During recruit training, an old gunnery sergeant explained to about 500 of us in a vast hall: "The purpose of a battle is to reach a *decision.*" This truth has troubled me to the present. We were trained to charge into machine gun fire—that was how the marines took Mount Suribachi on Iwo Jima. Surely, I thought, there must be a more rational way to reach a decision. During the prolonged tail end of the Vietnam War, when I was so fortunate as to be able to get a classical education at St. John's College, I came upon *A Constitution for the World,* the reprint edition by the Center for the Study of Democratic Institutions of the Chicago Committee's *Preliminary Draft of a World Constitution.* It suddenly dawned upon me that the reason why there are wars is that humanity has no government of the earth that could establish and enforce the rule of law. I discovered that there had been, in the 1940s, a rather popular political movement to remedy this very defect. I wondered, Was not world federalism the fundamental alternative to the containment policy? Was it not something for Americans to be *for,* in place of anti-communism?

This book began as a doctoral dissertation at Boston University over 20 years ago. Thanks go to the history faculty there, notably John Armstrong, Sidney Burrell, William Newman, and Arnold Offner, who first taught me the techniques of history. When I began, in the late 1970s, "world history" was not thought quite a proper study, and "U.N. reform" was a taboo term in the international community. Nevertheless, I pursued what on the face of it was a great and timely subject—the history of what has actually been attempted to politically unite the human race in order to establish the rule of world law and thus to abolish war. I collected material while working as director of the New York office of one of the nongovernmental organizations (NGOs) accredited to the U.N. (the World Association of World Federalists), and then brought the story up to date while trying to "strengthen the U.N." by building public support for it deep within one of its principal member states, the United States (through the Coalition for a Strong U.N., which hosted public conferences on U.N. issues at the Kennedy Library in Boston). I now teach world history, international relations, English history, and history of math and science at Worcester State College in central Massachusetts.

When a young scholar dares to enter a little worked field and undertakes to make an original contribution to knowledge, a little understanding and encouragement by older, more experienced people can be of immense help. Just a kind word or two every year can keep one going. I am deeply grateful to all those I have interviewed, as can be seen in Appendix E, especially, in the beginning, Louis B. Sohn, Elisabeth Mann Borgese, Richard A. Falk, Stewart Ogilvy, and Edith Wynner, and, later, Warren Kuehl, Saul Mendlovitz, Dr. Campbell Moses, Maurice Bertrand, Winston Langley, Gary Ostrower, Lawrence Wittner, Charles Chatfield, and Ralph Levering. I am honored to have interviewed so many surviving members of the old movement, but I have deliberately kept my distance in order to preserve my intellectual integrity. No one else is responsible for my historical judgments in this book.

Thanks, too, go to every reference librarian, as at the collections listed in Appendix D. They are among the most resourceful and generous of all professionals, like assistant professors. I cannot omit appreciation to the inventors of the Macintosh computer and the designers of ClarisWorks—what a dream is its handling of footnotes! In this book, we print them at the foot of every page, where the reader who wishes to check a fact can do so at a glance. I also am grateful to my late parents, good people who survived the Depression and the Second World War; they understood my project. And fulfilling an old promise to myself, I dedicate this book to the memory of my sister, Mary. I have missed her while researching and writing this book.

—Joseph Preston Baratta

Foreword

In December of 2000 as the books were closing on the Clinton administration, Samuel R. Berger, assistant to the president for national security affairs, in an article, "A Sovereign Policy for the Global Age," offered this opinion of the road ahead: "More tasks remain—from supporting new democracies to fighting international terrorism to reinventing the United Nations" *(Foreign Affairs, November/December 2000, Volume 79, Number 6).*

One of the principal questions surrounding the consequences of the inexorable tide of globalization is, How can the Charter of the United Nations, signed by 51 Nations almost six decades ago, fulfill its noble mandate of saving succeeding generations from the scourge of war? As Berger and many others have pointed out, the watershed event of the past decade, the end of the Cold War, with the implosion of the Soviet Union, presented the world with an incredible opportunity. The U.N., once immobilized by the threat of a Soviet veto in the Security Council, could hopefully be reconfigured in the new post Cold War era to take effective action on matters of international peace and security and help achieve the goals of the U.N.'s founders.

However, a new design for that kind of international order was not achieved, and precious time and momentum for change were lost as the Clinton administration was forced to spend most of its time trying to persuade a recalcitrant Congress to pay our delinquent dues to the world body before the invocation of Article 19 of the Charter deprived us of our vote in the General Assembly. Regrettably the advent of a new administration in 2001 has, as this foreword is being written, made it abundantly clear with its unilateral approach to world affairs that, although it favors payment on an annual basis of our U.N. dues, it does not view the world body as an institution with the capability of giving us either now or in the future world peace through world law.

My predecessor as president of the World Federalist Association was the late

Norman Cousins, former editor of the *Saturday Review of Books* and a co-founder of Americans United for World Government. It ultimately became the World Federalist Association, which from its inception was based on the fundamental premise that world peace could only be attained under world law which required the transformation of the United Nations, a membership organization of nation states, into a democratic world federation.

A few years ago when we celebrated the 50th anniversary of the U.N., it was my privilege to engage in a debate of sorts with Richard Armitage, a former U.S. ambassador and an assistant secretary of defense for international security affairs under President Ronald Reagan, and more recently undersecretary of state in the administration of President George W. Bush. His position was that in the 50th year of its existence the U.N. was an institution that had "run amok in terms of its Charter." He also opined that it had been formed simply as a "coalition of nations" who came together on the basis of "great power governance in an effort to prevent a third conflagration." Hence, "We should either bring the United Nations organization back to its roots or create a new membership reflecting the intent of the Charter and the vision of the founders."

My response to Mr. Armitage both then and now is that there must be a redefinition of security in a way that recognizes a simple truth: That we are interdependent on a planet that will perish, whether we are talking about the environment, violations of human rights, or peace and security. These are transnational problems that have to be within the jurisdiction of a revived, reformed, and restructured United Nations. That new structural framework must be based on a new organizing principle. Whereas he looked upon the United Nations as a mere coalition of nations united by a triumph over fascism in World War II whose organizing principle was "great power governance," I made the argument for something quite different—namely, a democratic world federation which would function as a system of governance based in the enactment, interpretation and enforcement of world law. My view in that regard followed the language of House Concurrent Resolution 64 introduced in 1949 with 111 co-sponsors, more than one quarter of the total membership of the U.S. House of Representatives. It read in part: "It is the sense of Congress that it should be a fundamental objective of the foreign policy of the United states to support and strengthen the United Nations and to seek its development into a world federation open to all nations with definite and limited powers adequate to preserve peace and prevent aggression through the enactment, interpretation and enforcement of world law."

Tragically, from the perspective of those of us who are world federalists, that expression of political will in favor of a United Nations with the capabilities described represents the apogee of what was then and now a truly new organizing principle for a world body designed to carry out far more than great power governance. The politics of global governance was very shortly submerged under the sweeping tides of the Cold War.

However, undeterred and undiscouraged the work of promoting the vision of a democratic, empowered U.N. system still continues.

As I write these words in the early spring of 2003, the crisis of superpower politics of the Cold War has been replaced by the second crisis in little more than a decade in the Persian Gulf, followed by the effort to disarm Iraq and free the world of the threat of the possession of weapons of mass destruction by the Iraqi dictator, Saddam Hussein. The United Nations Security Council has served as principal forum in which efforts to arrive at a solution to that problem has taken place. I perhaps may be on the side of wishful thinking and unrestrained optimism. Nevertheless, I believe that in however perverse a manner that historic intervention has served to refocus the attention of the entire world on the importance of having an effective and empowered world body as the site for decision–making in matters of war and peace. I believe that it can have enormous and positive consequences for the further evolution and eventual transformation of the present U.N. into a democratic world federation.

It is in the context of these ongoing developments in international affairs that Joseph Baratta's work on *The Politics of World Federalism* has newly arrived. It is not only enormously useful as an historical approach to the efforts to reach the goal of a world where world law has replaced the use of warfare as a means of maintaining peace and stability. His explanation of the role of politics in laying the necessary foundation for such a revolutionary transformation in both thought and action helps to close the gap between vision and reality that so often pervades discussions in this area of human affairs.

As the head of a non-governmental organization which has been in existence during most of the period that furnishes the material for the author's research, I am most impressed by his selection of materials that are relevant to his search for the truth about world government. He successfully challenges the notion that a mere aggregation in whatever form of purely sovereign nation states should be the limits of our horizon in the continuing search for peace and justice. World peace through world law should be our ultimate political goal. His book, I believe and more than that—hope and pray—brings us another step farther along the road toward that goal.

—John Anderson
Independent Candidate for U.S. President in 1980
(Winner of 5,719,437 votes—6.6% of electorate)

Introduction to Both Volumes

Truth passes through three stages: first, it is condemned, then it
briefly triumphs, and finally it ends as platitude.

—Arthur Schopenhauer, *The World as Will and Idea,*
Foreword to the First Edition (1818), p. xv

Summary Overview

This book is a history of the practical, political efforts to establish a constitutionally limited, democratically representative, federal world government in order to effectively abolish war. Historically, during the coming, waging, and aftermath of World War II, a number of people in and out of government in America and in the eventually 51 allied countries in the wartime "United Nations"
urged that the failed League of Nations not be simply revived, even with U.S.
membership, but be transformed into the beginnings of a representative world
government. In principle, they argued that the moment had come to guide international organization through a transition like that when the United States under
the Articles of Confederation (1781) passed to a more perfect union under the
federal Constitution (1787). Europeans, too, looked to federation as an end to
endemic wars, and in time the European Union would be the practical realization
of such dreams.

The basic idea is to do effectively for the world what has been painfully, but
proudly, done for well organized national states—establish peace under the rule
of law. Real liberty, as Immanuel Kant argued, exists only by obedience to law.
The consent of the governed for the enactment of that law is the basis of democratic states. But the new United Nations Organization (1945) remained in principle a confederation of states, so world federalists then aimed to reform it into a
representative federation of states and peoples.

The closest the United States has ever come to support for a world federation
was in the State Department during deliberations about the shape of the U.N. organization in 1942–43, and again, after first use of atomic bombs on Hiroshima
and Nagasaki, during negotiations over the Baruch plan for the international control of atomic energy in 1946. There were hearings on world federation in Congress in 1948–50, but amity among the victorious allies of World War II could

not be maintained, and the Cold War emerged as the reality of international life for 40 years.

In Europe, practical thought focused more on a regional union, though many recognized that world peace ultimately would require a union of all regions. The European Community (1951) and the European Union, established by the Maastricht Treaty (1992) and at time of writing a European Constitution (2003), are the most familiar examples of the practical federation of modern states. In Europe, powers to regulate commerce (common management of coal and steel industries, a common market, and now a common currency—the *euro)* have been vested in the central institutions, while powers to provide for the common defense and foreign policy have still been retained by the states or their peoples.

In national life, history shows many instances of the choice of federation as a form of government to create unity while preserving diversity, starting with the United States of America in 1787. Other federations include Canada, Mexico, Brazil, Switzerland, Germany, Nigeria, and Russia (30 historic federations to date). Unitary states like Britain, France, Italy, Spain, India, and even China have experienced devolution or decentralization recently in various degrees.

Very novel political institutions at regional and world levels are evolving at the beginning of the 21st century. The United Nations, in its basic brochures, defines itself as "not a world government," yet treaties on human rights (25 of which are currently binding), peacekeeping operations using national military forces, and treaties and protocols on the environment show the way to the future. The unity slowly being forged out of diversity in the future will probably be as novel in comparison to the historic national federations as the federations were to the confederations and monarchies that preceded them.

One World was the title of a book by Wendell Willkie, the Republican challenger in 1940, whom President Franklin D. Roosevelt sent around the world on a goodwill mission in the midst of World War II. "One World" gave a name to the aspirations of a generation of internationalists. Originally, the book before you was entitled, "What Happened to One World?" The short answer is that the ideal of a united, peaceful world is resurfacing in the public mind even while it remains utopian to scholars aligned with current trends in policy.

This book is properly entitled *The Politics of World Federation* because its whole burden is to treat world federation not merely as an ideal, nor as a proposal for the leaders of sovereign states to act upon, but as a popular movement, reflective of the general will, in the tradition of democratic politics. We begin to abandon the distinction between domestic politics (elections and the enactment of the laws) and world politics (relations between sovereign states that acknowledge no higher law). We remember that in all democratic theory (liberal and socialist) the *people* are sovereign. The view here, like that of Grenville Clark and the organizers of United World Federalists, is that until world federation becomes a matter for domestic politics, it will remain an idle dream. Hence, the climax of this book comes in the chapters on Henry Wallace, political action in the states, and the House and Senate hearings on world federalist bills in 1948, 1949, and

1950. The measure here of the movement is *influence*. The idea is treated as *practical policy* in the context, first, of the planning for the United Nations Organization in the midst of World War II, then, second, of the emerging containment policy at the start of the Cold War. Focus is on the *transition* and the formation, under public pressure, of an alternative foreign policy by the United States, allies, and adversaries. The hope is that the book will serve, not for easy imitation in the future, but as a reminder that greater things are possible than the current drift of policy.

Prominent World Federalists

The idea of creating a political union of states and peoples in order to abolish war may be traced back for centuries—back to Woodrow Wilson, Peter Kropotkin, Jeremy Bentham, Immanuel Kant, l'abbé de Saint–Pierre, William Penn, Henry IV, le duc de Sully, and even Dante—but until the collapse of the League of Nations in the 1930s most such proposals of international union were not strictly federalist. Kant, for instance, proposed only a *confederation* of free and independent states. The League of Nations (and its successor the United Nations) was the great realization of the dreams of a confederal system of nation states; for all its limitations, it was a triumph in the slow and painful progress of international law.

By 1939, however, as the League collapsed, bolder spirits began to call for establishment of a true world federal government, by delegation of sovereign powers at least for the maintenance of peace and security. They are the principal subjects of this book. They included Clarence Streit, author of the book that practically conjured up the movement, *Union Now*. Another was Tom Otto Griessemer, German émigré from Hitler's Reich, who edited *World Government News*. Griessemer, educator Vernon Nash, and advertising executive Mildred Riorden Blake founded World Federalists in New York in 1941. The Wall Street lawyer and "statesman incognito" behind the Wilson and Roosevelt administrations, Grenville Clark, had some influence when the times were auspicious, and later he and Harvard international lawyer Louis B. Sohn wrote one of the classics of the movement, *World Peace through World Law*.[1] U.S. Supreme Court Justice Owen J. Roberts retired from the Court in 1945 in order to publicly advocate Atlantic union as a stage to world union; he cooperated with both Streit and Clark. The world-renowned physicist and another émigré from Hitler's Germany Albert Einstein was an eloquent proponent of the idea. Atomic scientists Leo Szilard and J. Robert Oppenheimer supported it, too. The essayist, E. B. White, wrote a rare book of good humor about world government, *The Wild Flag*.[2] Chancellor Robert M. Hutchins at the University of Chicago and his dynamic professor of European literature Giuseppe Antonio Borgese led the Committee to Frame a World Constitution, which produced another classic, *The Preliminary*

---

[1] Grenville Clark and Louis B. Sohn, *World Peace through World Law* (Cambridge, MA: Harvard University Press, 1958; 2nd ed., 1960; 3rd, 1966).

[2] E. B. White, *The Wild Flag* (Boston: Houghton Mifflin, 1946).

Draft of a World Constitution.[3] His wife Elizabeth Mann Borgese (daughter of Thomas Mann) became a leader of the World Movement and later organized the *Pacem in Maribus* conferences on the Law of the Sea.

In the organized American movement, cofounder of Americans United for World Government, Thomas K. Finletter, was President Truman's secretary of the air force. Another cofounder of Americans United was influential editor of the *Saturday Review of Books* Norman Cousins. The only substantial money to come into the movement—$1 million from McCormick reaper heiress Anita McCormick Blaine—funded the Foundation for World Government, which was managed by Stringfellow Barr, former president of St. John's College, where the classics had been reintroduced in 1937. Among the University of Chicago group, the great books, which belong to no one nation, were read in that "great conversation," as Mortimer Adler put it, of man as a rational being. Barr used to say, "To flourish, liberal education must be universal.... Only a reign of law between nations will permit any government to concern itself seriously with the liberal education of its citizens."[4] Why the foundation failed is an instructive tale. The founder of Student Federalists was Harris Wofford, who would later serve the Kennedy administration as a regional director of the Peace Corps; he became briefly a U.S. senator from Pennsylvania. Wounded army veteran Remfer Lee ("Jack") Whitehouse, with veterans David McCoy and Paul Sauer, founded the most radical student and veterans' group at Northwestern University, in which briefly the flame of future world political union burned brightly. The "World Republic Boys," as they were called by admiring, but doubtful, adults, had just enough spunk to pressure Americans United and World Federalists to merge into United World Federalists (UWF) by February 1947. UWF's second president (1949–52) was Alan Cranston, later a U.S. senator from California (1969–93).

Outside the United States, world federalists included Lord Lothian (till 1930 Philip Kerr), who wrote another classic, *Pacifism Is Not Enough,*[5] before he became ambassador to the United States in 1939–40. Lothian was one of several English federalists, including Lionel Curtis, who had labored to transform the British Empire into an imperial federation as the nucleus of a world federation. Others followed them on European and world federation, including Sir William Beveridge, Lionel Robbins (later Lord Robbins), John Boyd Orr (later Lord Boyd–Orr), and Arnold Toynbee, the creative world historian. Prime Minister Winston Churchill made an actual offer, not often remembered, of British union with France on 16 June 1940; Toynbee was coauthor of this proposal. Then,

---

[3] Committee to Frame a World Constitution; Robert M. Hutchins, president; G. A. Borgese, secretary; "Preliminary Draft of a World Constitution," *Common Cause,* 1 (March 1948), 1–40. Reprinted as *A Constitution for the World* by the Center for the Study of Democratic Institutions, Santa Barbara, CA, 1965.

[4] Stringfellow Barr, "Education: For Nations or Human Beings," *Common Cause,* 1 (September 1947): 83.

[5] [Philip Kerr,] "The End of War," *The Round Table,* 5, 20 (September 1915): 772–96; Lord Lothian, *Pacifism Is Not Enough,* 219–63.

beginning with his speech at Zurich in September 1946, Churchill daringly proposed Franco–German reconciliation, which culminated with plans for the confederal Council of Europe in 1948. British member of Parliament Henry Usborne, elected to Clement Attlee's government in 1945, led a campaign to bring about a constitutional convention by unofficial popular elections, known as the peoples' convention. He was supported by Hungarian pacifist Rosika Schwimmer (moving spirit behind the Henry Ford Peace Ship in 1915), Edith Wynner, and Georgia Lloyd.

Jean Monnet, the French banker, was inspired by Churchill's offer and guided the process of creating the more federal European Community. Italy's Altiero Spinelli, who was impressed by the British federalists, deeply served European union; in 1984 as an elected member of the European Parliament, he chaired the group that produced the *Draft Treaty Establishing the European Union.*[6] That treaty, though not ratified, yet leading to the Council of Ministers' Single European Act of 1986 and the Maastricht treaty of 1992, which avoided early federation, was certainly the most significant recent draft constitution for the practical federation of modern states. At time of writing, still another constitution for the European Union has been drafted under the chairmanship of former French President Valéry Giscard d'Estaing, designed to incorporate another ten members into the Union (for a total of 25) by 2004. Pope John XXIII's encyclical, *Pacem in Terris* (1963), similarly maintained high principle in the depths of the Cold War with its profound argument for a "public authority ... on a world–wide basis."

In India, M. K. (Mahatma) Gandhi once said that world federation could be based only on a foundation of nonviolence. Later, India's first prime minister Jawaharlal Nehru echoed these views when approached by world federalists but shifted course toward nonalignment. In Japan, Morikatsu Inagaki was a leader by 1948, soon joined by the atomic scientist Hideki Yukawa. The World Movement for World Federal Government in 1950 consisted of 73 organizations within 22 countries, with a total individual membership of 151,000.[7] (The American UWF had a peak membership in 1949 of 47,000.) In a survey of the literature worldwide, *Strengthening the United Nations,* we have found substantial works from 72 nations and five intergovernmental organizations on systemic U.N. reform and world federalism. Outside of the United States, Canada, and Western Europe, the next most fertile countries for federalist thinking were, in this order:, India, Japan, Mexico, and so on down to Paraguay, Tunisia, and Zaire.[8] It has not been an "American" movement. Since the 1940s, prominent leaders have

---

[6] European Parliament, *Draft Treaty Establishing the European Union,* 14 February 1984, Directorate–General for Information and Public Relations, P.O. Box 1601, L–2920 Luxembourg. The vote was 237 to 31, with 43 abstentions.

[7] Reply to Questionnaire from the United Nations on Non–Governmental Organizations, n.d. [post September 1950], Robert M. Hutchins Papers (A), Box 158.3, Regenstein Library, University of Chicago. Hereafter, Hutchins Papers.

[8] Joseph P. Baratta, *Strengthening the United Nations: A Bibliography on U.N. Reform and World Federalism* (Westport, CT: Greenwood Press, 1987). A draft update has been prepared.

been much more reticent about such an ideal, but, as the Cold War ended, Mikhail Gorbachev of the Soviet Union and Václav Havel of Czechoslovakia began to write and speak in large terms reminiscent of old pleas for world federation.[9]

In the American political context, declared world federalists included Henry Wallace, last of the New Dealers, who challenged Truman on the policy of getting tough with the Russians in the presidential election of 1948. Senator Glen Taylor (D., Idaho), Wallace's running mate, introduced the most radical world federalist resolution in the U.S. Congress. Representatives Walter H. Judd (R., Minnesota) and Brooks Hays (D., Arkansas) introduced several more modest resolutions, including HCR–59 of 1948, which called on the president to convene the "general review conference" provided for in the U.N. Charter's Article 109, and HCR–64 of 1949, which still more modestly declared the "sense of Congress" that the fundamental objective of U.S. foreign policy should be the development of the U.N. into a "world federation." HCR–64 was co-sponsored by 111 representatives, including John F. Kennedy, Christian Herter, Peter Rodino, and Jacob Javits. Even Richard Nixon, then a freshman representative, supported a comparable bill. In the Senate, a world federalist bill was supported by senators Hubert Humphrey, Wayne Morse, and Claude Pepper. Senator J. William Fulbright supported the Atlantic union resolution. Hearings were held in the House in 1948 and 1949, and in the Senate in 1950.

Definition of Terms

What do we mean by world federal government, and how would we place it into the array of contemporary approaches to peace? What is contemplated is much more than voluntary *cooperation,* which Jean Monnet, father of the European Community, disparaged as inadequate to the exigencies of the modern world. As he wrote to French prime minister Georges Bidault on the occasion of the signing of the convention of the organization to implement the Marshall plan:[10]

> Efforts by the various countries, in the present national frameworks, will not in my view be enough. Furthermore, the idea that sixteen sovereign nations will co-operate effectively is an illusion. I believe that only the establishment of a *federation* of the West, including Britain, will enable us to solve our problems quickly enough, and finally prevent war.

The United Nations, like the League before it, is also based on cooperation —in the Security Council on great power unanimity—but since the League failed to prevent World War II, and since the U.N., although it has endured over

---

[9] Mikhail S. Gorbachev, Address to the General Assembly of the United Nations, *General Assembly Official Records,* Plenary. 43rd sess., 7 December 1988. A/43/PV.72; Václav Havel, *The Art of the Impossible: Politics as Morality in Practice* (New York: Fromm International, 1994, 1997).

[10] Jean Monet, *Memoirs,* trans. Richard Mayne (Garden City, NY: Doubleday, 1978), 272.

twice as long, suffers from similar disabilities like national refusal to pay assessments under plausible excuses, many people have been attracted to federalism.

World federal government does not mean *confederation*. In American usage, contrasted, say, with Swiss or French, a "confederation" is the kind of union achieved by the United States during the Revolution under the Articles of Confederation (drafted in 1777, ratified by all the 13 states not till 1781). It was a "league of friendship" or association of sovereign states, requiring unanimity for common decisions affecting the army or foreign relations. Congress was a unicameral legislature, laws reached only to the states, the "president" was president of the Congress and not an independently elected executive of the laws, there was no supreme judiciary, and every state had a veto.

The confederation of states was so weak that, as is well known in American history, the Founding Fathers by 1787 had to assemble in Philadelphia to form "a more perfect union." This they did by drafting the federal Constitution, which, by delegations of powers from the states and the people, established an originally very limited national government over the states with powers to enact laws reaching both states and individuals. In effect, sovereignty, or the supreme power in the state, was divided between the states and the federal government. The people were made citizens of both a member state and the union. *Sovereignty* was understood as *popular* sovereignty, that is, in Thomas Jefferson's terms, as "the Right of the People ... to institute new Government, laying its foundation on such principles and organizing its Powers in such form, as to them shall seem most likely to effect their Safety and Happiness."

One can think of world federal government by analogy with the government of the United States under the Constitution, or, as people in Canada or Switzerland or the U.S.S.R. tended understandably to do, of any of the 30 other federal states that have been founded since 1787. Canada is a federation, as are Mexico, Brazil, Venezuela, and Argentina. In Europe, so are Switzerland, Germany, Austria, and Russia; in Africa, Nigeria; and in Asia, Pakistan, Malaysia, and Australia. Some eight other countries have been influenced by federalist experiments in their history, including South Africa, Burma, Ethiopia, People's Republic of China, United Arab Republic, and Cyprus. Several unitary states have been experiencing decentralization short of federation: Italy, Belgium, Spain, France, and Great Britain. There have also been eight attempts at federation that failed, including most spectacularly the U.S.S.R., Czechoslovakia, and Yugoslavia, but also, tellingly, the United Provinces of Central America, Gran Colombia, the West Indies Federation, and the Mali Federation. For a complete list, with dates, see Appendix B.

The essence of the change from confederation to federation was abandonment of the fundamental flaw, found in the Articles of Confederation as in the U.N. Charter, of attempting to legislate for states or governments in their collective capacities, as distinguished from the individuals inhabiting the states, as Alexander Hamilton argued in *The Federalist*, No. 15. The idea is to establish the rule of law in place of the anarchy of states. Enforcement of the law would become a judicial matter within a civil society in place of threatened or actual military force among sovereigns. Hence, the level of violence necessary for the maintenance of order would be radically reduced.

Federation is also not a *unitary world state,* abolishing the nation states. Since the end of the Cold War, the term "world government," like "U.N. reform," has been creeping back into public consciousness, notably in fears of the new World Trade Organization or of the United Nations itself. But 99 writers out of 100 merely drop the term as if world government were a silver bullet to solve the problem of nationalism; a few, like evangelist Pat Robertson, treat the idea as a bogey for everything destructive of religion and diversity since the *Illuminati* of 1776.[11] But a unitary world state is a straw man. No historical figure known to us ever advocated the abolition of nation states and its replacement by a unitary world government, though some, like H. G. Wells and G. A. Borgese imagined so centralized a federal power that it would be much the same. All presume to save the liberties that the historic nation–states have so painfully won.

World federation has actually been proposed to *preserve* the national states, just as the United States preserved Massachusetts, Virginia, and the others; it is the strongest form of union consistent with preservation of the states. "Unity and diversity," the first motto of United World Federalists, has been the watchword. The states will be vital to a world federation as subordinate authorities more knowledgeable of local (national) conditions and hence more fit for legislation affecting every unique people. A unitary world state is another name for a world empire established by force—the very opposite of what World Federalists and their successors aimed at. Nevertheless, it is true that most federations tend over time toward unitary states, so every constitutional safeguard and eternal vigilance will remain necessary to preserve liberty.

World federal government is not undemocratic. A federation of the world could hardly be undertaken except on a democratic basis, but the powers to enact law reaching to individuals could be constitutionally limited to the most common concerns (like security and, next, regulation of trade), which would avoid radical redistribution of income from the global North to the South, though it should provide new means to begin to close global economic inequalities. Clarence Streit was the most vigorous proponent of proceeding only on the basis of *liberal democracy;* hence, he advocated a union of the Atlantic democracies, to which maximal powers could be granted, pending expansion to a world democracy.

After first use of atomic bombs in war, when the World War II alliance with the Soviet Union broke up, world federalists, on the other hand, felt that the acceleration of history required a *world* union at least to control nuclear weapons even before all peoples were prepared to responsibly act as world citizens. The United Nations was also a universal organization, so the world federal government devised by the Hutchins committee or Clark and Sohn was, like the U.N.,

---

[11] Pat Robertson, *The New World Order* (Dallas: Word Publishing, 1991).

shrewdly designed with minimal powers to accommodate the "people's democracies" as well as authoritarian states. The key point was to establish a common security system in place of all the competitive national defense establishments, so that preparations for war and the posture of war could be safely abandoned, thus providing resources for peaceful competition.

But the Cold War was fought on just this point of democracy. G. A. Borgese said the Cold War was a conflict about the nature of *justice,* on which the necessary world government of the future would be based. By the time it ended in 1990 (when President George H. W. Bush, at the signing of the Conventional Forces in Europe Treaty, said the words, "The Cold War is over") it was evident that humanity had made a great, inchoate decision that liberty was preferred to equality, capitalism to communism, markets to planned economy, liberal democracy to economic democracy. The Communist parties in the Soviet Union and East European Communist states, recognizing popular rejection, then voluntarily renounced their monopoly power. Streit was proved right, and Hutchins and Clark wrong, at least concerning universal membership. No future union of humanity is now conceivable except on a liberal democratic basis. The expansion of the international law of human rights, of which there are now some 95 instruments, 25 of which are binding treaties, is the advance agent of such democratic world union.[12] When the U.N. is made representative of peoples in at least a second chamber of the General Assembly, democracy will have arrived at the world level.

Revolution to Establish Politically the Brotherhood of Man

World federal government, therefore, is not an easy solution to the problem of war. It is in principle the same, familiar solution that has been achieved in every well organized state—namely, the monopolization of force by a single authority (in democracies by a representative legislature) that governs by law reaching the people. World federation plainly implies a revolutionary exercise of the sovereignty of the people, a new social contract comprehending the whole human race, the family of man. Harris Wofford, founder of Student Federalists, called it "man's greatest peaceful revolution, ... the revolution to establish politically the brotherhood of man."[13] To become a reality, the people of the world would have to establish a democratic, federal World Republic. Hence, the great difficulty is whether *world community* is sufficiently advanced to undertake the construction of a world republic. Are the people of the world "ready" for federal union?

By the end of World War II, a number of people in Europe and America judged that the problem of war and the world–wide spread of industry and democracy made so great an innovation in world affairs as the establishment of world federal government both *necessary* and *possible.* It is necessary to protect the

---

[12] United Nations, *Human Rights—Status of International Instruments* (New York: U.N., ST/HR/5, E.87.XIV.2, 1987); *Human Rights—Chart of Ratifications* (New York: U.N., ST/HR/4/–Rev.14, 30 June 1996).

[13] "Dead End: Federalism Limited," *Common Cause,* 1 (May 1948): 388.

people, to make a reality of collective security, and to solve global problems beyond the capacity of sovereign national states. It is possible because of the global expansion of Western industrialization, finance, and economic techniques, the spread of European forms of liberal and socialist democracy, the counterflow of non-Western cultural ideas from the postcolonial world, the shrinking of distances by modern transportation and communications, and, in short, the interdependence of civilized life today on the planet. The world is already one, federalists say; only law and politics lag behind.

This book is an examination of what they attempted and accomplished. European Union, which was conceived by the Resistance during the war, when it was seen as a stage toward world union, has had far more success to date—it has all but ended the history of war between Germany and France, with Britain playing the role of "balancer," even before full federation has been achieved—but the focus here is on the larger and more remote project of world union.

Another innovation with large implications is the recent establishment of the International Criminal Court. The institutions of the rule of effective and enforceable world law are still exceedingly rudimentary, but what is significant historically is the appearance of thousands of people who understood the project and were ready to assume the responsibilities and privileges of world citizens, ready to participate in the election of world legislators and to obey the new world laws. If the populations of even a few key countries were ready to start, it would not be difficult to draft a world constitution to incorporate them into a civil body politic. Today's responsible national leaders would suddenly realize there was a practical, fundamental alternative to the conduct of foreign policy.

We are looking at more than an idea: world federal government is a *project* and a *movement*. A movement of ideas and people is harder to trace and less dramatic than, say, a biography of Harry Truman or a history of a policy like containment or deterrence; but it is as real and just as important as the idea of government to James Madison or of a general association of nations to Woodrow Wilson. If the world ever passes through the transition to the Federation in Star Trek, people will be interested in the beginnings.[14] G. A. Borgese, the leading spirit of the University of Chicago's Committee to Frame a World Constitution, used to say that a constitution, like his committee's *Preliminary Draft,* was a *myth,* in the sense of a "proposal to history," for "a myth incorporates the faith and hope of its age, mediates between the ideal and the real, and calls the mind to action."[15] Similarly, the Constitution of the United States was a proposal to history, as was the Charter of the United Nations. What follows is a history of the progress of the myth of *a more perfect union* for the world.

In short, expressions that are synonymous with world federal government are "world union," "world republic," "world democracy," and "world federation." What is *not* meant is empire, unitary world state, alliance, league of sovereign states, or confederation. We will sometimes speak of federation in the context of

---

[14] Jill Sherwin, ed., *Quotable Star Trek* (New York: Pocket Books, 1999), 180–82.
[15] "To the Reader," *Common Cause,* 1 (March 1948): 327.

"international organization," for the latter can include a government of states and peoples, especially since the natural progression will be to reform the United Nations to include even one popularly representative legislative house and to limit the absolute veto in the Security Council. But it should be understood that we do not regard international organization as a final stage.

World federalists say that they, who wish to extend the rule of law, are the realists, while those who put their faith in a league of sovereign states or, worse, who suppose that peace can long be maintained by deterrence or competition in arms are the utopians.[16]

Delegations of Sovereignty

At first blush, most people cannot imagine that modern states and their peoples would ever delegate sovereign powers to a common, higher union. Yet some 36 states have declared their willingness to do just that, revealing that "sovereignty" is far less indivisible than theorists often maintain. For instance, shortly after World War II, the constitutions of France, Italy, and West Germany were expressly changed to permit limitations of sovereignty for their participation in a European federation (or, by legal implication, in a world federation); the constitution of Japan renounced war:

France

Preamble. On condition of reciprocity, France accepts the limitations of sovereignty necessary for the organization and defense of peace.

—Constitution of the Fourth Republic, 1946.

Art. 55. Treaties or agreements duly ratified and approved shall, upon their publication, have an authority superior to that of laws, subject, for each agreement or treaty, to its application by the other party.

—Constitution of the Fifth Republic, 4 October 1958.

Italy

Art. 11. Italy renounces war as an instrument of offense to the liberty of other peoples or as a means of settlement of international disputes, and, on conditions of equality with other states, agrees to the limitations of her sovereignty necessary to an organization which will ensure peace and justice among nations, and promotes and encourages international organizations constituted for this purpose.

—Constitution of 1 January 1948.

Germany

Art. 24. Entry into a collective security system:

(1). The [German] Federation may by legislation transfer sovereign powers to intergovernmental institutions.

(2). For the maintenance of peace, the Federation may enter a system of mutual collective security; in doing so, it will consent to such limitations

---

[16] Erich Kahler, "The Reality of Utopia," *American Scholar,* 15 (Spring 1946), 167–79.

upon its rights of sovereignty as will bring about and secure peaceful and lasting order in Europe and among the nations of the world.

(3). For the settlement of disputes between states, the Federation will accede to agreements concerning international arbitration of a general comprehensive, and obligatory nature.

—Constitution of 1949, confirmed by Unification Treaty of 31 August 1990.

Japan

Art. 9. Aspiring sincerely to an international peace based on justice and order, the Japanese people forever renounce war as a sovereign right of the nation and the threat or use of force as a means of settling international disputes.

In order to accomplish the aim of the preceding paragraph, land, sea and air forces, as well as other war potential will never be maintained.

The right of the belligerency of the State will not be recognized.

—Constitution of 3 May 1947.

The point is that the limitation of national sovereignty for the purpose of participating in higher unions, to secure the common defense and promote the general welfare, is not unprecedented but rather is quite widely recognized in the fundamental constitutions of numerous states. All members of the European Union, except Britain (which has no written constitution), have made similar provisions for the limitation of their sovereignty in order to participate in a higher union, as have states once or prospectively in other regional federations.[17] An effort to amend the U.S. Constitution to similar effect by United World Federalists failed in 1950. For texts, see Appendix C.

Hardly one of the constitutional lawyers or political leaders who drafted such clauses limiting the sovereignty of the state or who enacted federal constitutions could be identified as a world federalist, and almost every one of them would be surprised or even offended if so labeled. (The one exception we have found is Joe Heydecker, president of Weltstaat–Liga in Munich, who apparently influenced Germany's Article 24.)[18] As far as is known, the authors were simply responding to the threat of internal anarchy and foreign invasion, as in Switzerland after the Sonderbund War (1847) or in Russia faced with the nationalities problem after the Revolution (1922), and they seized upon the federal structure as providing the least necessary government of the whole while preserving the government of the parts.

Major Problems in Constructing World Federation

There are four major problems for world federalism: membership,

---

[17] Nations with such provisions include, in Europe: Austria, Belgium, Denmark, Finland, France, Germany, Greece, Ireland, Italy, Luxembourg, Netherlands, Norway, Portugal, Spain, Sweden, Switzerland; in Latin America: Argentina, Brazil, Colombia, Costa Rica, Cuba, El Salvador, Guatemala, Nicaragua, Peru, Venezuela; in Africa: Congo, Egypt, Guinea, Mali, Rwanda, Democratic Republic of the Congo (former Zaire); in Asia: India, Japan, Philippines, Singapore.

[18] *World Government News,* February 1949.

representation, powers, and approaches.

Membership

Should membership be open to all states as in the League and United Nations, or limited to the democracies? Virtually all world federalists are agreed that *universality* is the ultimate goal; most hold that it is the immediate goal. Universality is the great achievement of the United Nations. Every weakness of the U.N. has been tolerated rather than tamper with the principle of universal membership, and every attempt to evict one country (the Soviet Union in the early days, later South Africa or Israel) has been rejected as a threat to the peace. Most of the world federalist movement, including Grenville Clark and Louis B. Sohn as they worked out *World Peace through World Law,* and Robert M. Hutchins, G. A. Borgese, and the Chicago Committee to Frame a World Constitution, favored a universal approach, since "democracy," liberal or economic, had become the central issue of the early Cold War.

Clarence Streit, on the other hand, argued that even a modest federal union is not practical unless the people accept common values, and the minimum are shared values concerning liberty and responsible government. So he favored membership *limited to the democracies,* pending the development of democracy in all nations, when they could be admitted to a democratic world federal government. The movement for European Union, similarly, has limited itself to liberal democracies. With the collapse of the Soviet Union, there is now hardly any question about the necessity of beginning with democracies.

Representation

Granted that what is needed is a democratic republic of the world, should representation in the legislative body be *proportional to population,* which is the pure principle but which would give predominance to poorer, more populous, and less "politically experienced" countries like India, or should it be *weighted* somehow to reflect the widely differing experience of national peoples with democracy and to make active participation more attractive to the great powers? To this vexing problem, Grenville Clark and Louis B. Sohn proposed that the U.N. General Assembly be reorganized according to a system (subject to periodic amendment) of weighted representation cleverly scaled with respect to population, wealth, education, and traditional great power ranking: the U.S., U.S.S.R., China, and India would each be allocated 30 votes; mid-sized powers like Britain, France, West Germany, and Japan, 16; smaller nations, 8; and so on through seven steps to the smallest state, which would be granted 1. This scheme produced a total of 625 world representatives. Clark and Sohn urged that the representatives be elected by the people wherever possible, so that representatives develop a sense of responsibility to the people instead of to national governments; elsewhere, appointment by parliaments, national monarchs, or communist parties would have to be tolerated.

The Chicago committee earlier proposed an ingenious alternative scheme of regional popular elections and nine electoral colleges, which eliminated the invidious weighting scheme. But it had the same effect, since the nine regions (nicely coincident with the world civilizations that Arnold Toynbee distinguished) had different populations. These representatives were to be finally elected by all the electoral colleges in plenary session, so each representative would in principle represent the whole world. There were to be 99 of them.

Weighted voting has actually been introduced into the World Bank and other international financial institutions, where it avoids a great power veto or voting in accordance with sovereign equality. Federalists later proposed ingenious alternatives, like Richard Hudson's Binding Triad (majorities of states, populations, and economies) or Joseph Schwartzberg's Entitlement Quotients. (Appendix J.)

Streit, because he started with working democracies, provided for immediate proportional representation, while states not admitted were not represented at all. The European Parliament was made elective on the basis of proportional representation in 1979. At the world level, however, respect for sovereign equality of states has been so recently and painfully won that there is little movement for basing the world order on the true political equality of citizens. The one nation, one vote rule avoids facing the vexed problem of democratic representation.

Powers

Should the powers delegated to the world federal government be the minimum necessary to preserve the peace, as was intended in the United Nations, or the maximum desirable to make peace and promote justice throughout the world? Grenville Clark argued that only minimal powers were acceptable for delegation by the nations at present; amendment could provide for gradual expansion of powers as the world federation proved trustworthy. This was the doctrine of *minimalism.*

G. A. Borgese and the Chicago committee, at the other extreme, contended that a mere security government would be a world police state; the federation had to start with powers to achieve justice, for injustice was at the root of the crisis of modern civilization. Hence, in addition to powers to preserve the peace, the world federation would have to have powers to regulate world commerce, supervise world communications and transportation, lay world taxes, issue world money and control world finance, prepare plans for equitable economic development, regulate emigration and immigration, and supervise the rectification of borders and the creation of new states. Hence, this view with respect to powers was called *maximalism.*

Streit was a maximalist within his democratic Atlantic union. There has never been open resolution of this contentious issue of powers, but as the U.N. has entered the economic development field and peace workers everywhere have turned to development projects, since political progress toward federation seems so slow, virtually all federalists and internationalists are now maximalists.

Transition

Should the transition to world federation be a revolutionary act, as at Philadelphia in 1787, or a gradual series of steps, carefully building on innovation after innovation as each one proves workable? The greatest problem of world federalism is the political transition. Most federalists have argued that the only practical course is to conduct a campaign of public education to persuade people that it is in their own self-interest, particularly in peace, to reach an international agreement for the non-violent establishment of world federal government. Federalists have always resisted talk and hints of preventive war, use of force, and a national bid for empire. The preferred method is to convene a general review conference for the reform of the United Nations, as provided for in Article 109 of the Charter, or to convene a new world constitutional convention, like that in San Francisco in 1945.

This is commonly known as the approach of *U.N. reform*. The approach is official, legal, and "realistic." Appeal is made not to moral sentiments or to the sense of human brotherhood but to national interests. The politics of U.N. reform has consisted largely of lobbying with legislators and high executive officials to produce a resolution or other national initiative for a new conference. United World Federalists saw its purpose almost entirely as lobbying in Congress for a world federalist resolution. The World Federalist Association conducts a broader educational program but still attempts to influence Congress.

A variant on this official approach is the "parliamentary" approach, in which national parliamentarians, including members of the U.S. Congress, would introduce the federalist resolution themselves. The British Parliamentary Group for World Government, launched by Henry Usborne, began this approach. It is carried on, with more political "realism," by Parliamentarians for Global Action (formerly Parliamentarians for World Order).

A minority of federalists have argued that national governments are natural enemies of a project that would reduce national sovereignty, so an appeal must be made directly to the people in order to produce a wholly new social contract. They propose to hold popular elections of delegates to a world constitutional convention, using state electoral machinery wherever possible; these delegates, legitimated by their election, would then assemble in convention to draft the world constitution.

This is the *peoples' convention* approach. It is unofficial, revolutionary, and "utopian." Most proponents see it as an educational device to bring greater grassroots popular pressure to bear on officials, in order to move them to undertake U.N. reform. British Member of Parliament (M.P.) Henry Usborne led a difficult campaign to hold just such a peoples' convention in Geneva in December 1950. This extraordinary effort came to naught with the arrival of the Korean War in June.

Still another approach would be to form a transnational political party aimed at winning national offices for the purpose of carrying out a program of establishing world federation, as was once proposed by young Harris Wofford. A more modest variant would be to form an advisory committee of leaders of national political parties and trade unions on the model of Jean Monnet's Action

Committee for a United States of Europe.

Actually, all federalist approaches are revolutionary, in the sense that they all aim to create favorable political conditions for the transfer of sovereign powers from nations to a higher governing authority. What is proposed is no less than the dissolution of the external sovereignty of nations. But federalists argue that—since sovereignty is really the right of the people to institute new government, laying its foundations on such principles and organizing its powers in such form as to them shall seem most likely to effect their safety and happiness —there can never be a "sacrifice" or dissolution of sovereignty. Rather, sovereignty is *strengthened* by uniting governments. Far from being a loss, establishing federal world government would be a gain of immense powers of social cooperation, analogous to what has been achieved under the U.S. federal Constitution, which was bitterly opposed at first.

Even the provision in Article 109 that each of the Big Five must ratify any amendments to the Charter need not be a barrier, if there were overwhelming popular demand for a stronger United Nations. Delegates to a U.N. Charter review conference could provide that the new Charter should go into effect when ratified by some large majority of states plus, say, three or four of the five "permanent members," just as the delegates to the Philadelphia convention of 1787 provided that the new U.S. government should go into operation when the Constitution was ratified by 9 of the 13 states, and not unanimously, as required by the Articles of Confederation.

World federalists say that the times themselves are revolutionary. Nuclear weapons could end human civilization, a global economy is forming, the working classes and women have acquired political power in the West, the Communist countries are now in transition to bourgeois democracy and free market capitalism, the impoverished masses in Latin America, Africa, and Asia are discovering the rights of labor, the earth seen from space is fragile. These events reduce even the Cold War between Russia and America to a mere wave on the tide of history. Revolutionary times call for a revolutionary response.

Streit used to argue, in the early days of the Second World War and again in the early Cold War, that "the most dangerous way to cross a chasm is in two steps," but most of the movement has followed Clark and Sohn in favor of incremental U.N. reform. The primary focus of the world order school of thought led by Saul Mendlovitz and Richard A. Falk, who were originally inspired by Clark and Sohn, is on this transition, which they realistically call the "struggle of the oppressed."[19] A similar approach at time of writing is the 20–40 year program "Global Action to Prevent War," led by Jonathan Dean, Randall Forsberg, and Saul Mendlovitz. They propose forming a "coalition" of government officials and grassroots activists to support a series of four treaties to gradually reduce national defense forces while strengthening international ones under a functioning United Nations. In effect, a minimal transfer to the world organiza-

---

[19] Richard A. Falk, Samuel S. Kim, and Saul Mendlovitz, eds., *Toward a Just World Order* (Boulder, CO: Westview, 1982).

tion of powers affecting peace and security would be accomplished after an effort lasting as long as the Cold War.[20] Such struggle is contrasted to the public pressure on national political leaders practiced by United World Federalists and their successors.

World Political Creativity in the 21st Century

In the United Nations community today, we can detect a novel, somewhat inelegant but practical statecraft that in principle could be called federalist. In our survey, *The United Nations System,* on the literature since the end of the Cold War on U.N. reform, most writers seem to see three general directions for the future of the United Nations, analogous to the three fundamental bases of international politics—balance of power, collective security, and rule of law:

1. Cautious development of the state system, utilizing the U.N. as at present only when bilateral diplomacy must avail itself of the services of multilateral diplomacy.

2. A non-hierarchical system of perhaps 100 international organizations, including a much more effective United Nations empowered to achieve the purposes in its Charter.

3. A world federal government, preserving the nation–states but providing a higher level of legislative, executive, and judicial authority, probably on the model of the emerging European Union.

A non-hierarchical system (alternative 2) is now overwhelmingly preferred, not only because statesmen (and -women) are reluctant to part with national power, but also because the peoples of the states are fearful, after over 40 years of the Cold War, to centralize power in a world state, even if it could be designed as a federal system with such checks and balances as not to become a threat to liberty. But a non-hierarchical world system of organizations that could be *effective* in keeping the peace and in providing the negotiating forum for cooperating to solve global problems would practically amount to the same thing. If it keeps the peace and respects the independence and diversity of modern states and their restive peoples, what is its difference from a world federation?

The present world situation, we find, can be seen as a period of political creativity no less inferior to that at the founding of the United States, and the emerging world political order promises to be as different from any of the 30 historical federations as the U.S. federal government was from the confederation and colonial governments that preceded it. The European Union, with its five branches led by the European Council (the "summit" of heads of government), whose "policies" (delegations of sovereign powers) are continually reviewed by the Council of Ministers, is typical of the movement toward global governance.

[20] Dr. Randall C. Forsberg, Institute for Defense and Disarmament Studies, 675 Massachusetts Avenue, Cambridge, MA 02139; 617-354-4337; globalaction@idds .org.

Consider the following facts replete in the literature of U.N. reform:

- U.S. hegemony since 1973, like British hegemony after 1918, has been declining, marked by abandonment of the gold standard and decline of the U.S. portion of the world gross product from one half (1945) to one fifth (2000).[21]

- The absolute sovereignty of states, enshrined in the U.N. Charter's Article 2(7), no longer preserves states from war, economic disruption, or, now, humanitarian intervention.[22]

- International war is decreasing in incidence, while domestic and ethnic conflict affecting international peace and security is increasing. The U.N., which was designed to stop Hitlerite aggression across borders, is now increasingly charged with maintaining the peace among individuals, as if it were a world state.[23]

- Common security is supplanting national security as the first interest of states, and economic power is increasingly recognized as more of a reality than military power.[24]

- Nuclear weapons, which their most optimistic champions claimed undermined *Realpolitik,* are unusable.[25]

- Despite a public posture of ignoring or criticizing the U.N., the U.S. govern-

---

[21] Robert O. Keohane, *After Hegemony: Cooperation and Discord in the World Political Economy* (Princeton: Princeton University Press, 1984); Inis L Claude Jr., "American Values and Multilateral Institutions," in Claude, *States and the Global System: Politics, Law, and Organization* (New York: St. Martin's, 1988), 102–11.

[22] Edwin M. Smith, Keith R. Krause, and Brian Urquhart, "The United Nations: Meeting the Challenges of the Post–Cold War World," *American Society of International Law Proceedings,* 87 (1993): 268–99.

[23] Ernst B. Haas, *The United Nations and Collective Management of International Conflict* (New York: UNITAR, E.86.XV.ST.19, 1986; Ramesh Thakur, ed., *International Conflict Resolution* (Boulder, CO: Westview, 1988).

[24] Independent Commission on Disarmament and Security Issues, Olaf Palme, chairman, *Common Security: A Blueprint for Survival* (New York: Simon & Schuster, 1982; Mikhail S. Gorbachev, "The Reality and Guarantees of a Secure World" *Pravda* and *Isvestia,* 17 September 1987; U.N. Department for Disarmament Affairs, *Study on the Economic and Social Consequences of the Arms Race and Military Expenditures* (New York: U.N., Study Series No. 19, E.89.IX.2, A/43/368, 1982).

[25] U.N. Department for Disarmament Affairs, *Nuclear Weapons: A Comprehensive Study* (New York: U.N., Study Series No. 21, E.91.IX.12, A/45/373, 1991).

ment in particular recognizes the need for a general security system;[26] and, since the Persian Gulf War, many states have applauded the U.N.'s acquisition of greater enforcement powers.[27]

- Newer techniques of conflict resolution and more traditional means for the peaceful settlement of international disputes are combining and progressing rapidly—to the point where John Burton argues that they offer a universal ideology in place of liberalism and communism, mutually exhausted in the struggles of the Cold War.[28] Preventive diplomacy and all devices to prevent conflict, rather than contain or stop it, are held to be the elements of a mature international system.[29]

- The world is "governable," as Georgi Shakhnazarov wrote in 1988, for a strengthened United Nations no longer threatens to take sides in the struggle between East and West.[30]

- A global *problématique* of common problems beyond the powers of any one national state to solve for the protection of its people—ranging from defense against attack and cooperation for international financial and commercial interests to protection and promotion of human rights and preservation of the environment—requires common action by the U.N.[31]

- The General Assembly, even as presently constituted, has a quasi-legislative

[26] U.S. Department of State, *United States Participation in the United Nations*, Report by the President to the Congress for the Year 1991 (Washington, DC: U.S. Department of State, Bureau of International Organizational Affairs, Pub. No. 9974, 1992; Tobi Trister Gati, *The U.S. , the U.N., and the Management of Global Change* (New York: New York University Press for United Nations Association—USA, 1983).

[27] U.S. Commission on Improving the Effectiveness of the United Nations, Representative James A. Leach, co-chairman, *Defining Purpose: The United Nations and the Health of Nations; Final Report [to the President and Congress]* (Washington, DC: By the Commission, 1993); Edward C. Luck and Tobi Trister Gati, "Whose Collective Security?" *Washington Quarterly,* 15 (Spring 1992): 43–56; Marrack Goulding, "The Evolution of United Nations Peacekeeping," *International Affairs* (London), 69 (1993): 451–64.

[28] John W. Burton, *Conflict: Resolution and Provention* [sic] (New York: St. Martin's, 1990); Burton, *Global Conflict: The Domestic Sources of International Crisis* (Brighton, England: Wheatsheaf, 1984).

[29] Peter Stein, *Legal Institutions: The Development of Dispute Settlement* (London: Butterworths, 1984).

[30] Georgi Shakhnazarov, "Governability of the World," *International Affairs* (Moscow), 34, 3 (1988): 16–24; Georgi Shakhnazarov, "The World Community Is Amenable to Government," *Pravda,* 15 January 1988, p. 3.

[31] John G. Ruggie, "On the Problems of 'the Global Problématique': What Roles for international Organizations?" *Alternatives,* 5 (1979–80): 517–50; Ronald J. Glossop, *World Federation? A Critical Analysis of Federal World Government* (Jefferson, NC: McFarland, 1993), 49–95.

competence, which would be increased if a second chamber, representative of peoples like the European Parliament, were established.[32]

- Increasingly, consensus, rather than consent of every state willing to be bound, is recognized as the basis of international obligation laid down in the recommendations, or enactments, of the General Assembly.[33]

- The individual is being recognized as a "subject" of international law, particularly under the Nuremberg principles and now under some 95 human rights instruments.[34]

- An International Criminal Court, making permanent what began as *ad hoc* international tribunals at Nuremberg, Tokyo, Arusha, and The Hague for the prosecution of individuals for genocide, war crimes and crimes against humanity, was established in 1998 and entered into force in 2002, after 60 ratifications (not including the U.S.A.).[35]

When the *individual* is protected by international human rights law, is the beneficiary of humanitarian intervention by the international community despite the claims of the domestic jurisdiction clause of the U.N. Charter, has a role via non-governmental organizations accredited to the U.N. in the making of treaties and the hardening of customs, and has standing before world courts and international tribunals, have we not crossed the line from an association of sovereign

[32] Stephen M. Schwebel, "The Effect of Resolutions of the United Nations General Assembly on Customary International Law," *American Journal of International Law*, 73 (1979): 301–09; Dieter Heinrich, *The Case for a United Nations Parliamentary Assembly* (New York: World Federalist Movement, 1992).

[33] C. Wilfred Jenks, "Unanimity, the Veto, Weighted Voting, Special and Simple Majorities, and Consensus as Modes of Decision in International Organizations," in *Cambridge Essays in International Law: Essays in Honour of Lord McNair* (Cambridge: Cambridge University Press, 1965), 48–63; Jon M. Van Dyke, ed., *Consensus and Confrontation: The United States and the Law of the Sea Convention* (Honolulu: University of Hawaii, Law of the Sea Institute, 1985).

[34] U.S. Senate, Committee on Foreign Relations, *Strengthening the International Court of Justice*, Hearings, 93rd Cong., 1st sess., 10–11 May 1973 (CIS No. S381–22, SuDoc No. Y4.F76/2:In8/42).; Monroe Leigh and the Office of the Legal Advisor, "The International Court of Justice," in *Digest of United States Practice in International Law, 1976* (Washington, DC: Department of State, Pub. No. 8908, 1977), 650–80; Benjamin B. Ferencz, *An International Criminal Court: A Step toward World Peace; A Documentary History and Analysis* (Dobbs Ferry, NY: Oceana, 1980).

[35] Fanny Benedetti and John L. Washburn, "Drafting the International Criminal Court Treaty: Two Years to Rome and an Afterword on the Rome Diplomatic Conference," *Global Governance*, 5, 1 (January–March 1999): 1–38; Robert C. Johansen, "U.S. Opposition to the International Criminal Court: Unfounded Fears," The Joan B. Krok Institute for International Peace Studies, Policy Brief No. 7 (June 2001); Benjamin B. Ferencz, "Misguided Fears about the International Criminal Court," *Pace International Law Review* (forthcoming, Spring 2003).

states to a government of states and peoples? "We are living through the birth pangs of a world community," said C. Wilfred Jenks in 1969.[36] We are immersed in the "emerging constitutionalism of world order," said Edward Mc-Whinney in 1987.[37] Judging by current interest in what is termed "world governance," humanity is in search of some more stable, more peaceful world order, but few are ready to plunge into a world federal state in order to escape the fundamental flaw, found in the U.N. Charter, of attempting to legislate for states or governments in their collective capacities, as distinguished from the individuals of whom they consist, as Hamilton argued in *The Federalist*, No. 15.

If we look at the current movement toward world governance in terms of the world order school's preferred values of peace, social justice, economic plenty, preservation of the environment, and democratic participation,[38] the new creativity of world politics will be evident. Slowly the realism and practicality of *common security* recommended itself to national statesmen, until by 1987 Mikhail Gorbachev of the Soviet Union unilaterally and courageously affirmed the idea as he led his country and the world out of the Cold War.[39]

What is striking about *human rights* from a world constitutional point of view is that millions of people in all cultures have affirmed common definitions of such rights and often begun to adhere to common institutions to enforce them even before establishment of a world state.[40] The situation is reminiscent of the French Declaration of the Rights of Man and the Citizen *before* establishment of the French national government.

It is not generally appreciated that the *economic development* of the poorer parts of the world is generally a success and proceeds at a brisk pace. Average life expectancy in the last 30 years has increased by 16 years, adult literacy by 40 percent, and per capita nutritional levels by over 20 percent. Child mortality has fallen by half. Developing countries have achieved in 30 years what it took industrialized countries a century to accomplish.[41] Such a result looks like a vindication of G. A. Borgese's claim in 1948 that *justice* meant an end to colonialism, racism, and economic inequality and that the struggle between the two world systems eventually would result in a mixed system.

The *Apollo 11* photographs of earth from the orbit of the moon in 1969, the

---

[36] C. Wilfred Jenks, *The World beyond the Charter: A Tentative Synthesis of Four Stages of World Organization* (London: Allen & Unwin, 1969), 15.

[37] Edward McWhinney, *The International Court of Justice and the Western Tradition of International Law* (Dordrecht: M. Nijhoff, 1987).

[38] Richard A. Falk, "Contending Approaches to World Order," *Journal of International Affairs*, 31 (Fall–Winter 1977): 171–98.

[39] Mikhail Gorbachev, "The Realities and Guarantees of a Secure World," *Pravda*, 17 September 1987.

[40] Joseph P. Baratta, *Human Rights: Improving U.N. Mechanisms for Compliance* (Washington, DC: Center for U.N. Reform Education and U.S. Institute of Peace, 1990).

[41] U.N. Development Programme, *Human Development Report, 1994* (New York: Oxford University Press, 1994).

Club of Rome's publication *The Limits to Growth* of 1972, and the Brundtland Commission's report *Our Common Future* of 1986, which gave us the formulation of "sustainable development" for a rational development goal, may be taken as landmarks of the mobilization of political will to *protect the environment.* The U.N. Charter, like a workable constitution, has proved flexible enough to bring the new concern into the conduct of diplomacy and multilateral negotiation. Since the Earth Summit in 1992, *protection of the environment* has unmistakenly been put on the international agenda.[42]

The arguments for *political participation* or *democracy* in the U.N. and similar international organizations are exactly like those for widening the franchise in Britain 170 years ago or in the United States 220 years ago. Popular representation would bring *energy* into the U.N. as countless individuals around the world were given standing before the law, contributed to the work of monitoring agreements and aiding development, and undertook the responsibilities and privileges of world citizenship.[43] It is the task of this book to show the links between the world federalism of the past and such global governance in the future.

Placement of the Idea

To place the idea of world federal government into the context of other approaches to peace, it may be helpful to use the U.S. Institute of Peace's *Approaches to Peace: An Intellectual Map* (1991). There, some four large approaches are distinguished: traditional diplomacy, international law, conflict resolution, and systemic political approaches, including world federation. The contributor selected to explain the latter misunderstands it as a unitary and tyrannical world state, destructive of cultural diversity,[44] but federation truly is a systemic political approach. We regard the first three as transitional to the fourth, which indeed treats the nation state as a historical form of political organization (since the Peace of Westphalia in 1648) and looks forward to the political union of all humanity on the planet.

A second placement would be in the scholarship on peace, yet at time of writing, largely because the historic World Federalists failed to obviate the Cold War and even to rise to leadership in opposition to the Vietnam War, world fed-

---

[42] Stanley P. Johnson, *The Earth Summit: The United Nations Conference on Environment and Development* (London: Graham & Trotman and M. Nijhoff, 1993); Michael Keating, *The Earth Summit's Agenda for Change: A Plain Language Version of Agenda 21 and the Other Rio Agreements* (Geneva: Centre for Our Common Future, 1993).

[43] U.S. Senate, Committee on Foreign Relations, *Strengthening the International Court of Justice,* Hearings, 93rd Cong., 1st sess., 10–11 May 1973 (note testimony of Louis B. Sohn); Angus Archer, "Methods of Multilateral Management: Interrelationship of International Organizations and NGOs," in Tobi Trister Gati, ed., *The U.S., the U.N., and the Management of Global Change* (New York: UNA–USA, 1983), 303–26.

[44] Michael N. Nagler, "Ideas of World Order and the Map of Peace," in W. Scott Thompson, ed., *Approaches to Peace: An Intellectual Map* (Washington, DC: U.S. Institute of Peace, 1991), 382–83.

eralism is usually overlooked. Peter Wallensteen's survey of the literature does not even have an index item for "world government."[45] I have tried to rectify such mistakes and omissions in articles for the *World Encyclopedia of Peace* and *Peace and Change,*[46] but the peace field currently does not seem much given over to what Einstein called "sound pacifism" (the prevention of wars through a world order based on power, not through a purely passive attitude toward international problems).[47] Books of late that engage the scholarly community in the field of world politics are now quite rare; two of the best are Wesley Wooley's *Alternatives to Anarchy* in American history and Ronald Glossop's *World Federation* in philosophy.[48]

A third way to place federalism is to look at standard texts on international relations, such as that by Joshua Goldstein. There the absence of world government is abundantly shown as the essence of international anarchy, yet when he considers liberal alternatives to realism, federalism gets only brief mention after sections on feminism, postmodernism, and peace studies.[49] The attitude is not unlike that of Hans Morgenthau, who, with Carl J. Friedrich, Frederick Law Schuman, Nicholas Spykman, E. H. Carr, and Brooks Emeny, carried realism (politics as the struggle for power, especially military power) from Europe to America. Schuman wrote a serious book on world government, and Spykman at Yale taught Cord Meyer, who became first president of UWF.

Morgenthau wrote in *Politics among Nations* (1948), "Our analysis of the problem of domestic peace has shown that the argument of the advocates of the world state is unanswerable: There can be no permanent international peace without a state coextensive with the confines of the political world."[50] Since the achievement of a world state seemed to him unfathomably in the remote future, he concluded his book with suggestions for an indefinite "wise diplomacy." But by 1978, Morgenthau was becoming alarmed that in a nuclear age the pursuit of power was tending inexorably to a third world war, and, according to Francis Boyle, admitted to Louis Sohn that he had abandoned "Machiavellian power po-

[45] Peter Wallensteen, ed., *Peace Research: Achievements and Challenges* (Boulder, CO: Westview, 1988).

[46] Joseph P. Baratta, "Federalism, World," *World Encyclopedia of Peace*, ed. Ervin Lazslo and Jong Joul Yoo (Oxford: Pergamon, 1986): 311–21; "The International Federalist Movement: Toward Global Governance," *Peace and Change*, 24 (July 1999): 275–76, 340–72.

[47] Albert Einstein, response to a conscientious objector, 14 July 1941, in Otto Nathan and Heinz Norden, eds., *Einstein on Peace* (New York: Schocken, 1960), 319.

[48] Wesley T. Wooley, *Alternatives to Anarchy: American Supranationalism since World War II* (Bloomington: Indiana University Press, 1988); Ronald J. Glossop, *World Federation? A Critical Analysis of Federal World Government* (Jefferson, NC: McFarland, 1993).

[49] Joshua S. Goldstein, *International Relations* (New York: Addison Wesley Longman, 1999), 77, 88, 103, 111, 140, 287, 292, 314, 340.

[50] Hans J. Morgenthau, *Politics among Nations: The Struggle for Power and Peace*, 1st ed. (New York: Knopf, 1948), 398–99.

litics" for the more traditional American diplomacy in which respect for the Law of Nations and international organization was accorded a place alongside economic and military power.[51]

George Kennan set the tone for the scholarly consensus that continues to the present day on world federalism. In *American Diplomacy, 1900–1950,* the architect of the containment policy roundly condemned the "legalistic–moralistic approach to international problems." This included Woodrow Wilson's effort to establish the League of Nations, Secretary of State Kellogg's Pact for the Renunciation of War, Franklin Roosevelt's United Nations, and proposals of "World Law and World Government." Kennan explained:[52]

> It is the essence of this belief that, instead of taking the awkward conflicts of national interest and dealing with them on their merits with a view to finding the solutions least unsettling to the stability of international life, it would be better to find some formal criteria of a juridical nature by which the permissible behavior of states could be defined.

But these views did not prevent Kennan from accepting the Grenville Clark Prize in 1981. Somewhat chastened by the militaristic character of the more economic and political containment policy he had recommended a quarter century before, Kennan stated:[53]

> To many of us, these ideas [of *World Peace through World Law* for a program of universal disarmament and for a system of world law to replace the chaotic and dangerous institution of unlimited national sovereignty] looked, at the time (1958), impractical, if not naïve. Today, ... the logic of them is more compelling. It is still too early, I fear, for their realization on a universal basis; but efforts to achieve the limitation of sovereignty in favor of a system of international law on a regional basis are another thing; and when men begin to come seriously to grips with this possibility, it is to the carefully thought out and profoundly humane ideas of Grenville Clark and Louis Sohn that they will have to turn for inspiration and guidance.

It would be tedious to cite others in the "realist" tradition who basically argued, during the Cold War with the Soviet Union, that any notion of a union with a totalitarian power was profoundly unhelpful and misleading. Louis René Beres captured this attitude well when he argued that federalists neglect the realities of power; they write superficially and with more enthusiasm than use of evidence. "As a result," he wrote, "large numbers of people have been diverted from

---

[51] Francis A. Boyle, *The Future of International law and American Foreign Policy* (Ardsley–on–Hudson, NY: Transnational Publications, 1989).

[52] George F. Kennan, *American Diplomacy, 1900–1950* (New York: Mentor, 1951), 93–94.

[53] "Beyond the Shadow of the Atom," *Boston Globe,* 29 November 1981, p. A15.

a variety of potentially more productive courses to international order."[54]

Even authors in the world order school, like Richard Falk, tried to argue during the Cold War that "world order" was something different from "world government." Falk favored a kind of "central governance," in which a variety of existing international institutions and transnational popular peace movements—not a world government vested with powers to enact and enforce world laws against preparations for war—will restrain national governments from recourse to war.[55] Nevertheless, his own preferred world, in *A Study of Future Worlds*,[56] was, apart from the novel terminology, indistinguishable from maximal world government devoted to peace and justice, and in recent years appreciation for the ideal of world federal government has begun to creep back into such books as *The Constitutional Foundations of World Peace*.[57]

In short, as the "realist" school of thought gives way to the functionalists, transnationalists, internationalists, and world order theorists and activists, the consensus on world federalism is loosening, if not yet deeply fractured. The theorists of world order, European union, functionalism, and the United Nations have developed a new vocabulary that avoids the historically loaded connotations of federalist terms. These may help to overcome groundless fears during the transition. Some equivalents are:

Subsidiarity	=	Federalism
Competence	=	Sovereignty
Consensus	=	Majority rule
Norms	=	Laws
Cooperation	=	Friendly relations
Common action	=	Binding law
Policies (E.C.)	=	Powers
Integration	=	Economic, social, and political union
Union	=	Government
Legitimacy	=	Lawfulness, consent of the governed
Multilateralism	=	Internationalism
Coalitions	=	Groupings of states outside the U.N.
Political will	=	Unanimity of will of great powers
Preventive diplomacy	=	Effective international organization
Peace making	=	Pacific settlement of disputes
Peacekeeping	=	International police operations
Enforcement	=	Use of international armed force
Collective security	=	Threat or use of international force

[54] Louis René Beres, "Examining the Logic of World Federal Government," *Publius*, 4 (Summer 1974): 75–87.

[55] Richard A. Falk, "Contending Approaches to World Order," *Journal of International Affairs* (New York), 31 (Fall–Winter 1977): 171–98.

[56] Richard A. Falk, *A Study of Future Worlds* (New York: Free Press for the World Order Models Project, 1975).

[57] Richard A. Falk, Robert C. Johansen, and Samuel S. Kim, eds., *The Constitutional Foundations of World Peace* (New York: SUNY Press for the World Order Models Project, 1993).

Implementation of decisions	=	Coercion of governments
Human rights	=	Justice
Regime	=	Rule of law
Mandate	=	Grant of powers
Central governance	=	World government

The Bahá'í faith, which developed in Iran after 1844, is the only religion that teaches as a point of doctrine that world peace can practically be achieved by a political union or federal world government. Such a government will abolish war by the familiar instrument of the rule of law, which Bahá'ís call the Lesser Peace. But world federation will provide the minimal political, economic, and social order for the full realization of the potentialities of every human being, that is, for the perfection of religion, which they call the Most Great Peace.[58] This is a book about the Lesser Peace. When the oneness of humanity is established on a working basis, then the great work of education, science, democratic politics, industry, business enterprise, sport, art, and religion will begin to succeed.

The achievement of the rule of world law will largely depend on new, enlightened national leadership and on massive public opinion ready to undertake the responsibilities no less than the benefits of world citizenship. Jean Monnet used to say that, for the hard work of uniting sovereignties, people will act only when faced by a crisis. Thomas Jefferson said much the same when he wrote, "All experience hath shewn that mankind are more disposed to suffer, while evils are sufferable, than they are to right themselves by changing the forms to which they are accustomed."

The world now is faced by a massive crisis, symbolized by the threat of nuclear war, economic depression, ecological collapse, new pandemics, terrorism from the global South, and all the problems of the global *problématique*. At the moment it is only a crisis of the mind. Until there is another disaster on the scale of World War II, demonstrating the failure of the old ways of internationalism, we probably cannot expect revolutionary action. Small changes must continue to suffice. "We are trying to hoist a sail," wrote G. A. Borgese in 1947. "It greets the good wind." The wind in the 1940s amounted to only scattered gusts. By 2002, the atmosphere lay becalmed, certain to stir into storms again, as happened by September 11, 2001. We hope this book will offer the pilots of the future some charts to steer by. World federation offers a positive vision of peace. Its history exhibits a new kind of world political wisdom.

---

[58] J. Tyson, *World Peace and World Government: From Vision to Reality* (Oxford: Ronald, 1986).

1

Precursors from Dante to Wilson

Πάθει μάθος. [Man must learn by suffering.]
—Aeschylus, *Agamemnon*, l. 177, 458 B.C.
Motto of Arnold Toynbee's *Study of History*

Where there is no vision, the people perish.
(Also translated as:)
Where there is no prophecy the people cast off restraint,
But blessed is he who keeps the law.

—Proverbs, 29:18, c. 1000 B.C.

The Perennial Idea of Union

The idea of world federal government did not spring up in a vacuum, nor was it the culmination of a linear progression. Even now, the idea recurs to people who have no notion of its history yet are perplexed by the drift of world history. Its lineage is more like countless rivulets joining tributaries to a river flowing to the sea than the course of a single raindrop. Nevertheless, the idea of a union of states to achieve peace is an old one, and successive thinkers and politicians often had some dim recollection that they were treading in the footsteps of precursors. Even if our focus is on a union of states *and peoples,* which cannot be said to have been seriously proposed until the 19th century or definitely until the manifest interdependence of the world and another general war by the mid–20th, it may be useful to briefly trace the lineage. Many historians of internationalism do so; our merit is only not to let a few socialists escape notice.

Historians of federalism go back to ancient Israel (a kingdom of 10 tribes) or to the Delian League of the Greek city–states. But Israel was carried off by Assyria after defeat in 722 B.C., and Judah, which survived until 587, was composed of a *single tribe;* it gave its name to the Jews. The Delian League degenerated into an empire under Athens, which was destroyed by Sparta in the Peloponnesian War. Greece never united until it was conquered by Macedonia and then Rome. The Romans finally united the ancient world under a centralized empire, though with local autonomy under law.

Dante

During the High Middle Ages, Dante wrote *De Monarchia* (1310–13), which was translated at the height of the federalist movement in 1949 as *On World Government*.[1] He wrote it in celebration of the entrance of Henry VII of Luxembourg into Italy in order to be crowned Holy Roman Emperor in Rome. Dante hoped that Henry would restore civil order to the fractious city–states, and he expressed this hope in a vision of the revival of the Roman Empire, bringing peace to all of Christendom. In this little book may be found such Renaissance and even modern political doctrines as the unity of man, the perfection of the human mind as the shared end of life, liberty under law, and the necessity of a third power ("world government") to resolve disputes between city or state governments.

Henry IV

The modern doctrine of world government begins during the Reformation and Wars of Religion and extends into the Enlightenment and our own violent 20th century. The *Grand Design* of Henry IV of France (1610), which his trusted minister the duc de Sully published and Jean–Jacques Rousseau celebrated for its realism, was another step forward in conception. Henry, by hard campaigning and an opportune conversion to Catholicism, ended the civil wars of religion in France and then for the last 15 years of his reign meditated a war to end war with the Habsburgs of Austria. Rousseau claimed that Henry's object was the same "armed league" or "European republic" that 100 years later the abbé de Saint–Pierre advocated in order to bring perpetual peace to Europe. But this was no federation established by consent. Rousseau delighted in Henry's secret diplomacy to unite all the other sovereigns of Europe by treaties of alliance and promises of gain—James I of England to be rescued from Spanish Catholic conspiracies, the king of Sweden to gain Pomerania, and the pope, Naples—while France would gain nothing but the hegemony *(primauté)* of the resultant confederation. The project came to naught on the eve of an aggressive allied attack when Henry was assassinated by a religious fanatic in 1610.[2]

William Penn

William Penn's *Essay towards the Present and Future Peace of Europe,* written after the Glorious Revolution in England (1688) and during King William's War (War of the League of Augsburg, 1689–97), was another source of thinking about a political union to make and keep the peace.[3] Penn was inspired by Hen-

---

[1] Dante Alighieri, *On World Government (De Monarchia,* c. 1311), Herbert W. Schneider, trans. (Indianapolis: Bobbs–Merrill, Library of Liberal Arts, 1949; 2nd ed., 1957).

[2] Jean–Jacques Rousseau, *A Project of Perpetual Peace* (1761), Edith M. Nuttall, trans. (London: Richard Cobden–Sanderson, 1927), 119–29.

[3] William Penn, "An Essay towards the Present and Future Peace of Europe" (1693), in Penn, *The Fruits of Solitude and Other Writings* (London: Dent, Everyman ed., 1915), 3–22.

ry IV's Grand Design. The Father of Pennsylvania argued in favor of a federal European state, which would govern the foreign relations of the existing sovereign states on the basis of the philosophy of the social contract. A common parliament to enact rules of justice and meeting yearly was proposed. Princes would remain sovereign within their territories (no interference in domestic relations). Like other plans for Europe, Penn's had no direct influence on events until the League of Nations was established (1919).

Abbé de Saint–Pierre

The abbé de Saint–Pierre's plan, *Perpetual Peace,* which he published with much uneasiness in 1713 after the War of the Spanish Succession ended in the Peace of Utrecht, marked a distinct advance. Despite Rousseau's ironical criticism, Saint–Pierre proposed the establishment of a European confederation not by secret stratagem but by open agreement of all European states of the time, in accordance with their supreme interests in avoiding the costs of war and preserving their sovereignty against other dynastic claimants. Saint–Pierre, an early *philosophe* from the age of Fontenelle, Pascal, and Malebranche, condemned "the perpetual dissensions, the brigandage, the usurpations, the rebellions, the wars, the murders which daily distress this venerable abode of sages, [Europe]."[4] The cause he found in the lack of a common superior power, able to extend public law over the inhabitants of Europe. His solution, which he called *un gouvernement confédérative,* amounted to what we would call a strong collective security system.

Its essence, Saint–Pierre explained, was that "all its members must be placed in such a mutual state of dependence that not one of them alone may be in a position to resist all of the others."[5] It is effectively true, as Rousseau claimed, that Saint–Pierre envisioned a *rational* process of transition to such a league, but, if he neglected the passions of men in statecraft, he did plainly appeal to their *interests.* This has been the basis of all proposals of voluntary agreement to unite states and peoples in order to abolish war from that day to this. Saint–Pierre's argument, basically, was that the very preservation of sovereign states required their confederation.[6]

Founders of the United States of America

The foundation of the United States under the federal Constitution of 1787 has been a landmark for all traditions of federalist thinking—national, European, and world. The 13 states were legally independent after the Declaration of Independence in 1776, and the Articles of Confederation (unanimously ratified and in force only by 1781) were, strictly speaking, a treaty in international law between sovereign states. So their "more perfect union" under a federal government has exerted a powerful example on other peoples seeking to establish peace, even though the American states were far less diverse and riven by national jealousies

---

[4] Rousseau, *Perpetual Peace,* 19, 21–25.

[5] Ibid., 39.

[6] Ibid., 51–81.

than those of Europe.

The Founding Fathers at Philadelphia were acutely conscious that the eyes of monarchical Europe were upon them. James Madison, chief architect of the Constitution, once remarked at the convention that the delegates were "deciding forever the fate of Republican Government," and he contrasted a union based on law, as was being proposed in America, with mere treaties based on voluntary compliance, as had been tried for centuries without success in Europe.[7] Benjamin Franklin, after the Constitution was signed, wrote to a friend in France:[8]

> If the Constitution succeeds, I do not see why you might not in Europe carry the project of good Henry IV into execution, by forming a Federal Union and One Grand Republick of all its different States and Kingdoms by means of a like Convention, for we had many interests to reconcile.

The essential elements of the U.S. Constitution drafted at Philadelphia were:

- A strong central government (as opposed to a continued association of sovereign states);
- Legislation for individuals (as opposed to pretended legislation for states);
- Popular representation in at least one house of the legislature to bring "energy" into the government (as opposed to state representation, though this was eventually accepted for the Senate, in the great "federal" compromise);
- Majority rule of popular and state representatives to determine the "public interest" for enactment of the laws (as opposed to the rule of unanimity in the old unicameral Congress of the Confederacy);
- Enforcement of the laws by courts on individuals (as opposed to use of the army or military force against states);
- Delegation of enumerated powers from the states or the people to the common government (as opposed to reservation of all powers by the sovereign states);
- Separation of executive, legislative, and judicial powers (as opposed to the highly unitary system that had evolved in the British Parliament);
- Checks and balances to set special interest against interest so that, even in the absence of republican virtue, only the general interest would prevail (as opposed to the supremacy and corruptions of Parliament);
- The federal structure representing states in the Senate and the people in the House of Representatives (as opposed to a unitary state); and a
- Bill of political and civil rights demanded during the ratification conventions and designed to protect the people from any abuses of power by the federal government.

All of these elements have been present in the minds of those who have looked to world federation as a solution to the problem of war.

---

[7] Max Farrand, ed., *Records of the Federal Convention of 1787*, 4 vols. (New Haven, CT: Yale University Press, 1937, 1967), 1: 423, 446. Cf. 464.

[8] Franklin to Grand, 22 October 1787, ibid., 3: 131.

The necessity of a *government* was set out clearly in the debates on the formation of the United States. The great debate at Philadelphia and during the ratification period (1787–88) was about the necessity for an "energetic" (or "strong" or "national") government, enabled, by delegation of powers from the states or their people, to rule by law reaching to individuals. The debate was not originally about the *federal* form of government, in which the states are given equal representation in one of the two houses of the legislature. That developed later as a solution to the problem of representation. John Jay later set out very eloquently in the *Federalist*, Nos. 2–5, the inadequacies of the Confederation against foreign force and influence; and Hamilton, in *Federalist*, Nos. 6, 15–17, 23, and 51, set out its inadequacies against war between the states and internal disorder.

Again and again Hamilton explained that the essence of a confederation was pretended legislation for states, which rapidly degenerated into anarchy or a war of all against all; while the essence of government was legislation for individuals, or real law, which amounted to accepting, as the price of civil society, the "mild and salutary *coercion* of the magistracy" in place of the "destructive *coercion* of the sword."[9] Hamilton commented often on the necessity for such a power. "Why has government been instituted at all?" he asked. "Because the passions of men will not conform to the dictates of reason and justice, without constraint."[10] To meet the *ends* of a government for the United States, he insisted, we must will the *means,* that is, a national republic so designed that a free people can safely delegate their personal and state powers to it.[11] When Hamilton discussed the principle of separation of powers, he remarked:[12]

> It may be a reflection on human nature, that such devices should be necessary to control the abuses of government. But what is government itself, but the greatest of all reflections on human nature? If men were angels, no government would be necessary. If angels were to govern men, neither external nor internal controls on government would be necessary. In framing a government which is to be administered by men over men, the great difficulty lies is this: you must first enable the government to control the governed; and in the next place oblige it to control itself.

In an international context, the necessity of a government of the world is generally demonstrated similarly for a national government, since it makes possible the rule of law. The difficulty lies in the degree of world community needed to undertake a popular government—a point to which we will often return. Readers of the *Federalist Papers,* who may wonder why its arguments do not instantly apply to the United Nations in the modern world, must bear in mind that Madison, Hamilton, and Jay were writing for a community in which the Patriots outweighed the Tories and those indifferent to the Revolution.

---

[9] *Federalist,* No. 20, p. 124.
[10] *Federalist,* No. 15, p. 92.
[11] *Federalist,* No. 23, pp. 142–46.
[12] *Federalist,* No. 51, p. 337.

Federalism has been the unique "American contribution to politics," historians find,[13] and its influence has spread throughout the New and Old Worlds. Some 30 federal states have been established on the U.S. model. Even more influential has been the model of a written constitution, especially the American example of the deliberate establishment of a state in order to secure the rights of the people. The "struggle for constitutionalism" of modern democratic states has become part of world history.[14]

Immanuel Kant

Following establishment of the United States, Jeremy Bentham wrote his *Plan for Universal and Perpetual Peace* (1786–89; published in 1838), which was written in the depths of the European wars for empire not long after Britain had won Canada, lost her American colonies, and was engaged in taking India. But his ideas were no match for the challenge of the Napoleonic wars that soon engulfed Europe.

Far more adequate, fundamental, openly published, and studied for their penetration to this day were Immanuel Kant's "Idea for a Universal History from a Cosmopolitan Point of View" of 1784 and *Perpetual Peace* of 1795—the first written at the height of the Enlightenment, the second in the continuing enthusiasm among liberal Europeans for the French Revolution. Here are found the great arguments for the rule of law as the moral and political basis of freedom, the necessity of government to escape the state of nature, the need for a league of nations or confederation of free and independent states to escape the international anarchy, the development of mankind from lawless freedom through the rule of law provided by government (what Kant called the "halfway mark"), and finally to the perfect use of reason, that is, to self–government by individuals and citizens of free republics.[15] Such mature self–government was Kant's definition of Enlightenment. *Sapere aude!* (Dare to be wise) he took as its motto.[16]

In *Perpetual Peace,* Kant dealt with the difficulty, internal to his philosophy, that once men have protected their freedom under law in organized states, the moral duty to extend the rule of law as the area of freedom and of treatment of human beings as ends in themselves is largely satisfied—yet wars continue between states. Kant's solution was to establish a "league of peace" to make an end of all wars. Such a league he opposed to a "treaty of peace" that terminates only one war. Kant explicitly rejected the notion that individuals within the states so leagued together would be subject to laws commonly enacted in the

---

[13] Gordon S. Wood, *The Creation of the American Republic, 1776–1787* (New York: Norton for University of North Carolina Press, 1972), 519–64, 593–615.

[14] Albert P. Blaustein and Gisbert H. Flanz, eds., *Constitutions of the Countries of the World,* 18 binders (Dobbs Ferry, NY: Oceana, 1971–present).

[15] Immanuel Kant, "Idea for a Universal History from a Cosmopolitan Point of View" (1784), in Lewin White Beck, ed. and trans., *On History* (Indianapolis: Bobbs–Merrill, Library of Liberal Arts, 1963), Fifth to Eighth Theses, 16–23 (Berlin edition, 22–28).

[16] Immanuel Kant, "What Is Enlightenment?" ibid., 3 (35).

league—which is the essence of a federation like that of the new United States of America:[17]

> This league does not tend to any dominion over the power of the state but only to the maintenance and security of the freedom of the states itself and of other states in league with it, without there being any need for them to submit to civil laws and their compulsion, as men in a state of nature must submit.

Kant made very clear that any closer union was impractical in the Europe of his day—torn by struggles between absolute monarchs, constitutional monarchs, principalities, monarchical republics (his own preference), and democratic republics. The Concert of Europe, following the Treaty of Vienna (1815), or the League of Nations, after World War I (1919), may be taken as the great achievements of a confederal vision of a league of sovereign states.

But Kant did indicate that he could conceive of what we would understand as a world federation of states and peoples under the rule of law. In a footnote to *Perpetual Peace,* he distinguished between:

1. The constitution conforming to the civil law of men in a nation *(ius civitatis);*
2. The constitution conforming to the law of nations in their relation to one another *(ius gentium);*
3. The constitution conforming to the law of world citizenship, so far as men and states are considered as citizens of a universal states of men, in their external mutual relations *(ius cosmopoliticum).* [18]

A universal state of world citizens living in freedom under cosmopolitan law was very near to the modern concept of world federation.

Lionel Curtis

From the perspective of the union of once hostile states into an eventual world federation, one of the most important developments by the late 19th century was the undoing of American ill will toward Great Britain dating back to the Revolution. This reversal was very largely the work of American Atlantic federalists, particularly John Fiske, and British imperial federalists, J. R. Seeley, W. T. Stead, Lionel Curtis, and Philip Kerr (later Lord Lothian), as Atlantic union historians Ira Straus and Tiziana Stella have shown.[19] The Anglo–American *rapprochement* began with British appreciation for the success of the Union during the Civil War, continued through granting Canada its effective independence as a dominion under a federal constitution a few years later, and culminated with the *Alabama Claims* international arbitration in 1873.

---

[17] Kant, *Perpetual Peace,* Second Definitive Article, 18.

[18] Ibid., Concerning the Definitive Articles, 10, n. 1.

[19] Ira Straus, "Atlantic Federalism and the Expanding Atlantic Nucleus," *Peace and Change,* 24 (July 1999): 282–84; Tiziana Stella, "Roots of Atlantic Federalism, 1860–1900," unpublished paper, Conference on the History of International Federalism after Fifty Years, Washington, June 1997. Stella's work has since been completed in her doctoral dissertation, University of Pavia, 1999.

To Lionel Curtis, a federal union of the British Empire, with a common imperial parliament, promised to hold all the eventual dominions securely together. The Imperial Federation League was founded in London in 1884; it was a tiny group of publicists including Seeley, Stead, E. A. Freeman, and James Bryce, author of *The American Commonwealth* (London, 1888). Americans John Fiske and Andrew Carnegie supported them. The consequence was that, although Curtis's term "commonwealth" stuck in official usage in place of "empire," the Empire never legally united, which nearly left Britain isolated in World Wars I and II. Nevertheless, the mutual admiration for federation had made friends of Britain and America by 1914.

Proudhon, Bakunin, Kropotkin

Following the French Revolution and the origins of the socialist movement in the egalitarian doctrines and conspiratorial tactics of François–Noël Babeuf, socialism broke into three broad branches, each of which had an influence—mostly negative—on the emerging concept of world federal government. The first was the ill–named and widely maligned social and political philosophy of "anarchism," as upheld by Pierre–Joseph Proudhon, Mikhail Bakunin, and Peter Kropotkin. Far from being simply the repudiation of all government and an incitement to revolutionary violence—though it lent itself to that—philosophical anarchism affirmed the values of small self–governing communities, in which *contract* between free and responsible individuals would replace *law* enacted by a centralized, even "democratic" state. Moreover, philosophical anarchism profoundly affirmed federalism on national, European, and world levels—so much so that a more accurate name for its adherents might be *federalist socialists*.

The other two contentious branches were international socialism, as reflected in the four working–class Internationals, and world communism, as preached and promoted by Lenin and the Communist party. Bakunin was the great antagonist of Karl Marx in the first International (1864–76); the main point of contention between them was whether the goals of the social revolution could best be achieved by acquiring power in a strong, centralized state (a proletarian dictatorship in place of the liberal democratic bourgeois state) or by a decentralized federation of self–governing factories, communal farms, service companies, and towns.

Lenin extended Marx's vision of an authoritarian socialist state as far as that of a world union of soviet socialist republics. Only since 1991, with the collapse of the Communist party and worldwide repudiation of the methods of Marxist–Leninist communism, does it seem that socialism has definitely discarded the authoritarian, centralized state as a means for the achievement of its ends at national or world levels. Hence, new attention may now focus on the federalist alternatives of Proudhon, Bakunin, and Kropotkin.

Such a reexamination is also useful because much of "pop politics"—contemporary popular music, peace movements opposed to traditional foreign policy, and emerging transnational civil society—are unconsciously anarchistic in the federalist sense. "That government is best which governs least," wrote Thoreau in his essay "On Civil Disobedience" (1848). "And when men are prepared for it," he added, "that government is best which governs not at all." As John Lennon put it in his song "Imagine" (1971):[20]

> Imagine there's no country,
> It isn't hard to do.
> Nothing to kill or die for,
> And no religion too.
> Imagine all the people
> Living life in peace!
> You may say I'm a dreamer,
> But I'm not the only one.
> I hope someday you'll join us,
> And the world will live as one!

Lenin and Stalin

It remains to provide some brief account of how federalism fitted into the Communist party program. Lenin, in "On the Slogan for a United States of Europe" (August 1915), thought that the idea, politically, could be useful if it advanced the establishment of democratic republics in Europe, "accompanied by the revolutionary overthrow of the three most reactionary monarchies in Europe, headed by the Russian." World War I accomplished this objective for him. If European imperialism continued, Lenin admitted that a U.S. of Europe could only amount to "an agreement on the partition of colonies" or merely "an organization of reaction to retard America's more rapid development."[21]

In the struggle of socialism with world capitalism, Lenin, like Marx, envisaged "a period of turbulent political and economic upheavals, the most intense class struggle, civil war, revolutions, and counterrevolutions." Against the opposition of the capitalist class and the bourgeois state, Lenin argued, the working class had to aim at the creation of a socialist *state,* first in one country, then in others. This view led him to reflect on a United States of the World:[22]

> A United States of the World (not of Europe alone) is the state form of the unification and freedom of nations which we associate with socialism—until the time when the complete victory of socialism brings about the total disappearance of the state, including the democratic.

The socialist state, then, national and world, was in Lenin's eyes to be the instrument of the revolution, pending the time when it could "wither away," as

[20] Words and Music by John Lennon. © 1971 (Renewed 1999) LENONO.MUSIC. All rights Controlled and Administered by EMI BLACKWOOD MUSIC INC. All Rights Reserved. International Copyright Secured. Used by Permission.

[21] V. I. Lenin, "On the Slogan for a United States of Europe," August 1915, *Selected Works* (Moscow: Progress Publishers, 1963), 1: 629–32; *Collected Works,* 21: 339–43.

[22] Ibid., 631.

free, working individuals took increasing responsibility for their own lives. Lenin generally was contemptuous of "the petty–bourgeois ideal of federal relationships,"[23] but at the Russian level (Russian Socialist Federative Soviet Republic) and even the international (Comintern), he was forced to acknowledge its value as a "transitional form."[24]

The First Congress of the Comintern (March 1919) could only call for the establishment of soviets (popular councils) among the working people everywhere. The Second Congress (July 1920), however, issued a clear call for a *world communist state*. There Lenin ridiculed the new Covenant of the League of Nations, which failed to terminate the Allied invasion of Russia and was already being repudiated by the Big Four capitalist victors over Germany. Lenin predicted that the inevitable failure of the League would prove that capitalism could not reform itself. He looked forward not to an improved international organization of sovereign states, nor to a constitutionally limited world federation respecting national differences, but to the "world proletarian revolution, the creation of a world soviet republic."[25]

The only softening of this line came with the establishment of the Russian Soviet Federated Socialist Republic in 1922. Stalin was commissar of nationalities at the time, and federation seemed like the only available political device to keep the more than 100 nationalities in the former Russian empire voluntarily in a socialist republic. Even the *right of secession* was formally granted in the constitution of the Union of Soviet Socialist Republics of 1924. Lenin and Stalin certainly never imagined that the constituent republics and autonomous regions in the union would ever exercise their right, and the Communist party of the Soviet Union rapidly transformed the federation into virtually a unitary state. But the form was always there—even as a model for a world soviet republic— and since 1991 we have seen what potential lies latent in a federal union for self–government and national independence.[26]

Internationalism before World War I

Opposed to Lenin was Woodrow Wilson. There were several roots of what is now remembered as "Wilsonianism"—that is, President Wilson's foreign policy and its continuing legacy. In order of influence, these were religious pacifism, international law, conference diplomacy, and the beginnings of international organization. The Concert of Europe following the Congress at Vienna had introduced the practice within diplomacy of meeting in international conferences to

[23] V. I. Lenin, "On the National Pride of the Great Russians," December 1914, *Selected Works*, 1: 625–28; *Collected Works*, 21: 102–6.

[24] V. I. Lenin, "Theses for the Second Congress of the Communist International," 5 June 1920, *Selected Works*, 3: 374; *Collected Works*, 31: 154.

[25] V. I. Lenin, "Report on the International Situation and the Fundamental Tasks of the Communist International," 19 July 1920, Second Congress of the Communist International, *Selected Works*, 3: 397–98, 404; *Collected Works*, 31: 225–26, 234.

[26] Vernon V. Aspaturian, "The Theory and Politics of Soviet Federalism," *Journal of Politics*, 12 (1950): 20–51.

settle grave issues of war and peace, as in the Berlin conference in 1878, which reversed Russian gains in the recent war in Bulgaria, or again in 1884, which provided for the partition of Africa. One acute scholar, Warren Kuehl, counts more than 350 international conferences in the 19th century.[27] The Pan–American conference of 1889 and the first Hague conference on international arbitration in 1899 were typical. By the Paris peace conference in 1919, the diplomatists, of whom Wilson is usually accounted one, as by Arthur S. Link, were in the best position to determine the shape of the Covenant of the League of Nations.

Also influential on Wilson, there was a diverse group of authors, advocates, elected representatives, public speakers, and members of citizens' organizations who sought to establish some form of permanent international organization acceptable to national states yet effective in preventing war. These were the internationalists. The internationalists struggled for international arbitration, conciliation, processes for the peaceful resolution of disputes, a court of justice applying international law, annual congresses for regular consultation, a world assembly to enact law, sanctions to enforce international decisions against aggressor states, some kind of executive council, and a secretariat or continuing administration. The Rhine River Commission, first of modern international organizations, was created in 1815. The International Telegraphic (now Telecommunications) Union was established in 1865, and the Universal Postal Union in 1874. The first *non*governmental organization was the World Evangelical Alliance, founded in 1846.

It is striking that, in the period before the establishment of the League of Nations, the world federalists of the time played a leading role. This is made abundantly clear in Warren Kuehl's *Seeking World Order* (1969), the standard history of the internationalists before 1920. One of them was Hamilton Holt, the moving spirit of the League to Enforce Peace in 1915–20, which had a definite influence on Wilson's League of Nations. From 1903 to his death in 1951, Holt was a tireless advocate of an international system with the United States at its core. One of Holt's last acts was to host the Rollins College conference in 1946 in response to first use of atomic bombs in war.

League to Enforce Peace
The League to Enforce Peace rapidly became the leading American citizens' organization in favor of creation of a league of nations in which the United States would be a full participant. With former U.S. president William Howard Taft as president and Harvard's A. Lawrence Lowell as chairman, the league drew together prominent figures in the peace movement, business, law, education, and government, including Wilson's secretary of war Newton D. Baker.[28]

At its height in 1919, the League to Enforce Peace had over 300,000 mem-

---

[27] Warren F. Kuehl, *Seeking World Order: The United States and International Organization to 1920* (Nashville: Vanderbilt University Press, 1969).

[28] Ibid., 191; Ruhl J. Bartlett, *The League to Enforce Peace* (Chapel Hill: University of North Carolina Press, 1944), 39.

bers[29] and well organized chapters in 20 states[30]—which was three times the membership of the American Association for the United Nations in 1949, and six times that of United World Federalists at its height that same year. The league had a budget in 1916 of nearly $300,000, which in real terms was even higher than that of the subsequent organizations.[31] It drew so many people to the cause that in May 1919, when President Wilson called a special session of Congress, in part to ratify the Peace Treaty, including the Covenant of the League of Nations, *12,000 speeches per day* under the auspices of the League to Enforce Peace were given in its favor across the country.[32]

The policy of the League to Enforce Peace at its founding included four rather modest proposals: (1) that the United States create a league of nations in which "justiciable" questions of international law would have to be submitted to a judicial tribunal; (2) that members "jointly use their military force to prevent any one of their number from going to war" before submitting the question to the tribunal; (3) that "non-justiciable"—that is, *political*—questions be submitted to a council of conciliation before members go to war; and (4) that occasional international conferences be held to codify international law, including precedents set by the tribunal.[33] Hence, war was not absolutely abolished: nations were only to be constrained to undergo processes of conciliation and adjudication before resorting to war. As Theodore Marburg wrote, the proposed league "was fundamentally a league to compel inquiry before nations are allowed to fight."[34] The eventual League of Nations was just so modestly structured.

Weakness of the Covenant despite the Internationalists

The internationalists, then, primarily through the League to Enforce Peace, certainly popularized the idea of a league and had some influence among national leaders. But President Wilson remained cautious about any constitutional departures, and the Senate remained close to the "no entangling alliances" tradition. The history of the drafting of the Covenant can be told almost without respect to the internationalists—so independent was Woodrow Wilson. This fact explains why the resultant Covenant appeared so strange, with its renewed emphasis on arbitration, its lack of an integral world court, and its pledge to defend the territorial integrity and political independence of every state member by force if need be. Apart from one speech to the League to Enforce Peace in 1916, Wilson generally remained aloof, not wishing to provoke opposition abroad or at home by descending into details.[35] But as Senator Lodge said, "Everything depends on the details."[36]

---

[29] Kuehl, 314.
[30] Bartlett, 62.
[31] Ibid., 61.
[32] Kuehl, 313–14.
[33] Kuehl, 190; Bartlett, 40–41.
[34] Kuehl, 192.
[35] Ibid., 254.
[36] Ibid., 222.

The drafting of the Covenant of the League of Nations began within a group called the Inquiry, assembled by Wilson's trusted advisor, Colonel Edward M. House, beginning in mid–1917.[37] The State Department was hardly involved as it would be 25 years later for the drafting of the U.N. Charter.[38] One of the Inquiry's members was the brilliant young journalist Walter Lippmann, who had written an interpretation of Wilson's Fourteen Points that was widely respected at the Paris peace conference.[39] He also was on record, in 1915, that a "world state" had to be the ultimate objective for a peaceful and prosperous world.[40] In 1946, in response to the advent of atomic energy, Lippmann wrote a similar essay for the atomic scientists' manifesto, *One World or None*, in which he eloquently called upon the American people to commit themselves to the "formation of a world order of universal law!"[41] Lippmann was typical of sophisticated internationalists who retained all his life the standard of ultimate world federation.[42]

But pressures of the last year of war and of the threat of Bolshevism produced haste. Neither British nor French plans provided for the firm abolition of war. In just *two days* (13–14 July 1918),[43] House produced a plan that Wilson later rather hastily modified by eliminating the court of justice, casting aside at a stroke the object of years of internationalists' efforts, and adding military sanctions, in addition to economic sanctions, against states that resorted to war in defiance of an arbitral award or league recommendation.[44] At the Paris peace conference, the diplomatists Sir Robert Cecil (later, Lord Cecil) and General Jan Christiaan Smuts had the most influence on the shape of the Covenant.[45] The actual drafting of the Covenant was accomplished by 19 commissioners (including Wilson and House for the U.S.A., Cecil and Smuts for Britain, Léon Bourgeois for France, Vittorio Orlando for Italy), who met for the astonishingly brief period of *10 days* (3–13 February 1919), often in the evenings after hard days of bargaining at the peace conference. There was a second period of about

[37] Ibid., 256–57.

[38] Lawrence E. Gelfand, *The Inquiry: American Preparations for Peace, 1917–1919* (New Haven: Yale University Press, 1963).

[39] *Papers Relating to Foreign Affairs, 1918*, Supplement 1: *The World War*, 1: 405–13; *The Annals of America, 1916–1928: World War and Prosperity* (Chicago: Encyclopedia Britannica, 1976), 14: 151–57.

[40] Walter Lippmann, *The Stakes of Diplomacy* (1915), 177–78.

[41] Walter Lippmann, "International Control of Atomic Energy," in Dexter Masters and Katharine Way, eds., *One World or None* (New York: McGraw–Hill, 1946), 66–75. Emphasis his.

[42] Anwar Hussain Syed, *Walter Lippmann's Philosophy of International Politics* (Philadelphia: University of Pennsylvania Press, 1963); D. Steven Blum, *Walter Lippmann: Cosmopolitanism in the Century of Total War* (Ithaca, NY: Cornell University Press, 1984).

[43] Kuehl, 259.

[44] Ibid., 260–62.

[45] Francis P. Walters, *A History of the League of Nations* (London: Oxford University Press, 1952), 23.

three weeks (18 March–11 April 1919), when Wilson had to negotiate four amendments demanded by the U.S. Senate, but the substantial frame of the Covenant had already been laid down in February.[46]

Collective Security

The distractions of the conference drafting the peace treaty, the consequential lower priority of the Covenant, the haste of the drafters, the influence of Smuts, Cecil, and the diplomatists in the commission, their lack of direct accountability to the people by election for the drafting of what was to be a world constitution to preserve the peace, the secrecy in which they conducted their deliberations, and their general isolation from the thinking of most internationalists in Europe and America—all help to explain why the Covenant of the League of Nations was so surprising and so weak.

The term "sovereignty" did not appear prominently in the Covenant, but the preamble made clear that this covenant was an agreement between "High Contracting Parties." Article I provided that only *states* would be members; Articles III and IV granted each state but one vote; and Article V laid down a rule of unanimity for decisions in either Assembly or Council (except for admission of new members or selection of permanent members of the Council). That is, each state had an absolute veto.

The heart of the Covenant, in Wilson's view, was its assertion of the new principle in international relations of collective security (Article X):

> The Members of the League undertake to respect and preserve as against external aggression the territorial integrity and existing political independence of all Members of the League.

Wilson had affirmed this principle in his proposal of a Pan–American union in January 1916, even before he addressed the League to Enforce Peace, and he often repeated it in his wartime addresses.[47] At Paris, the French and the smaller powers saw it as the bulwark of their safety against a resurgent Germany and other great powers, but the British, particularly Cecil, feared it would become a bastion of the status quo. Cecil therefore proposed an additional section allowing the Assembly to recommend changes in treaties, including the peace treaties then being drafted with very harsh provisions, in order to permit rectification of injustices and peaceful change. A relic of this "statesmanlike plan" barely survived in Article XIX. That article was the last hope for rectifying the Versailles Treaty and hence removing Germany's grievances that Hitler exploited on the road to World War II. In the U.N. Charter, the substance of Article X was restored not as a guarantee but as a "principle" or pledge (Article 2(4)).

Gap in the Covenant

The Covenant contained several provisions for the peaceful settlement of in-

---

[46] Kuehl, 270–71; Walters, 33–37; David Hunter Miller, *The Drafting of the Covenant* (New York: Putnam, 1928).

[47] Walters, 48–49; Kuehl, 275–76.

ternational disputes that had grown out of enlightened state usage and reflective internationalist discussion: inquiry (Article XI), arbitration and adjudication (Articles XII–XIII), and conciliation (Article XV). But *war* remained a legitimate option for the state, since it was provided that, should a state complete the process of peaceful settlement, lasting six months, and wait another three months, if the dispute were still unsettled, then the state may "resort to war" (Article XII). Or, if the Council were unable, unanimously, to recommend a settlement, the member states "reserve to themselves the right to take such action as they shall consider necessary for the maintenance of right and justice" (Article XV).[48]

This was the famous "gap" in the Covenant. Even though Wilson claimed that the Covenant abolished aggressive war, it had not done so. Perhaps this process would have obviated the precipitous beginning of the Great War, but in later years conditions were never so similar, and no nation ever exercised its right to resort to war in the manner provided under the Covenant. The *right* to wage war as an instrument of national policy was not abolished *in international law* until the Kellogg–Briand Pact of 1928 and thereafter in Articles 2(3) and 2(4) of the U.N. Charter. The *possibility* of war has never been eliminated. The provisions for disarmament in the Covenant (Article VIII) were a dead letter without effective collective security and peaceful settlement.

The Illusion of Military Sanctions

Lastly, the Covenant provided for seemingly effective economic and *military* sanctions against states that "break the covenant" or commit acts of aggression (Article XVI).[49] It is surprising that the Senate did not object so vigorously to this article, which is the one that in principle could have visited boycotts, freezes, blockades, and acts of war upon the United States. The difference was that Article X laid down the offense, and Article XVI the punishment. But read closely, Article XVI applied only to violators of the three articles on peaceful settlement. Were, then, sanctions available for violators of Article X? Not strictly. The Council then would only "advise" members of appropriate action. If the offender entered the process beginning with Article XII, and if Article XVI were invoked, the Council, if unanimous (except for parties to the dispute), could only "recommend" action.

The whole enforcement section was set up so loosely that we may wonder that anyone, like Senator Borah, was ever afraid of League sanctions,[50] or, like President Wilson, expected they would deter aggressors. The federalist solution of creating a world legal system to provide enforcement of the laws upon individuals was never considered. Sanctions could have worked only if there were overwhelming *will* among the states members of the League to apply the Covenant's deliberately ambiguous provisions. Against Japan's invasion of Manchuria, Hitler's reoccupation of the Rhineland, and Mussolini's attack on Ethiopia, such will could not be found. By the 1930s, League sanctions were a hol-

---

[48] Walters, 52; Kuehl, 277.

[49] Walters, 53.

[50] Kuehl, 293.

low threat.

Essentially, therefore, the Covenant of the League of Nations was an attempt to achieve peace by associating states within an organization that would oblige them to conform their traditional pursuit of power for security and prestige within forms commonly agreed upon—war remaining an ultimate right. It was not a new union or federal government to which states and peoples would delegate powers for common purposes, starting with the absolute abolition of war.

The "political" organs of the Council and Assembly—that is, new organs of power politics—would henceforth dominate the international organization, in place of "judicial" organs symbolized by the optional Permanent Court of International Justice. The vision of the internationalists, including the federalists, of a world gradually, yet decisively, expanding international law and creating new law by world legislation, under standards of justice derived from the highest traditions of the civilizations and religions throughout the world, had very little influence.[51]

As Warren Kuehl concludes, "The belief in an imposed peace seemed more important to the draftsmen at Paris than the vision of a world adjusting to new conditions under a system of justice and law."[52]

Wilsonianism

Although the Covenant was deeply flawed, the very attempt of President Wilson to bring the United States into the League of Nations was an event of world significance. The national leadership and world statesmanship of Woodrow Wilson mark a new beginning in the history of international organization designed to maintain world peace. With Wilson, the ideal enters the realm of practical politics. Wilson deserves more credit than any other political philosopher or practical politician for the actual establishment of the League of Nations. Though due to some of Wilson's own misjudgments the United States remained outside the League, and though the League proved too weak to stem the course of events leading to World War II, the very establishment of the League of Nations was a break in sovereign national traditions. It was, as Wilson himself said in his last public address, a "revolution" in received ideas about international relations—like the state's "right of conquest," or its internationally "legal" recourse to war as an instrument of policy—that in many ways was more of a triumphal break with the past than the subsequent establishment of the United Nations. If ever humanity unites still more closely in a world federation, that will only be a refinement of the U.N., which itself was a modest improvement on the League. Wilson was the great innovator. "Wilsonianism," the sum of his international doctrines, remains a source of inspiration or an object of attack for idealists or realists to this day.

Wilson delivered at least 10 significant speeches on an "association of nations" that deserve to be singled out as classics of Wilsonianism analogous to the works of Kant or Rousseau that we have already noted. In these speeches,

[51] Kuehl, 285, 336, 344.
[52] Ibid., 286.

Wilson set out his international doctrines with a clarity that has never been equaled. Even President Franklin Delano Roosevelt, who brought about U.S. participation in a revived League and who quietly guided the official processes leading to the establishment of the United Nations, never spoke so clearly. Grenville Clark, the elder statesman of the federalist movement, rarely wrote about "justice." The only comparable publicists, in our judgment, have been Robert M. Hutchins, G. A. Borgese, and their colleagues in the University of Chicago's Committee to Frame a World Constitution from 1945 to 1951. But they were not elected national leaders nor statesmen responsible to the public.

In his speeches Wilson emphasized the principles of the sovereignty of the people (self–determination), the interdependence of nations (against isolationism), the acceleration of history in the industrial age ("the day of conquest and aggrandizement is gone by"). He spoke of not a balance of power but a union of peoples, not equality of nations but equality of rights, and international cooperation as emerging respect for the rule of world law. For instance, he argued, especially in his last great address at Pueblo, Colorado, on 25 September 1919, that the League, like governments, would have to rely on the loyalty, "moral forces," and judgment of the people, for armed force was only "in the background"[53] as a "last resort."[54] He also hoped that the establishment of the International Labour Organisation would build solidarity among the workers of the world and thus undercut the appeal of Bolshevism.[55] He looked forward to a concert of peaceful, democratic states as autocracies like the German, Austro–Hungarian, and Turkish Empires were replaced by free, self–governing states based on nationality. (The era of Communist party dictatorships and Fascist totalitarianisms was hardly expected.) Ultimately, Wilson implied, the League of Nations itself would become democratic. "The world," said Wilson in a famous phrase (with the emphasis on "world"), "must be made safe for democracy."[56]

Justice above "Interests"

Wilson did speak at great length about "evenhanded and impartial justice,"[57] the last of the ideal objectives of an association of nations that we will discuss here. What did Woodrow Wilson mean by *justice?* He often used this term to describe whole lists of U.S. war aims or the larger objectives to come out of the Great War. In 1916, it included self–determination, the rights of small nations, and international security.[58] In 1918, it included all the Fourteen Points, introduced as the "interest" of all the peoples of the world in "justice and fair

---

[53] *Public Papers of Woodrow Wilson,* Ray Stannard Baker and William E. Dodd, eds. (New York: Harper, 1927), *War and Peace,* 1: 426. Hereafter: Baker.

[54] Ibid., 2: 402–03.

[55] Ibid., 1: 543.

[56] Ibid., 14.

[57] *The Papers of Woodrow Wilson,* Arthur S. Link, ed. (Princeton: Princeton University Press, 1981), 37: 115. Hereafter: Link.

[58] Ibid.

dealing."[59]

That meant open diplomacy, freedom of the seas, free trade, disarmament, impartial adjustment of colonial claims, the defeat of Germany, settlements in Russia, Belgium, France, Italy, Austria–Hungary, Romania, Serbia, Turkey, and Poland, and finally a league of nations to guarantee the political independence and territorial integrity of great and small states alike. These objectives were necessary, Wilson said, for "the right" to prevail.[60] On leaving for the peace conference in Paris, he added and qualified these points of "impartial justice": no favorites among states, no special interests favored over the common interest, no economic favoritism, no partial alliances within the league, no secret treaties.[61]

Justice, then, like right, in Wilson's mind was conceived as the comprehensive objective of the general association of nations, without ever quite implying a world state to protect it. Yet *justice,* as Wilson understood it, was very far from the "interests" that before and after him were held to be the highest standards for national conduct.

American Leadership

Wilson expressed many objectives for the peoples engaged in the World War and then in the making of the peace—justice and right, liberty, equality, solidarity, security, a league of nations. He commented at a midpoint in the Paris negotiations that the wounded soldiers and crowds of ordinary people demanded these things but "had no particular notion of how it was to be done."[62] That was the task of leadership at a great, chaotic opportunity for statecraft. Wilson responded with new expressions of *American idealism,* and this peculiar idealism deserves a prominent place in Wilsonianism.

Over 100 years before, Presidents Washington and Jefferson had left office with profound warnings to the citizens of their small republic against entangling alliances with Europe. President Wilson was well aware that this isolationist tradition had long served to preserve and protect the United States. But the republic had grown into a great power, and it was tied by countless threads of industry and commerce to the whole world. When the World War drew the United States into the general disaster, Wilson courageously attempted to show the way to a new tradition of American foreign policy—what is now called *internationalism.* His arguments were basically that American liberty could no longer be preserved in isolation, that the republic was founded to make all men free, that America was trusted everywhere and was the hope of the world, that the League of Nations was consistent with American principles, and that failure to lead would have disastrous consequences for America, Europe, and the world.

Senator Borah's Rejection of League Enforcement

This is not the place to retrace the dramatic story of Wilson's struggle with

---

[59] Baker, 1: 158.
[60] Ibid., 161.
[61] Ibid., 256–57.
[62] Ibid., 454.

the Senate over ratification of the Covenant or the tragic history of the League, as other scholars have done,[63] but a few observations may be made from a federalist perspective. First of all, Senator William E. Borah's "irreconcilable" opposition deserves to be remembered not as mindless devotion to Washington and Jefferson's no entangling alliances tradition, but as a clearheaded, if not a forward looking, assertion of abiding principle for the preservation of the republic. His views are relevant for the history of the idea of world federalism.

Borah instantly saw that the mode of enforcement of international decisions contemplated under the Covenant was *war* or measures comparable to war (threats, boycotts, blockades), waged by the collectivity of states against other states. To him, collective security meant not peace but war. It continued the "war to end war." The United States could not be associated with such a scheme without losing its liberties and character as a democratic nation.

Borah expressed himself eloquently in his speech opposing ratification even with the Lodge reservations before the first Senate vote on 19 November 1919:[64]

> You cannot yoke a government whose fundamental maxim is that of liberty to a government [the League] whose first law is that of force and hope to preserve the former. These things are in eternal war, and one must ultimately destroy the other. You may still keep for a time the outward form, you may still delude yourself, as others have done in the past, with appearances and symbols, but when you shall have committed this republic to a scheme of world control based upon force, upon the combined military force of the four great nations of the world [United States, Great Britain, France, Japan], you will soon have destroyed the atmosphere of freedom, of confidence in the self–governing capacity of the masses, in which alone a democracy may thrive. We may become one of the four dictators of the world, but we shall no longer be master of our own spirit. And what shall it profit us as a nation if we share with others the glory of world control and lose that fine sense of confidence in the people, the soul of democracy?

Borah consistently opposed the use of force by an international organization, preferring instead the appeal to public opinion in preparation for the rule of law, as in his later leadership of the "outlawry of war" movement. However unrealistic and impractical for short–term foreign policy that a demand for reliance on world public opinion and voluntary acceptance of the decisions of an internation-

---

[63] Thomas A. Bailey, *Woodrow Wilson and the Lost Peace* (Chicago: Quadrangle, 1944); Bailey, *Woodrow Wilson and the Great Betrayal* (Chicago: Quadrangle, 1945); Arthur S. Link, *Wilson the Diplomatist: A Look at His Major Foreign Policies* (Chicago: Quadrangle, 1957); Francis P. Walters, *A History of the League of Nations* (London: Oxford University Press, 1952); Gary B. Ostrower, *The United States and the League of Nations in the Early Thirties* (Lewisburg, PA: Bucknell University Press, 1979); John M. Blum, *Woodrow Wilson and the Politics of Morality* (Boston: Little, Brown, 1956); Robert E. Osgood, *Ideals and Self– Interest in America's Foreign Relations* (Chicago: University of Chicago Press, 1953).

[64] *Congressional Record*, 66th Cong., 1st sess., 19 November 1919, p. 8,783; *The Annals of America: 1919*, 14: 204.

al organization was then and still is, the relatively nonviolent rule of law contemplated in some subsequent, federal stage of world organization can rest on no
other basis.

Senator Lodge's Reservations to Nullify the Covenant

Second, it seems a reasonable historical conclusion that the reservations of
Senator Lodge in no way corrected the inadequacies of the Covenant but rather,
as the president wrote to his Democratic intermediary Senator Gilbert M. Hitchcock (D., Nebraska) on the day before the first crucial vote, they would have led
to "nullification" of the treaty. Lodge himself knew that the reservations had
binding significance, as they generally do in international law. A reader of the
14 reservations today cannot escape the impression that they made a mockery of
the national pledges in the Covenant. One reservation, for instance, provided
that the "United States assumes no obligation to preserve the territorial integrity
or political independence of any other country" unless Congress, in the exercise
of its power to declare war, authorizes the international employment of the military or naval forces of the U.S. (destructive of Covenant Article X).

Considering how hedged and qualified the Covenant already was with respect
to state sovereignty, the Lodge reservations would have destroyed not only the
spirit of the League but also the last measure of its binding substance. Reservations have since become a regular feature of Senate ratification of multilateral
treaties like the International Covenant on Civil and Political Rights. One significant exception was the U.N. Charter, which was ratified *without reservations*
in 1945, at a moment of great faith in the future. If ever a world federation is
established, it must be based on a firm moral and political commitment, like
Wilson's imaginative League, without equivocations and exemptions expressed
in reservations.

Wilson's Resolute Leadership Not to Compromise

Third, from a federalist viewpoint it seems a reasonable historical conclusion
that Wilson, when directing the Democratic and moderate Republican senators to
vote for the Covenant without the Lodge reservations and against the Covenant
with them, was exercising the highest political leadership to save what little international organization he had been able to win assent to by painful negotiations in Paris and by partisan political struggle domestically in the United
States. He certainly made many tactical political errors in struggling for U.S.
assent to the Covenant, which were not repeated when Franklin Delano Roosevelt tried again with the Charter of the United Nations. Wilson should not have
allowed the drafting and ratification of the Covenant to descend into a partisan,
Democratic–Republican party conflict, he should have separated the Covenant
from the Peace Treaty, and perhaps he should have even have accepted the earlier
mild reservations like those he later worked out with Senator Hitchcock in order
to maneuver the moderate Republicans into temporary alliance with the loyal
Democrats while public support was still high.

The personal animosity between Lodge and Wilson was not so large a factor as their difference in principle over what kind of international organization the United States should accede to. Lodge was willing to accept one that could not automatically involve the U.S. in war; Wilson wanted one in which international diplomatic pressure and economic sanctions would in most cases be sufficient while military sanctions remained as an ultimate threat. Nor was Wilson's illness, after his collapse in Pueblo, so incapacitating as to cause him to lose sight of the main issue—the salvaging of a league with some real powers—and he refused to compromise with Lodge, very evidently in expectation that enough senators would see the "right."

A league of nations to maintain the peace had become a necessity in the modern world. A new order of international relations based not on a balance of power but on a community of power was long overdue. America was in the world, and international organization was consistent with her ideals. "Justice, liberation, and succor," as Wilson expressed American ideals in his Metropolitan Opera House address in March 1919, were the great ideals in the "vision of the people."[65] These were the large themes of Wilson's international leadership. Whatever tactical compromises he may have had to make, strategically Wilson was very right. The world has not seen his political courage since. That is why world federalists will always look back to Wilson for inspiration.

Federalist ideals were at work among internationalists and behind Wilson's own genius; but neither Wilson nor Lodge nor any European statesman gave the slightest thought to actually establishing a world federal government, empowered to enact law reaching to individuals, in order to keep the peace after the Great War. All their energies were expended to break the traditions of isolationism and nationalism. The resulting League was pitifully weak. Even so, it was too much for the Senate, which rejected the Covenant without reservations by 53 nays to 38 yeas on 19 November 1919, and again by a margin of seven votes on 19 March 1920. The public, too, by the last date had lost its former enthusiasm.[66]

Implications of U.S. Isolation for the Coming of World War II

Would U.S. entry into the League of Nations have saved the organization and prevented World War II? Many historians seem to assume so when they portray Wilson's defeat by the Senate in 1919 and again in 1920 as a tragic setback for the United States and ultimately the world.[67] No doubt the participation of the U.S. along with that of Britain, France, Italy, and Japan in the League would have radically altered world history. One of the Council's greatest concerns at the time it was deliberating whether to apply sanctions against Italy in 1935—the issue that decided the fate of the League—was whether the United States (not a member and hence not bound) as the world's greatest economic and potentially

---

[65] *Public Papers of Woodrow Wilson*, Ray Stannard Baker and William E. Dodd, eds. (New York: Harper, 1927), *War and Peace*, 452.

[66] Bailey, *Woodrow Wilson and the Lost Peace*, 57, 117, 199–201, 204–5, 322, 324; *Woodrow Wilson and the Great Betrayal*, 120–22, 272–74.

[67] Walters, *League*, 72–74; Blum, *Politics of Morality*, 197; Link, *Diplomatist*, 125; Bailey, *Great Betrayal*, 277, 356–61.

military power would honor them.[68]

But to assume that the main fault with the League was not its structure but the absence of the United States is to imply that Article XIX would have led to early revision of the Treaty of Versailles, obviating Germany's grievances.[69] It implies that an effective League would have supplied the need for the promised treaty of guarantee with France (1919),[70] the Treaty of Rapallo establishing diplomatic relations between Germany and Russia (1922),[71] and the Treaties of Locarno between Germany, Belgium, France, Italy, and Britain (1925),[72] which seemed to guarantee the signatories' borders and to collectively guard them against aggression by one another. Moreover, this easy assumption implies that the Protocol on the Peaceful Settlement of Disputes (1924) would have been ratified and have entered into force,[73] that there would have been no occasion for the Anglo–German naval agreement once Hitler embarked on rearmament (1935),[74] or the Hoare–Laval agreement on the dismemberment of Ethiopia (1935),[75] or the capitulation at Munich (1938),[76] or the Hitler–Stalin nonaggression pact (1939).[77]

All this is too much to hope for. Judging by the strength of lingering sovereign and military traditions, even with the United States as a member, the League of Nations by all odds would still have failed, as the United Nations, its successor built on the same principle of sovereign equality did for its largest purposes by the end of 1946. But then, if a second world war had still come, it could not have been claimed at the end of it, as in 1945, that the reason why the League failed was that the United States had refused to join.[78] The weaknesses of a league of sovereign states would have been much more evident to all, and hence the arguments of the internationalists and the federalists for a much stronger world organization based on justice and law, even a constitutionally limited, world federal government, might, at humanity's second chance, have prevailed.

---

[68] Walters, *League,* 660.
[69] Walters, *League,* 49, 54–55.
[70] Ibid., 55, 222.
[71] Ibid., 165.
[72] Ibid., 291–94.
[73] Ibid., 268–76, 283–85.
[74] Ibid., 613–14.
[75] Ibid., 669.
[76] Ibid., 777–83.
[77] Ibid., 796.
[78] Ibid., 72–74, 385–87, 711.

2

Clarence Streit: Federal Union of Democracies

What we are trying to do is to keep peace without war. To succeed in that we have to do something dramatic. We have to step ahead of our time. We have to jump over a certain space. The most dangerous way to leap a chasm is in two steps.

—Clarence K. Streit, testimony at House hearings on the world federalist resolutions, 12 May 1948

The Coming of World War II

By the 1930s, after a decade of historic development, the League of Nations began to fail in keeping the peace. In principle, the reason was that the League, by the terms of its Covenant, did not limit the sovereign independence of its members.[1] When the League protested the Japanese invasion of Manchuria in 1931, Japan withdrew from the League and contemptuously proceeded to incorporate conquered Manchuria into her imperial domains. This was followed in the decade by futile League fulminations against Italian aggression in Ethiopia in 1935, German reoccupation of the Rhineland in defiance of the Versailles Treaty in 1936, and intervention by fascist and democratic great powers in the Spanish Civil War in 1936-39. The British settlement with Nazi Germany over Czechoslovakia at Munich in 1938 took place with hardly any respect for the League. The Munich settlement then was taken as the occasion for further German aggression against Poland, which in turn unloosed the Second World War.

It was in this context of the portended failure of the League of Nations that a few stronger voices began to be raised in behalf of world government. H. G. Wells added a prophetic Chapter 41 ("Man's Coming of Age. The Probable Struggle for the Unification of the World into One Community of Knowledge and Will") to *The Outline of History* in 1920 and wrote one of the original books of the movement, *The Shape of Things to Come* in 1933. Some of his writings found their way into the U.S. State Department. Small "Wellsian

---

[1] "The limitation of its membership and possibility of withdrawal apart, the most serious institutional weakness of the League was the requirement of unanimity of action by the Council or the Assembly." C. Wilfred Jenks, *The World beyond the Charter: Four Stages of World Organization* (London: Allen & Unwin, 1969), 70.

Societies" sprang up in various parts of the world, but their inaction earned for them from the press the new epithet "utopian," that is, one who wills the end but not the means.[2]

Union Now

In November 1938, Clarence K. Streit, *New York Times* foreign correspondent at the League of Nations in Geneva, returned to the United States with a heavy manuscript that Harpers in New York had agreed to publish the next March. Streit believed that Hitler was not satisfied with the Munich agreement but would start a general war in August or September 1939. Streit was racing against time, for he had a proposal in his manuscript that he believed, if it were well promoted upon publication, would stop Hitler. The proposal was a federal union of the democracies against the Axis powers. The book was called *Union Now*.[3]

Union Now was a book that combined, in the words of a professor of political science who reviewed it at Oberlin College in April 1939, "the acute, realistic analysis of a Hamilton with the exuberant vision of a Walt Whitman."[4] It was a book to move hearts. It assembled a political will. Streit, who had had the experience of covering the national disruptions of the League for 10 years, looked out realistically at the world with the spirit of Americans at the time of their Revolution:[5]

> Now when man's future seems so vast, catastrophe threatens to cut us from it.... depression, dictatorship, false recovery and war are hemming us in.... I believe there is a way through these dangers, and out of the dilemma, a way to do what we all want, to keep both peace and freedom.
>
> The way through is Union now of the democracies that the North Atlantic and a thousand other things already unite—Union of these few peoples in a great federal republic built on and for the thing they share most, their common democratic principle of government for the sake of individual freedom.

Streit proposed a union of 15 nations, like that of the 13 states of the United States in 1787. He suggested the union be granted maximal powers to provide for common citizenship (rights), defense, regulation of interstate commerce,

---

[2] H. G. Wells, *The Shape of Things to Come* (New York: Macmillan,1933). Wells returned, obliquely, to this theme in a science fiction work, *Star Begotten* (New York: Viking, 1937), dedicated to Winston Churchill. On the eve of World War II, Wells saw hope for man only in a eugenic improvement of the race, caused by cosmic rays.

[3] Clarence K. Streit, "A 44-Year Marathon against War," Address to Triple Anniversary Celebration, Washington, DC, 21 January 1978, *Freedom & Union,* Summer 1978, pp. 4-6; Clarence K. Streit, *Union Now* (New York and London: Harper & Bros., 1939).

[4] Oscar Jaszi, Introduction to *Union Now,* postwar ed., by Clarence K. Streit (New York: Harper & Bros., 1949), xiii.

[5] Streit, *Union Now,* 1-2. Emphasis omitted.

union money, and uniform postal, transportation, and communication systems.[6] The "founder democracies" to be united he listed as the United States, the British Commonwealth (including the United Kingdom, Canada, Australia, New Zealand, Union of South Africa, and Ireland), France, Belgium, the Netherlands, Switzerland, Denmark, Norway, Sweden, and Finland. These democracies, if united, would acquire a preponderance of force far in excess of the military forces of the fascist states, and thus they could deter war.[7]

The Sovereignty of the People

But such a union of peoples was not an easy accomplishment in 1939. Streit was most forceful in those passages in which he reminded his readers that the modern democracies were established to secure the rights of the people, especially liberty, through the operation of laws that regard all the people as equals. The sovereignty of the state was created by the sovereign people only as a means to protect their individual freedom. State sovereignty was not absolute in the beginning. But the history of the Atlantic democracies by 1939 indicated to Streit that they had fallen into the same "heresy of absolute national sovereignty" as had the 13 states under the League of Friendship (Articles of Confederation) before establishment of the U.S. Constitution. If the peoples of the Atlantic could "cease sacrificing needlessly our individual freedom to the freedom of our nations, be true to our democratic philosophy and establish that 'more perfect Union' toward which all our existing unions explicitly or implicitly aim," they *could* unite. "Are not liberty and Union, now and forever, one and inseparable, as in Webster's day?" Streit asked.[8]

Streit himself saw the advantages of union in the positive terms of increasing individual liberty, reducing the expense and artificial impediments of duplicate national governments, giving scope to individual enterprise and creative ability in a greater, more united civilization. "Then," he concluded broadly, "Man's vast future would begin."[9]

The Union's Preponderance of Power

Streit argued that union would prevent war first by example and then by overwhelming social, economic, and military force. He thought that the citizens of Germany or Italy or Japan, "to attain the equality they crave," would see how needless was the sacrifice of their freedom to their nations' military power, overthrow their autocrats, establish democracies at home, and bring their nations too into the "Great Republic." In the interim, to deter them from following their autocrats in making war on democracies to bring about a new order based on state supremacy, the democratic union would present an insuperable preponderance of power.[10] Streit was quite explicit about this and returned to it again

[6] Ibid., 2, 160-68.

[7] Ibid., 6-7, 86-113, 171-83.

[8] Ibid., 4-5, 30-35.

[9] Ibid., 3.

[10] Ibid., 9-10.

and again.[11]

> Together these fifteen [democracies] own almost half the earth, rule all its
> oceans, govern nearly half mankind. They do two-thirds of the world's trade,
> and most of this would be called their domestic trade once they united.... The
> Union's existing and potential power from the outset would be so gigantic,
> its bulk so vast, its vital centers so scattered, that Germany, Italy, and Japan
> even put together could no more dream of attacking it than Mexico dreams of
> invading the American Union now.

Later Streit calculated the "overwhelming power of the fifteen" and found that
in population they had 280 million to the Axis's 189 million; with dependencies, 914 million to 264 million. In land area the democracies had 62 million
square kilometers to the other's 6 million. In percent of control of critical raw
materials and productive capacity, petroleum, steel, and the like, the democracies
were superior on the order of 60 to 10 percent. In bank deposits, the democracies
had $99 billion; the autocracies, $14 billion. In armed forces, they compared as
$3.3 billion to $1.3 billion for defense expenditures, 3.6 million tons to 1.8 for
naval vessel displacement, 14,000 to 8,500 for air force aircraft, 2.4 million men
to 1.3 million in army effectives.[12]

Streit's Early Attitude toward Russia

This was powerful and encouraging analysis at a time when faith in democracy was faltering, when defenses against Nazi Germany and Imperial Japan were
lacking.[13] The rub was whether the "Atlantic" peoples could be welded into a
political community quickly, even in the face of a deep challenge to their continued existence. One great unknown was the course of the Communist Soviet
Union. In early 1939, it seemed unlikely that the Soviets would side with the
liberal, capitalist democracies, yet it could not be imagined that they would make
common cause with their professed enemies the Nazis. Streit's attitude toward
the Soviet Union is instructive. Russia and its constituent republics were not
lumped in with the Axis, as in the preceding calculations, but were regarded cautiously and fairly as a nation whose social democracy might yet develop into a
form where individual freedom was respected and so permit her admission to the
union.

Streit recognized that the political theory and practice of Soviet Russia admitted no divine–right monarch, as in Japan, and denied the supremacy of the
race or nation over the working man, as in Germany or Italy. "These three
countries make the accident of birth the all important thing in politics, and Soviet Russia shares the democratic abhorrence of this theory that makes men bow
down before blind arbitrary force outside them." Streit recognized that commun-

---

[11] Ibid., 7.

[12] Ibid., 94-104.

[13] Streit explicitly repudiated the idea of the Union's initiating a war or a "crusade
against autocracy abroad," in the spirit of making the world safe for democracy.
Ibid., 9.

ism did not discriminate among men, for their acquisition of power over others, on the basis of nation or race, color or sex, but rather only on that of ideas or possessions, and he was quite courageous, for 1939, in protesting against discrimination by color. He recognized that collective machinery in economics was not incompatible with democracy and indeed had been introduced by democracy in the form of collective political institutions, but he objected to extending state ownership and administration, no less than private enterprise, to every level of economic life without regard to the effect on individual freedom. It was a mistake to identify democracy with either capitalist or socialist economics. He recognized that Russia had had a long history of absolutism and that the Marxists tended to confuse laissez-faire economic theory with democracy, but he was unable to decide whether Russia's rigidity in collective enterprises was a matter of temporary expediency or permanent principle. He thought she could *not* be included in the nucleus of the union at the beginning.[14]

Ultimate World Government

Lastly, Streit believed that the ultimate objective for the democracies was world government. This was definitely a secondary objective for him, after the formation of the nucleus of 15 democracies and the arrest of the trend toward the Second World War. But he placed a chapter on world government early in the book, and he often used the term in contexts that were more clearly about his partial union. When he discussed the difference between league or union, for instance, Streit meant mainly to distinguish the choices for his union of 15.[15]

World government was necessary only because of the progress of the "machine"—telephones, airplanes, world economy—and because of the "interdependence" of peoples. It was necessary because no nation any longer is self-sufficient, because freedom cannot be further extended until anachronistic national barriers are removed, because recourse to war, in a world so interdependent, tends to involve all and so must be replaced by "effective means of making, enforcing, interpreting and revising law."[16]

Streit did little thinking on the complex problem of establishing world government in his own time, but the trend of his arguments, especially his eloquence on the two American revolutions and the failure of the League of Nations, clearly pointed in that direction. For a time a sizable fraction, certainly a creative minority, of his readers took him to be a prophet of world government.

Union Now's Influence

If ever a book made a movement, *Union Now* was such a book. It went through seven editions by 1949: a privately printed edition of 300 (distributed to influential people) in August 1938; the New York and London editions of March 1939; a French translation, *Union ou Chaos?*, in June 1939; a Swedish translation, *Union Nu,* in August 1939; and then, after the war broke out, U.S. edi-

---

[14] Ibid., 109-11.

[15] Ibid., 5-6; Chap. VII, 128-59.

[16] Ibid., 37-39, 46-49.

tions of 1940, 1941, 1943, and 1949. Streit estimated, on publication of his eighth edition in 1961, that over 250,000 copies had been sold.[17]

Streit's ideas led directly to the founding of his own organization, Federal Union.[18] In Britain, his book supported the organization with the same name, Federal Union, though the British had independent founders following the Munich crisis.[19] Streit inspired Grenville Clark to write his first draft of a minimal world constitution in December 1939.[20] Union Now committees and committees of correspondence, hearkening back to those of Samuel Otis, sprang up in the United States and Europe. A number of prominent Americans, including John Foster Dulles, Robert Sherwood, and William Allen White, in 1941 signed an appeal in favor of a "stable system of international relationship which does not periodically break down into worldwide war," adding a favorable reference to Streit's plan.[21]

Later, in 1941, a split in Federal Union over partial versus universal federation led to the formation of World Federalists, who brought a populist line into United World Federalists in 1947.[22] The book came to the attention of historian

---

[17] Streit, "Marathon against War," *Freedom & Union,* Summer 1978, pp. 4-6; Clarence K. Streit, *Freedom's Frontier—Atlantic Union Now* (Washington, DC: Freedom & Union Press, 1961), viii, n. There were also a "pirated" Chinese edition and a Dutch Indonesian edition of 1941.

[18] Mildred Riorden Blake, Reminiscences, Oral History Research Office, Columbia University, 1980, pp. 7-9. Federal Union was legally established by that name on 31 July 1940. Robert J. Weber, "Proposals Involving World Federation Supported by U.S. Nongovernmental Political Action Organizations since World War II" (Ph.D. dissertation, School of International Service, American University, Washington, DC, 1969), pp. 45-46, New York Public Library, Schwimmer–Lloyd Collection.

[19] Richard Mayne and John Pinder, *Federal Union: The Pioneers: A History of Federal Union* (London: Macmillan, 1990).

[20] Grenville Clark, "A Memorandum with Regard to a New Effort to Organize Peace and Containing a Proposal for a 'Federation of Free Peoples'..." (New York: Author, 30 December 1939), pp. 7, passim, Joseph Regenstein Library, Robert M. Hutchins Papers (A), 35.8. Clark provided for legislative and judicial (binding) powers only to maintain the peace; he added recommendatory (nonbinding) powers to deal with disarmament, trade, labor conditions, and the "excesses of competitive nationalism." Hence, in respect of powers, he was already a minimalist. But he admitted certain Latin American countries to the initial membership, and, while he still required new members to have "free institutions," he liberalized the rules for admission of new members. This was his first step, in respect of membership, toward universalism. He showed the proposal to a few highly placed friends. One, Lord Tweedsmuir (John Buchan), governor–general of Canada, advised at the beginning of the war, "I do not think it should be too much broadcast." Tweedsmuir to Clark, 23 January 1940, Baker Library, Grenville Clark Papers, 21.9.

[21] John Gunther, "The Story of Clarence Streit and Union Now," Book of the Month Dividend Announcement, n.d., ante September 1941, pp. 7, 4-5, Stephen Benedict Papers; Clarence K. Streit, *Union Now with Britain* (New York: Harper & Bros., 1941), vi.

[22] Blake, Reminiscences, 10-11.

Merrill Jensen, who was moved to set the record straight (as he thought) on the "critical period in American history" by his first book on the period under the Articles of Confederation.[23] In 1941, according to legend, apparently true, Harris Wofford, while doing his Latin lesson in the bathtub, heard Streit give a speech on the radio, and Harris was so inspired he founded Student Federalists.[24] In the same year U.S. Supreme Court Justice Owen J. Roberts became an ardent advocate of union with the democracies, and he never wavered from that position for the rest of his life.[25]

There were once sanguine hopes to build a membership of 1 million, which could have led to greater achievement, but Streit's following declined through the war, and at the Pittsburgh convention of November 1945, after Hiroshima, Federal Union all but disbanded to permit the universalists to find their own way in other world government organizations.[26] Streit became editor of the journal that continued to express his views, *Freedom & Union*. The universalists eventually formed United World Federalists (UWF). Then, after the Cold War had begun and after the North Atlantic Treaty was signed (April 1949), Roberts and former under-secretary of state Will Clayton formed the Atlantic Union Committee (AUC), which introduced legislation rivaling that of UWF in Congress.[27] Streit re-edited *Union Now* in 1949 so that Russia emerged in place of the Axis as the autocracy against which the union was aimed.[28]

The universalists saw such a partial union as a vital threat to the Soviet Union, liable to precipitate the very war that world government was intended to prevent.[29] It may be said that UWF's whole political accomplishment was the de-

---

[23] Merrill Jensen, *The New Nation: A History of the United States during the Confederation, 1781-1789* (New York: Knopf, 1950), x-xii. Jensen admitted only that the "weakness" of the U.S. Congress under the Articles was due to its constitutional reliance on "persuasion" rather than "coercion" (pp. 348, 428). This is precisely the difference between a confederation and a federation, between a league and a union. Although Jensen made clear the achievements of the Confederation, he did not illuminate why the Founding Fathers felt it so necessary to change it for the federal government.

[24] Harris Wofford Jr., *It's Up To Us: Federal World Government in Our Time* (New York: Harcourt, Brace, 1946), 3-5.

[25] "Justice Roberts to Join Debate on Post-War World Federation," *New York Herald Tribune,* 13 June 1943.

[26] Resolution, Federal Union Convention, Pittsburgh, n.d., c. 18 November 1945, Lilly Library, UWF Papers, 9.Fed. Union.

[27] Owen J. Roberts to Gentlemen, Invitation to become charter member of AUC, 8 July 1949, Regenstein Library, World Republic Papers, AUC.

[28] Clarence K. Streit, *Union Now,* postwar ed. (New York: Harper & Bros., 1949), 262-27, 281, 313-20. In the 1943 edition Streit had already hardened his position against Russia.

[29] Grenville Clark, Statement for the Hearings before the Foreign Affairs Committee of the House of Representatives on the World Federation Resolution (HCR-64, Introduced 7 June 1949), 10 October 1949, Regenstein Library, Hutchins Papers (A), 35.8.

feat of AUC legislation, at the cost of its own program.[30]

Throughout the 1950s, however, the Streit group remained a kind of gadfly on the right, and in 1960 they succeeded in getting an act passed by Congress and signed by President Dwight Eisenhower authorizing a "United States Citizens Commission on NATO" to hold a "Convention of Citizens of the North Atlantic Democracies" to "explore" and "recommend" how they might better unite their peoples.[31] In 1972, his Atlantic union resolution actually passed in the Senate after 23 years of efforts, though it failed in the House, while the public was preoccupied with the Vietnam War and the landslide for Richard Nixon.[32] Throughout the years, Streit tested many leaders for the qualities necessary to lead to Atlantic federation: Franklin Delano Roosevelt, Winston Churchill, Paul Reynaud, Harry Truman, Dean Acheson, George Marshall, John Foster Dulles, Estes Kefauver, Dwight D. Eisenhower, Paul-Henri Spaak, Richard Nixon, Robert Schuman, John F. Kennedy, Walter F. George, Hubert Humphrey, Charles de Gaulle, Christian Herter, J. William Fulbright, Nelson Rockefeller, Eugene McCarthy, Robert Kennedy, and Paul C. Findley. His journals remain replete with the record of high-level contacts on a practical policy toward Atlantic federation. He died in 1986.

World Federalists

In 1941, shortly before Pearl Harbor and U.S. entry into the war, the Streit organization split over the issue of partial versus universal federation as a peace proposal and soon enough as a war aim. The splinter group, led by Vernon Nash, Millie Blake, and Tom Griessemer, became World Federalists, who by 1947 were to contribute the largest and most active membership organization to the United World Federalists. Streit's group, Federal Union, though the center of much press attention, slowly declined in numbers, as we have seen.[33] From the point of view of humanity's historic formation of a political union, the origins of this first organized *world* federalist movement are worth tracing.

Vernon Nash was a World War I veteran, Rhodes scholar, and journalist with

---

[30] "Four Plans for U.N. Reform Rejected by State Dept.," *New York World Telegram,* 16 February 1950.

[31] Streit, *Freedom's Frontier,* 4, passim. The Convention has not been held.

[32] *Freedom & Union,* August-September 1972; ibid., November-December 1972.

[33] The goal of acquiring 1 million members, set at the Federal Union Peoria convention of 1943, was never remotely approached. The reason, in the view of the chairman of the action committee, was that "there was no definite program or action which provided work for the membership." L. H. Schultz, Proposals for Plan of Consideration and Criticism of the Action Committee and the Board of Directors of Federal Union, n.d., ante 4 December 1943, Lilly Library, UWF Papers, 9.Fed. Union. To Harris Wofford, the reason was "lack of organizational leadership and backing." *It's Up To Us,* 42.

12 years experience in China.[34] Mildred Riorden Blake, whose roots went deep into Quakerism and abolition of slavery in Illinois and Michigan, was an advertising writer for Young and Rubicam.[35] The third figure was Tom Otto Griessemer, an émigré from Nazi Germany, surviving and discovering America in a New York law firm.[36]

Union Now had hardly appeared in the bookshops when this group was stirred into action. Blake tells the story: "We were all reading it, and we quickly wrote to Streit and said, 'What can be done about this? What can we do for you?' And I don't know whether he would have done anything about it himself. He was the kind who carried his mail around in his hat and seldom got around to answering it." But R. Frazier Potts, a broker on Wall Street, kept after Streit until finally Streit agreed to come to a meeting of activists in Potts' apartment on 7 March 1939. Fourteen people were present, mostly strangers to one another but "united in believing that it has now become a practical possibility to make an effective start toward effective world government."[37] There was already a division beginning between the members and Streit, for the title of their original organization was "Committee of Correspondence for *World Federal Union,*" but the goal of their program statement was, more narrowly, "To bring about UNION NOW of the United States of America with other Democracies."[38]

By May 1939, Streit's first organization was established with the rather ambiguous name of Inter-Democracy Federal Unionists. It continued until it was renamed Federal Union in 1940. "[We] did what all Americans always do," recalled Blake; "elect a chairman and a vice–chairman and a secretary and treasurer." Offices were found on East 40th Street. A speakers' bureau was run there, Vernon and Clarence the principal speakers. William Blake, Millie's husband, went to work for them. "He was carried away, as I was, with this whole idea and he began to answer all this correspondence that had accumulated. It was growing so fast that we all had fanciful ideas about how influential we were going to be and how fast things were going to go." By the summer of 1939 a similar committee of correspondence had sprung up in Boston, under the leadership of Thomas H. Mahony, a prominent lawyer who would organize the strongest state group for merger into UWF in 1947. Another sprang up in Washington, D.C., and "else-

---

[34] Vernon Nash, comp., "Yes, But—Questions and Answers about Federal World Government" (New York: World Federalists, U.S.A., n.d., c. 1946), p. 2; Vernon Nash, comp., "It Must Be Done Again" (New York: Federal Union, 1940), p. i, New York Public Library, Schwimmer–Lloyd Collection; "Vernon Nash," Speakers bureau circular, n.d., c. 1950, UWF Papers, 26.Nash.

[35] Blake, Reminiscences, pp. 4-5.

[36] "The World Is My Country," *World Government News*, July 1948, pp. 15-16.

[37] Committee of Correspondence for World Federal Union, Announcement of Organizational Meeting, 25 March 1939, UWF Papers, 9.Fed. Union.

[38] Ethel Johnson Kelly, Secretary, Temporary Committee for Organization, Report, 27 March 1939, UWF Papers, 9.Fed. Union.

where around the country as people read Clarence's book."[39]

Split to Form World Federalists

The imminence of war no doubt explains the sudden rise of so radical a group as world federalists. After Hitler invaded Poland, recalled Blake, the movement became even more "prosperous and burgeoning." Streit and his associates felt that they "were working against time as nobody ever had before. Saving the world [laughter]." But with the conquest of France in June 1940, there could no longer be any thought of averting the war, and Streit, "giving up on France for the time being," typed out a new book, *Union Now with Britain.* This book widened the division between the idealistic members and their pragmatic founder. At the Federal Union convention in Cleveland in the summer of 1941, Streit advocated union only with Britain; the members preferred "union of everybody who would join, with the emphasis on world federalism." And so a split occurred, as would happen several times in a movement to unite people around the globe! In retrospect, Streit was realistic enough, but others preferred in the midst of so terrible a war to uphold an ideal peace. The difference was really over timing. The convention voted for world federalism.

"But this," recalled Blake, "made no difference to Clarence Streit, who was always a loner more than an organization man. And he went right on advocating union with Britain in all his speeches and everything he wrote. And by fall the division was severe, because the rest of us were not in sympathy with what he was saying in his lectures." The New York group apparently was so vocal in its opposition that the board of Federal Union, despite the convention vote, sided with Streit and revoked the charters of the New York and Washington groups in November 1941.[40] The disgruntled New Yorkers then met on 14 December 1941, a week after Pearl Harbor, and formed World Federalists. About 50 people signed the founding document. Tom Griessemer, who had been executive director of the New York chapter of the Streit organization, went to work as secretary of the World Federalists. The office at first was in Tom and Stewart Ogilvy's apartment on Sullivan Street in the Village.

Throughout the war years, World Federalists grew slowly as a decentralized membership organization. Its models were the movements in American history for the abolition of slavery, for women's suffrage, temperance, and repeal of the

---

[39] Blake, Reminiscences, pp. 1-9. Mahony was a close confidant of Grenville Clark.

[40] Ibid., pp. 9-11. Streit was acting in the spirit of *Realpolitik,* of realistic transition stages to world government, for what he proposed was essentially what Winston Churchill offered to France on the eve of her downfall on 16 June 1940—a federal union. (Paul Reynaud, then prime minister, accepted, but his other ministers refused. Acceptance would have meant continued French resistance in North Africa, it was feared without British aid, since Marshal Petain and General Weygand both predicted England would be defeated in three weeks.) Both Churchill's and Streit's proposals were war measures, mainly in Britain's interest, which is why they were rejected generally.

18th amendment. These movements had simple, easily understandable goals and aimed to keep so active a popular following that national leaders would be forced to take note and their own leaders would not be tempted to betray the cause.[41] Their methods were typified by the speaking career of Vernon Nash, who by 1947 had made about 1,000 speeches on behalf of world federation throughout the country, leaving behind him a trail of federalist chapters.[42]

Tom Griessemer's Influence

Nash, Blake, and Ogilvy, however, agreed that the primary credit for building up World Federalists, even for keeping any world government movement going through the war, goes to self-effacing Tom Griessemer. He had a thick German accent, which was awkward for uniting the world during and after World War II. It was Griessemer who built up World Federalists from the disarray of the split with Federal Union. He worked full time for the smallest salary. He offered "penetrating analysis and relentless logic" in behind-the-scenes policy discussions. He had remarkable practical ability in doing things or managing volunteers to do the chores of a growing movement—arranging meetings and dinners, producing literature and advertising, organizing committees and chapters. It was he who brought Mark Van Doren and his older brother Carl into the movement.

Griessemer, with Stewart Ogilvy, founded *World Government News* in 1943. Ogilvy, himself a modest man, gave credit to Griessemer for whatever editorial "bite" it had. The little monthly remained editorially a journal of the whole far-flung movement, rather than become the house organ of any one group, and so it remained until UWF abandoned it in 1951, after which it folded in the general collapse of the movement.

In 1945, after Hiroshima, Griessemer secured the endorsements for Emery Reves' *Anatomy of Peace* by many distinguished persons, including former Justice Owen J. Roberts and Senator J. William Fulbright. Reves' book was the most influential book on world government in its time. During the World Federalists, U.S.A., period, Griessemer's efforts were largely responsible for several large gifts, which enabled the organization to buy World Government House, a four-story stone house at 31 East 74th Street, which became the most valuable tangible asset ($75,000) of the merged United World Federalists in February 1947. Griessemer was a key figure in the formation of UWF.

Later, in August 1947, his fluency in European languages and his skill in organizing world government groups made him a natural choice as first secretary–general of the World Movement for World Federal Government, which was formally established in part through his efforts. He stayed in Europe for 18 months.

---

[41] Vernon Nash, *The World Must Be Governed* (New York: Harpers, 1949), 152-53, 182-83.

[42] Statistical Summary of Speaking Engagements by Vernon Nash on "Federal World Government," 1939–1947, UWF Papers, 43.National Executive Council; Vernon Nash, Report to the Executive Council, 20 April 1947, ibid., 42. Vernon Nash, "Yes, But—" (1946), p. 2, Schwimmer–Lloyd Collection. By 1950, Nash had made a total of 2,200 speeches. "Vernon Nash" (1950).

"I don't think we could ever have developed World Federalists without him," recalled Millie Blake. "I am certain in my own mind that without him the movement would never have attained the influence it did," confirmed Stew Ogilvy. "Griessemer deserves far greater credit than he is ever likely to get for his sound building of the foundations of organized work for world government in this country," added Vernon Nash.[43]

Roosevelt Will Do Something About It

The great problem for the World Federalists during the war was to counter the popular feelings that "we can't do anything about it until the war is over" and "Roosevelt is going to do something about it. Just wait and see."[44] For this reason the dispersed federalists did not take up an effective critical view of the Dumbarton Oaks proposals for the U.N. Charter in 1944. World Federalists did not become a national organization until another Cleveland convention in October 1945, after Hiroshima, when the atomic bomb and the delay of the U.S. government to establish world controls aroused feelings of unprecedented urgency. The national group was then briefly known as World Federalists, U.S.A., before merger into United World Federalists in 1947. By that time its enrolled membership came to 6,033.[45]

Student Federalists

Another group that arose within Streit's Federal Union then split to join United World Federalists was Harris Wofford's Student Federalists. The story is apparently true that 15-year-old Harris Wofford Jr. was inspired by hearing Streit on the radio in 1941 while in the bathtub. "Defense is not a destiny for Democracy." said Streit. "It is 'Union Now,' the nucleus of a world government." Soon young Harris began talking of a United States of the world "in our time" with his family and schoolmates. He read *Union Now,* took Mary Ellen Purdy to the Federal Union office in New York City to ask what students could do to help, got literature, and recruited seven members in his hometown of Scarsdale, New York. They received the first student charter of Federal Union on 24 March

---

[43] *World Government News,* hereafter *WGN,* July 1948, pp. 15-19; Stewart Ogilvy, Interview with the author, Yonkers, New York, 21 October 1980; Ogilvy to Author, 14 July 1981; Statement of Income and Expenses for the Period 1 January 1946, to 30 September 1946, UWF Papers, 22.WF,USA; Blake, Reminiscences, pp. 31-32; Nash, *World Must Be Governed,* p. 181. *World Government News* (1943–52) ranks with *Common Cause* (1947–51) as a running, inclusive, and illuminating primary source, invaluable for the history of the movement.

[44] Blake, Reminiscences, p. 12.

[45] Tom Griessemer to Credentials Committee, 3 February 1947, UWF Papers, 57.Asheville Convention Reports. World Federalists changed its legal name to Federal World Government, Inc., in September 1943, to avoid confusion with Ely Culbertson's new World Federalists, Inc. "New Name," *World Government News,* October 1943, p. 7. At the Cleveland convention in October 1945, the group changed it back again.

1942.[46]

The history of Student Federalists in the beginning, as Tom Griessemer reported in *World Government News,* was very much the history of this "enthusiastic, bright and energetic lad from Scarsdale." Wofford seems to have been motivated by the discovery—which has often been made in similar circumstances by upper middle class youths—that most of the world had yet to enjoy the advantages and tranquility of life in a Westchester County suburb. When he was 11, his grandmother took him on a trip around the world, where he heard Mussolini harangue the crowds in Rome and arrived in Shanghai a few weeks after the Japanese had captured the city. "Too soon the trip was over," wrote a biographer, "but a young boy had learned many lessons and seen many things which had started him thinking about the world." Four years later, after "the Fascist pot boiled over in Europe," he joined William Allen White's Committee to Defend America by Aiding the Allies and heard Streit. Then the Japanese attacked Pearl Harbor, and he organized Student Federalists.[47]

Wofford later analyzed, with remarkable perceptiveness, the conditions American youth found itself in on the eve of what Churchill called the "Unnecessary War." He concluded that the political unification of the world was the great cause of his generation in war and peace.[48]

> This is the rendezvous which my generation holds with destiny. For this we were born. Whether we shall be men enough to stand up to the challenge and end world anarchy by building a World Federal Democracy in our time, only the future can say.

Starting in the High Schools

Young Wofford plunged into a flurry of activity. He took 16 members of the Federal Union student chapter to hear Clarence Streit. Students set up literature displays in the village and school libraries. Wofford, Purdy, Michael Bache, and Ed Sproull spoke before their 10th grade class in ancient history on World Federal Union. The period ended in an uproar. A heckler charged that Federal Union must be a new variety of onion! The group began issuing a one-page weekly *Chapter Bulletin* on Harris's father's mimeograph machine. By June 1942, they had 50 members, and Harris went to Federal Union's national convention in St. Louis as the only student delegate. An office was set up in the Woffords' home. Letters were written. The *Bulletin* became the four-page *Scarsdale Student Federal Unionist.* An opponent who tried to set up a "Union Never" club failed. The principal, Lester Nelson, did not give in to parents in conservative Scarsdale who demanded he break up the student chapter.

Students at other high schools then began to form chapters. Joe Wheeler,

---

[46] Wofford, *It's Up To Us,* 3-7.

[47] "American Youth in the Van," *WGN,* March, 1944, p. 1; Wofford, *It's Up To Us,* 8-16. The Committee to Defend America later became Americans United for World Government.

[48] Wofford, *It's Up To Us,* Chap. 6, "Heritage," 50-79.

later to be a president of World Student Federalists, organized a chapter in Concord, Massachusetts. Tom Hughes independently organized a chapter in Mankato, Minnesota. Jerry Miller followed Scarsdale in organizing a chapter in Sarasota, Florida. By the time of Federal Union's national convention in Peoria in November 1943, there were nine chapters in six states with about 150 members. The Scarsdale group began having printed the monthly *Student Federalist*.[49]

Wofford became first president of the Student Federalist Council in Streit's national organization. He was already becoming a bit of a national figure; in July 1943, he took his vacation in Washington, D.C., interviewed Arkansas Representative J. William Fulbright and Wisconsin Representative Howard J. McMurray, talked late into the night with Clarence Streit during Washington blackouts, and received an invitation to the White House from Mrs. Roosevelt. "She believes that probably the next generation will be able to bring about federation," he wrote his friends, "but not this one."[50]

Student Federalists at the National Level

Wofford was slated to enter the army air force in May 1944, after early senior graduation, but before he did so, he made the first national speaking trip in behalf of Student Federalists. He traveled to Ohio, Indiana, Missouri, Illinois, Wisconsin, Minnesota, and North Dakota, speaking to about 25,000 students. Topics were "We Challenge the Elder Statesmen," "Youth's Stake in the Peace," and the like. This tour caught the attention of *Newsweek*, which counted 30 chapters and 1,000 Student Federalist members. On 31 March 1944, stimulated by the tour, over 100 delegates from 20 states assembled in New York City for the first national Student Federalist convention. U.S. Representative McMurray gave a "hard-hitting and crystal-clear" speech on the real cause of war—anarchy—and the necessary solution—world government. A model world constitutional convention was held, and a ringing Streitian "Challenge to Our Elder Statesmen" was adopted:

> We call for decisive action on the elementary necessity of beginning world government ... by uniting ... in a *democratic federal union* to cooperate as a freely expanding nucleus within an all-inclusive world organization.

Tom Hughes was elected second Student Federalist president, and Wofford went off to training camp. He received a furlough to attend the United Nations convention in San Francisco the next year. Later, mustered out of the army, he became, just out of his teens, a kind of elder statesman himself of the student

---

[49] Wofford, *It's Up To Us*, 17-27; "Why Can't We Do It?" *Student Federalist*, Vol. 1, No. 1, 15 May 1943; *Student Federalist*, October 1943.

[50] Wofford, *It's Up To Us*, 29.

movement.[51] Streit made a characteristic remark about Student Federalists to *Newsweek:* "[The student movement] has grown up of itself, not pushed by us—rather, they are pushing us."[52] The same could be said of the students later, under the adult regime of UWF. They had energy, knowledge, and will—everything but money.

Massachusetts Committee for World Federation

A third group that would merge to form UWF was the Massachusetts Committee for World Federation. It was largely the creation of Thomas H. Mahony, a Boston lawyer, graduate of Harvard and Boston University, and prominent Catholic. In the early 1940s, convinced that world peace depended on world order and world law, he joined Streit's Federal Union and was elected to its Board of Directors.

The branch later separated from the Streit organization for the same reason World Federalists did, became the Massachusetts Committee for World Federation, and made Mahony its co-chairman. Other leaders included Elizabeth Cady, executive secretary; William Stoddard, chairman; Conrad Hobbs, president; and Endicott Peabody, headmaster of Groton, honorary chairman. Mahony's reputation attracted Grenville Clark to him, and they worked together before the Dublin conference of 1945 and thereafter.[53]

Catholic and Protestant Opinion on World Federation

Catholic opinion during World War II slowly shifted toward the necessity of international organization. Pope Pius XII, in his first Christmas message of 1939, as Reverend Robert F. Drinan, S.J., later a U.S. representative from Massachusetts, once pointed out, called for an international organization "which, respecting the rights of God, will be able to assure the reciprocal independence of nations big and small." In 1944, the American bishops went even further to demand "that positive international law govern relations in the international community."[54] So Mahony was at the extreme edge of this shifting Catholic opinion but not beyond bounds.

Protestant opinion, too, during the war shifted far toward world federation, only to be constricted again after 1950. The World Council of Churches, founded tentatively in Utrecht in 1938, issued a statement on "The Church and Inter-

---

[51] Wofford, *It's Up To Us*, 27-30, 35-41, 84; "Challenge and Inspiration," *WGN*, April 1944, pp. 2-3; "Wofford Talks to 15,000 Students in First Three Weeks," *Student Federalist*, March 1944; "First Convention Maps Student Action Campaign," *Student Federalist*, April 1944.

[52] "Student Federalists," *Newsweek*, 21 February 1944, pp. 76-77.

[53] A.J.G. Priest, "In the Great American Tradition [Thomas H. Mahony]," *WGN*, June 1950, pp. 13-16.

[54] Reverend Robert F. Drinan, *Pius XII's Legacy to World Federalism* (The Hague: World Association of World Federalists, 1958); Robert M. Hutchins, Aquinas Lecture, Marquette University, 1949, reported in "Catholic Teaching and World Government," *Brooklyn Tablet*, 17 June 1950.

national Reconstruction" from Switzerland in January 1943, which was widely circulated in the European Resistance, Britain, and America. It contained this statement: "VI. *We believe that the Church is to proclaim that international relations must be subordinated to law.*"[55]

In the United States, the Commission on the Bases of a Just and Durable Peace of the Federal Council of Churches, led by John Foster Dulles, issued "A Message to the Churches" in 1942.[56] Vernon Nash said of this report, "No other publication of comparable length, before or since, has so balanced a statement of all the spiritual, social, economic, and political problems involved in the establishment and maintenance of a just peace." Similarly, *The Christian Century* often lent its pages to the cause, notably in a series of editorials in 1948.

Measuring Public Opinion

Mahony's group was a strong advocate in the movement for arousing public opinion. The Massachusetts Committee, by a diligent signature campaign, was able to get the following question on the ballot for the November 1942 election:[57]

Shall the Representative in the General Court from this district be instructed to vote to request the President and Congress to call at the earliest possible moment a convention of Representatives of all free peoples, to frame a Federal Constitution under which they may unite in a Democratic World Government?

At the time when the Russians were fighting the battle of Stalingrad, and Americans, the battle of Guadacanal, the results were impressive: 202,726 voted yes to 67,205 no, or about 3-1 in favor! Three Streitist resolutions were then guided through the Massachusetts Legislature, resulting in passage of a moderate bill "to study and formulate plans for the enforcement of world peace by and through international cooperation and a council of nations," on 26 April 1943. The matter was considered serious enough for the *Boston Globe* to print the debate and the yeas and nays.[58] The Boston group would mount another meaningful referendum in 1946 and attempt to do so in 1949, as we will recount later in the chapter on state federalist activity.[59]

---

[55] Walter Lipgens, ed., *Documents on the History of European Integration*, Vol. 1: *Continental Plans for European Union, 1939–1945*. European Union Institute, Series B (History) (Berlin: De Gruyter, 1984), II. Views of Churches and Other Christian Groups [W. A. Visser 't Hooft], 737.

[56] *The Churches and a Just and Durable Peace: A Handbook* (Chicago: Christian Century Press, 1942.

[57] *Election Statistics, 1942*, p. 361.

[58] *Globe*, 15 April, 27 April 1943; *World Government News*, May 1943.

[59] World Government Campaign in Massachusetts, 1946–47, Indiana University, UWF Papers, 36.

Americans United for World Organization

A fourth organization that would later merge with United World Federalists was the rather prestigious Americans United for World Organization, founded in 1944. It was a continuation of the Committee to Defend America by Aiding the Allies under *Emporia* (Kansas) *Gazette* editor William Allen White in 1940. In debate with isolationists at that time, the Committee to Defend America had come out on the right (interventionist) side in World War II, and the continuing group had a reputation for the same kind of realistic, military–minded vision about keeping the peace. In 1944, Americans United geared up for a major public effort to win Senate approval of U.S. participation in the United Nations *Organization*. The Senate fight failed to materialize in 1945—so deeply had the United States been integrated into the wider world. Or perhaps we should say so weak was the U.N.O.

Americans United for World *Government*

But after Hiroshima, Americans United became transformed into the most influential, if not the first, mass organization dedicated to the establishment of world federal government. "Yesterday was a thousand years ago," their internal bulletin stated in August 1945. Then on 21 February 1946, after six months convincing the membership that atomic bombs required more radical international organization, board chairman Raymond Gram Swing announced that the organization was changing its name to Americans United for World Government (AUWG).[60] World Federalists were not much convinced there had been a genuine change of heart. "Here come the *atomic* federalists," Millie Blake said of them, not overlooking the Committee to Defend America mentality that still lingered in the organization. The board, however, she admitted, "saw the light."[61]

The leadership of Americans United, it is clear enough, shared the membership's reluctance to take the big step toward the abolition of war. The political error in gearing up the organization for the Senate fight over the U.N. Charter that failed to materialize certainly caused much embarrassment. The money that had been wasted on lobbying, dinners, and publicity left a defensive, overcompensating atmosphere in headquarters. In mid-1945, Americans United was spending about $1,000 per week on payroll alone; its monthly receipts and debits, then at their highest ever, were on the order of $38,000. Grenville Clark naturally appealed to Americans United for political support behind his various reforms, for Americans United was much more prominent than World Federalists, but his appeals always fell on deaf ears. He concluded that his relationship

---

[60] Bulletin, No. 5, 30 August 1945, UWF Papers, 9.AUWG; "The People's Reaction," *WGN*, September 1945, p. 3; Resolution, 15 November 1945, UWF Papers, 9.AUWG; "U.S. to Assist U.N.O. Set Up Its Office Here," *New York Herald Tribune*, 22 February 1946.

[61] Blake, Reminiscences, p. 25, emphasis added. The history of Americans United is handicapped by the failure to place all its records in UWF files following merger, as Stewart Ogilvy reports. Some evidence remained behind, but most of what is known comes from AU's critics.

to Americans United had been a "hindrance."[62]

AUWG Growth

Americans United had all of the normal difficulties of building up a mass political organization on a new principle. The organization saw its responsibility to offer constructive alternatives for the political decisions of the day in order to move the nations toward the novel goal of world government. Americans United began editing its "Washington Bulletin" to give a world government slant on every current issue, such as the U.N. Relief and Rehabilitation Agency appropriation, the Negro rights Fair Employment Practices Commission, and the British loan.

World Federalists criticized this as an "omnibus" approach, and even Clark thought it "diffused" their efforts. But how else can a serious political movement guide the transition from power politics to world government? World Federalists could in turn be criticized for never taking a stand on the momentous issues after the war that were to determine whether world government would ever be an option in their time. Americans United, like Clark, saw the significance of the Baruch plan, for instance, and supported it, though federalists did not.[63]

After the name change in February 1946, Americans United for World Government drew the most prominent—meaning not only well-connected but also responsible and cautious—leaders working politically for the establishment of world government. A who's who of the movement served on its board of directors: Charles Bolté, Harrison Brown, Henry B. Cabot, Mrs. John Alden Carpenter, Alan Cranston, Russell Davenport, David Dubinsky, Clifton Fadiman, Marshall Field Jr., Thomas K. Finletter, Paul S. Henshaw, Thomas H. Mahony, Cord Meyer Jr., Edgar Ansel Mowrer, Philip Murray, Bishop G. Bromley Oxnam, A.J.G. Priest, Robert E. Sherwood, Rex Stout, Leland Stowe, James P. Warburg, and Sumner Welles. In 1946 total income from contributions was $83,669; total disbursements, $105,616. Membership rose to some 9,000.[64]

Ely Culbertson and the Quota Force Plan

In 1943 there appeared an advocate of what he called "world federation" who was so famous a personality that his plan for postwar world order could hardly

[62] Payroll for Week Ending 6 July 1945; Receipts and Disbursements, June 1945, UWF Papers, 59; Clark to Ulric Bell and Arthur Goldsmith, 13 March 1946, Clark Papers, 15.3; Clark to Cranston, 16 May 1946, ibid., 15.1.

[63] "Washington Bulletin," 15 May 1946, 11 July 1946, AORES Papers, 9.6; "Noted in Passing," WGN, March 1946, 5; Clark to Bass, 11 March 1946, Clark Papers, 15.1.

[64] "Let's Stop the Atomic War Now," ad, New York Herald Tribune, 24 March 1946; Schedule of Contributions Received from January 1 to September 10, 1946, ... September 11 to October 21, 1946, ... November 1 to December 31, 1946; Schedule of Contributions Dispersed from January 1 to September 10, 1946, ... September 11 to October 21, 1946, ... November 1 to December 31, 1946, U.S. Special Committee to Investigate Senatorial Campaign Expenditures, Questionnaire for Independent Political Committees, 1946, UWF Papers, 59.

not attract widespread public attention. But by the nature of his plan—exhaustive in detail but superficial in concept—he aroused the most extreme support and opposition within the minuscule federalist movement. Max Eastman, the disillusioned Russophile and conservative political commentator, praised him in print as a "genius for combining theory with practice, mathematics with psychology." Rosika Schwimmer called him privately the "fakest of fakers, ... the Hitler of the peace movement." He was Ely Culbertson, internationally known expert in contract bridge, whose system of approach-force bidding had set off the bridge craze of the Depression and made him a millionaire.[65]

Ely Culbertson was born in 1891 to an American petroleum engineer developing the oil fields of the Caucasus and to the daughter of a Cossack *ataman,* or chief. The family became rich, and young Ely followed the life of aristocratic Russian sons in the decades before the revolution, when he was first imprisoned. Ely's father then sent the boy to Yale University in America, but he quit to live in the Bowery with the "people." He worked in Canada as a railroad laborer, tried to join Zapata's revolt in Mexico in 1912, got caught up in an anarchist plot in Spain to assassinate the king, was again imprisoned, then was expelled to France. He studied government in Paris, escaped the World War in Zurich, where he studied psychoanalysis, left behind a trail of mistresses, and, after the Russian Revolution of 1917, in which his parents' oil holdings were confiscated, found himself cut off. He returned to New York in 1921, desperately poor. He was 30 years old.[66]

Culbertson's Bidding System

Culbertson began to play auction bridge in Greenwich Village bistros for money. He developed theories of bidding and play that were unusual and soon was playing at the Knickerbocker Whist Club, then the stronghold of the recognized experts of the game. "His strange theories and unusual personality caused a turmoil there," it was said. He married the leading lady in the club, founded *The Bridge World* magazine on what he earned in play, and formed a Bridge World team in 1930. The team won the national championship in Asbury Park, New Jersey, that summer, the Vanderbilt Cup in November, and an international match in London against P. Hal Sims's team in December. Culbertson published *The Blue Book,* written in two frantic weeks, which set out the principles which still underlie most bidding systems. Its sales were soon paying royalties of $2,000 *a day.* In December 1931, Culbertson and his team began a match with Sidney S. Lenz and his team of anti-Culbertsons. They

---

[65] Ely Culbertson, *Summary of the World Federation Plan; An Outline of a Practical and Detailed Plan for World Settlement* (Garden City, NY: Doubleday, Doran, 1943), 1; Rosika Schwimmer to Lola Maverick Lloyd, 3 February 1943, Schwimmer–Lloyd Collection, U8; *Encyclopedia Britannica,* 15th ed. (1979), s.v. "Bridge," by Charles H. Goren, 3: 168.

[66] *Current Biography—1940,* 211-13; "An Ace World Planner," *New York Post,* 10 April 1943, Schwimmer–Lloyd Collection, N305.438; Ely Culbertson, *The Strange Lives of One Man* (Chicago: John C. Winston, 1940).

played 150 rubbers in 33 days; the story made front pages of hundreds of newspapers and was taken up by radio and newsreels. His decisive victory in this match made contract bridge on Culbertson principles a national fad. A rich man again, he built a magnificent town house, with adjoining club, on East 62nd Street, New York, and maintained a million-dollar estate in Ridgefield, Connecticut.[67]

Culbertson's World Federation Plan

By 1943, Ely Culbertson had long since felt the need to redeem his easy riches by service to some revolutionary cause. He began work on the *World Federation Plan* in 1939. He seems not to have consulted any of the small but growing literature on federation, but rather to have based the book on his own observations of the conduct of foreign policy and on his success in manipulating what he called "mass psychology." He even explained, in a full-length book on the plan published late in 1943, how cards influenced his views of power politics:[68]

> I had always been fascinated by the bizarre world of cards. It was a world of pure power politics where rewards and punishments were meted out immediately. A deck of cards was built like the purest of hierarchies, with every card a master to those below it and a lackey to those above it. And there were "masses"—long suits—which always asserted themselves in the end, triumphing over kings and aces. In bridge every play was in itself a problem of force and timing.

The plan called for three treaties: a Treaty of Defensive Alliance among the United Nations then at war with the Axis, a Treaty of Peace with Germany and her allies to come into effect upon their surrender, and a Treaty of Perpetual Cooperation or Quota Limitation Treaty to maintain the peace. This latter treaty was fundamental for the plan. The world was to be divided by the victors into 11 regions, each consisting of a dominant sovereign state and subordinate sovereign states in its sphere of influence, including their colonies and possessions, if any. The map of the world, so divided, exhibited some novel groupings. The American region, for example, was to include all of Latin America but not Canada. The British included Canada, Australia, New Zealand, Burma, Singapore, all of East and South Africa, but not Hong Kong, India, and certain islands in the West Indies. The Russian included the U.S.S.R. plus strategic frontiers next to Finland and Poland, but not Central Europe, which was a region by itself. Culbertson called such a treaty-based system a "federation," but it was more accurately a confederation or, since there were hardly any ties but threats of force to bind the sovereign states together within their regions, a balance of power sys-

---

[67] *Encyclopedia Britannica,* "Bridge," 3: 168; "Ely Culbertson, Bridge Expert and Peace Advocate, Dies at 64," *New York Times,* 28 December 1955.

[68] Ely Culbertson, *Total Peace: What Makes Wars and How to Organize Peace* (Garden City, NY: Garden City, 1943), 8.

tem, solemnized by international law. The system was not to contain even a revived League of Nations.[69]

The "Quota Force Principle"

The central feature of the Treaty of Perpetual Cooperation was the "quota
force principle." This was Culbertson's version of an international police force,
about which there was much confusion in the public debate of 1943-44, before
the Dumbarton Oaks conference. He proposed creation of a "World Police,"
alone armed with the heavy weapons of land, sea, and air forces by which modern
wars are won. It would be composed of 11 "National Contingents" (from each
of the dominant sovereign states in the eleven regions) plus one "International
Contingent" (from the smaller nations in the regions). The latter, called the
"Mobile Corps," would be stationed throughout the world, owe its allegiance
solely to the "Government of the World Federation," and be first to come to the
defense of a small nation or a great one. The other national contingents would
then be federalized, just as the militia of the United States can be.

The percentages of power to be allowed each dominant state and the mobile
corps were specified in some detail. The United States was to have 20 percent,
Britain 15 percent, Russia 15 percent, Germany (though it was to be supreme in
the Germanic region) 3 percent, Turkey (supreme in the Middle East) 3 percent,
and the mobile corps 22 percent. Thus, the mobile corps would have a preponderance of force over even the most powerful national contingent, should it begin
a course of aggression, yet the three most powerful nations would still have
comparable forces to resist the mobile corps, should the world federation become
tyrannical. Furthermore, additional national contingents could be mobilized to
overwhelm the balance.

Thus, war would be averted, Culbertson claimed, and the system preserved
from corruption. What if a combination of, say, the United States, Britain, and
Germany decided to rebel against the world federation and to conquer the world?
By the quota force principle, they would have only 38 percent of the forces,
while the world would have 62 percent. How could Russia expand, with only 15
percent? As a deterrent the plan was perfect. All the statesmanship of modern
times, Culbertson exulted, had failed to discover so simple a solution to the
problem of war.[70]

"Not a Government at All"

Culbertson did not provide for a true government to control the system's
forces. There was to be a "World President" (the first to be selected by the U.S.
Senate), but it was not stated if he was to be commander–in–chief. There was to
be a house of "World Trustees" (appointees of the presidents of 11 regional federations also provided for), but they had recommendatory and "educational" functions only—no legislative powers. Similarly, there was to be a "World Supreme
Court," without laws to interpret. Culbertson even explicitly denied that he was

---

[69] Culbertson, *World Federation Plan*, 14, 45, 18, 6-7, 23-27.

[70] Ibid., 33-35, 40-42.

providing a government:

> Thus, the Government of the World Federation is in reality not a government
> at all, but a Peace Trust to which every nation entrusts a part of its sovereign-
> ty (the right to wage war), receiving in exchange a greater value (the right to
> be defended against aggression).

He understood that the quota force principle could not work unless nations adhered to the treaty rigidly defining their power allotments, so he made amendment of the treaty virtually impossible. Such a legalistic stricture was a fatal departure from Culbertson's notion of *Realpolitik*. It was also contrary to the theory and practice of federalism, which provides for orderly change of the status quo by legislation and administration.[71]

But in the middle of World War II, when people were desperate for some means to effectively prevent another general war and were unimpressed with the rather idealistic proposals of the *bona fide* World Federalists, Culbertson offered a seemingly tough minded alternative. The Culbertson plan at least described the world as it would become under the United Nations: the system of national forces to be on call to the world "federation" was very like that established in the U.N. Charter, Articles 42 and 43; the U.N. Expeditionary Force that Secretary–General Dag Hammarskjöld was first to field in 1956 resembled nothing so much as Culbertson's mobile corps; and arms control treaties such as SALT I (1972) set down a kind of quota of permitted arms.

Criticism of Culbertson's Plan

Critics in the movement and without were quick to find flaws in Culbertson's proposal. "An international house of cards," Louis Fischer called it in the *Nation*. "The same old game," said Elsa Maxwell in the *New York Post*. "Captivating and deceptive," said Milton Mayer, who criticized the unreality of assuming that nations will limit their armaments to their quotas, that colonial peoples will not demand independence, that economic justice is not a demand in the world, that the status quo need only be fixed. A "paleo–Utopian," he called Culbertson. "A Menshivik Ivy Lee, a Nostradamus in pinstripes," Eunice Clark called him in *Common Sense*.[72]

"Successful publicist that he is," wrote Edith Wynner in an article not ac-

---

[71] Ibid., 47-54, 50, 36. In his larger book Culbertson maintained that his plan offered the only workable compromise to both nationalists and internationalists. "The nationalists may scoff at the pound-foolishness of the internationalists' proposed system of collective defense, but they will be paid off in the national coin of the American Strategic Zone and safeguards of the national sovereignty. The internationalists may scorn the penny–wiseness of the nationalists, but they will be paid off in the international coin of a world order." *Total Peace*, 17.

[72] Louis Fischer, "The Culbertson Plan," *The Nation*, 24 April 1943; Elsa Maxwell, "Party Line," *New York Post*, 14 April 1943; Milton Mayer, "The Horrors of Peace," *The* (Madison, Wisconsin) *Progressive*, 12 July 1943; Eunice Clark quoted in Emmet Crozier, "The World Ahead," *New York Herald Tribune*, 16 May 1943;

cepted in the liberal *Common Sense,* "Mr. Culbertson has cunningly taken advantage of the current popularity of 'federalism' ... to the already existing confusion on the subject." She methodically criticized his plan for not providing a popular government, for relying only on punitive measures to maintain the peace instead of on legislative powers to eliminate the causes of war, and most of all for conceiving international police power as a capacity to wage war on whole nations rather than to apprehend the guilty individuals, as with any civil police. She continued:[73]

> Real World Federation is not a mere grouping of cells in the body politic as Mr. Culbertson seems to think. It is a redivision of political control into local, national, and supranational units, each of which, within its own limited and delegated sphere, operates directly on the individual. Peace will be served with nothing less.

Influence of Culbertson's Plan

Despite this criticism, the Culbertson plan cast a long shadow. For years it was the only precisely written out plan for practical federation with respect to the power realities of its time, even if its "federalism" was deceptive. Streit had an "illustrative constitution" in an annex of *Union Now,* but it was seldom referred to. Not till 1948, when the Chicago Committee to Frame a World Constitution published its draft of a maximal constitution, was there a comparable document. Grenville Clark did not publish his model minimal U.N. Charter (essentially complete by 1949) until 1958.[74]

Culbertson devoted the rest of his life to his plan for world peace. In early 1946 his presence on the scene influenced the early growth of the radical veterans group at Northwestern, Students for Federal World Government (World Republic).[75] In late 1946 some spontaneous grassroots support in Ohio for giving the U.N. a police force on the quota force principle moved him to found the Citizens Committee for United Nations Reform (CCUNR), apparently funded by himself and consisting of a committee of correspondence with his many admirers.[76]

Culbertson recast his plan as the "ABC plan" in 1947:[77]

---

[73] Edith Wynner, Ely Culbertson's So-called Plan for World Federation, n.d., c. 29 March 1943; Alfred M. Bingham to Wynner, 18 February 1943, Schwimmer–Lloyd Collection, U8; Edith Wynner, "Mr. Culbertson Proposes to Internationalize Punishment," *World Federation—Now,* June 1943, p. 1. Similar critiques in *World Government News,* February 1943 and January 1944.

[74] Robert M. Hutchins, G. A. Borgese et al., "Preliminary Draft of a World Constitution," *Common Cause,* 1 (March 1948): 325-46; Grenville Clark and Louis B. Sohn, *World Peace through World Law* (Cambridge, MA: Harvard University Press, 1958).

[75] "Tonight! Hear These World-Famous Authorities: Ely Culbertson," Ad for Chicago Stadium Rally, *Chicago Sun,* 30 May 1946, World Republic Papers.

[76] Ely Culbertson to Friend, 9 December 1946, UWF Papers, 9.CCUNR.

[77] Ely Culbertson, "The Truman Doctrine Is Not Enough," *Readers Digest,* June 1947.

A: Eliminate the Security Council veto;

B: Negotiate the Baruch plan for the international control of atomic energy;

C: Establish a world police force.

The American Legion accepted the ABC plan *in toto* as their foreign policy program.[78] By 1948 support was strong enough for an ABC resolution to be introduced in Congress—Representative Richard M. Nixon (R., California) was a co-sponsor (HCR-170)—and in 1949 Culbertson's bill was a major contender with Streit's and United World Federalists'.[79]

[78] Foreign Relations Committee, American Legion, "To Promote Peace and Goodwill on Earth," Position paper, n.d., c. July 1947; *New York Post*, 23 July 1947, UWF Papers, 9.CWG [sic].

[79] CCUNR, "Congressional Resolution for Revision of the United Nations," n.d., post 12 April 1948; U.S. Congress, House, *Requesting the President to Initiate Measures for a Revision of the United Nations Charter*, HCR 163-176, 80th Cong., 2nd sess., 16 March 1948; "American Congress and World Federation: A Report on the Hearings of the House Foreign Affairs Committee," *Common Cause*, 3 (February 1950): 344, 352-54.

3

Winston Churchill's Offer of Anglo–French Union

In this crisis we must not let ourselves
be accused of lack of imagination.

—Winston Churchill, 16 June 1940

The Mainstream British Federalist Organization

We now turn to another broadly popular movement for a federation of democratic nation–states—Britain's Federal Union. Its goal was a European union first, then an "Atlantic" union (Europe plus the United States and Canada), and ultimately a world federal union. Federal Union was founded by three young men—Charles Kimber, Derek Rawnsley, and Patrick Ransome—in London during the Munich crisis of 1938. They attracted very prominent intellectuals and politicians to their cause, including Lord Lothian and Lionel Curtis, who were linked to the older imperial federalist movement, and Clement Attlee and Ernest Bevin, who would lead the postwar Labour government.[1] Avoidance of war was their principal motivation.

As the Second World War approached—especially during the so–called "phony war" between Hitler's invasion of Poland in September 1939 and his invasion of the low countries and France in the spring of 1940—Federal Union grew "astonishingly," as Kimber recalls, to about 10,000 people in 239 chapters within the British Isles. Its immediate accomplishment was to create a climate

---

[1] Charles Kimber, "Federal Union," *The Federalist* (Pavia), 26 (December 1984): 205; Andrea Bosco, "Federal Union, Chatham House, the Foreign Office, and Anglo–French Union in Spring 1940," in Bosco, ed., *The Federal Idea*, vol. I, *The History of Federalism from the Enlightenment to 1945* (London: Lothian Foundation Press, 1991), 295; Andrea Bosco, "Lothian, Curtis, Kimber and the Federal Union Movement (1938–40)," *Journal of Contemporary History*, 23 (1989?): 495; Andrea Bosco, "National Sovereignty and Peace: Lord Lothian's Federalist Thought," in John Turner, ed., *The Larger Idea: Lord Lothian and the Problem of National Sovereignty* (London: Lothian Foundation Press, 1988), 118; John Pinder and Richard Mayne, with John C. de V. Roberts, *Federal Union: The Pioneers, A History of Federal Union* (London: Macmillan, 1990), 27.

of public opinion favorable to Prime Minister Winston Churchill's offer to unite Britain and France at the darkest hour of Nazi Germany's invasion of France on 16 June 1940.[2]

Popular Precursors to Federal Union

There had been earlier popular movements for international organization, which give us some basis for taking the measure of Federal Union. Certainly, millions of people around the world hung on Woodrow Wilson's speeches in 1918–19. The League to Enforce Peace, which pressed Wilson and foreign statesmen to establish the League of Nations, grew to about 300,000 adherents by 1919, the year before it disbanded after U.S. Senate rejection of the League Covenant.[3]

Again millions rallied around the Kellogg–Briand Pact for the renunciation of war in 1928–29, but the core activist group around Senator William E. Borah, Charles C. Morrison, and Salmon O. Levinson was very small.[4] French Foreign Minister Aristide Briand then made the first offer of what could more strictly be called European federation in 1929–30. He built on the small Pan–Europa movement of Count Richard N. Coudenhove–Kalergi, who was never able to mount enough public pressure to convince national leaders to begin the process of uniting sovereignties; his movement, however, survived the war.[5]

In Britain, Lord Cecil and Cambridge don Gilbert Murray's League of Nations Union (LNU), whose membership peaked at about 407,000 in 1931, organized the famous "Peace Ballot" of 1934–35. In it, over 11 million people voted that Britain should remain in the League, and nearly 7 million that aggression should be resisted by international military force. But by 1938 the League no longer inspired such hopes, and membership in the LNU fell to 264,000 by 1938 and 100,000 by 1940.[6]

The Reverend H.R.L. (Dick) Sheppard's Peace Pledge Union, founded in 1934, grew within two years to over 30,000 and climbed to a peak of 136,000

[2] Leon Noel, "Le Projet d'union franco–britannique de juin 1940," *Revue de la Deuxième Guerre Mondiale*, 21 (janvier 1956): 35; P.M.H. Bell, *A Certain Eventuality: Britain and the Fall of France* (Farnborough: Saxon House, 1974), 7; Max Beloff, "The Anglo–French Union Project of June 1940," in Beloff, *The Intellectual in Politics* (London: Weidenfeld & Nicolson, 1970), 175; Avi Shlain, "Prelude to Downfall: The British Offer of Union to France, June 1940," *Journal of Contemporary History*, 9, 3 (1974): 31; David Thomson, *The Proposal for Anglo–French Union in 1940* (Oxford: Clarendon, 1966), 10–11.

[3] Warren F. Kuehl, *Seeking World Order: The United States and International Organization to 1920* (Nashville, TN: Vanderbilt University Press, 1969), 314.

[4] Joseph P. Baratta, "The Kellogg–Briand Pact and the Outlawry of War," in Richard Dean Burns, ed., *Encyclopedia of Arms Control and Disarmament* (New York: Scribner's, 1993), 2: 695–705.

[5] Arnold Zurcher, *The Struggle to Unite Europe, 1940–1958* (New York: New York University Press, 1958), 5, 7, 8.

[6] Donald S. Birn, *The League of Nations Union, 1918–1945* (Oxford: Clarendon, 1981), 129–30, 201; Pinder and Mayne, *Federal Union*, 13.

by early 1940. Its members included the eloquent Aldous Huxley; he and many courageous pacifists continued to have a slow and deep influence.[7] But pacifism, though it continues to inspire war resisters, was no immediate answer to the threat of Nazi Germany.

Still another British movement was Lord (David) Davies' New Commonwealth Society (1932), which never grew to more than 3,000 élite members. But year after year, in conferences of prominent people (Winston Churchill was its president) and in well supported books and a journal, the New Commonwealth group urged establishment within the League of a world equity tribunal to settle *political* disputes beyond the capacity of the World Court and establishment of an international police force to enforce decisions of the League or equity tribunal.[8] The police force was enacted in principle with Chapter VII of the U.N. Charter and effectively was being realized by the 1990s; the equity tribunal became a key feature in Grenville Clark and Louis B. Sohn's magisterial proposal for U.N. reform, *World Peace through World Law* (1958), and it is still unrealized.

Federal Union was much smaller than all but the last of these predecessors. What set it apart was that Federal Union clearly and with increasing distinctiveness maintained that, to secure the peace, humanity had to move beyond a league of sovereign states to a federation of states and peoples based on common *citizenship,* for the league principle was a proven failure; moreover, such a federation could not rely on mere sentiment against war but had to *organize power* superior to that of national states that so far had been established in history. Kimber recalls the essential point:[9]

Why, we asked ourselves, had the League of Nations failed? It was too easy an answer that its members had let it down—would they not always do so? We found that we no longer had any faith, where national self interest was involved, in gentlemen's agreements, treaties, alliances, solemn declarations or covenants. What was needed, we concluded, was not a League but an assembly elected by the people of the member nations which could not only take decisions on behalf of all but which also had both the authority and the power to give effect to them. I don't recall that the word federation was ever mentioned.

Federal Union's Creative Response to War
Since the statesmen and the diplomats had failed, the people had to undertake the work of federal government to protect their common interests, particularly in peace. This was, in world historian Arnold Toynbee's terms, the creative response that Federal Union made to the drift of international events in the 1930s —the Great Depression, higher tariffs and protectionism in accordance with economic nationalism (which deepened the Depression), Japanese aggression in

[7] Martin Caedel, *Pacifism in Britain, 1914–1945: The Defining Faith* (Oxford: Clarendon, 1980), 318, 183–87.

[8] Ibid., 318; Alan de Rusett, *Strengthening the Framework of Peace* (London: Royal Institute for International Affairs, 1950), 26; Bosco, "Lothian," 481.

[9] Kimber, "Federal Union," 200.

Manchuria and China, failure of the Disarmament Conference of 1932, collapse of the League of Nations over Italy's aggression in Abyssinia, German rearmament and defiance of the Versailles Treaty, Hitler's demands on the Rhineland, Austria, Sudetenland, and the Polish corridor to Danzig, and finally World War II.

Federal Union made substantial contributions to bringing international relations under the rule of law. As already mentioned, it contributed to the favorable climate of opinion preceding Churchill's offer to unite Britain and France. It drew together earlier federalist intellectuals, like Lionel Curtis, Lord Lothian, and Arnold Toynbee, and inspired many more new ones, like Lionel Robbins, John Boyd Orr, William Beveridge, C.E.M. Joad, William Curry, Melville Chaning–Pearce, R.W.G. Mackay, Ivor Jennings, Kenneth Wheare, Georg Schwarzenberger, and Barbara Wooton—all of whom created a large federalist literature still of great value.

Federal Union cooperated with the American journalist Clarence Streit, author of the best–selling *Union Now* (1939), whose organization in the United States, also called Federal Union (independent), was the font and source of the American Atlantic Unionists and the World Federalists. The latter, as we have seen, formed as a splinter group from America's Federal Union when, all of Europe in Hitler's power, Streit narrowed his focus to federal union with Britain.

At the lowest ebb of Britain's Federal Union in the first years of the war, its "clean, precise" literature—notably Lionel Robbins' works—came to the attention of Altiero Spinelli, an Italian anti-Fascist prisoner of Mussolini on the island of Ventotene, and it worked a "revolution" in his mind. That led to substantial federalist influence within the Resistance in many German–occupied countries by 1944, though the idea also arose spontaneously throughout Europe.

Federal Union raised up new Parliamentary leaders, like Henry Usborne, M.P., elected in the Labour landslide of 1945. Immediately, another slender thread of influence reached New York, when Usborne began discussions with World Federalists in the apartment of Noel and Violet Rawnsley, parents of Derek (killed in the Royal Air Force flying over North Africa), leading to a flood tide of radical federalism in America. Usborne tried courageously, yet in some desperation, in 1947 to expand the world federalist movement (organization and sympathizers) from the U.S. to Britain, Europe, and India in order to head off the Cold War.

Another M.P. was the Australian–born barrister R.W.G. ("Kim") Mackay, who led the European federalists from 1940 through the Hague Congress of 1948, when Churchill lent his immense prestige to the movement. Mackay then led the effort within the Constituent Assembly of the Council of Europe to transform the Council into a European government—a project not fully defeated until 1954. The Federal Trust for Education and Research (1945) and then its Regional Commission (1955) maintained a small but ultimately successful advocacy campaign in favor of Britain's entrance into the Common Market; despite de Gaulle's veto in 1963, entry was achieved in 1973.

New scholars and activists, like John Pinder, professor and long–time president of the Union of European Federalists, and Richard Mayne, colleague of Jean Monnet, have continued resolutely and graciously to advocate the transformation of the European Community into a federal union with full British participation. Their book, *Federal Union: The Pioneers, A History of Federal Union,* is a major contribution to federalist literature, helping to restore the memory of the British movement to the history of recent times.

Though many of the old organizations no longer exist—Federal Union was formally disbanded in 1963, with the death of Lord Beveridge and the veto of de Gaulle—the European and World Federalist groups began effecting a reunion in the mid–1980s during the Gorbachev era. One of the new signs was the establishment of the Lothian Foundation in the office of the Federal Trust by the young Italian scholar Andrea Bosco, in cooperation with John Pinder and others in 1987. The idea is not dead.

Organizing in London and the Country

After September 1939 in response to the war, Federal Union grew rapidly. Because hostilities did not immediately develop on land, apart from those at sea and in the air—the "phony war"—people still had hope for a short war. Perhaps Hitler would relent from releasing the pent–up forces of modern total war. So all over Britain, like tiny bulbs being lit on a topographic map, little groups of Federal Unionists continued to form in people's homes, at their offices, in churches, in schools, at the universities. Someone would start a conversation, which would lead to calling a meeting. People got information from pamphlets provided by the little Federal Union office in Gordon Square, and some pamphlets circulated in "chain letter" fashion.[10]

The BBC broadcast a short debate on Federal Union between Clarence Streit in America and Sir Alfred Zimmern in Geneva on its "Questions in the Air" series.[11] Serious articles on the immense issues of federalism immediately began appearing in *Federal Union News*—the first was Hoyland's "Federate or Perish," which may have influenced Attlee, since he later used the famous phrase.[12] William B. Curry's answer to Streit, *The Case for Federal Union,* appeared in November and sold 100,000 copies in six months.

People spread the word by leaving slips of paper on which was printed, "Have you heard of Federal Union?" on trams, trains, and bus seats, in waiting rooms, telephone books, and library books.[13] Stamps were printed up for pasting on letters, lampposts, Christmas parcels, and telephone books in restaurants.[14] Blackout posters that allowed the words "Federal Union for World Peace" to show through faintly (permitted by regulations) were prepared.[15] Money was

---

[10] Ibid., 11 (2 December 1939).
[11] Ibid., 1 (5 September 1939).
[12] Ibid., 6 (28 October 1939).
[13] Ibid.
[14] Ibid., 11 (2 December 1939).
[15] Ibid., 27 (23 March 1940).

raised, at least in Horwich, by that very English institution, a jumble sale (£4 profit).[16] One young lady in Melbourne, Derbyshire, was typical of those fired with the spirit:[17]

> Miss Piper is busily forming a nucleus for a South Derbyshire group. Letters to the local newspapers and to personal friends have brought several prospective members. "One advantage of the present situation," she writes, "is that it sets people talking, and it is quite possible to get into a conversation with anybody—on a 'bus, for instance. Then by the Socratic method, it's very easy to manoeuvre them into an untenable position where FEDERAL UNION can be introduced as the only way out. I try to make two converts a day.

The bulk of organizing took place in London, of course, by virtue of its concentration of population and talent. Eventually, 37 groups were formed in London.[18] Professor Joad often hosted gatherings at his house in Hampsted.[19] Joad, Wootten, Law, Kimber, and Ransome spoke all over the city and sometimes beyond, as *Federal Union News's* weekly feature "The Coming Week" records.[20] The group in Peckham, led by Howard Fox, was especially dynamic. They were the ones who came up with the slips in trams and later in library books. They established a Federal Union bookshop on Heath Street and by January had grown so that they decentralized.[21] M.P. Kim Mackay drew so many to a series of lectures on European union that the Central London chapter split into four: Westminster, Chelsea, Marylebone, and Holborn.[22] Clubs for Federal Unionists were established on Fleet Street (one guinea per year fee) and at 101 Piccadilly.[23]

Ernest Bevin

One of those who paid a call at the Gordon Square office in this early period was gruff, square Ernest Bevin, prominent trade union leader, soon to be minister of labour in Churchill's wartime coalition government, then foreign minister in Attlee's Labour government after victory. Kimber recalls: "He came stomping across the room and he asked a lot of very searching questions. At the end of it he said, 'I will do what I can to get any articles in the Union magazine, and I'll send you the names of anybody who I think might be interested.' And he did."[24]

---

[16] Ibid., 5 (21 October 1939); 9 (18 November 1939).

[17] Ibid., 4 (14 October 1939).

[18] Ibid., 25 (9 March 1940).

[19] Ibid., 4 (14 October 1939).

[20] Ibid., 7 (4 November 1939)

[21] Ibid., 5 (21 October 1939); 9 (18 November 1939); 16 (6 January 1940).

[22] Ibid., 16 (6 January 1940).

[23] Ibid., 7 (4 November 1939); 17 (13 January 1940); R.W.G. Mackay, *Federal Europe: The Case for European Federation, Together with a Draft Constitution for a United States of Europe*, Foreword by Norman Angell (London: M. Joseph, April 1940).

[24] Quoted in Pinder and Mayne, *Federal Union*, 12.

After the war, however, in a political atmosphere transformed by the world dominance of the United States and the Soviet Union, Bevin found it prudent to guide Britain into alliance with the United States *and* the Western democracies in what he called "Western Union," which was anathema to the remnants of Federal Union. Churchill, too, opposed Bevin with the alternative of "European Union" (what became the Council of Europe and the European Community).

Henry Usborne

Another case, with special significance for the world federalist movement, was the way Birmingham manufacturer Henry C. Usborne, a member of the advisory group, went about organizing in the Midlands. He and Reverend Leyton Richards made a list of about 20 likely converts, called a meeting in Usborne's office on Macdonald Street to which 15 came, handed out literature, formed a committee, decided to approach the most influential people in the district, held a second meeting, which was packed, signed up 46 people on membership forms, charged one shilling for membership, decided to form satellite groups, and ordered 2,000 basic pamphlets from London. A group formed in Leamington; the Rotary Club devoted three successive lunches to discussing federal union in Birmingham; John Hoyland, an expert on India and Gandhi,[25] was brought in as a speaker on 15 occasions; the Women's Luncheon Club in Wolverhampton discussed the idea; and so did the Bridge Club in Burnt Green. So successful was the outreach that Usborne scheduled a "monster meeting" for Digbeth Institute (capacity 1,400) in mid–December, which drew the cream of the Birmingham business community.[26]

William Beveridge

The most lasting development at Oxford University was the involvement of Sir William Beveridge. Former director of the London School of Economics and future author of the two famous "Beveridge Reports" on social insurance and full employment that would lay the foundations of the British welfare state,[27] Beveridge in 1937 had become master of University College, Derek Rawnsley's *alma mater*. When Federal Union was founded, young Rawnsley, Kimber, and Ransome approached Beveridge for support, as they did many prominent people. "I'm too busy to do anything about that now," Sir William replied. "But if there's a war, come and see me." In the fall of 1939 there was a war, and Derek

---

[25] John S. Hoyland, *Gandhi and World Government* (London: Crusade for World Government, 1948).

[26] *Federal Union News,* 5 (21 October 1939); ibid., 11 (2 December 1939); ibid., 16 (6 January 1940).

[27] William Beveridge, *Social Insurance and the Allied Services* (London: HMSO, 1942); Beveridge, *Full Employment in a Free Society* (London: Allen & Unwin, 1944). There was also a "third Beveridge Report"—*The Price of Peace* (London: Pilot, 1945)—in which he argued for a supranational authority to prevent the use of force for national purposes and to enforce international economic cooperation in order to secure all national welfare states.

returned to receive a generous response.

Beveridge called a conference on economic problems of European and world federation in October 1939 that drew such prominent economists as London School of Economics professor F. A. von Hayek, Lionel Robbins, brilliant young Harold Wilson (later a prime minister), and Barbara Wootton. With Patrick Ransome's assistance as research director, Beveridge put together the Federal Union Research Institute (FURI to historians who claim it was no dundering "academic" exercise), which produced the excellent *Federal Tracts* by L. Robbins, K. C. Wheare, C.E.M. Joad, A. L. Goodhart, George Catlin, Barbara Wootton, and others.[28] They began appearing in 1941—too late to influence Churchill— but Beveridge wrote the first one, *Peace by Federation?*, in time by February 1940.[29] Beveridge spoke on federalism many times at Oxford, once, for instance, debating Gilbert Murray of the League of Nations Union; in April 1940 he traveled to France with the new gospel, contributing to the links preceding Churchill's offer; and in general he lent his prestige to the cause.[30]

Sir William Beveridge must be credited with doing more than any other other academic figure to make world federalism—in addition to European federalism—a respectable field of study. English scholars like K. C. Wheare did not expand the field very far beyond their specialties nor sustain the effort as long. Beveridge wrote in his memoirs that after meeting Rawnsley, Kimber, and Ransome in late 1939, he became a Federal Unionist for life. "The choice is between Utopia and Hell," he concluded in a speech to the students and tutors in the University College Hall in November 1939. After the war, he belonged to that faction in Federal Union that favored the "Utopia" of world government. He took virtually no interest in Jean Monnet's European Communities or in the European federalists; and he left the welfare state, which he had helped to create, to its fate at the national level in Britain. He seems to have believed that Europe, even if federated, was too small a region to solve the problem of war. Aging and disappointed, Beveridge wrote in 1963 about U.S. President Eisenhower and the coming of the Cold War:[31]

> But disappointment of nearly all the hopes and aims which led his nation into war under Franklin Roosevelt had long been implicit; 1945 was a year of defeat, not of victory, for the United States and Britain and all who think like them.

[28] *Federal Union News*, 6 (28 October 1939); Pinder and Mayne, *Federal Union*, 19, 34, 46; Patrick Ransome, ed., *Studies in Federal Planning* (London: Macmillan, 1943; Lothian Foundation Press, 1990).

[29] William Beveridge, *Peace by Federation?* (London: Federal Tracts, No. 1, April 1940).

[30] *Federal Union News*, 7 (4 November 1939); idem, 16 (6 January 1940).

[31] William Beveridge, *Power and Influence* (London: Hodder & Stoughton, 1953), 266, 357, passim. Beveridge's biographer passes off Federal Union as just a temporary aberration in a career divided between civil service and pure research. It was merely another "point upon the compass of liberal philosophy." Jose Harris, *William Beveridge: A Biography* (Oxford: Clarendon, 1977), 2, 367, 469.

European Federation as a War Aim

At the end of March 1940, Federal Union published a full policy statement that provides the most succinct record of the movement's balance between European and world federalism, which it offered as a practical policy to the British government as the phony war drew to a close:[32]

FEDERAL UNION

The objects of Federal Union are:

(1) To obtain support for a federation* of free peoples under a common government, directly or indirectly elected by and responsible to the peoples for their common affairs, with national self–government for national affairs.

(2) To ensure that any federation so formed shall be regarded as the first step towards ultimate world federation.

(3) Through such a federation to secure peace, based on economic security and civil rights for all.

To this end the present policy of Federal Union is:

(1) To work for an Allied statement of Peace Aims challenging the idea of race superiority with a declaration of the rights of man, and the method of aggression with a declaration of readiness to federate with any people whose government is prepared to recognize these rights.

(2) To welcome any steps towards such a federation of the Allies or any other groups of peoples, provided that at the time of its formation the federation is declared open to accession by other nations, including Germany.

*Note: The federation would control foreign policy, Armed Forces and armaments. It would have substantial powers over tariffs, currency, migration, communications and similar matters. It would also have the power to ensure that colonies and dependencies were administered in the interests of the inhabitants and not for the benefit of any particular country.

Hence, by the time of Churchill's offer, the balance of opinion in Federal Union had shifted very definitely away from Atlantic or world federation on the U.S. model, which was seen as impractical before or after the war, to some novel and uncharted European federation as the more realistic approach to an admittedly necessary, eventual world union. Man would have to learn by suffering. This split, which would continue for decades, was evident from the beginning, for Curtis and Lothian, too, had maintained during their own struggle with the problem of peace that what was vitally necessary was not immediate world federation, but a more limited federation of the Commonwealth and the United

---

[32] *Federal Union News*, 29 (6 April 1940).

States.[33] By 1940, Curtis had withdrawn from the new organization, and Lothian had died in harness as British ambassador to the U.S. So Britain's Federal Union turned toward Europe.

As Kimber recalls,[34]

> To us Europe held the key to war and peace, and we were thinking only of European democracies.... We were Europeans. For centuries England has never been sure whether it was a part of Europe or not and the effect of Streit's book [*Union Now,* which called for an immediate union of 15 democracies around the globe] was to bring into Federal Union a large number of members who actively preferred the idea of Anglo–American union rather than of European union of which Britain was a part.

Nevertheless, the British federalists on the whole preferred to focus on Europe, as in the new statement of policy just quoted in which world federation was placed definitely after European federation as an Allied peace aim.

In retrospect, this hardly mattered as the world plunged into war, but after the war, when atomic bombs and U.S. power had utterly changed the situation, Federal Union's fixation on Europe meant that the British federalists were on the whole uncooperative with the more radical American world federalists, who argued that immediate transformation of the United Nations into a constitutionally limited, world federal government would provide the military security and economic cooperation necessary for all regional federations, including European union. Since at time of writing, European federation remains a distant dream, who can we say was right?

Churchill's Offer to Unite Britain and France, at Peak of Federal Union

Did all this popular activity have any influence on British policy? Yes. One case was Clement Attlee's statement of Labour Party peace aims, which included the phrase, "Europe must federate or perish," in November 1939.[35] But a much more telling case was Prime Minister Winston Churchill's offer to unite Britain and France on 14 June 1940, which was a stepping–stone to the establishment of the Council of Europe in 1949, the European Communities in 1951 and 1957, and the still unconsummated European federal union.

Churchill's offer of British union with France came at the peak of public interest in Federal Union as well as at the deepest crisis of France during the German invasion. The offer has long been studied by historians, who have sorted out the conflicting records and accounts by the principal actors and have come to general agreement on the basic chronology—though they differ about the origins of the offer, its importance to the fall of France in World War II, and its signifi-

---

[33] Bosco, "Lothian," 487.

[34] Kimber, "European Union," 203.

[35] C. R. Attlee, "The Peace We Are Striving For," Speech of 8 November 1939, in C. R. Attlee, Arthur Greenwood, et al., *Labour's Aim in War and Peace* (London: Lincoln's Praeger, 1940), 101, 102. Cf. *Labour, the War, and the Peace* (London: Labour Party), 9

cance for the North Atlantic Treaty, the Council of Europe, the European Community, and the still more distant projects of European and world federation.
The diplomatic historian Avi Shlaim concludes, for example:[36]

> Even in the subsequent history of European unity, no Government ever proposed a more radical and far–reaching plan for supranational integration.... The thesis advanced here is that the British offer, despite its respectable intellectual parentage and its potentially staggering ramifications, was no more than a last and desperate effort to keep France in the war against the common enemy; [and] that it was not conceived as part of any long–term political objective but dictated by the strategic imperatives of winning the war.

On the other hand, the federalist historians John Pinder and Richard Mayne find:[37]

> In 1940 it was not the British who "shirked a bold decision" for a union of nation states. After the war France was to lead the way in building the European Community, while Britain held back. But the fact that the Anglo–French union so nearly succeeded in 1940 was a proof that federalist ideas need not be academic pipe dreams. In desperate days, men and women were able to shake off old habits of thought and try new ways to solve age–old problems, looking beyond the traditional barriers that kept nations apart.

Jean Monnet, who made the most demonstrable claim of influence on the offer of union, summed up:[38]

> So our generation shirked a bold decision that could have changed the course of the war and, what is more, the course of men's minds. "One Parliament, one Cabinet, one flag"—that stirring vision, put into words by Horace Wilson, was to remain for many years an impossible hope.... All too often I have come up against the limits of mere co-ordination: it makes for discussion, but not decision.... It is the expression of national power, not a means of transforming it: that way, unity will never be achieved. At the same time, I had come to realize that the quest for unity, even if it were limited to material problems such as production, armaments, and transport, had effects far beyond administrative matters and involved the whole political authority of the countries engaged in a common struggle. When people are threatened by

[36] Avi Shlaim, "Prelude to Downfall: The British Offer of Union to France, June 1940," *Journal of Contemporary History,* 9, 3 (1974): 27–28. Cf. David Thomson, *The Proposal for Anglo–French Union in 1940,* the Zaharoff Lecture (Oxford: Clarendon, 1966), 4; Max Beloff, *The Intellectual in Politics* (London: Weidenfeld & Nicolson, 1970), 172.

[37] John Pinder and Richard Mayne, with John C. de V. Roberts, *Federal Union: The Pioneers* (London: Macmillan, 1990), 29. Cf. Andrea Bosco, "Federal Union and the Foreign Office," in Bosco, ed., *The Federal Idea,* vol. 1, *The History of Federalism from the Enlightenment to 1945* (London: Lothian Foundation Press, 1991), 319.

[38] Jean Monnet, *Memoirs,* Richard Mayne, trans. (Garden City, NY: Doubleday, 1978), 35.

the same danger, it is no good dealing separately with the various interests that determine their future.

A World Federalist Account

From a world federalist point of view, the European federalist histories cast the widest net for the causes influencing Churchill's offer, but federalist influence on policy apparently comes to an end with Sir (later, Lord) Robert Vansittart, who drafted the penultimate document of union on June 15th. Diplomatic historians, generally but not completely unsympathetic to federalism, provide the best blow–by–blow account, but they cannot seem to explain why the government of a great power would suddenly offer to surrender—or more accurately, pool—its sovereignty over armed forces, foreign policy, finance, and economic policy. Monnet's account, though clearly that of one principal actor, seems to spring full bloom from his own brow in the slim tradition of international economic cooperation on June 14th, the day before the Vansittart draft.

We will not provide a full account of the negotiations, but we must recognize the federalist roots of ideas. We make no undemonstrable claims for what by the time of the actual offer was clearly an act of sovereign power. Churchill may have been surprised by what was in principle a federalist proposal, but that he went on to offer it to the French proves that federal union was once an immensely practical proposal.

The principal contributions of the federalists were as follows. Arnold Toynbee, who had been writing the *Yearbooks* for the Royal Institute of International Affairs and was even then struggling with the idea of world government, which would fill out the completion of his *Study of History,* wrote the first draft of the "Act for the Perpetual Association between the United Kingdom and France" in February 1940.[39] Lionel Curtis, one of the founders of the Royal Institute, critiqued "association" as a mere "inorganic system," like an alliance or the League of Nations, based on a compact among sovereign states whose interests were sure to soon divide them. What was needed was an "organic system," like the sovereign state or a true union, where the loyalties of individual citizens would not be divided between separate states but could be united politically, thus increasing the union's stability.[40] The French translation of Clarence Streit's book *Union ou chaos* came to the attention of Emmanuel Monick, a former governor of the Bank of France then attached to his country's embassy to Britain, and then to Ambassador Corbin and hence Jean Monnet, chairman of the Anglo–French Co-ordinating Committee.[41] The influence of these ideas on the French is uncertain, but at the end of 1939 Premier Daladier did allow himself to say, "It will be

---

[39] Bosco, "Federal Union," 295; Beloff, "Anglo–French Union," 177–78; Public Record Office, Foreign Office, 371/24299, 134921.

[40] Bosco, "Federal Union," 315–17; Beloff, "Anglo–French Union," 179–80; Curtis Papers, Bodleian Library, 100, 19–31.

[41] Monnet, *Memoirs,* 18–19; Noël, "Projet d'union," 34; Beloff, "Anglo–French Union," 175 n. Cf. Michel Debré et Emannuel Monick, *Demain la paix* (Paris: Librairie Plon, 1945); Monick, *Pour mémoire* (Paris: Mensil, 1970).

necessary ... perhaps to envisage federal ties between the various states of Europe."[42] The ideas were certainly in circulation in France, probably to some extent in official circles.[43]

After the fall of Finland, a new French government pledged to vigorous conduct of the war was formed under Paul Reynaud, who brought his ministers to London for a meeting of the Supreme War Council on March 28th. They issued a ringing "Solemn Declaration," promising never to seek a separate armistice or peace and concluding with the final goal of "an international order which will ensure the liberty of peoples, respect for law, and the maintenance of peace in Europe."[44] The Anglo–French proposal was made to the Reynaud government during its desperate defense of France in June.

On May 10th, the long awaited German invasion of the Low Countries and France began. The Dutch army surrendered in the field on the 14th, allowing the government to escape to London. The Belgians held out for 18 days. On the 10th, adding to the confusion, the Conservative government under Neville Chamberlain fell in Britain, ending a long course of first trying to satisfy the German *Führer,* then belatedly preparing for inevitable war. Sir Winston Churchill then came to power, and during those days of disaster in Holland and Belgium he resolutely assembled the national coalition government of Conservatives, Labour, and Liberals that would guide Britain to victory.

The astonishing evacuation of British and some French and Belgian troops from Dunkirk began on May 26th and continued to June 4th. The Germans then turned their full fury on France. General Maxime Weygand, who had been hastily recalled from Syria to be made commander in chief of French forces on May 19th, found his forces reduced to 49 divisions to the German's 130, including 10 panzer tank divisions. Weygand fell back. Then on June 10th, Italy, hungry to share the kill, declared war on France and Britain.

Negotiations to Save France

The French government was forced to retreat with the army to Orléans, Tours, and Bordeaux. Churchill flew back and forth across the Channel, trying to keep France in the war, avoid repudiating the Solemn Declaration, or at the very least keep the French fleet out of the hands of the Germans. On the 11th, Weygand first suggested that to save the country from further destruction France might have to ask for an armistice. Marshal Pétain, then a vice–president of the council, could see only defeat. As Pétain said to Churchill when urged to defend Paris, "Making Paris into a ruin would not affect the final event."[45] Churchill prepared for a last stand in western France (the "Breton redoubt"), and he took care at the time to extract a promise from Admiral Darlan never to surrender the

---

[42] Quoted in Thomson, *Proposal for Anglo–French Union,* 10.

[43] Pinder and Mayne, *Federal Union,* 26.

[44] Llewellyn Woodward, *British Foreign Policy in the Second World War* (London: HMSO, 1970), I: 284–88.

[45] Shlaim, "Prelude," 33.

French fleet.[46] Premier Reynaud was determined to maintain the alliance and to continue the defense of France from North Africa if necessary.[47] He hoped for a promise from President Roosevelt of the United States, then neutral, for emergency military aid in return for a French pledge to continue to fight for democracy even if it meant withdrawal to North Africa or to the Atlantic. "There is no light at the end of the tunnel," Reynaud said gloomily. Churchill again was full of devices for continuing the war, but, back in London, he concentrated very prudently on home defense.[48]

Roosevelt's message, dated June 13th, arrived via Ambassador Joseph Kennedy. It promised no commitment of American military participation. Only Congress could declare war, the president reminded Reynaud.[49] Churchill immediately wrote to Reynaud a "message of good cheer," late on the night of the 13th, in which he struck the note again of *indissoluble union of our two peoples and of our two Empires.*[50] This did not yet mean a constitutional union. It was Churchill's way of reaffirming Britain and France's alliance in the defense of civilization against Nazi Germany.

During the next three days, an astonishing sequence of behind–the–scenes diplomatic efforts to save the situation by a union of Britain and France was made by Jean Monnet; Arthur Salter, his British counterpart; Major (later Sir) Desmond Morton, Churchill's personal assistant; René Pleven, Monnet's assistant and later a Premier of France, and Sir Robert Vansittart, former under–secretary and now diplomatic advisor to the government.[51] At a meeting of Churchill's war cabinet on June 15th, a revision of Monnet's draft of union, edited by Vansittart, was discussed. It provided for *one Franco–British nation,* with common citizenship, a *united Parliament,* joint organs of defense, foreign affairs, finance, and economic policy, a single war cabinet with unified command over British and French armed forces, and shared responsibility for war debts and reconstruction.[52] Churchill thought of it as "giving M. Reynaud some new fact of a vivid and stimulating nature with which to carry a majority of his Cabinet into the move to Africa and the continuance of the war."[53]

But it would arrive much too late, with the Germans past the gates. In France on the afternoon of the 15th, at a desperate meeting of the Reynaud council,

---

[46] Churchill, *Second World War,* 2: 136.

[47] Shlaim, "Prelude," 34; Beloff, "Anglo–French Union," 181–82.

[48] Churchill, *Second World War,* 2: 154–57; Shlaim, "Prelude," 33–38.

[49] Churchill, *Second World War,* 2: 158, 161.

[50] Ibid., 160.

[51] Monnet, *Memoirs,* 19, 21–23; Shlaim, "Prelude," 43; Beloff, "Anglo–French Union," 185; Thomson, *Proposal,* 11; Draft entitled, "Anglo–French Unity," dated 14 June 1940, in Vansittart Papers.

[52] Monnet, *Memoirs,* 23; Shlaim, "Prelude," 43; Beloff, "Anglo–French Union," 185; Thomson, *Proposal,* 11. Draft entitled, "Anglo–French Unity," dated 14 June 1940, in Vansittart Papers.

[53] Churchill, *Second World War,* 2: 176; Monnet, *Memoirs,* 24; Noël, "Projet," 32; Shlaim, "Prelude," 43–45; PRO, FO, C7375/9/17.

deputy premier Camille Chautemps made the fateful motion that the government seek from the Germans their terms for an armistice. Reynaud, worn down by his ordeals, still succeeded in postponing a decision until the next day, in order to inquire officially with the British government for a release from the March 28th pledge.

The Declaration of Union

Now came the *coup de théâtre* of Sunday, 16 June 1940. The main new player in the drama was General Charles de Gaulle. He had been sent to London late on the 15th to arrange transportation for the French government and military units of its army to retreat to North Africa or, if necessary, to Britain. Monnet asked him to carry the full plan to Churchill. De Gaulle perceived the practical difficulties of real union, but the grandeur of the scheme appealed to him at that supreme hour of French peril. The plan was further reduced from one parliament to an *association* of the two national parliaments. Vansittart found a red binding required for submission of a document to the cabinet, and the proposal of union came formally before Churchill's government. The document was still very impressive, and it must be accounted one of the principal initiatives in the history of supranational unions. Churchill says:[54]

> All the difficulties were immediately apparent, but in the end a Declaration of Union seemed to command general assent. I stated that my first instinct had been against the idea, but that in this crisis we must not let ourselves be accused of lack of imagination. Some dramatic announcement was clearly necessary to keep the French going.

This is the text:[55]

THE DECLARATION OF UNION

At this most fateful moment in the history of the modern world, the Governments of the United Kingdom and the French Republic make this declaration of indissoluble union and unyielding resolution in their common defence of justice and freedom against subjection to a system which reduces mankind to a life of robots and slaves.

The two Governments declare that France and Great Britain shall no longer be two nations, but one Franco–British Union.

The constitution of the Union will provide for joint organs of defence, foreign, financial and economic policies.

Every citizen of France will enjoy immediately citizenship of Great Britain, every British subject will become a citizen of France.

Both countries will share responsibility for the repair of the devasta-

---

[54] Churchill, *Second World War*, 2: 178; Monnet, *Memoirs*, 28; Noël, "Projet," 23–24; Shlaim, "Prelude," 49–50; Beloff, "Anglo–French Union," 192; Thomson, *Proposal*, 11–12; John Colville, *The Fringes of Power: 10 Downing Street Diaries, 1939–1955* (London: Hodder & Stoughton, 1985), 158–59.

[55] Woodward, *British Foreign Policy*, 1: 278, 280.

tion of war, wherever it occurs in their territories, and the resources of both shall be equally, and as one, applied to that purpose. During the war there shall be a single War Cabinet, and all the forces of Britain and France, whether on land, sea or in the air, will be placed under its direction. It will govern from wherever best it can. The two Parliaments will be formally associated. The nations of the British Empire are already forming new armies. France will keep her available forces in the field, on the sea, and in the air. The Union appeals to the United States to fortify the economic resources of the Allies, and to bring her powerful material aid to the common cause. The Union will concentrate its whole energy against the power of the enemy, no matter where the battle may be.

And thus we shall conquer.

Everyone involved knew that time was short. De Gaulle and Pleven, who had been waiting outside the cabinet room, quickly translated the document into French.[56] By 4:30, "with an air of unwonted enthusiasm," de Gaulle telephoned Reynaud directly and read out the text. Reynaud recalls that as he heard it, "this sensational turn of events could only fill me with joy since it was to give me a new argument for keeping France in the alliance."[57] Ambassador Campbell, who with Major General (Sir) Edward Spears, Churchill's personal representative, was talking to Reynaud at that very moment, reports that the offer "acted like a tonic on M. Reynaud who said that for a document like that he would fight to the last."[58] The premier took it down in longhand, "in a frightful scrawl," as may be seen on the frontispieces of both volumes of his memoirs.[59]

Premier Reynaud's Final Council

The council did not buy it. Reynaud writes that he was left "absolutely alone," deserted by President Lebrun and even Georges Mandel, minister of the interior, and Louis Marin. Deputy Premier Chautemps declared that the proposed union would reduce France to the status of a British dominion. Others saw it as a scheme to carry off France's colonial empire. Marshal Pétain, expecting British defeat within weeks of France's, called such a union "fusion with a corpse." Senator Charles Reibel, close to General Weygand, declared that if France remained in the war under the pretenses of this empty union with Britain, now girding for invasion, German armies would lay waste the entire country. Jean Ybarnegaray exclaimed, "Better to be a Nazi province. At least we know what that means." Mandel said only that being a British dominion was better than a German *Gau*. As Lebrun commented in his memoirs, "The project fell of

---

[56] Noël, "Projet," 24–25.

[57] Quoted in Shlaim, "Prelude," 51; Noël, "Projet," 28; Colville, *Fringes of Power,* 159–60; Reynaud, *Thick of the Fight,* 537–38.

[58] Churchill, *Second World War,* 2: 180; Woodward, *British Foreign Policy,* 1: 281; Shlaim, "Prelude," 51.

[59] Paul Reynaud, *La France a sauvé l'Europe* (Paris: Flammarion, 1947); Reynaud, *Au Coeur de la mêlée, 1930–45* (Paris: Flammarion, 1951).

itself with a sort of indifference."[60]

By 8 o'clock the stormy meeting was over. Chautemps's proposition that the Germans should be approached immediately for an armistice was accepted. Officially, British consent had not been received. Reynaud, at the end of his resources, then went through the proper motions of resigning, and by 10 P.M. President Lebrun asked Marshal Pétain to head a new government. He had his ministers already selected, notably the Anglo–hater Pierre Laval for foreign affairs (a hitch prevented his taking office until October).[61]

Consequences of Rejection of Union

But rejection had consequences. Pétain immediately asked the Germans for terms. Baudouin, however, announced on the radio on the 17th that the new French government would never accept "terms that would deny our honor or our national independence," and for another day there was still potential for evacuation to North Africa. Monnet made one last flight with Churchill's approval on the 18th to save the situation; he found that Pétain was supporting a plan for President Lebrun, Senate president Jules Jeanneney, Chamber president Édouard Herriot, and other members of the government to withdraw to North Africa, while he and Baudouin stayed in France to preserve order during the occupation.[62] But on the 22nd they accepted liberal terms from the Führer. Hitler did his jig of joy before signing the armistice at Compiègne, in the same railroad car used for signing the German armistice in 1918.[63]

In Britain, every heart expected an invasion. After Dunkirk, the British people were defiant, determined never to give in. Churchill, whose wartime rhetoric perfectly captured their spirit, himself admits that, had he wavered, he would have been "hurled out of office." "There was a white glow, overpowering, sublime, which ran through our island from end to end.... This was a time when all Britain worked and strove to the utmost limit and was united as never before."[64] Hence, his concern about the disposition of the French fleet, technically in Vichy hands but always subject to German treachery and *force majeure*, is understandable.

British Naval and Air Attacks on the French Fleet, 3 July 1940

Churchill now conceived one of the most extraordinary actions of World War II, troubling to anyone who imagines that democracies do not make war on democracies. Although he had received assurances from the Pétain government and

---

[60] Churchill, *Second World War*, 2: 182–83; Noël, "Projet," 29; Shlaim, "Prelude," 53; Beloff, "Anglo–French Union," 194; Thomson, *Proposal*, 12–13. In this period Weygand made the remark, which got to Churchill: "In three weeks, England will have her neck wrung like a chicken." Later in the war, speaking in the Canadian Parliament, Churchill rejoined: "Some chicken, some neck."

[61] Churchill, *Second World War*, 4: 185.

[62] Monnet, *Memoirs*, 32; *Thomson, Proposal*, 23.

[63] Churchill, *Second World War*, 2: 263.

[64] Ibid., 2: 87, 142.

from Admiral Darlan that the French fleet would never fall into German hands, he set in motion naval maneuvers ("Operation Catapult") to end the threat. An ultimatum was prepared for the French to sail their warships to British ports or scuttle them. On July 3rd, this ultimatum was delivered in the morning to French admirals at Mers–el–Kebir (near Oran) and Alexandria. Meanwhile, French vessels in Portsmouth and Plymouth were commandeered by surprise (much in the way Churchill feared the Germans would do) with the loss of two seamen, one French, one British. When the French in North Africa, no doubt informed of the actions in Portsmouth, still maintained an attitude of defiance by late afternoon, at 5:54 P.M., well before dark, Admiral Somerville opened fire on the French fleet.

In the *mêlée*, the battleship *Bretagne* took two 15–inch shells and capsized, the top–of–the–line battle cruiser *Dunkerque* was hit in the engines and immobilized, the battleship *Provence* was beached, and smaller vessels were damaged or sunk. The *Strasbourg*, sister ship to the *Dunkerque*, escaped through the fire to Toulon on the French coast. Seven cruisers at Algiers also escaped to Toulon. In Alexandria, the French disabled their ships by dumping their fuel oil, removing key parts of their gun mechanisms, and repatriating some crews. At Dakar four days later, the new battleship *Richelieu* was put out of action by air and motor torpedo boat attacks. At Casablanca, the partly completed battleship *Jean Bart*, which lacked her big guns, was immobilized at dockside. In Martinique, a French aircraft carrier and two light cruisers were immobilized with the cooperation of the United States.[65]

These were dreadful events, especially coming so soon after an offer of union. As many as 1,297 French sailors perished with their ships. Was it necessary? It seems not, except as an extreme case of how far even democratic independent sovereign states will go in their own defense, for there was never a threat to hand over the French fleet to the Germans. Churchill himself admits, "No French ship was ever manned by the Germans or use against us by them in the war." Even as late as 1942, after Allied landings in North Africa had provoked the Germans into speedily occupying all of Vichy France, French sailors, well trained by Admiral Darlan, refused to allow their ships to be captured. On 27 November 1942, to avert an anticipated German *coup de main* against the Mediterranean Fleet, Admiral de Laborde and his officers scuttled 61 ships in the port of Toulon, including the *Strasbourg*.[66]

End of the Third French Republic

Rejection of the offer of union was catastrophic. The day after Operation Catapult, 4 July 1940, the Pétain government severed diplomatic relations with Britain, and by the 12th the *constitution of the Third Republic was abolished.* In its place was created a semifascist state directly under the personal authority of

---

[65] Ibid., 2: 202–4; Raymond de Belot, *The Struggle for the Mediterranean, 1939–1945* (Princeton: Princeton University Press, 1951), 15–32.

[66] Churchill, *Second World War*, 2: 197, 4: 545–46; de Belot, *Struggle for the Mediterranean*, 191–95.

Pétain, who, at age 84, feeling betrayed by the democracies and in the power of the totalitarianisms, tried to prevent his country from being ruled directly by Nazi Germany.

If we take a broad view, Pétain was faced with dreadful choices between two primitive unions produced by modern forces of integration but in protean political forms whose consequences could barely be foreseen. Churchill's Anglo–French union meant that France would remain in the war and suffer a violent and tyrannical German occupation. The alternative was Hitler's "New Order," in which national boundaries would be opened and economies integrated under the hegemony of a "master race." That he chose wrong is shown by the sentence of death given to the aged marshal by a French court of justice in 1945 (commuted to life imprisonment). But the peaceful integration of Europe under free, democratic governments, only a dream in the 1940s, was unrealistic then and is still, at the time of writing, unrealized.

Significance of the Offer of Franco–British Union

This whole affair was hardly a historical mayfly. On overhearing the war cabinet's Declaration of Union being translated to Reynaud in his office on 16 June 1940, Churchill's assistant private secretary Sir John Colville later recorded in his diary: "There would have been great difficulties to surmount, but we had before us the bridge to a new world, the first elements of European or even World Federation."[67] Paul Reynaud thought that the proposition to unite Britain and France aimed "to constitute the kernel of a new Europe."[68] Monnet's experience with the offer was the direct inspiration for his subsequent efforts to establish the European Coal and Steel Community in 1951 and to develop it into the European Economic Community and Euratom in 1957.[69]

Winston Churchill concluded the second volume of his history of the war with some astonishing reflections on the offer of Anglo–French union, which he thought might have radically shortened the war and left the peace that followed less likely to so rapidly collapse into the Cold War. Perhaps because historians do not like counterfactual history, none of the diplomatic historians cite this passage, but the federalist historian must, since it clearly indicates the probable effects of union, if it had been accepted in the circumstances of 1940:[70]

> Although vain, the process of trying to imagine what would have happened if some important event or decision had been different is often tempting and sometimes instructive. The manner of the fall of France was decided on June 16th by a dozen chances, each measured by a hair's breadth. If Paul Reynaud had survived the 16th, I should have been with him at noon on the 17th, accompanied by the most powerful delegation that has ever left our

[67] Quoted in Pinder and Mayne, *Federal Union*, 28, and Bosco, "Federal Union," 318; Colville, *Fringes of Power*, 161; cf. ibid., 30, 159.

[68] Quoted in Noël, "Projet," 29; Shlaim, "Prelude," 53; Reynaud, *In the Thick of the Fight* (1955), 541.

[69] Memoirs, passim.

[70] Churchill, *Second World War*, 2: 189–91.

shores, armed with plenary powers in the name of the British nation. Certainly we should have confronted Pétain, Weygand, Chautemps, and the rest with our blunt proposition: "No release from the obligation of March 28 unless the French Fleet is sailed to British ports. On the other hand, we offer an indissoluble Anglo–French Union. Go to Africa and let us fight it out together." Surely we should have been aided by the President of the Republic, by the Presidents of the two French Chambers, and by all that resolute band who gathered behind Reynaud, Mandel, and de Gaulle. It seems to me probable that we should have uplifted and converted the defeatists around the table, or left them in a minority or even under arrest.

But let us pursue this ghostly speculation further. The French Government would have retired to North Africa. The Anglo–French Super–State or Working Committee, to which it would probably in practice have reduced itself, would have faced Hitler. The British and French Fleets from their harbours would have enjoyed complete mastery of the Mediterranean, and free passage through it for all troops and supplies. Whatever British air force could be spared from the defence of Britain, and what was left of the French air force, nourished by American production and based on the French North African airfields, would soon have become an offensive factor of the first importance....

France would never have ceased to be one of the principal belligerent allies and would have been spared the fearful schism which rent and still rends her people. Her homeland no doubt would have lain prostrate under the German rule, but that was only what actually happened after the Anglo–American descent in November 1942....

Federalist Analysis

What, in conclusion, is the federalist analysis of the proposed Anglo–French union in 1940? In a nutshell, the proposal has to be accounted federalist in nature and partly in inspiration, but it was made too late, or too early, to be accepted, and the citizens of both countries were hardly prepared for a political and legal union that would rest upon their consent and loyalty. Federalist historians John Pinder and Andrea Bosco have argued that the offer came "too late," for the time to unite peoples and prepare adequate common defenses was in the 1930s, even before the rise of Hitler.[71] On that reading, the failure to accept Aristide Briand's federal proposal of 1929–30 was the tragic lost opportunity. But later, as the Cold War was beginning, a European Defense Community and European Political Community were seriously proposed in 1950–54. Was European federalism then again timely? Probably no time for so revolutionary a departure in international relations as the federation of sovereign national states will ever be "right." If in time of peace, neither the populace nor their leadership will feel the necessity for uniting, so nations will continue, like the proverbial British, to muddle through. If in time of war, the danger will be so great that nations will experiment only so far as combined co-ordinating committees and war cabinets, like those of Britain and France in 1940. Nevertheless, as Monnet always said,

[71] John Pinder, "Prophet Not Without Honour: Lothian and the Federal Idea," *The Round Table*, 286 (1983): 216; Bosco, "Federal Union," 318.

for the hard work of uniting sovereignties, negotiations require a crisis.[72]

Failure Because of Lack of Public Preparation

There were many causes of failure, particularly in the demoralization of French counsels, which the diplomatic historians have closely traced. But from a broader, federalist perspective, the cause of the rather hasty support for the plan of union among British leaders and of the generally incredulous reactions among the French—the cause that would have made the knitting together of national hearts very difficult even if the plan had been approved by the leadership—was the almost total lack of popular participation in the making of the "union." Charles Kimber did not even learn of the high–level maneuverings until he read about them in the newspapers on June 18th.[73] Federal Union had made impressive gains, then with a peak membership of about 10,000 in 239 chapters, but it was very far from the 1 million that Lionel Curtis had advised would be necessary to make a political force on a scale like that of Lord Cecil's League of Nations Union at the time of the Peace Ballot of 1935, now almost forgotten.[74]

In France, the movement for federal union, though existent, was even smaller. With such shallow roots, even supposing that the French government had escaped to Oran or London, how would the absolutely vital sense of *common citizenship,* and hence the reality of federal union, have developed? Without popular support, as federalist historian Andrea Bosco has emphasized, projects of federal union inevitably fail.[75] There was an immense task of European and world political education ahead.

On this issue, Lord Gladwyn, at the end of his career as he turned to the cause of European union, draws an appropriate conclusion:[76]

> If the supranational thesis is to prevail, it needs as an exponent a man of power who can, as I could never hope to do, capture, when the time is ripe, the imagination of the people.

---

[72] Monnet, *Memoires,* 13.
[73] "Union with France," *Federal Union News,* 39 (22 June 1940).
[74] Bosco, "Federal Union," 303.
[75] Bosco, "Lothian," 470.
[76] Gladwyn, *Memoirs,* 371.

4

U.S. State Department Planning for the United Nations Organization

It is much easier to see a thing from the point of view of abstract principle than from that of concrete responsibility.

—Dietrich Bonhoeffer, *Letters and Papers from Prison,*
January 1943

[T]here will no longer be need for spheres of influence, for alliances, for balance of power, or any other of the special arrangements through which, in the unhappy past, the nations strove to safeguard their security or to promote their interests.

—Cordell Hull, the secretary of state on returning from the
Moscow conference on the future of the United Nations,
November 1943

The Advisory Committee on Post-War Foreign Policy

If ever there was an opportunity for world federalists, it was *before* the United States, Great Britain, and the Soviet Union became committed to a United Nations organization based on the sovereign equality of states. Shortly after the Japanese attack on Pearl Harbor and then Nazi Germany's declaration of war, which brought the United States into World War II on both Pacific and European fronts, President Franklin Roosevelt characteristically began planning for the peace. He approved on 28 December 1941 formation of a new planning group in the State Department, the Advisory Committee on Post-War Foreign Policy. Led by venerable Secretary of State Cordell Hull and his vigorous Undersecretary Sumner Welles, the group's mission was to devise an international organization to maintain peace and security. Arms might make peace, but then the problem would be to keep it. All participants were determined to avoid Woodrow Wilson's mistakes in negotiating the Versailles Treaty and Covenant of the League of Nations then precipitating Senate rejection, which they felt were among the principal causes of the war.

The United Nations

On 1 January 1942, the United States, Great Britain, Soviet Union, China, and 18 more nations at war with the Axis formed a grand alliance under a name suggested by Roosevelt, the "United Nations." They pledged to fight until victory, not to make a separate peace, and to adhere to the principles of the new Atlantic Charter, one of which set the goal of establishing "a wider and permanent system of general security." (By 1945, 51 states had joined the United Nations.) Hence, from the beginning the State Department planning group assumed they would devise a universal organization of these allies, open eventually to their reconstructed enemies and to all neutral and independent states. The times were hardly auspicious. Imperial Japan had conquered a vast arc of the Western Pacific from Manchuria to Singapore and the East Indies and was threatening New Zealand, Australia, and India, while Nazi Germany had conquered or controlled all of Europe from the English Channel to the front in Russia and was approaching Leningrad, Moscow, and Stalingrad.

The Advisory Committee—and particularly its Permanent International Organization subcommittee, which did most of the deliberating and drafted what became the U.N. Charter—included, from the department, Undersecretary Welles, Hull's special assistant Leo Pasvolsky, assistant secretaries Dean Acheson and Adolf Berle, legal advisor Green H. Hackworth, and research director Harley Notter (who assembled the invaluable historical record). From private life, it included former undersecretary of state and now director of the American Red Cross, Norman F. Davis; Columbia University historian and founder of the Commission to Study the Organization of Peace (CSOP), James T. Shotwell (he favored federation in the first, "Preliminary" report of CSOP in 1940); founder of the Committee to Defend America and executive director of CSOP, Clark M. Eichelberger; editor of *Foreign Affairs,* Hamilton Fish Armstrong; geographer and president of Johns Hopkins University, Isaiah Bowman; general counsel to the National Power Policy Committee, Benjamin V. Cohen; the president's special representative to the Vatican, Myron Taylor; and trusteeship expert, Benjamin Gerig. Generals and admirals and a dozen or so others came in when needed. Thus, the drafters represented the most responsible and informed citizens in government, not of course elected by the people, but appointed by State Department officials who had to live with the results.[1]

Judging by the record, the participants were conscious of their duty and expressed frankly the probable concerns of the Senate, Midwestern isolationists, medium and small states, individuals denied their rights, the poor, Russia, and more radical internationalists. They conducted their meetings in secret, as did the Philadelphia convention in 1787 and, for that matter, the University of Chicago's Committee to Frame a World Constitution after 1945. Secrecy allowed the State Department's advisory committee members to express themselves frankly, often on matters affecting traditional state sovereignty, at a time when democracy was fighting for its life. Secrecy meant that, when the draft text of the U.N. Char-

---

[1] Records of Harley A. Notter, Advisory Committee on Post–War Foreign Policy, Permanent International Organization Minutes 1, U.S. National Archives. Hereafter, Notter Records, Advisory Committee, PIO–1, 17 July 1942.

ter finally met the light of day, which it did at the San Francisco conference in the spring of 1945, it was strong enough to withstand public reaction. The records would make an instructive book for students who wonder about the next step of international organization. Records we have seen were declassified only in 1994.

"Federalized Government" to Succeed the League

A "federalized international organization—or government," in the terms of Harley Notter's published account of the advisory committee,[2] was in the minds of the drafters from their first meeting in mid–1942 right up to the Moscow conference of October 1943. At that point an international organization based on collective military enforcement by the Big Four (the United States, Great Britain, Soviet Union, and China) was definitely agreed to. *Great power unanimity was then presumed*—to be guaranteed by some form of veto. World federation was not thereafter explored as an alternative form of organization, for it was judged "infeasible" at the time, but it expressly formed the bounds of what was actually done. Federation served to render realistic an association of sovereign states. After the Moscow conference and Welles's departure from the department in August, expressions about federation drop out of the record.

Why, after the manifest failure of the League of Nations, was some form of world federal government rejected? In the words of the subcommittee that presented the draft (secret) Charter of the United Nations to the president on the eve of the Moscow conference:[3]

> The document which emerged is not a radical departure from national and international experience. Two, and perhaps only two, alternatives in the basic form of organization were open: (1) the cooperative form, or (2) the federal form. The latter, while urged by many prominent individuals and groups, was rejected by the drafting committee as politically not feasible. The various governments and peoples are not believed to be ready for an international federal government even if it were theoretically desirable. Yet the name of the organization and the provisions of the Charter itself provide a basis for steady growth toward closer relationships and even toward more unified forms of world cooperation.

Historically, there can hardly be a doubt that in 1943 the various nations were not ready for world federation. Clarence Streit's Federal Union organization in the United States had attracted only a few thousand adherents, not the million aimed at in 1943, and Britain's Federal Union, also aiming at a million, grew to a bit more than 9,000 in 1940, then rapidly declined. The great days of United World Federalists, after use of the atomic bomb, when they would have resolu-

---

[2] Harley A. Notter, *Postwar Foreign Policy Preparation, 1939–1945* (Washington, DC: U.S. Department of State, Pub. No. 3580, General Foreign Policy Series 15, 1949), 113.

[3] Notter Records, Commentary on the Tentative Draft Text of the Charter of the United Nations, PIO–UND 7a, 7 September 1943.

tions favoring world federal government in half of the United States and in the Congress, were five years in the future. That would be too late.

Clarence Streit's draft constitution for a federation of free peoples and a similar one by Grenville Clark found their way into the State Department files, but federalist plans at the time were very inadequate. (Years later, Clark and Louis B. Sohn sought to remedy this defect with their magisterial study, *World Peace through World Law.*) Other comparable plans in the files included Tom O. Griessemer's *World Affairs* article, "An International Police Force," Oscar Newfang's book *World Government,* Minnesota governor Harold Stassen's speeches on international government, Justice Owen Robert's speeches, and writings by such English federalists as R.W.G. Mackay, Sir Walter Layton, W. I. Jennings, and C. B. Fawcett.[4] The main concern of the drafters, Secretary Hull, and President Roosevelt was hardly world federation, however logical it might be, but isolationism, particularly after the elections of 1942 had returned a number of isolationists to Congress. They were also plainly concerned about winning the advice and consent of the Senate. Not to mention Russia.

The drafters did not simply revive the League of Nations, in the sense of conceiving amendments to its Covenant; they rethought what sort of cooperative organization might solve the world political problems with which they were familiar or had watched the League address, like abuses of the rights of minorities; they made numerous changes, like permitting an absolute veto only for the Big Four where the League had granted one to every state member; and so they recreated a general security organization on the same fundamental basis. From the point of view of the history of the idea of world federal government, we need to examine a bit of this debate on points of structure, representation, powers, and transition.

Constitutional Debate in the State Department

That "law forms the basis of organized society" and that "security measures cannot be applied effectively unless they are in accord with a decision of the merits of the dispute bearing a sufficient resemblance to justice to command public support" was recognized at least in the Legal subcommittee (composed of the same people).[5] Drafters saw that "international society is dynamic and that a static law in such a society cannot fulfill its proper role"; hence, the law must grow with the society. To update the law, they discussed an equity tribunal (still not tried 50 years later) and a world legislature, the "natural solution of the problem of revision," for "the legislature would be closer to, and presumably more responsive to the will of the people." The reason they admitted was that "popular sentiment of what is just in a given situation may be something different from the official policy of states."[6] The alternative of a world legislature as the

---

[4] Notter Records, PIO–152.

[5] Notter Records, H–2010, International Law: Establishment and Promotion of Legal Order, 2 June 1943.

[6] Notter Records, H–2011, International Law: Role of Law in International Relations, 19 May 1943.

foundation of a successor international organization was fully discussed. From a historical perspective, it is worth quoting at length a critical passage:[7]

> Provision for full legislative powers, involving the right to pass laws binding on nationals of member states
>
> This proposal is integral to plans based on the principle of federalism, and occurs in schemes which emphasize the analogy between international developments and the historical evolution of the United States of America. It has the advantage of assuring direct and expeditious procedures for urgent problems, and if the legislative body was backed up with adequate authority, this proposal would make possible the enforcement of policies dependent for their success on action by the citizens of all states.
>
> Unless a broadly federal scheme of international organization is adopted, which is unlikely, it would be difficult to secure support for this proposal, particularly in the United States. This proposal would create a serious constitutional problem in the majority of states. It seems probable that a less ambitious scheme will be adopted, particularly in view of the fact that the common views, traditions, and institutions essential to the success of a federal scheme have not yet evolved.

An International Bill of Rights

Nevertheless, a bill of human rights was drafted in the absence of a government to enforce it. Did the drafters think that the new international organization (U.N.O.), if it guaranteed human rights, would have to have some of the nature of a world federal government? No, they seem to have proceeded "pragmatically," in the American way, aiming to meet post–World War II needs, fully realizing the implications "in the direction of international government."[8] Roosevelt had announced the Four Freedoms (freedoms of speech and religion, freedoms from fear and want) in January 1941, reaffirmed in the Atlantic Charter in August. Americans and the allies were fighting for these rights. Moreover, abuse of these rights in Germany was regarded as another principal cause of the war. The drafters had before them the great English, American, and French national bills, as well as novel ones recently devised by H. G. Wells, Clarence Streit, and the American Law Institute. The *right of petition* to an international court was briefly made the keystone of the draft. That fundamental right (Art. 21 in the draft of 31 July 1942), which gave meaning to the enforcement of all the others, disappeared from the final bill,[9] and then the bill itself was omitted from the U.N. Charter as presented to the San Francisco conference in 1945.

The main reason was fear of its implications for American Negro, Jewish,

---

[7] Ibid., H–1047, International Organization: Deliberative Body: Basis and Nature of Powers, 29 September 1943.

[8] Notter Records, H–1034, International Organization: Basic Objectives of Permanent Organization, 15 July 1943.

[9] Ibid., Bill of Rights, Preliminary Draft, Legal Document 2, 31 July 1942; Bill of Rights, Draft Approved by Legal Subcommittee, 3 December 1943.

Mexican, and Nisei minorities and even for women, as Hackworth explained.[10] Other states would have their own fears about such an instrument affecting their domestic jurisdiction. Commitments to human rights, however, were made in the Preamble and Articles 1, 55, 56, and 62 of the U.N. Charter. Later, the international bill of rights, in the form of two covenants on liberal and economic rights, was finally signed in 1966 and it entered into force in 1976. The right of petition is now provided for in an optional protocol, to which, at time of writing, few states were parties.

Such proposals made for a bit of conflict between the legal subcommittee and the political ones. Both Adolf Berle and Benjamin Cohen argued that the former subcommittee should restrict itself to consideration of problems submitted by the other subcommittees. That meant that international law would be subordinated to political, military, and economic policy, as treated by the others. "Otherwise," Cohen said, "the law might preempt the entire field, as a great many of the problems of international organization and of international political institutions could be treated as primarily legal in character."[11] But even in the policy subcommittees, some extraordinary concessions were made that were relevant to an eventual legal world organization. At one point a qualified veto was proposed —two vetoes necessary to defeat a measure, even "in case one of the states members [in what became the Security Council] was the aggressor." Weighted voting —indexed by population, trade volume, defense budget, or even "degree of contribution to the defeat of the Axis nations"—was also explored.[12] Weighted voting later would actually be introduced into the Bretton Woods financial organizations. Both these measures for decades to follow would be alternatives for effective U.N. reform.

Devolution of Great Power to World Democracy

"Devolution" of power from the Big Four (understood as historically transitory) to all states and their people was expected. By the fall of 1942, the drafters had decided on a U.N. structure of an executive committee of the great powers, a council composed of distinguished *individuals from the regions* (not state representatives), and an assembly of all the other nation–states. But what would committee, council, and assembly do? Bowman set out the "philosophical basis" for this concept of international organization. People and nations relate to each other on levels of culture, welfare, and security, he began. The assembly, representative of all states, would assemble the *will* of the world community and protect every cultural, religious, national, and human interest against destruction. The council, representative of regions, would be better fitted to supervise economic, social, and technical matters that require more constant control than the intermittent assembly could give, though both should share in the control. The executive committee of the great powers must take responsibility for security because

[10] Ibid., Legal Minutes 5, 5 November 1942; Legal Minutes 8, 3 December 1942.

[11] Notter Records, Legal Minutes 1, 21 August 1942.

[12] Ibid., H–1010, International Organization: Executive Body: Voting, 22 May 1943.

no other means are available or effective. But, while in anarchic situations power must be concentrated in a few hands, in the course of time as weaker states developed a comparable sense of responsibility for the whole, there would develop, Bowman expected, a "devolution of power." "The day might come when you have all countries exercising equal rights, but that is perhaps utopian," he concluded. "It will surely not be the case at the end of the war and probably not within our lifetime."[13]

Democracy, therefore, would be the conclusion of a historical process. Bowman's thesis led to a world constitutional debate. Sumner Welles wanted to know just what provisions in the Charter would encourage such a development. Portugal might regard the executive committee as a condominium of imperialists. Perhaps it would be better to admit to the council the small powers in order for them to learn how to manage "welfare." Bowman admitted that, in the present scheme, "the only bond of unity [among the nations] is that relating to economic processes." Notter pointed out that the functional agencies (Universal Postal Union, International Telecommunication Union, International Labour Organisation, etc.) are the ones that actually "do" things; what power is there to shift from assembly to council to committee? The assembly, replied Welles, is the democratic foundation of the organization, since there the equality of states is recognized. Only two things can happen: either the great powers will tell the small what they must do, or the small will tell the great within limits what they ought to do. The latter is preferable. The executive committee should avoid the appearance of dictation.[14]

A Transitional International Organization

The drafters all began to think in terms of a transitional organization and a permanent one. Bowman argued that victory in war would create a psychological moment when the great powers could lead the small into the kind of organization that could evolve; one of its first functions would be disarmament, so, as the nations became militarily more equal, powers could devolve to the council and even the assembly. Eichelberger added that in principle the process could continue to *individual* representation in the assembly, and Bowman stated that the principle at work here was the consent of the governed. Shotwell urged that descriptions of the new U.N. organization should emphasize the "democratic thing to follow," for "unless that is there, you are going to have a large movement of opposition in this country against imperialism." One of their models was the International Labour Organisation (ILO), which since 1919 had been based on representation from labor, business, and governments; Shotwell imagined that U.S. senators would attend the assembly rather as state senators did the Congress before the 17th Amendment. Welles concluded that for the foreseeable future, the assembly would be a "debating society," the council a policy advisor, and the executive committee the great powers responsible for military security.[15]

[13] Notter Records, PIO–18, 27 November 1942.
[14] Notter Records, PIO–18, 27 November 1942.
[15] Ibid.

By the end of 1942, a popularly representative world legislature and a world judiciary competent to hear much broader categories of legal disputes had been rejected. The drafters proceeded inexorably toward the international organization now found in the United Nations. The fundamental structure was that of Roosevelt's Four Policemen, set within a two-thirds majority–rule policy making council, accompanied by a diplomatic conclave for debate, functional agencies, and a revived world court restricted to the narrowest legal disputes affecting states.[16] In the end, this structure became the Security Council, with its inner circle of permanent members (five with the addition of France in 1945), the General Assembly, Specialized Agencies, and International Court of Justice. In retrospect, since we know that the unanimity of the permanent members broke down within one year or at most two (by 1947), we probably must admit that no plan to effectively abolish war was possible by the mid–20th century. The only acceptable plan was at best transitional.

The Police Power

The absurdities to which the State Department planning group were driven is well indicated by their extended debate in March 1943 on the proposed police power. A whole draft U.N. "constitution" was ready, without veto in the executive committee (it then had recommendatory powers only).[17] There were two key articles, "7. Maintenance of Security" and "7a. Police Power," rather like Chapter VII of the eventual U.N. Charter. In the latter were two operative articles:

> (1) In order to assure compliance with arms limitation agreements and the maintenance of international peace and security, the Members of the International Organization mutually undertake to make available such of their military, naval, and air forces, and other resources and facilities, as the Executive Committee and the Council may deem to be necessary for this purpose. Forces designated by Member States in compliance with this obligation shall be held in readiness at all times....

> (5) All forces acting on behalf of the International Organization shall be permitted during the period of such action freely to use national facilities and installations of Member States in such a manner and to such an extent as the Executive Committee, after consultation with the Permanent Security and Armaments commission, shall determine to be necessary.

Sumner Welles, normally a believer in collective security, thought that the whole approach of the draft was inherently wrong. Paragraph 1 was tantamount to making a protectorate of all small nations, subjecting them to the control of the four big powers, and paragraph 5 was tantamount to permitting control by the major powers of the facilities and installations of smaller independent nations. "If the League of Nations had done away with the theory of neutrality,"

---

[16] Notter Records, Memorandum for the President, PIO–161f, 29 December 1943.

[17] Ibid., Draft Constitution of the International Organization, PIO Document 123e, 26 March 1943.

he said, "this draft would do away with the theory of sovereignty." The Dutch were already on record as opposed to such a scheme; in Panama, which he knew well from his days at the Latin America desk, it would be "confusion worse confounded."[18]

Enforcement upon States

The problem, from our perspective, was that, in the absence of the rule of world law, "enforcement" effectively meant war waged by the international organization against aggressive states. Shotwell drove this point home ironically by proposing "reliance principally on the use of an air force as an international police," to get around the problem of bases and free passage. If the Germans returned to belligerency, he not so ironically suggested, the peace–keeping body should send bombers back as an "instrument of terror." But General George V. Strong objected that "war could not finally be won in the air." So Leo Pasvolsky drew the logical conclusion, in support of Article 7a, that the Big Four would have to maintain bases and their own forces around the world to maintain the peace. But he was uneasy, since 7a "went much too far in the direction of opening up one country to the occupation of other countries. It virtually means," he concluded, "that a peaceful country could be occupied on the decision of the Executive Committee."[19] Norman Davis summed it up in a similar context: "The big powers would run the world."[20]

A relic of this baffled search for effective enforcement in an international organization based on the sovereign equality of states can be seen in the U.N. Charter's Article 45, which still provides for air force operations in response to breaches of the peace. So indiscriminate and violent is such a measure that Chapter VII has historically been employed for international suppressive operations only twice—once against North Korean aggression in 1950 and second against Iraq in 1990.[21] Meanwhile, over 150 international wars took place from 1945 to 1990,[22] and the count of civil wars affecting international peace since

---

[18] Notter Records, PIO Minutes 33, 26 March 1943.

[19] Notter Records, ibid.

[20] Ibid., PIO Minutes 35, 16 April 1943.

[21] Seven times, if we count all declarations of threats to international peace and security: Cease–fire in Palestine (July 1948); Korean War (June 1950–53); mandatory sanctions against Rhodesia (May 1968); extension of these sanctions (March 1970); decision against South African rights in Namibia (January 1970); sanctions on arms trade to South Africa (1977); Gulf War (1990–91). Evan Luard, *The United Nations: How It Works and What It Does* (New York: St. Martin's, 1979), 23; David J. Scheffer, *The United Nations in the Gulf Crisis and Options for U.S. Policy* (New York: UNA–USA, Occasional Paper No. 1, February 1991), 7–11.

[22] Count of wars through 1982. Hanna Newcomb, *Design for a Better World* (Lanham, MD: University Press of America, 1983), 231–34. Count of 50 through 1971. F. S. Northedge and M. D. Donelan, *International Disputes: The Political Aspects* (London: Europa Publications for the David Davies Memorial Institute, 1971), pp. 343–44. Count of 86 by 1977. K. Venaka Raman, ed., Dispute Settlement through the United Nations (New York: Oceana for UNITAR, 1977), pp. xv–xix.

then is several score more. To remedy the probable unworkableness of the universal measure, Welles while in the State Department supported regional security schemes, which were provided for in Article 51 of the Charter. That was the loophole that permitted the formation of NATO in 1949.

Wisdom in 1943

Was the State Department unwise to rely on Big Four unanimity and enforcement by armed force? In retrospect, it is striking how confident the planners were in moving toward so unworkable a design of a general international organization charged with the maintenance of world peace and security. No doubt it would have been defeatism to suggest in 1943 that the wartime alliance with the Soviet Union would not last, and it would have been lacking in realism to suppose that the peoples of the world were ready for world federal government. The alternatives to the universal U.N. Organization in the spirit of Wilsonianism were Churchill's regional councils and Stalin's straight tripartite military alliance.[23] Churchill got his Council of Europe in 1949 after one last public appeal in Amsterdam (the Council of Asia has never materialized), and Stalin's alliance would surely have fared no better than the U.N. by 1947.

From a world federalist perspective, State Department planning in 1942–43 did achieve a *universal* world organization. However weak, the U.N.O. did get the United States, Great Britain, U.S.S.R., and eventually virtually all states *in*. The next problem would be to reform its structure, at some auspicious period of building world community, along the lines of popular representation (democracy) and to grant it powers to enact law effectively to maintain international peace and security.

---

[23] Townsend Hoopes and Douglas Brinkley, *FDR and the Creation of the U.N.* (New Haven: Yale University Press, 1977), 70, 85, 100, 102.

5

World Federalists' Response to the United Nations

Federalists of the World, Unite!

—E. B. White, *The New Yorker*, 21 October 1944

What you should do is go home and try to figure out a way to
stop the next war and all future wars. Think of what war will
be in twenty–five years. It is intolerable.

—Henry L. Stimson, the secretary of war's last assignment
to Grenville Clark after the successful Normandy invasion,
July 1944

Drafting the United Nations Charter

The years 1942–1944 were the crucial ones for the creation of the permanent United Nations Organization. In 1943, despite national preoccupation with the war effort, a wide range of public legislation on the shape of the future international security organization was introduced in the U.S. Congress. The Fulbright resolution (without reference to "sovereign states") passed in the House (360–29), and then the Connally resolution passed in the Senate (85–5), after being amended to reflect exactly the language of the Moscow declaration of 1 November 1943. Thus, president, State Department, House and Senate, and particularly Russia among the allies were agreed about establishing, in the language of the Moscow declaration, a "general international organization, based on the principle of the sovereign equality of all peace–loving states." What this meant was not yet quite clear.

A year later, in the fall 1944, formal discussions between diplomatic representatives of the United States, Great Britain, and Soviet Union and, separately, the U.S., Britain, and China (since the U.S.S.R. was still observing its 1941 non-aggression pact with Japan) met at the Dumbarton Oaks estate in Washington to review exactly the draft Charter of the United Nations, including its still secret veto provisions. Then in the spring of 1945, spanning Victory in Europe (VE) Day and first use of atomic bombs at Hiroshima and Nagasaki, the great San Francisco conference was held with all 51 members of the United Nations alliance, where final agreement was reached on the U.N. Charter.[1]

Among the congressional resolutions (see Appendix H), the expression "sovereign equality" tended to be code for a league rather than a federation. The Fulbright resolution did not use this expression and hence was much more flexible; neither at first did the Connally resolution, which was held up in the Senate until the fourth paragraph, using the code, was introduced. But Representative Fulbright, perhaps not exceeding the views of the House majority that passed his resolution, made some very timely, clarifying remarks about sovereignty at a meeting in the New York Times Hall in September 1943:[2]

> The oft-repeated objection to any system of collective security, that we must never sacrifice our sovereignty, is, in my opinion, a very red herring. If sovereignty means anything, and resides anywhere, it means control over our own affairs and resides in the people. The people, according to our republican principles, are sovereign. They may delegate all, or any part, of the power to manage their affairs to any agency they please. So far they have delegated part to their city government, part to the county, part to the State, and part to the Federal Government.
>
> Certainly it cannot be denied that twice within twenty–five years we have been forced, against our will, into wars which have seriously threatened our free existence. To this extent, the supreme control over our affairs, over our destiny, is at present imperfect. Therefore, if we can remedy this defect, by a delegation of limited power to an agency designed to prevent war, to establish law and order, in which we participate fully and equally with others, how can this be called a sacrifice, a giving up of anything?

There is not the slightest evidence that President Roosevelt ever supported an international organization that might by the power of world public opinion restrict the freedom of action of the United States. His professed ideal was the "Four Policemen"—a continuing alliance of the principal World War II allies. "World government," in a rare interview for the *Saturday Evening Post* in 1944, he called "nonsense" without more ado.[3] He was plainly on record as dreading Senate rejection of any plan reminiscent of Woodrow Wilson's League of Nations.[4] Secretary of State Hull shared these views exactly and was alarmed by isolationist support for New York governor Thomas E. Dewey.[5]

The Russians, of course, no less demanded the "sovereign" language. Sta-

[1] Townsend Hoopes and Douglas Brinkley, *FDR and the Creation of the U.N.* (New Haven: Yale University Press, 1997), 64–82.

[2] "Quotes," *World Government News,* October 1943, p. 6.

[3] Forrest Davis, Washington Editor, *Saturday Evening Post,* May 1944, quoted in "Great Design," *World Government News,* June 1944, p. 1.

[4] Franklin Delano Roosevelt, "The Spirit of This Nation Is Strong—The Faith of This Nation Is Eternal," Address to Congress on the State of the Union, Samuel I. Rosenman, ed., *The Public Papers and Addresses of Franklin D. Roosevelt,* 13 vols. (New York: Harpers, 1938–50), 11: 32–33; Willard Range, *Franklin D. Roosevelt's World Order* (Athens, GA: University of Georgia Press, 1959), 27–48.

[5] Cordell Hull, *Memoirs,* 2 vols. (New York: Macmillan, 1948), 2: 1686–95.

lin's main concern at the Moscow conference in 1943 was to win Western commitment to open a second front in 1944. When he understood that the contemplated U.N. Organization was to be based on "sovereign equality," implying no binding powers on the principal members, he thought it innocuous. His League of Nations representative Maxim Litvinov had been thoroughly disillusioned with the League by 1938, and Stalin was barely willing to see its revival. But there was some indication of Russian flexibility. Former ambassador to the Soviet Union Joseph E. Davies reported in 1943 that the Soviets "would be willing to give up so much of their sovereignty as would assure a strong federation to outlaw war, aggression and conquest," adding, in the confusion of the time over how a lawful *federation* would operate, "and to establish an international police force to keep the peace for the world community of nations."[6] In retrospect, this view of the Soviets seems mostly to reflect the great hopes of the time.

Federalist Response

Where was the world federalist movement during these discrete congressional and diplomatic moves so fateful for the future peace of the world? The answer seems to be that the movement still consisted of scattered, rather visionary individuals who had yet to discover the great national initiatives being taken, around which they could organize an opposition. The atomic bomb, which would bring the movement to a peak, still lay shrouded in the future.

William Bross Lloyd Jr., American director of the Campaign for World Government and editor of its newsletter, was about to report for alternative service as a conscientious objector.[7] Edith Wynner and Georgia Lloyd were working on their massive *Searchlight on Peace Plans*, which was timely published in March 1944, when it attracted enough attention in Washington for Mrs. Roosevelt to invite the "girls" (as the press cavalierly referred to them) to a White House dinner.[8] Clarence Streit spoke before the resolutions committees of the Democratic and Republican party conventions in 1944 but failed to get either to accept a Union of the Free plank.[9] The World Federalists had no more success with their campaign to "put a World Government plank in every party platform for '44."[10] G. A. Borgese had just returned to the States after teaching a course in political science at the University of Puerto Rico.[11] University of Chicago philosophy

[6] Quoted from *Life Magazine*, in "Quotes," *World Government News*, April 1943, p. 4.

[7] Georgia Lloyd, Interview with the author, 30 May 1981.

[8] Ibid.; Edith Wynner to Friend, 1 January 1944, UWF Papers, 9.CWG; W. Wallace A. Deuel, "Compendium of Hopeful Cures for War," *New York Times Book Review*, 4 June 1944; Malvina Lindsay, "Girls Present Peace Plans in Capsules," *Washington Post*, 17 June 1944, Schwimmer–Lloyd Collection.

[9] Clarence K. Streit, "Robot Political Platforms Cannot Launch Peace," Statement before the Resolutions Committee of the 1944 Democratic National Convention, Chicago, n.d., c. 30 July 1944, Stephen Benedict Papers.

[10] "New Campaign," *World Government News*, October 1943, p. 7; "Tweedle-dee–Tweedledum," ibid., August 1944, pp. 2–3.

[11] Current Biography—1947, p. 55.

professor Mortimer J. Adler, who would later, with Borgese and Hutchins, become one of the leading figures of the Committee to Frame a World Constitution, published another classic of the movement, *How to Think about War and Peace,* in 1944.[12] Robert Lee Humber got his seventh state legislature (Louisiana) to pass, in June 1944, his Declaration and Resolution on the Federation of the World.[13]

The Period of Flux, 1944–1946

A few federalists realized that they were in the midst of a historic opportunity. On 1 April 1944, at the first national Student Federalist convention in New York City, Harris Wofford made an eloquent address on the immediate future. He asked if all the fighting and the dying in the war will have been in vain again. He referred to the progress made in convincing at least many thousands of Americans "that anarchy brings on war, that world peace will come through world government." He thought that past educational efforts had taught many what world citizenship would mean and thus had helped prepare the future of the "great World Federal Union." Then he spoke of the historic opportunity opening up in 1944:

> As Ambassador [to the Soviet Union, 1934–36, William C.] Bullitt explained it at Federal Union's third nation–wide convention in Peoria last November [1943,] after a great war like this there comes a brief moment when world affairs are in a period of flux, are malleable to the extent that we can mold the world the way we want it, or as Tom Paine would have put it, when "we have it in our power to begin the world over again."

Wofford replied to the worldly heads who said, You federalists are going to be terribly disillusioned: "We can't be disillusioned, because we are taking the realistic, practical course. We see grimly that our present course in foreign policy is leading us into another worldwide war." He concluded that, in the coming period of flux, when the suffering, fighting men and women of all lands will demand an end to war, some degree of federal world government *could* be established. "There is a tide in the affairs of men," Wofford quoted from Shakespeare's *Julius Caesar,* "which, taken at the flood, leads on to fortune."[14]

These words, from the mouth of a man so young, were to prove to have a certain prophetic rightness. From a historical perspective, can we not imagine that there *was* a "period of flux," a period when the remaining sovereign powers at the end of the Second World War were willing to eliminate war from the conduct of their foreign policy, if it could be done in some way without jeopardizing

---

[12] "The *only* cause of war," he wrote, "is anarchy." "It is the only cause we can control." Mortimer J. Adler, *How to Think about War and Peace* (New York: Simon & Schuster, 1944), 69, 75. The author first discovered this powerful book in an outlying post library of Camp Pendleton, California.

[13] "Humber's Seventh," *World Government News,* July 1944, p. 1.

[14] Harris Wofford, Convention Address, 1 April 1944, Stephen Benedict Papers.

their domestic affairs? Judging by professed national initiatives, the period lasted from the Fulbright Resolution of 21 September 1943, to the take–it–or–leave–it vote on the Baruch Plan for the international control of atomic energy in the U.N. Atomic Energy Commission on 30 December 1946. After that, the Cold War followed rapidly. The very *last* date for the historic opportunity might be 25 June 1950, when the Korean War broke out and the Cold War became accepted as a new reality of international relations, not to change until 1990.

Grenville Clark

World federalists were still very few and far between, but they were to be weighed rather than counted, including Grenville Clark and Cord Meyer Jr. Clark is particularly important, for he had thought through the world federalist alternative well before the period of flux, unlike so many others. He was the "elder statesman" of the federalist movement and a "statesman incognito" in American government. Even before the Dumbarton Oaks conference, he published an outstanding article on the fundamental need to establish a popularly representative world legislature in order to inaugurate the rule of world law.[15] By example, he led the opposition to the Dumbarton Oaks plan.[16] Even before Hiroshima he was organizing a conference of world government advocates and distinguished American leaders, which took place near his home in Dublin, New Hampshire.[17] He submitted major proposals for Charter revision to the United Nations General Assembly in time for its first session in London in February 1946.[18] He was a background eminence at the formation of United World Federalists in 1947 and was from the first the most respected counsel of the presidents of UWF.[19] We will often have occasion to refer to his views in this history.

Grenville Clark was born to the New York aristocracy in 1882. He was much influenced by his maternal grandfather, Colonel LeGrand B. Cannon, pioneer railroad financier, Union officer, and acquaintance of Abraham Lincoln. Cannon often quoted Lincoln, in words that Clark remembered: "The people will save their government, if the government itself will do its part only indifferently well."[20] He deeply instilled in the boy the democratic maxims of self–help: "Don't wait for the government to act in a crisis, my boy. Let the people take

[15] Grenville Clark, "A New World Order—The American Lawyer's Role," *Indiana Law Journal*, 19, 4 (July 1944): 289–300.

[16] Clark to Editor, "Dumbarton Oaks Plans Held in Need of Modification: Viewed as Repeating Essential Errors of League of Nations and Offering No Assurance of International Security—Some Remedies Suggested," *New York Times*, 15 October 1944, Clark Papers, 21.9.

[17] Clark to Justice Owen J. Roberts, 7 July 1945, ibid., 15.2.

[18] Alan Cranston, Grenville Clark, Thomas H. Mahoney, Dublin Conference Committee, "Proposals for Amendment of the United Nations Charter" (New York: Authors, 1 February 1946), Clark Papers,15.2.

[19] Cord Meyer to Clark, 1947.

[20] Abraham Lincoln, *Message to Congress*, 4 July 1861, in Nicolay and Hay, eds., *The Complete Works of Abraham Lincoln* (New York, 1905): 6: 312; Grenville Clark, *A Plan for Peace* (New York: Harper & Bros., 1950), 3.

hold when there is need. That is the way this country was built up. Move yourself."

After graduation from Harvard Law, Clark briefly worked in the same law office with Franklin Delano Roosevelt, before setting up his own office near Wall Street with Elihu Root Jr. In 1915, Elihu Root Sr.—former secretary of state, secretary of war, and New York senator—joined the growing Root, Clark firm as general counsel. Through the senior man, Clark met Henry Stimson and many of the ablest men in law and government of their generation.[21]

The Plattsburgh Movement

Grenville Clark soon began a career as public citizen that had important implications for his later advocacy of world federalism. In 1915, when the Wilson administration did not dare to undertake preparations for what a suspicious public might have regarded as entry into World War I, Clark proposed and then organized a series of Army training camps (the first was at Plattsburgh, across the lake from Colonel Cannon's estate) to train army officers in case of U.S. entry into the war. Eventually, some 60,000 line officers were commissioned. They made a decisive contribution to the combat effectiveness of the American forces that had to be suddenly raised after 1917. Clark himself was commissioned a major (later promoted to lieutenant colonel) and was decorated with the Distinguished Service Cross. The experience of the Plattsburgh movement convinced Clark of the power of timely citizens' action, when the government was preoccupied with urgent day–to–day detail or set in its "grooves" by training and tradition. He contributed significantly to U.S. victory in war.[22]

Henry Stimson and the Selective Service Act

In 1940, after World War II had begun but before the fall of France, Clark again came to the aid of his country. Isolationist pressure was so strong, President Roosevelt could not act. So Clark organized a prestigious committee to sponsor a selective service law. In the course of their behind–the–scenes work —particularly with Justice Felix Frankfurter—former secretary of state Henry L. Stimson was proposed as secretary of war, and the younger Robert P. Patterson (formerly of Root, Clark) was suggested as assistant secretary. Roosevelt's eyes lit up at these names, which solved a difficult political problem. He appointed Stimson and Patterson, the congressional opposition was overcome (by one vote), and in September, before the election, the draft became law. The appointments and the act proved wise and enduring for the American war effort.[23]

Clark himself became an advisor to Stimson. Throughout the war, Clark worked in the War Department on civilian national service legislation, the

    [21] "The Legacy of a Great American: An Interview with Grenville Clark," *McCall's*, April 1967, p. 64ff; World Order—Reasonable Hope or Illusion, draft, 28 September 1966, Clark Papers, 21.33.
    [22] Clark, *Plan for Peace*, 4; *Memoirs*, 14, 59–60, 114–15; Clark to Theodore Roosevelt, 19 November 1914, ibid., 267–69.
    [23] *Memoirs*, 15, 17–18, 55, 60, 115, 209–10.

"Work or Fight" bill. Wartime Britain and Russia had similar programs, and Clark argued that national service would speed up American mobilization and hence save lives. He organized another citizens' committee, but this time, largely because Roosevelt shrank from so radical a war measure until January 1945, he failed. Whether such a measure, if passed, would have enabled the Western allies to open a second front in 1943, or even 1942, as General Marshall wanted, is one of those might–have–beens that will never be known. An early second front might well have reduced the Soviet distrust that was deeply at the root of the subsequent Cold War. Clark, in any case, for his wartime services to the United States earned the unofficial sobriquet of "Statesman Incognito."[24]

Figuring Out a Way to Stop All Future Wars

Why, then, did Grenville Clark turn from the works of war to those of peace? For him, there was no inconsistency. He was trying to save the United States. He advocated military preparedness in 1915, and again in 1940, as prudent measures of national defense. In each case, his proposals were radically at variance with the current state of popular and official opinion, but history has largely proved the wisdom of his course, especially with regard to World War II. By 1944, however, the possibility of a military defense for preserving the life and liberties of the American people seemed deeply in doubt to Clark—and to Stimson, too, for that matter.[25]

The world in which nations could protect themselves by force of arms was passing away. Industrialization was creating a world where war was an intolerable calamity, and science was putting weapons into the hands of national leaders that meant total destruction if used in the traditional manner for resolving international disputes. World War II, even before revelation of atomic bombs, convinced Clark that a third general war would be the end of civilization. Stimson, who of course knew all about the Manhattan project, sent Clark home after D–Day 1944, saying:[26]

What you should do is go home and try to figure out a way to stop the next

[24] *Memoirs,* 20–21, 27; Stimson to Clark, 2 September 1941, Stimson Papers, 104; Clark to FDR, 30 December 1943, ibid., 108; Stimson to FDR, 16 May 1944, ibid., 110; Clark to Stimson, 13 June 1944, ibid.; Clark to Stimson, 2 January 1945, ibid., 111; Clark to Stimson, 9 January 1945, ibid.; FDR to Stimson, 11 January 1945, ibid.; Stimson to FDR, 13 January 1945, ibid.; "Grenville Clark: Statesman Incognito," *Fortune,* February 1946, pp. 110–15ff; James MacGregor Burns, *Roosevelt: The Soldier of Freedom,* 1940–1945 (New York: Harcourt Brace Jovanovitch, 1970), 183–89, 364–74.

[25] Stimson to Stettinius, 23 January 1945, Stimson Papers, 111; Discussion with Truman, 25 April 1945, Stimson Diaries, 51:70–72; Stimson, "Reflections on the Basic Problems which Confront Us," 19 July 1945, ibid., 52:42–44; Stimson to George Wharton Pepper, 27 October 1948, Stimson Papers, 118.

[26] Clark, World Order—Reasonable Hope or Illusion, pp. 9–10; *Memoirs,* 20; Irving Dillard, "Grenville Clark: Public Citizen," *American Scholar,* 33 (Winter 1963–64): 97–104.

war and all future wars. Think of what war will be in twenty–five years. It is intolerable.

Clark then, in July 1944, published and circulated among prominent internationalists and officials "A New World Order," the first of his proposals for a limited world government as a new basis for national security. That it was radically at variance with prevailing ideas did not daunt him.[27] This proposal of 1944 contained four essential principles found in all of Clark's and his colleagues' proposals of world federation. Indeed, these principles determined the shape of the whole federalist movement, for in each case there was a fundamental alternative that, if chosen (and others did choose), gave an entirely different character to the contemplated world government.

1. Membership. The world government should be universal in membership, or at least should not omit any major power nor present conditions that would prevent the early admission of any major power.

2. Representation. There should be established a unicameral world legislature, representative of peoples according to a "well balanced and fair" system of weighted representation. The enactments of the popular world house would, therefore, have the character of law, binding on individuals. As in any legislature, decisions would be reached by majority rule (no national veto). Executive and judicial branches then follow from creation of the legislative.

3. Powers. The sovereign powers delegated by the world's peoples or their states to the world government should be limited to those necessary to provide for the common defense. All other powers would be retained by the states or their people. Hence, the world government would be limited in power (minimal) and federal in jurisdiction.

4. Transition. The goal of establishing the rule of law under a common, federal world government must become the official policy of national governments; the actual establishment should be by negotiated agreement.

In August 1944, Clark sent reprints to President Roosevelt, Secretary of State Hull, Undersecretary Edward R. Stettinius Jr., Secretary of War Stimson, former ambassador to Japan Joseph C. Grew, presidential candidate Thomas E. Dewey, his foreign affairs advisor John Foster Dulles, members of the Dumbarton Oaks delegations including Soviet ambassador Andrei A. Gromyko, and selected friends.

Though respected, Clark received little support. Stanley K. Hornbeck, special assistant to Secretary Hull, replied that planners for a new world order too often gave little thought to the problem of creating prior conditions of social life that would "incline" the people toward peace and away from the use of force.

---

[27] Grenville Clark, "A New World Order—The American Lawyer's Role," *Indiana Law Journal,* 19 (July 1944): 289–300.

One of Clark's friends criticized with some merit Clark's proposal of a world court, like the Supreme Court in the U.S., to settle all international disputes. These disputes are usually of a "political" nature and cannot be settled by familiar processes of law, he said. There needs to be a kind of political council, too, to settle disputes peacefully. The same correspondent also drew attention to the fundamental problem of enforcement, after court or council reached a decision. If world forces remained under the commands of the great powers, he doubted that any power would acquiesce to a decision that went against it. Another correspondent criticized Clark's fixed system of representation, arguing that the history of the federal system in the United States showed a tendency of power gravitating toward the center, so provision should be made for such change, lest it take place contrary to principle. He also questioned Clark's assumption that the colonial system would continue.[28]

But the most penetrating objections came from Lewis W. Douglas, a friend in a neighboring law office on Nassau Street and former ambassador to Great Britain. Douglas began with the "basic problem" of how to restrain the exercise of sovereignty by the nation–states. Two types of "contract" have been used: the one most frequently agreed to by sovereign states is a contract covering a single or limited number of subjects; the second, less used, is a contract covering a potentially unlimited number of subjects. The first is the *treaty* method; the second, the *constitutional.* "Neither has a historic record that commends itself to us as a perfect device," Douglas argued, "but the constitutional method in international affairs as between peoples of varying races, languages, philosophical inheritances, economic interests, creeds and colors has been less effective than the first." The only example of the constitutional method in the international field that he could think of was the British Commonwealth and Empire. The example of the United States, he thought, could not be stretched to cover the world.

Douglas went on to ask the most difficult questions that could be posed to advocates of world government in 1944. Would the world government have power to use force even against the United States, if, in the opinion of the world body, the U.S. was exercising its power in too unrestrained a fashion? If so, from whence is it going to derive its power? Will the people become citizens of the world state as, after the Constitution of 1787, the people of the states became citizens of the United States? Will the world government have powers to tax and otherwise to coerce individuals? Will it not, to be respected in any era of nation–states, have to abolish the military establishments of the nations and set up both world police and world military forces? Douglas was not sure, but he thought the treaty method might have to serve somewhat longer, "embellishing

---

[28] Grew to Clark, 7 August 1944; Hornbeck to Clark, 14 August 1944; Dewey to Clark, 22 August 1944; George Rublee to Clark, 8 September 1944; Eduard C. Lindeman to Ethan Alyea, 14 August 1944, Clark Papers, 21.9. Clark later incorporated Rublee's suggestions in his revised U.N. Charter, Articles 11, 24, 25, and 42, and the World Equity Tribunal and World Conciliation Board. Lindeman's may be found in revisions to the amendment procedure and to the trusteeship system. See *World Peace through World Law*, passim.

it with councils and parliaments of man and courts of international justice," until decisive common interests developed.[29]

Nevertheless, Clark was convinced that the magnitude of modern war necessitated at least a limited extension of the method of government over the whole world, that is, over the victorious wartime United Nations when the opportunity was at hand. So he pressed on with his high–level intercessions. The right opportunity emerged immediately.

Dumbarton Oaks

The Dumbarton Oaks conference began, in secret, on 21 August 1944. The introductory addresses of Secretary Hull, leader of the United Kingdom delegation Sir Alexander Cadogan, and Ambassador Andre Gromyko were released to the press the next day, but thereafter the progress of the negotiations could be followed only indirectly through the dispatches of James Reston to the *New York Times*.[30]

Hull based the United States' proposals on the "unity" forged by the "forces of freedom" in the war and on the "common interest" of the nations to maintain the peace. He suggested the creation of the "institutions" that became the Security Council to settle disputes and the Economic and Social Council to guide the development of stable material and social conditions (pointedly omitting reference to an all–powerful representative assembly). He repeated the language of the "sovereign equality of all peace–loving states," and he rather inconsistently referred to the whole as a "system of order under law."

Gromyko, more conscious of Russian sacrifices in the war, repeatedly referred to the common struggle against "Hitlerite Germany." Also using the language of the "sovereign equality of all freedom–loving countries," he emphasized the responsibilities of the nations to prevent repetition of another general war.[31]

Clark immediately saw that what was being proposed was a revival of the League of Nations. He wrote to Stettinius the very day the opening speeches were published in the papers:[32]

> Whatever is done at Dumbarton Oaks, I hope the error will not be made of assuming that the principle of the "sovereign equality of all peace–loving states, irrespective of size and strength" (Mr. Hull's phrase) requires or implies equality of *voting power* in a representative international Assembly or Congress.

[29] Douglas to Clark, 10 August 1944, Clark Papers, 21.9.

[30] James B. Reston, "Plans Are Outlined for World Security by Three Great Powers," *New York Times,* 22 August 1944; Reston, "World Body Asked to Maintain Peace by Its Joint Force," *New York Times,* 10 October 1944.

[31] "International Organization for the Maintenance of Peace and Security," Remarks ... at the Opening of the Informal Conversations on the General Nature of an International Organization for the Maintenance of Peace and Security, Washington, DC, 21 August 1944, U.S. Congress, Senate, Presentation by Senator Connally, 78th Cong., 2nd sess., 23 August 1944, Doc. No. 231.

[32] Clark to Stettinius, 22 August 1944, Clark Papers, 21.9. No reply.

Still thinking that an effective assembly would be included in the future organization, Clark argued that voting power must be proportional to population and other factors, as in the U.S. Congress, while a great power veto, protecting their absolute sovereignty, would reduce the whole system to impotency.

The next day a Reston dispatch revealed that in two executive sessions the "American plan" of three plans submitted was chosen as a basis for discussion. Stettinius was selected as permanent chairman of the meetings. The American plan provided for only an advisory assembly "to assist the executive council," which had the real power. The assembly was to represent nations (on the principle of one nation, one vote), not peoples (on the principle of voting proportional to population and other factors). The executive council, far from being the branch of government to enforce the laws enacted by the legislature, was to be an organ of the four (later five) great powers, who, as permanent members, had to be unanimous (on the principle of their sovereign equality) to take action for the enforcement of the peace. The implied veto vitiated the whole system.[33]

At this point Clark wrote boldly to the executive director of Americans United for World Organization and urged him to fight the American plan. This began his long association with popular movements outside the government working for a strong international organization. He analyzed the lack of legitimacy in the proposed assembly, the unreliability of a council whose significant members had to be unanimous to take action, the lack of judicial bodies with powers beyond those of the World Court to settle all disputes without artificial distinctions of "legal" or "justiciable" jurisdiction. Clark wrote:[34]

> Feeling strongly as I do that the Dumbarton Oaks conference is on the wrong track and is likely to bring out a plan that is weak, ineffective and hardly worth while, I urge that "Americans United" ought not to wait until an ineffective plan is produced and then begin to oppose or try to improve it. It might then be too late. I think that *now* is the time to tackle the problem.

But Americans United still supported an international *organization*. Clark was chagrined. Said he later: "I got into the wrong pew."

Clark next, continuing to develop his threefold analysis of the weakness of the assembly, the paralysis by veto of the council, and the virtual elimination of a judicial branch, made many efforts to find a leader to "bring the great issue before the people." He wrote to Dewey, then entering the final stretch of the presidential race of 1944, and suggested that his advocacy of a "constructive" alternative plan would increase his chances of election.[35] He answered John Foster Dulles, who had written that new plans might be regarded as "obstruction in the

[33] Reston, "Plans Are Outlined for World Security by 3 Great Powers," *New York Times*, 23 August 1944. Reston later wrote Clark to the effect that the Russian position on the veto was even more favorable to a sovereign power than the American. Reston to Clark, 13 November 1944, Clark Papers, 21.9.

[34] Clark to Ulric Bell, 24 August 1944, ibid..

[35] Clark to Dewey, 4 September 1944, Clark Papers, 21.9.

guise of perfectionism": "Surely it is not obstruction to ask reconsideration of a plan that is demonstrably inadequate to the purpose. It is good sense and a service to the world."[36] Clark wrote to Cordell Hull, reminded him of his statements at the time of the Moscow declaration—that "there will no longer be need for spheres of influence, for alliances, for balance of power"—and asked him if the proposed organization was not so "defective" that nations will be forced to return to power politics. He plainly referred to the expected Senate opposition that some of the secretary's advisors may have "feared" but that could be overcome by a direct appeal to the people, as in his Plattsburgh and Selective Service Act successes. "[The people] have, I believe, the intelligence to know that something stronger is needed and will support those who advocate really effective plans," he argued. Clark went so far as to suggest that Hull support a call for a "Constitutional Convention of the United Nations" to draft a stronger charter.[37]

Clark's Proposed World Constitutional Convention
Soon after the close of the Dumbarton Oaks talks on 9 October 1944, Clark published a full–page letter to the editor of the *New York Times* in which he presented his more fully considered threefold criticism of the proposed charter. He outlined, in the familiar language of government, his alternative plan. Then he proposed the calling of a "World Constitutional Convention," which would draft a constitution to replace the admittedly "exploratory" and "preliminary" Dumbarton Oaks charter. He even named illustrative Americans, the likes of Washington, Hamilton, Madison, and James Wilson, to be delegates to such a constitutional convention. Clark's list included Hull, Chief Justice Harlan Fisk Stone, Harvard president James B. Conant, and columnist Anne O'Hare McCormick. He concluded: "Let us all hope and pray that, as our people have in other crises summoned their intelligence and resolution, they may do so again and rise to the height of this supreme occasion."[38]

But no public leader of stature responded. Roosevelt endorsed the Dumbarton Oaks plan, calling on the nations "to complete the structure in a spirit of constructive purpose and mutual confidence." Hull and Stettinius "commended" their own work. Dewey led no opposition and called the plan a "fine beginning." Senator Connally of the powerful Foreign Relations Committee said the plan deserved the "support of the American people, irrespective of party affiliations." Sumner Welles called it "wise." The editor of the *Times* recognized it as a "beginning" of a "new union capable of enforcing law and order in a world which had paid the terrible price of two great wars for its failure to organize

---

[36] Clark to Dulles, 21 September 1944, ibid.

[37] Clark to Hull, 16 September 1944, ibid.

[38] Grenville Clark, "Dumbarton Oaks Plans Held in Need of Modification," *New York Times*, 15 October 1944.

peace."[39]

Besides the president, his opponent, the major party leaders, and most congressional candidates, there was representative public support from 12 internationalist organizations, including Americans United for World Organization, the Commission to Study the Organization of Peace, the Council for Democracy, and the Christian Conference on War and Peace. The National Peace Conference, the Carnegie Endowment for International Peace, and even Federal Union also gave at least qualified support.[40]

Other Critical Opinion

Workers in the small movement for world government saw much the same defects in the Dumbarton Oaks plan as did Clark. Tom Griessemer saw no beginning toward world federation, since the assembly had no power to make binding laws, the council no authority to act independently and outside of the national governments composing it, and the court no jurisdiction like that of ordinary courts. To take the first step to an effective organization, there would have to be changes in the "fundamental structure" of the plan. He doubted that the movement could effect such changes but asked for readers' views so that a protest at least could be made.[41]

Similar opposition was voiced in the liberal press. The *Nation* commented editorially (2 September 1944), "No mechanism has even been proposed for curbing aggression on the part of Britain, Russia, China, or the United States." The *New Republic* warned (4 September) that "the peoples of the world would deceive themselves if they took an arrangement of this kind to represent the real hope of future peace." Dorothy Thompson in her syndicated column (15 September) explained, "In the absence of law, binding on all, there will therefore be the maintenance of peace by force and diplomacy dividing the world into spheres [of influence]."[42]

E. B. White of the *New Yorker*, who was for a time the most droll and brilliant of journalists in favor of world government, had this comment:[43]

---

[39] Franklin D. Roosevelt, Endorsement, in Robert E. Summers, comp., *Dumbarton Oaks,* The Reference Shelf, vol. 18, no. 1 (New York: H. W. Wilson, 1945), 116; Reston, "United Nations, as New League, Chartered at Washington with Power to Avert War," *New York Times,* 10 October 1944.

[40] "Dewey Lauds Dumbarton Plan ," *New York Times,* 10 October 1944; "Connally Urges Peace Plan Unity," *New York Times,* 10 October 1944; "Oaks Plan Called 'Wise' by Welles," *New York Times,* 12 October 1944; "The United Nations," *New York Times,* 10 October 1944; "Pros and Cons on D.O.," *World Government News,* November 1944.

[41] "The United Nations," *World Government News,* October 1944, pp. 1–3.

[42] "Dumbarton Oaks," *World Government News,* September 1944, pp. 2–3.

[43] "The Talk of the Town," *The New Yorker,* 21 October 1944. White's editorials on world government from 1943 to 1946 were later collected into *The Wild Flag* (Boston: Houghton Mifflin, 1946), a little gem of a book.

The name of the new peace organization is to be the United Nations. It is a misnomer and will mislead the people. The name of the organization should be the League of Free and Independent Nations Pledged to Enforce Peace, or the Fifty Sovereign Nations of the World Solemnly Sworn to Prevent Each Other from Committing Aggression. These titles are clumsy, candid, and damning. They are exact, however. The phrase "United Nations" is inexact, because it implies union, and there is no union suggested or contemplated in the work of Dumbarton Oaks.

Referring to Wendell Willkie's ideal of "One World," White urged federalists to unite into an effective political movement: "Therefore we say, Federalists of the world, unite!"

San Francisco

The San Francisco conference on international organization opened on 25 April 1945 and continued to 26 June. The United Nations Charter was then signed, pending later ratification. Hardly a fundamental change had been allowed in the Dumbarton Oaks agreements, due to the national delegations' shrewd management of popular enthusiasm at San Francisco. Federalists, it must be admitted, made a rather weak showing. The State Department did not invite any of them to join some 42 private consultants accompanying the official delegation, such as James Shotwell, Clark Eichelberger, and Barnard College Dean Virginia Gildersleeve.[44] A start had been made toward democracy in the U.N., but not to the point of including world federalists. One potential exception was marine first lieutenant Cord Meyer Jr., who went as an assistant to delegate Harold Stassen.

Thomas H. Mahony's Massachusetts Committee for World Federation published a half–page ad in the *Boston Globe, Christian Science Monitor,* and *San Francisco Chronicle,* urging the gathering diplomats to "discard the false doctrine that exalts the Sovereignty of the State." New York's World Federalists sent resolutions to the delegates, urging them to introduce "federal principles" into the charter. Federal Union, Ltd., of England sent a memo to the British delegation in favor of European federation. William Bross Lloyd, then in a conscientious objector camp in Belden, California, sent an illustrative world constitution to American delegates. Georgia Lloyd attended, and she presented petitions in favor of an elected world legislature. Robert Lee Humber attended. Ely Culbertson came and soon left in disgust, saying that the conference was nothing but an assembly of "mice presided over by a few cats."

Harris Wofford got a furlough and, thanks to Clarence Streit and the publisher of the *Los Angeles Daily News,* received a press pass. At the end of the conference, when Senator Connally declared to the press, "We aren't going to lose

---

[44] Dorothy Robins Mowry, *Experiment in Democracy: The Story of U.S. Citizen Organizations in Forging the Charter of the United nations* (New York: Parkside Press, 1971). I am indebted to retired foreign service officer T. Patrick Killough in 1991 for this source.

any of our sovereignty. As a matter of fact America is coming out of this conference stronger than ever, with more bases, with a veto over everything," a soldier who had lost a leg turned to Wofford and said, "We can lose our legs, but the
diplomats can't lose any of their sovereignty."[45]

Signs of Willingness to Limit Sovereignty

From a world government perspective, there were a few significant developments at San Francisco. In response to a letter from Grenville Clark enclosing
his "Memorandum as to Weighted Representation," the Chinese, one of the Big
Four, of course, and representing the most populous country in the world, were
"very favorably inclined." On 26 April 1945, Dr. T. V. Soong, China's foreign
minister, declared before the first plenary session of the conference that "we must
not hesitate to delegate a part of our sovereignty to the new International Organization in the interests of collective security." He followed this on 1 May with a
statement to the press that China would be willing to give up the right of "unilateral veto" in the Security Council, provided the other sponsoring powers
would do the same.[46] The other powers were not willing, so nothing came of
this initiative, but it remains significant as the highest level declaration of a willingness to create a truly effective United Nations.

The reason that the veto power was introduced was not just because the Russians demanded it but because *all* the great powers did, as was plainly said during
the crisis over the voting rule:[47]

> It should be stressed that during the debate the representatives of the spon-
> soring powers made it clear that they were neither prepared to accept any
> modification to the Yalta formula nor to agree to a more liberal interpreta-
> tion thereof than that contained in their joint declaration of June 7, 1945,
> and that any unfavorable action of the Committee on the voting formula
> would imperil the whole work of the Conference. It was on this understand-
> ing that many delegations voted for or abstained from voting against the
> Yalta formula.

It is worth noting that, except for the Big Five (Article 27), all the other nations at San Francisco accepted a limitation on *their* sovereignties, since they accepted two–thirds majority rule (modified by big power veto) in the Security
Council. And *all* nations, including the United States and the Soviet Union, accepted majority rule in the subordinate General Assembly, Economic and Social
Council, and Trusteeship Council.[48]

Nevertheless, France approved the Dumbarton Oaks plan in February as only

---

[45] "World Federalists at San Francisco," *World Government News,* June 1945, p. 1;
Georgia Lloyd, Interview, 30 May 1981; Wofford, *It's Up To Us,* 88, 97.

[46] Victor Chi–tsai Hoo to Clark, 21 May 1945, Clark Papers, 21.10; "Quotes,"
World Government News, May 1945, p. 5.

[47] Verbatim Minutes of the Fifth Meeting of Committee III, UNCIO, 20 June 1945.
UNCIO Documents, 1150, 22 June 1945.

[48] Charter of the United Nations, Articles 18(2), 27(2), 67(2), 89(2).

an "imperfect" step toward security, expressing in proposed amendments that there be further limitations of sovereignty. One amendment specified a modified veto (two–thirds majority rule when the council makes recommendations, as opposed to decisions). The Dutch at the Yalta conference warned that to give the great powers a veto in the council would render the whole organization useless in disputes between great powers or between a great power and a small one. The Polish exile government in London about the same time objected to the proposed veto power of nations that were themselves parties to a dispute. Mexico and eight other Latin American countries at the Inter–American Conference objected to the Big Four veto power. At San Francisco, Colombia joined China in expressions of willingness to delegate some external sovereignty to the international organization. Australia's Justice Herbert V. Evatt (later president of the General Assembly in the crucial year of 1948) and New Zealand's Peter Fraser led an opposition of 17 small nations to the veto. But in the final vote, once the United States and the Soviet Union led the (now) Big Five in conveying the attitude that without their veto there would be no charter, 15 abstained and only 2—Colombia and Cuba—voted against.[49]

There was also a move to strengthen the assembly. Venezuela, Ecuador, and the Philippines proposed to make it a legislative chamber. France and 13 other nations sought amendments to give it more power. Other nations sought compulsory jurisdiction for the World Court.[50]

The "federalist" delegate Harold Stassen, supported by seven nations including Australia, did what he could against predominant nationalist attitudes to introduce an automatic 10–year amendment convention provision, but this was watered down so that it would apply only to the *first* 10–year period ending in 1955 (Article 109, Paragraph 3). Stassen was forthright on the necessity to "delegate a limited portion of our sovereignty" to the United Nations to make it effective, but to no avail.[51] (The review conference in 1955 was never held, as the times were "not appropriate.")

John F. Kennedy at San Francisco

Young John F. Kennedy, newly discharged from the Navy after his heroic service on PT–109, attended the San Francisco conference and encountered various world federalists. His comments are essentially ours in this history: "Admittedly world organization with common obedience to law would be the solution," he noted. "Not that easy. If there is not the feeling that war is the ultimate evil, a feeling strong enough to drive them together, then you can't work out this internationalist plan." To a fellow veteran he said, "Things cannot be forced from

---

[49] *The United Nations Conference on International Organization, San Francisco, California, April 25 – June 26, 1945, Selected Documents* (Washington, DC: Department of State, Pub. No. 2490, 1946), 147–51, 257, 740–42; Carlos P. Romulo, *Romulo: A Third World Soldier at the U.N.* (Westport, CT: Praeger, 1986), 13–17.

[50] "Small Nations on Dumbarton Oaks," *World Government News,* February 1945, pp. 5–6; "The United Nations Conference," *World Federation—Now,* July 1945.

[51] "Door Ajar," *World Government News,* May 1945, pp. 1–2, 6.

the top."[52]

> The international relinquishing of sovereignty would have to spring from the people—it would have to be so strong that the elected delegates would be turned out of office if they failed to do it.... We must face the truth that the people have not been horrified by war to a sufficient extent to force them to go to any extent rather that have another war.... War will exist until that distant day when the conscientious objector enjoys the same reputation and prestige that the warrior does today.

Cord Meyer Jr.

One of Stassen's two veteran assistants was a U.S. Marine first lieutenant who had lost an eye while leading his machine gun platoon in the assault on Guam. He was Cord Meyer Jr., an able young man who would later become the first president of United World Federalists. After the quick Senate concurrence on the Charter on 28 July 1945 (by a vote of 89 to 2), Meyer looked back on the San Francisco conference in an *Atlantic* article, "A Servicemen Looks at the Peace." It was one of the most powerful tracts looking toward world government ever written. Meyer began with the experience of the fighting men in the war, "who know what it is and who have no illusions about it, the members of the assault battalions, the front line fighters." Tautly, coolly, he described their common experience of coming upon a slain enemy soldier and discovering on the body letters and pictures of loved ones much like their own and of seeing the best and bravest of their friends destroyed by chance shell bursts or well aimed fire:

> When one's first battle is done, when the inexhaustibly patient wounded have been cared for and those past caring have been buried, one feels no exaltation in the victory. Rather, there is no one who does not ask himself what beneath the sun could possibly be worth it.

So Meyer asked what had the fighting men achieved in the opportunity presented to the statesmen at San Francisco? To him, only one purpose could have justified all the sacrifices of the war—"the opportunity to construct by intelligent and radical reform a more equitable society and a peaceful world." By this standard the San Francisco conference was found wanting. Meyer searched (in an argument apparently not influenced by federalist critiques) for the reasons:

> The death of more than sixty million men and women in two wars within a single generation is the concrete result of basic conditions in international society that must be changed if we are not to see the experience repeated on a larger scale.

The basic condition, he saw, was international anarchy. The cycle of increas-

---

[52] Arthur M. Schlesinger Jr., *A Thousand Days: John F. Kennedy in the White House* (Boston: Houghton Mifflin, 1965), 88–89.

ingly destructive wars was "the direct and inevitable result of the attempt to prolong the political system of absolute national independence" in a world of such
increasing interdependence that the scientific weapons being given to national
authorities make war a threat to all civilization. But the system of absolute national independence had been prolonged:

> The limits of what was accomplished at San Francisco are evident in the veto
> power. The Security Council, which has the power and authority to keep the
> peace, can take no enforcement action without the concurring votes of the
> five permanent members. If a major nation is not a party to a dispute, it can
> prevent even the investigation of the case by the Security Council. Any
> amendment to the Charter requires ratification by the five major powers be-
> fore it can take effect, with the result that one of the Big Five can forever
> prevent any change.

This view led then to an incisive analysis of the remainder of the Charter, all
of whose provisions, especially those establishing the so–called "world police
force," which consisted simply of national military contingents made available
to the Security Council, emphasized the unworkability of the voting rule in the
Security Council. Meyer recalled a question of a friend of his just back from the
Pacific theater, who asked what could the organization do in case of a civil war
in China with Russia favoring one side and the United States the other. "Obviously," he answered, "the product of San Francisco is totally unable to deal with
such a situation." Meyer's judgment of the statesmen who produced the Charter
was balanced, but his indignation was unmistakable. He acknowledged that the
U.S. delegation expected the Senate to reject any charter that conceded even a
portion of American sovereign independence. His account of the Senate hearings
both explained why there was no opposition and reflected again on the weakness
of the final Charter:

> The record of the hearings in the Senate Foreign Relations Committee is a
> tragicomic commentary on what was achieved at San Francisco. To allay the
> fears of even the most unregenerate isolationist, every impotent inadequacy
> of the Charter was stressed as a positive assurance that in ratifying it we were
> committing ourselves to nothing.

Meyer concluded that the goal had to be "government on a world level," but,
since there was not yet wide agreement on the "principles and values" of world
government, for some time hence all that could be achieved was recognition that
"the continuation of national egotisms is at the root of our misfortunes." The
Charter had to be supported as "all we have won from the war."[53]

The last word on the Charter from elements of the still diffuse world government movement may have come from Morgan Harris in the Methodist student

---

[53] Cord Meyer Jr., "A Serviceman Looks at the Peace," *Atlantic Monthly*, September 1945, pp. 43–48.

magazine *Motive,* in which he took a broad historical view:[54]

> Perhaps the greatest tragedy of this century stems from the refusal of the United States to join the League of Nations. If we had joined, it would not have prevented World War II, but it would have prevented people from believing that the League of Nations failed because we were not a member. Then World War II would have had a good chance of driving us to see that the League failed because it was a league—i.e., an organization lacking power and authority to administer justice. Thus we would not today be trying to get the United States to join another league of nations ... but instead would likely be setting up a world federal government.

Robert A. Divine, in his history of the founding of the United Nations, closes his book with a quotation from E. B. White's *Wild Flag:* "The preparations made at San Francisco for a security league of sovereign nations to prevent aggression now seem like the preparations some little girls might make for a lawn party as a thunderhead gathers beyond the garden gate."[55]

---

[54] Morgan Harris, *Motive,* May 1945, quoted in "Books and Publications," *World Government News,* June 1945.

[55] *Second Chance: The Triumph of Internationalism in America during World War II* (New York: Atheneum, 1967), 315.

6

A New Age: Hiroshima and Nagasaki

We must never relax our efforts to arouse in the people of the world, and especially in their governments, an awareness of the unprecedented disaster which they are absolutely certain to bring on themselves unless there is a fundamental change in their attitudes toward one another as well as in their concept of the future. The unleashed power of the atom has changed everything save our modes of thinking, and thus we drift toward unparalleled catastrophe.

—Albert Einstein, first appeal of the Emergency
Committee of the Atomic Scientists, 24 May 1946

A Theological Problem

Then there occurred an event that was to have the greatest influence on the movement for world federal government and on the history of the victorious United Nations for the next several years. On Monday, 6 August 1945, President Truman called the press to the White House, and at 10:45 A.M. he announced that 16 hours earlier an American airplane had dropped a new type of bomb—"harnessing the basic power of the universe"—on the Japanese city of Hiroshima.

Three days later, a second atomic bomb was dropped on Nagasaki. Humanity entered the atomic age. Total immediate deaths are estimated at 130,000; lingering deaths due to injury, burns, and radiation at twice that number. The Russians entered the war in the East on 8 August, and within a month Japan surrendered. World War II ended.

As he received the Japanese surrender on the deck of the U.S.S. *Missouri* in Tokyo Bay on 2 September 1945, General Douglas MacArthur made a historic address about the ending of the war:[1]

Men since the beginning of time have sought peace. Various methods through the ages have been attempted to devise an international process to prevent or settle disputes between nations. From the very start workable methods were found insofar as individual citizens were concerned, but the mechanics of an instrumentality of larger international scope have never been successful. Military alliances, balances of power, Leagues of Nations all in

---

[1] Inscribed on the walls of MacArthur Hall, the Pentagon, Washington, DC.

turn failed, leaving the only path to be by way of the crucible of war. The utter destructiveness of war now blots out this alternative. We have had our last chance. If we do not devise some greater and more equitable system, Armageddon will be at our door. The problem basically is theological and involves a spiritual recrudescence and improvement of human character that will synchronize with our almost matchless advance in science, art, literature, and all material and cultural developments of the past 2,000 years. It must be of the spirit if we are to save the flesh.

The use of atomic bombs in war mobilized the atomic scientists behind the international control of atomic energy. It led to an unprecedented initiative by the United States to place its ultimate weapon under the control of an international authority that necessarily would have had many of the attributes of a world government. It set leading scholars at the University of Chicago, where the first sustained nuclear reaction was achieved, to thinking about a constitution for the world aiming at both peace and justice. It changed the course of Grenville Clark and his many friends toward United Nations reform. It provoked Henry Usborne, radical students and veterans, and many people abroad to attempt to convene a "peoples' convention" to exercise the sovereignty of the people and demonstrate their will and readiness to support a participatory world federal government. It united the World Federalists, as they urged the nations to do, and, under American inspiration, it brought about the founding of the World Movement for World Federal Government, in cooperation and then in rivalry with the European federalists. It led to Henry Wallace's challenge to Truman in the presidential election of 1948 on the issue of getting tough with the Russians. It was the first step in the nuclear arms race. It inaugurated the Cold War.

TWENTY CENTS   MARCH 27, 1950

TIME

THE WEEKLY NEWSMAGAZINE

ATLANTIC UNION'S STREIT
Nationalism is the poison.

Clarence K. Streit, Federal Union (1939), Atlantic Union Committee
(1949). *Time Magazine*, Copyright © Time Inc./Timepix.

Emery Reves, *The Anatomy of Peace* (1945). "The purpose of a world-wide legal order is to avoid a third world war, and make it possible to solve the endless conflicts between nations, races, and classes by legal methods."

San Francisco Conference for the Founding of the United Nations Organization (26 April 1945). At center: Cmdr. Harold Stassen, U.S. Delegate; at left: Lt. Cord Meyer, Jr., aide.

Morikatsu Inagaki at ground zero of atomic bomb explosion at Hiroshima (1945; photo taken in 1952).

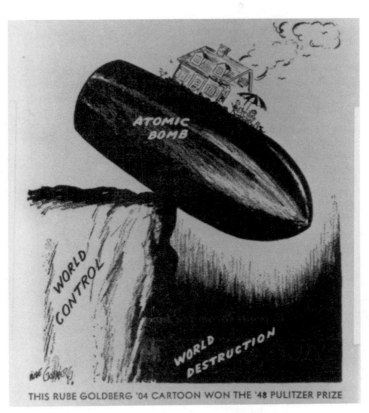

THIS RUBE GOLDBERG '04 CARTOON WON THE '48 PULITZER PRIZE

Rube Goldberg, "Atomic Bomb," *California Monthly* (June 1948). On failure of Baruch plan for the international control of atomic energy. Rube Goldberg is the ® and © of Rube Goldberg Inc. Used by permission.

Emergency Committee of the Atomic Scientists (1946). Seated left to right: Harold C. Urey, Albert Einstein, Selig Hecht; Standing: Victor Weisskopf, Leo Szilard, Hans Bethe, Thorfin Hogness, Philip Morse.

Dublin Conference (October 1945). Grenville Clark, U.S. Supreme Court Justice Owen J. Roberts, former New Hampshire Governor Robert P. Bass, Robert H. Mahony.

"Dublin Group Discusses Peace Plans," Christian Science Monitor (17 October 1945).

Harris Wofford, founder of Student Federalists (1943).

Professor G.A. Borgese, University of Chicago.

Trygve Lie, first U.N. Secretary-General, and Carlos P. Romulo, President, Fourth U.N. General Assembly, Lake Success (2 November 1949).

Jack Whitehouse, founder of Students for Federal World Government (1946) and World Republic (1947).

World Republic headquarters, Evanston Illinois (1947).

Founding of United World Federalists (UWF), Asheville, North Carolina (21-23 February 1947).
From 11 o'clock: Thomas H. Mahony, Mrs. J.T. Pitnam, Colgate Prentice, T.K. Finletter,
George Holt, Mildred Blake.

World Government House, 31 East 74th Street,
New York (1948).

World Government House.

7

The Atomic Scientists' Movement

Oh, weh! *[Alas!]*

—Einstein's first worlds on hearing of
the atomic bomb attack on Hiroshima,
6 August 1945

Origins of the Atomic Scientists Movement

After Hiroshima, the atomic scientists were the new group on the political scene to speak with authority and *in time* to have an influence on national policy on the atomic bomb. Many of the top leaders called their objective world government, but the majority of the atomic scientists aimed at what they called the international control of atomic energy, which amounted to almost the same thing. The scientists formed spontaneously, despite wartime rules of secrecy and compartmentalization, at the dozen or so sites of the code–named Manhattan District. By October 1945, they were issuing public statements on national policy, especially for use by the hastily organized Federation of Atomic Scientists (FAtS) in Washington. Their earliest public statement read:[1]

Representatives of the Associations of Scientists on the three major branches of the atomic bomb project at Los Alamos, Chicago, and Oak Ridge, have met at Chicago on October 24 [1945]. They have agreed that a joint statement of the fundamental views of their groups is appropriate....

We want to lend our collective support to the statements made earlier by separate groups and informed individuals, that no measures of secrecy can guarantee our exclusive possession of atomic bombs for more than a few years, and that there can be no defense which would effectively protect our cities against an attack by atomic bombs. Even leadership in an atomic armament race will in no way assure our safety against sudden attack by an aggressor, who might easily have enough bombs to destroy every one of our major cities in a single day. Therefore, we are convinced that the achievement of international controls over the military aspects of atomic power

[1] Simpson et al. to Higinbotham, telegram, 25 October 1945, Regenstein Library, ALAS Papers, 2.9, punctuation added.

must remain the paramount objective of our national policy.... There is no time to lose.

—J. A. Simpson, Chairman, Executive Committee, ASC
[Atomic Scientists of Chicago]
—W. A. Higinbotham, Chairman, Executive Committee, ALAS
[Association of Los Alamos Scientists]
—Paul Henshaw, Chairman, Executive Committee, AORSCL
[Association of Oak Ridge Scientists at Clinton Labs]

The atomic scientists were united on the three stands that there was no secret, that no defense could be complete, and, therefore, that international control was necessary. Their organizations never went so far as to advocate world government. That was implied, however, in international control, and it was often expressed in position papers at the start and throughout to the end of their movement. Certain of their most prominent leaders did openly advocate world government: Leo Szilard,[2] Harold Urey,[3] Harrison Brown,[4] Edward Teller,[5] Eugene Rabinowitch,[6] and Albert Einstein.[7]

Einstein had not worked officially on the bomb, but he had, with Szilard, sent the letter to President Roosevelt in August 1939 that started the project, and he had in 1905 discovered the fundamental equation for the equivalence of mass and energy that was, of course, the theoretical basis of all projects to release atomic energy. He was such a clear and influential advocate of world government —the only one ever to elicit a considered response from Russia—that he will have a chapter in this history of world federal government. But first there remain

---

[2] Szilard proposed a "25–year plan," providing for a "durable peace, implemented by a definite schedule for international developments to lead to a stable world government over a period of 25 years," during his early FAtS lobbying activity. He presented the plan at a dinner for friends in Congress, including Senator Brien McMahon (D., CT), director of science service Watson Davis, Senator Kilgore's aide Herbert Schimmel, and Representative Helen Gahagan Douglas (D., CA), on 31 October 1945. Joe Keller, Report of Meetings in Washington, October 31 to November 1, 1945, ALAS Papers, 2.9. See also Leo Szilard, "Calling for a Crusade," *Bulletin of the Atomic Scientists,* April–May 1947, pp. 102–5.

[3] Harold C. Urey, "Atomic Energy and World Peace," *Bulletin of the Atomic Scientists,* 1 November 1946, pp. 2–4.

[4] Harrison Brown, *Must Destruction Be Our Destiny? A Scientist Speaks as a Citizen* (New York: Simon & Schuster, 1946), 83ff; Harrison Brown, "The Dilemma of the Scientists," n.d., post June 1947, ECAS Papers, 1.16.

[5] Edward Teller, "Comments on the 'Draft of a World Constitution,'" *Bulletin of the Atomic Scientists,* July 1948, p. 204.

[6] Eugene Rabinowitch, "International Aspects," 27 October 1945, ASC Papers, 4.16.

[7] Albert Einstein, as told to Raymond Swing, "Atomic War or Peace," *Atlantic Monthly,* November 1945, pp. 43–45.

to be said a few words about the Promethean atomic scientists' movement.[8]

Motivation of the Atomic Scientists

Well before the first test of the atomic bomb, when it was apparent that the bomb would work and would revolutionize warfare, the scientists creating it became aware of their awesome responsibility. Discussions consistent with military security were under way by early 1945. Topics included the probable destructive effects on cities, the "political effects" to be expected if the United States were to use the bomb first against Germany or Japan, the possibility of an atomic armaments race leading to a general cataclysm, the need for international controls, and the alternative applications in peacetime of a force analogous to fire.

In March 1945, well before the Hiroshima attack, Leo Szilard of the University of Chicago's Metallurgical Laboratory (Met Lab) prepared a memorandum for Roosevelt about the danger to the U.S. of using the bomb against Japan and then beginning an atomic armament race with Russia. Keeping ahead in the quantity and quality of bombs, he wrote, would not guarantee U.S. security. In a war, enough bombs were certain to be emplaced by sabotage or to get through by rockets to destroy all cities of over 250,000 population. Szilard urged that the United States, "immediately after we [have] demonstrated the potency of atomic bombs," approach the Soviet Union with a proposal for the establishment of a "control system" much stronger than that of the Inter–Allied Commission supervising Germany after World War I. Szilard's memo, however, never reached the president, who died on April 12. It was given by Szilard to secretary of state designate James F. Byrnes in May, where it languished.[9]

In June 1945, still before Hiroshima, James Franck, also of the Met Lab, prepared a similar report for the secretary of war, Henry Stimson. Franck was more explicit than Szilard about the motivation of the atomic scientists:

> Scientists have often before been accused of providing new weapons for the mutual destruction of nations, instead of improving their well–being.... We feel compelled to take a more active stand now because the success we have achieved in the development of nuclear power is fraught with infinitely greater dangers than were all the inventions of the past.

Like Szilard, Franck foresaw no military defense against "a Pearl Harbor repeated in thousand–fold magnification in every one of our major cities." There was no physical secret that Russian scientists did not know from the scientific literature to 1940. He estimated (correctly, as it turned out) that Russia could

---

[8] The history of the atomic scientists is told with great care for the inchoateness of the movement by Alice Kimball Smith, *A Peril and a Hope: The Scientists' Movement in America, 1945–47* (Chicago: University of Chicago Press, 1965).

[9] Leo Szilard, Excerpts, "Atomic Bombs and the Postwar Position of the United States in the World—1945," *Bulletin of the Atomic Scientists,* December 1947, pp. 351–53; John A. Simpson, "The Scientists as Public Educators: A Two Year Summary," *Bulletin of the Atomic Scientists,* September 1947, p. 243.

acquire an atomic capability in "three or four years." The only military defense that might make sense would be forced dispersal of American industry and population, entailing a "radical change in the social and economic structure of our nation." But Franck could see a political solution—what he called the "political organization of the world"—in which, threatened by mutual destruction, the United States, Western Europe, and Russia could come to an "efficient agreement for the prevention of nuclear warfare." He even added that such an agreement would depend on the "readiness to sacrifice the necessary fraction of one's own sovereignty" in order to live in "one world." Hence, Franck urged a demonstration of the new atomic bomb on the desert or a barren island before its use against a Japanese city in order to prove to the world the United States' willingness to renounce a weapon that would soon threaten all civilization. [10]

After the bomb was used against Japanese cities, however, the scientists could no longer confine themselves to official channels. John A. Simpson of the Met Lab called the movement "revolutionary," which, if the scientists had been able to sustain the movement to attain their primary goal of the international control of atomic energy, might have been the historically accurate description. But as it happened, the movement showed only the *way* to the truly revolutionary innovation. The scientists remained politicized for at most two years, while national leaders determined events. [11]

ORES World Government Committee

Groups of scientists and engineers formed independently at all the sites of the Manhattan project except Hanford—notably at Chicago, Oak Ridge, and Los Alamos. They all struggled over the political implications of the atomic bomb but generally could agree only on some form of international control, as by the new United Nations. But one group in Tennessee looked toward a more radical solution—the Oak Ridge Engineers and Scientists (ORES). In January 1946, Edith Wynner spoke to them. Mortimer Adler's "Definition and Principles of World Federal Government" and Thomas K. Finletter's "Timetable for World Government" also came to their attention. In March 1946, William R. Kittredge and others formed the World Government Committee. It had a life of about 14 months and was especially active in the latter half of 1946, when the Baruch plan negotiations for the international control of atomic energy began to fail. Jack Balderston, second chairman, claimed the World Government Committee

---

[10] [James Franck,] "A Report to the Secretary of War, June 1945," *Bulletin of the Atomic Scientists,* 1 May 1946; Simpson, "Scientists as Educators," p. 243. There was also a poll taken at the Met Lab in July 1945, in which 46 percent of the scientists favored a demonstration in *Japan;* another 26 per cent favored a demonstration in the U.S. with Japanese observers present; both to be followed by "opportunity to surrender." Such moves were too weak and too late to influence decisions and were recalled later, when the armament race was on in earnest, to assuage the scientists' guilt. "A Poll of Scientists at Chicago, July 1945," *Bulletin of the Atomic Scientists,* February 1948, pp. 44, 63.

[11] Simpson, "Scientists as Educators," p. 243.

was the "most active and the loudest and [wrote] many more words than any other AORES committee." (AORES, the Association of Oak Ridge Engineers and Scientists, was the eventual umbrella organization of all those who met at the several plants of "Atomic City.")

The World Government Committee conducted surveys and studies, was given the assignment to critically examine the Russian counterproposals to the Baruch plan, prepared reports on world government proposals, participated in the merger movement that brought about United World Federalists, and, as the Cold War was beginning, almost succeeded in placing world government among the policy objectives of the AORES.[12]

Association of Los Alamos Scientists

At the remote atomic bomb lab of Los Alamos, New Mexico, where the first three atomic bombs were assembled, the Association of Los Alamos Scientists (ALAS) began forming three weeks after the third bomb was dropped on Nagasaki. Director J. Robert Oppenheimer gave quiet encouragement within the constraints of his office. Philip Morrison had just returned from a military damage assessment flight over Hiroshima. He galvanized the group with his report on what they had done: "One bomber, and one bomb, had, in the time it takes a rifle bullet to cross the city, turned a city of three hundred thousand into a burning pyre."

At a general meeting of about 500 on 30 August 1945, ALAS was formed. A draft statement on the significance of atomic energy was considered, and on 7 September, under the signature of Victor F. Weisskopf, chairman of the drafting committee, the statement was delivered privately to Oppenheimer, who passed it on to the War Department. The statement elaborated the arguments of no secret and no defense. It surveyed the history of voluntary arms limitations and found no support for the "unrealistic" hope that nations will renounce the use of the atomic bomb if so effective an offensive weapon is available to them. It called for "the control of this weapon by a world authority." The scientists boldly added that such a world authority must be given sole right to produce fissionable materials and also to manufacture atomic weapons. The world authority's atomic weapons should be held in readiness "in a military establishment of its own,

---

[12] Wynner to Balderston, 18 June 1946, AORES Papers, 9.3; Mortimer J. Adler, "Definition and Principles of World Federal Government," Committee to Frame a World Constitution, Doc. 4; Thomas K. Finletter, "Timetable for World Government," *Atlantic Monthly,* March 1946; Norton Gerber to Adler, 15 February 1948; World Government Committee, ORES, First Report, 16 May 1946, AORES Papers, 8.9; Balderston to Tom Rockwell, 17 October 1946; Gerber to E. E. Minett, 8 January 1947; AORES Executive Committee Minutes, 13 February 1947, AORES Papers, 8.8. Wynner spoke to the scientists at Chicago and Los Alamos in January 1946. She seems to have made clear the alternatives of league or federation but not to have moved her hearers toward the step of a peoples' convention. *Bulletin of the Atomic Scientists,* 15 February 1946, p. 12; ALAS Minutes, 1 February 1946, ALAS Papers, 2.16.

responsible to it and not to the individual nations," in order to "enforce international law."

Los Alamos' State Paper

This statement—earliest by a few days of all those by the atomic scientists —became, in the view of ALAS, a "State Paper." Followed by similar statements from other sites, it seems to have had some influence in postwar Washington. On 7 January 1946, the new secretary of state, James F. Byrnes, appointed a committee, chaired by the undersecretary Dean Acheson, to study the international control of atomic energy in terms similar to those of the scientists. Acheson, in turn, appointed a board headed by Tennessee Valley Authority chairman David E. Lilienthal, and the board produced recommendations incorporated by June into the Baruch plan.

Meanwhile, the Los Alamos scientists plunged into novel political activity. Meetings were held sometimes daily, and general meetings weekly. William Higinbotham, a young electronics man without a doctor's degree, became chairman; he soon went to Washington to organize the Federation of Atomic Scientists. Later he led its successor, the more inclusive Federation of American Scientists. On 21 September 1945, while the scientists were still voluntarily refraining from making *public* statements, the army engineer commanding the Manhattan District, Major General Leslie R. Groves, made a speech in New York to the effect that the United States could maintain its monopoly of atomic bombs for many more years than the two to five years estimated by the scientists. Senator Tom Connally, too, about this time made an opposing statement that every offense had generated a defense and that civilization could withstand atomic war as it had other wars and natural catastrophes.[13]

First Public Statements at Los Alamos

These official statements, so contrary to what the atomic scientists knew, provoked them to go public. Waiting only for President Truman's message to Congress on 4 October 1945, in which he made guarded references to "international arrangements" implying "renunciation" of the atomic bomb, the Los Alamos group issued their first press release for 14 October. There was no secret, and bombs "even thousands of times more powerful" than the atomic bomb were likely to be manufactured in a few years (hydrogen bombs). There was no defense, for rockets developed from the German V–2 type would, again within a "few years," be able to deliver atomic explosives "thousands of miles" in a heavy

---

[13] Higinbotham to J. R. Oppenheimer, 27 September 1945, ALAS Papers, 3.2; Minutes, 21 September 1945, ALAS Papers, 2.5; Higinbotham to John Trischka, 11 November 1945, ALAS Papers, 2.17; Minutes of Meetings at George Washington University, 7–8 December 1945, FAS Papers, 1.1; Smith, *A Peril*, 120, 106, 102, 117; "Keep Bomb Secret, Gen. Groves Urges," *New York Times,* 22 September 1945, p. 3; "Atom Bomb Defense Indicated by Navy—House Group Report Envisions Detonation of Missile at Great Distances by Radio," *New York Times,* 12 October 1945, p. 1.

attack "lasting a matter of minutes." An arms race could only lead to war, preventive or accidental.

The scientists explained:[14]

> A world in which nuclear weapons are owned by many nations and their use held back only by fear of retaliation will be a world of fear, suspicion, and inevitable final explosion....
>
> We are convinced that we are left but one course of action. We must cooperate with the rest of the world in the future development of atomic power, and the use of atomic energy as a weapon must be controlled by a world authority.... Such conditions will demand the loss of some degree of national sovereignty. This makes it imperative that we have the good will of all nations, for it must be realized that we are dealing with a deadly challenge to civilization itself.

This was followed on 9 November by a fuller statement on the "world authority." The scientists appreciated the "spirit" of the United Nations but they did "not believe that world control of nuclear energy necessarily must be a United Nations function." A long paragraph on "World Government" gave support to world government organizations, but it cautioned that the next step had to be "international agreements between existing states." Yet what was needed was not some mere convention of international law, like a Geneva convention to "outlaw" the atomic bomb: "Our aim is a material unification of the nations of the world for the purpose of controlling and exploiting the potentialities of nuclear energy."

The scientists announced an educational campaign on the significance of the atomic bomb to counter "national isolation and suspicion." They opposed policies of "unilateral control," explaining, "the problem of nuclear energy is not an American problem; it weighs on the whole world." On interim domestic legislation, they urged that the primary consideration was future international control; hence, the U.S. government, not private business, should develop atomic energy; and civilians, not the military with their "stultifying" secrecy regulations, should head the U.S. control agency.[15]

Other Scientists' Organizations

In addition to the atomic scientist organizations at Chicago, Oak Ridge, and Los Alamos, similar organizations formed at other project sites: the Association of Manhattan Project Scientists, New York Area (Columbia); the Association of Cambridge Scientists (Harvard and Massachusetts Institute of Technology); the Association of Philadelphia Scientists (University of Pennsylvania); the Univer-

---

[14] Statement of ALAS for Release 14 October 1945, ALAS Papers, 3.2; "400 Experts Decry Lone Atom Policy; See 'Unending' War," *New York Times,* 14 October 1945, p. 1.

[15] Statement of ALAS Policy, 9 November 1945, ALAS Papers, 2.16; printed in ALAS "Newsletter" and again in *Bulletin of the Atomic Scientists,* 10 December 1945.

sity of Rochester Rocket Group; the Dayton Association of Scientists (Monsanto Chemical Plant); the Rocket Research Group at the Allegheny Ballistic Lab; and the Washington Association of Scientists. (Their acronyms may be spared the reader.) Oddly, no atomic scientist group formed at the plutonium production plant at Hanford, Washington. Its remoteness combined with the smallness of its scientific staff may have been the reason.

There were also organizations forming of scientists who were not technically qualified as "atomic," notably the American Association of Scientific Workers, the New York Association of Scientists, the Northern California Association of Scientists (Berkeley), and the Association of Pasadena Scientists (California Institute of Technology). Simpson of Chicago estimated that by early 1946 between 1,800 and 2,400 natural scientists had joined these groups. The potential had been some 4,170, judging by a tally at the Washington University conference of November 1945. An estimate, then, of 50 percent would be about right for the proportion of atomic scientists, admixed with natural scientists closely connected, who associated themselves politically after the war to establish the international control of atomic energy.[16]

Organizing in Washington for International Control

The scientists' goal then, minimally, was some form of shared, international control of atomic energy. The "material unification of the nations of the world for the purpose of controlling and exploiting the potentialities of nuclear energy" was articulated, but the majority did not aim so high. After great struggles, they failed at even the minimal goal—international control is unachieved to this day —and when, by 1947, they realized they were failing, Einstein and others took up vigorously the more extreme goal of world federation to control atomic energy, but they were too late. Nevertheless, the scientists did achieve within the United States domestically the *civilian* control of atomic energy, and that story we must tell for its larger relevance.

The May–Johnson Bill

On 4 October 1945, the May–Johnson bill for U.S. domestic control of atomic energy, which threatened to continue wartime military control, was introduced in Congress. The bill provided for a control commission of nine, on which military officers could sit and which was not subject to congressional checks. The bill did not require government ownership of atomic materials and plants, but it gave the commission broad licensing and contractual powers over private enterprise. It provided for broad powers over scientific research into atomic energy, including the strictest secrecy and security regulations yet. It made no reference to the sharing of information with other countries as would be required under an international control system.[17]

---

[16] Description of Papers of AORES and Related Groups, Regenstein Library; Simpson, "Scientists as Educators," p. 245; Report on the Conference of Scientific Associations, 16–17 November 1945, ALAS Papers, 2.9.

[17] Smith, *A Peril,* 128–30.

Federation of Atomic Scientists

The atomic scientists were quick to take alarm at the implications of this bill. Szilard, Urey, and E. U. Condon went to Washington to prolong hearings, which the bill's sponsors, apparently to rush the bill through an unsuspecting Congress, had limited to *one day*. On 25 October 1945, the Federation of Atomic Scientists (FAtS) was formed. The member associations were those of Chicago, Clinton Labs, Los Alamos, and the New York Area Manhattan Project Scientists. FAtS found a little office in the Washington quarters of Harvard astronomer Harlow Shapley's Independent Citizens Committee (ICC) of the Arts, Sciences and Professions at 1018 Vermont Avenue. The various sites began sending representatives there, usually on a one–week rotational basis.

Higinbotham came from Los Alamos and stayed. He wrote on 11 November a hurried note to John Trischka, who had replaced him as chairman of the Los Alamos group, and captured the hectic, responsible spirit of the beginning of the scientists' movement:[18]

> We have taken over the office of the I.C.C.... The office is a dumpy suite of rooms, 4th floor walkup. Furniture very meager. The secretary is very good, works about 70 hours a week.... So far she hasn't been paid. No one has got any money. Szilard is getting $1,000 from Chicago for such expenses....
>
> Politically it looks haywire, too. Szilard, Schimmel [Senator Kilgore's aide,] etc. are the only permanent parties. Consequently any policy and action is up to them entirely....
>
> The boys in Washington under Szilard's direction are doing 2 things: 1) doing a good job from the international standpoint.... 2) They are trying to break the Johnson bill & get something else....
>
> Everyone is on the run every minute they can stay awake. I admire the spirit but it is a hell of a way to do things. I intend to stay out of the politicking as much as possible & try to get the big organization [FAtS] going....
>
> Also the boys are anxious for considered opinions on international control. There is no doubt that this is tough. But Congressmen and press are clamoring for dope on this. Leo & the boys tried to settle it over a couple of cocktails. You can't do things that way!

By the date of this letter, the May–Johnson bill had been fought to a standstill, but it threatened to be brought out of committee for months to come. Another bill, more acceptable, was introduced by Senator Brien McMahon (D., Connecticut) on 10 December 1945. The atomic scientists by then were getting themselves more regularly organized. Their early success had been based, as Simpson said, on the "magic" and "prestige" of the word "atomic"—also on their disinterestedness in not lobbying for their own benefit. Now they brought method and numbers into their movement.

---

[18] Higinbotham to Trischka, 11 November 1945, ALAS Papers, 2.17.

Federation of *American* Scientists

The larger group of American scientists who had not worked on the bomb yet felt similarly qualified to speak with the authority of science on the implications of atomic energy. The formation of the Federation of American Scientists (FAmS or FAS) was begun at the Washington University Conference of 16–17 November 1945. Delays in ratifying its constitution kept FAmS from undertaking official action until 6 January 1946.

FAtS–FAmS Contention

The delays were caused by what was, in miniature, a conflict over a league or a federal structure for the wider organization. The Federation of Atomic Scientists was, constitutionally, a league or *confederacy* of sovereign associations. The key clause of its founding document read:

> Each of the four Associations shall retain its identity and independence of action. The Federation will provide a central office and staff for the purpose of aiding and coordinating the activities of the several member associations.

The Federation of American Scientists, on the other hand, was a true *federation*. This was indicated in the section of its constitution on the central council's authority and powers:

> Voting power of a member association in the Council is proportional to the number of "qualified members" [persons enrolled in the associations holding a bachelor's degree or equivalent in natural science, mathematics, or engineering]. The Council shall determine the general policy of the Federation.

The newer scientists' organization, then, recognized member associations and, more fundamental to them, *individual* members, who by the rule of voting proportional to population were ultimately sovereign. In the older organization, the council would only "aid and coordinate" the activities of the member associations; in the newer, the council would "determine the general policy of the Federation," appoint an administration committee, submit reports, assess dues, and even by two–thirds vote make amendments to its constitution.[19]

The matter is relevant in this history, since most professed world federalist organizations (like United World Federalists) were able to federate (merge) nationally, but internationally (in the World Movement for World Federal Government) they were never able to practice what they preached. In short, in the FAtS, the original organizations remained sovereign; in the FAmS, the individual scientists by a second sovereign delegation created a federal organization superior for

---

[19] Smith, *A Peril,* 192–97; Simpson, "Scientists as Educators," p. 245; Minutes of FAS Council Meeting, 5–6 January 1946, FAS Papers, 1.1; "The Federation of Atomic Scientists," *Bulletin of the Atomic Scientists,* 10 December 1945; Constitution of the Federation of American Scientists, 8 December 1945, FAS Papers, 1.1. A similar conflict delayed the federation of AORS and ORES into AORES. Report of the Joint Committee, 17 December 1945, AORES Papers, 1.3.

general purposes to their local organizations. The greater strength of the latter
was a proof of the power of federation.

FAmS Achievements

The Federation of American Scientists had an active life of about two years.
It continued the coordination, begun under the FAtS, of scientists appearing before Senator McMahon's Special Committee for Control of Atomic Energy. It
guided the scientists' "crusade" for McMahon's own bill, which provided for less
oppressive security regulations, more public and congressional accountability,
and sole government production and distribution of fissionable materials. With
the help of a citizens' group, the National Committee for Civilian Control, the
scientists were able effectively to defeat Senator Vandenberg's amendment, which
would have given a military liaison committee virtual co-authority with the
civilian control commission.

The McMahon bill was reported out on 19 April 1946, passed by Senate and
House, and signed into law by President Truman on 1 August. This was the act
that created the U.S. Atomic Energy Commission (U.S. AEC, not to be confused
with the U.N. AEC). Thus the goal of U.S. *civilian* control, argued as necessary
for ultimate international control, was achieved.[20]

One World or None

The Federation of American Scientists conducted a vigorous publicity campaign, including correspondence with congressmen and government officials,
public news releases, policy statements, appeals to national leaders, forums,
conferences, lectures, articles, films, and radio programs. One of its largest pro-
ductions was the compilation *One World or None* in 1946. The authors were the
"biggest names" of the Manhattan project, including Arthur H. Compton, Niels
Bohr, Philip Morrison, J. Robert Oppenheimer, E. U. Condon, Hans Bethe, Harold Urey, and Leo Szilard.[21]

In the first and longer section, they discussed the implications of atomic energy for civilization, the dangers of atomic war, and the threat of an atomic arms
race. In the last, short section, solutions were advocated. Leo Szilard presented
the technical argument for an inspection system, which he saw as a transition to
world government:

> The breathing spell that we might secure by averting an arms race would give
> us the opportunity to establish a world community.... What matters is to

[20] Smith, *A Peril,* 271–75, 388–407, 365; *Bulletin of the Atomic Scientists,* 10
December 1945, p. 3; 24 December 1945, pp. 3–5; 1 February 1946, pp. 1–3; 1
March 1946, pp. 1–2, passim. Hearings on the McMahon bill took place during national preoccupation with Senate investigations into the Pearl Harbor surprise attack.
[21] Description of AORES Papers, Regenstein Library; Dexter Masters and Katharine Way, eds., *One World or None* (Whittlesey House, McGraw–Hill, [March] 1946;
reprinted by Books for Libraries Press, 1972), p. 64. The first printing of *One World
of None* came to 100,000 copies.

create at once conditions in which the ultimate establishment of a world government will appear as inevitable to most men as war appears inevitable at present to many.

Walter Lippmann, in an article rather uncharacteristic for him that nevertheless showed his clear grasp of the proposal of world government in 1946, presented the political argument for international control. He plainly rejected new schemes of "international law," which are dependent for their enforcement on the agreement of sovereign states ultimately to wage war against violators. He recalled the "known" principle of making individuals, not sovereign states, the objects of international agreements, that is, "to have laws operate on individuals." He referred to the application of this principle at the Nuremberg trials of German aggressors then under way. The traditional theory of the "absolute sovereign state that is subject to no higher law, and is itself the source of the highest law of its people" Lippmann called an "aberration and heresy" that was at its peak during the closing decades of the nineteenth century and the opening ones of the twentieth. The United Nations Organization, he hoped, would not be "rendered impotent by the veto," but, the nations having learned the lessons of the League, would become the "constituent assembly of a world state already directed to establish a universal order in which law, designed to maintain the peace, operates on individual persons."

Lippmann recommended that, during the upcoming U.N. negotiations on the international control of atomic energy, the American people make the "formation of the world state" the primary goal of their foreign policy:[22]

> Never was there such an opportunity for any people as is ours, though briefly if we do not seize it. We can use the preeminence of our military power so that an ideal for all mankind, not the United States of America as a nation state, may dominate and conquer the world. The issues of territory and of resources and all the other knotty problems of settling the war and of making peace will still have to be dealt with. The struggle of civilized men with the primitive, the stubborn, the malign, and the stupid, within each of us and all about us, will not end. But how different would be the assumptions and the expectations of diplomacy if, as a great power, in the company of other nations who would surely be with us, we were committed to the formation of a world order of universal law!

Albert Einstein, whose utterances on politics to some seemed to partake of his universal authority in science, amplified Lippmann's internationalist arguments. Einstein wrote very briefly and succinctly. He recounted the "illusion of security" under the League between the world wars. He referred to the "testing" since World War II of the new United Nations. Einstein found two circumstances that militated against the "moral" powers of the U.N. One was that the national states, despite their official condemnation of war, still had to consider the possibility, in their own defense, of waging wars. Hence, they would have to

[22] Masters, *One World or None,* 66–75.

continue to educate their youth to be ready to serve as soldiers in the event of war and to "implant a spirit of national vanity" in the whole citizenry to secure their support for another war. The other circumstance was that atomic bombs gave a decisive advantage to the offense, so that even responsible statesmen, at some moment of grave national peril, would feel compelled to launch a "preventive war." There was, in Einstein's view, "only *one* way out":[23]

> It is necessary that conditions be established that guarantee the individual state the right to solve its conflicts with other states on a legal basis and under international jurisdiction.
> It is necessary that the individual state be prevented from making war by a supranational organization supported by a military power that is exclusively under its control.

Einstein concluded with specific suggestions for the transition: inspection, denationalization of military establishments, great power agreement on a world constitution, operation of the "supranational security organization," and, lastly, inviting in the remaining national states.

---

[23] Ibid., 76–77. Walt Disney, on being approached by a Los Alamos representative, W. Bradford Shank, was interested in getting the "collaboration of the entire movie industry" for a feature film from the atomic scientists' point of view. Samuel Marx of MGM was also interested. Nothing came of these offers, apparently for lack of money. W. E. Cohn to S. C. English, telephone call notes, 1 November 1945; Minutes of Executive Committee Meeting, 5 November 1945, AORES Papers, 1.6.

8

Grenville Clark: U.N. Reform

It will be just as easy for nations to get along in a republic of
the world as it is for us to get along in the republic of the
United States.

—Harry S. Truman, address at the University of Kansas City,
28 June 1945, after signing the United Nations Charter

It is almost axiomatic that there can be no peace without order
and no order without law.

—Dublin Declaration, 17 October 1945

Critical Political Responses to the Atomic Bomb

Emery Reves' *The Anatomy of Peace* was in people's hands on the day of the
Hiroshima attack. Written in a "holy rage" (said Tom Griessemer) against the
sovereign state system and the international anarchy, which had produced World
War II and was preserved in the Charter of the United Nations, the book un-
flinchingly examined the problem of peace and set out the solution of the rule of
law under world government. Reves was the founder in 1930 of Cooperation
Press Service, which published counter–propaganda to Hitler until the dictator
nearly caught him after the conquest of France. In New York by 1945, he
wrote:[1]

> We have always been able to solve the problem of peace *within* sovereign
> groups of men. We have never been able to solve this very same problem *be-*
> *tween* sovereign groups of men, today between nations. The reason is obvi-
> ous. Trying to solve international problems by diplomacy or foreign policy,
> through alliances or the balance of power, is like trying to cure cancer with
> aspirin....
>   Peace in a society means that relations among the members of the society
> are regulated by law, that there is a democratically controlled machinery of
> lawmaking, of jurisdiction, and that to carry out these laws the community
> has the right to use force, a right which is denied to the individual members of
> the community. Peace is order based on law. There is no other imaginable
> definition.

---

[1] Emery Reves, *The Anatomy of Peace* (New York: Harper & Bros., [June] 1945),
146–47.

The Anatomy of Peace was widely endorsed and was on the best–sellers lists for six months. It sold 70,000 copies in eight printings in 1945 alone. It was widely excerpted, serialized, and translated into 20 languages (including Czech and Arabic). *Reader's Digest* excerpted it in three installments—the first time the *Digest* had accorded such treatment to any book. By 1948, the book had appeared in 30 editions in 24 countries, and often it was the only book people had read about world government. But Reves was pessimistic. He saw the future as a great struggle to unite the world either as an *empire,* in which the United States and the Soviet Union were the only remaining sovereign contenders, or as a lawful *federation,* in which the people of the world would have to exercise *their* sovereignty. He inclined to think that a bid for empire would be made and the world plunged into a third world war. So he urged the popular movement to prepare to make world government a *war aim* and thus prevent a third miscarriage of reason like the League and the United Nations.[2]

Norman Cousins

On the night after the news of the bombing of Hiroshima, Norman Cousins poured out his mind and heart in an editorial, "Modern Man Is Obsolete," which was published in the next issue of the *Saturday Review of Literature.*[3] What was "obsolete" was "modern man," in the sense of man who by 1945 had discovered the means for his own destruction but not yet the means for his preservation. Atomic power left man with two alternatives: ultimate destruction of civilization or, within the United States, development of atomic power as a "government utility or public service" and, within the world, a "centralized world government."

This editorial aroused much comment throughout the country. "It is the best thing I have seen since the atomic bomb came to light," said Justice Owen J. Roberts. The *New York Herald Tribune* printed an abridged version on 23 August. The Board of Education of New York City sent copies to 700 high school principals in the U.S. World Federalists distributed 12,000 reprints. Some 50,000 reprints in all were distributed by readers, churches, schools, and organizations. Before Christmas an expanded version came out in a slim little book. Cousins continued for several years to write world government editorials for the *Saturday Review,* which, like *Reader's Digest* and the *Atlantic* at least through 1946, often had room for world government opinion.[4] Cousins at this time was chairman of the executive committee of Americans United for World Organization (AUWO).

---

[2] Ibid., 257–61, 262–75.

[3] Norman Cousins, "Modern Man Is Obsolete," *Saturday Review of Literature,* 18 August 1945, pp. 5–9; Raymond Swing, *In the Name of Sanity* (New York: Harper & Bros., 1945–46), vii.

[4] "Radioactive Words," *New York Post,* 20 September 1945; "Books and Publications," *World Government News,* November 1945, p. 11; Norman Cousins, *Modern Man Is Obsolete* (New York: Viking, 1945).

Raymond Gram Swing

On the morning of Friday, 24 August 1945, prominent radio broadcaster Raymond Gram Swing took a long walk. He was thinking that the atomic bomb compelled him to take an editorial view in at least some of his news reports. He had been struck by President Truman's comparison of the United Nations to a "republic of the world" in his recent Kansas City speech. He explained:[5]

> During the walk I saw certain problems clearly. The atomic bomb had changed warfare, and must change all social life. I recognized that I should have to discuss world government, since only through a world sovereignty could war be abolished, and civilization preserved. It would not be easy for me to do this. As a news analyst I had never espoused any cause or doctrine in my broadcasts, as I believed that I did not have the right to do so. Now I should do so because I did not have the right not to do so.

Swing then devoted every Friday night's broadcast for 35 weeks to the implications of the news for world government. His first broadcast was entitled "One World or No World." Swing covered the history of the Manhattan project, the revolt of the atomic scientists, President Truman's wavering on leading the world to what he had called in his Kansas City speech a "republic of the world," the fight over the May–Johnson bill, Einstein on world government, and the events leading toward the Baruch plan. These broadcasts, delivered matter–of–factly, brought the idea of world government into more homes at an earlier moment than any other medium. Swing at the time was chairman of the board of AUWO and became a principal organizer of United World Federalists.

Albert Einstein

After Hiroshima, the world's most famous scientist actively led the movement for world government. He endorsed Emery Reves' *Anatomy of Peace* and recommended it to the Los Alamos atomic scientists, whose policy statement of November openly set forth world government as the goal after international control of atomic energy. Einstein cosigned, with Justice Owen J. Roberts, Senator J. William Fulbright, Mortimer J. Adler, American Veterans Committee founder Charles Bolté, Cord Meyer, and Mark and Carl Van Doren, a letter to the *New York Times* on 10 October 1945:[6]

> The first atomic bomb destroyed more than the city of Hiroshima. It also exploded our inherited, outdated political ideas.... The [U.N.] Charter is a tragic illusion unless we are ready to take the further steps necessary to organize peace.... The San Francisco Charter, by maintaining the absolute sovereign-

---

[5] Swing, *In the Name of Sanity*, vi, passim. Raymond Gram Swing, *Good Evening! A Professional Memoir* (New York: Harcourt, Brace & World, 1964), 241–43, 249.

[6] Otto Nathan and Heinz Norden, eds., *Einstein on Peace* (New York: Schocken, 1960), 340–41.

ties of the rival nation–states, thus preventing the creation of superior law in world relations, resembles the Acts of Confederation of the thirteen original American republics. We know that this confederation did not work. No league system ever attempted in human history could prevent conflict between its members. We must aim at a Federal Constitution of the world, a working world–wide legal order, if we hope to prevent an atomic war.

In the November 1945 issue of the *Atlantic Monthly*, Einstein published a major world government proposal in an article entitled "Atomic War or Peace." He saw atomic bombs not as creating a new problem but as increasing the destructiveness of war, which remained "inevitable" as long as sovereign nations held their military powers in readiness. Use of atomic bombs in future wars would mean mutual destruction. National interest in self–preservation, therefore, required abolition of all war.

Einstein recommended that the "secret of the bomb," in the formulation of the time, be given not to the United Nations, which as a league was impotent, but to a "world government." What was distinctive about his proposal was that he suggested the world government be initiated *first* by the three remaining great powers—the United States, the Soviet Union, and Great Britain. To show good faith to the Soviet Union, which then had not yet developed the bomb, Einstein even suggested that the government of the U.S.S.R. prepare the first draft of a world constitution. He admitted that in the Soviet Union a minority rules, but not oppressively so considering the long history of Russian autocracy. A limited federal world government, Einstein thought, would not require changes in the "internal structure" of the three member states. The alternative to a world government established by agreement was one imposed by force "in a much more dangerous form" by a nation bidding for world empire. But the political unification of the world "will come anyway," he concluded. If the method of agreement is chosen, a gradual process would not work, since unilateral retention of atomic capability would create "fear and suspicion." It was necessary to create world government at one step, "quickly."[7]

Disagreement was expressed by Sumner Welles, now a private citizen. Welles defended the U.N. structure he had been instrumental in creating during his days in the State Department in a sharp dissent in the January 1946 *Atlantic*. He perceived Einstein's inconsistency in advocating powers to intervene against a minority government yet accepting the minority government in Russia. Russia could hardly be expected to accept so powerful a world government, Welles

---

[7] Albert Einstein as told to Raymond Swing, "Atomic War or Peace," *Atlantic Monthly*, November 1945, pp. 43–45; Nathan, *Einstein on Peace*, 347–51; Albert Einstein, *Ideas and Opinions*, Carl Seelig, ed. (New York: Dell, 1954), 121–34. The essentials of the article were reprinted in *Reader's Digest*, December 1945, and in an ad of World Federalists, U.S.A., "Here Is One Einstein Theory You Can Understand," *New York Times*, 9 December 1945.

stated. He saw no alternative to working with the new United Nations.[8]

The Dublin Conference

These radical views of the implications of atomic energy culminated in a dissenting conference of the most highly placed internationalists hosted by Grenville Clark. After Hiroshima, Clark had hardly missed a day in continuing his preparations to hold a conference of distinguished Americans to propose improvements to the United Nations Charter. His efforts brought about the Dublin (New Hampshire) conference of 11–16 October 1945.

Clark had conceived his élite Dublin conference while proposing a "world constitutional convention" the year before. After that, in March 1945, Clarence Streit, through his highly placed colleague Supreme Court Justice Owen J. Roberts, proposed a three–week conference of about 40 internationalists "to consider further steps toward world organization." The site proposed was Clearwater, Idaho, near Streit's hometown. Clark met with Roberts that month to discuss efforts to insert a regular amendment provision into the Charter at the upcoming San Francisco conference. He began to move the justice deftly away from a subsequent U.N. reform conference sure to result in a high declaration favoring Streit's divisive "nuclear union" of the liberal democracies. By May, formal agreement had been reached to put the conference off until the fall, when the justice would have freed himself by resigning from the Court, which he did.

By July, Clark proposed a site in Peterborough, later changed to Dublin, New Hampshire, near his home. He cited "travel difficulties" (gas rationing was still in effect) against a meeting anywhere but in the East. Streit was expected to come, disappointment over his Clearwater project notwithstanding. The justice was still writing that the purpose of the citizens' conference was "to remedy the weaknesses of the United Nations Organization ... by creation of a nuclear union or unions."[9]

In effect, the Dublin conference was conceived as a test, when time was very pressing, of whether leading federalist opinion would support a partial, democratic union or a universal one in response to atomic energy. The two legalists collaborated on the list of invitees. Clark brought in Thomas H. Mahony, chairman of the Massachusetts Committee for World Federation, and Robert P. Bass, former governor of New Hampshire (1911–13) and soon to be made chairman of the board of the Brookings Institution. These four, Roberts (chairman), Clark (secretary), Mahony, and Bass, sent out the formal invitations. There was much subdued suspense about whether the issue would go to the Streitists or to the

---

[8] Sumner Welles, "The Atomic Bomb and World Government," *Atlantic Monthly*, January 1946, pp. 39–42.

[9] Grenville Clark, "Dumbarton Oaks Plans Held in Need of Modification," *New York Times*, 15 October 1944; Roberts to Clark, 27 March 1945; Clark to Roberts, 28 May 1945; Clark to Roberts, 7 July 1945; Roberts to Clark, 7 August 1945; Streit to Clark, 28 August 1945, Clark Papers, 15.1. Roberts resigned from the Supreme Court on 1 July 1945. He later became dean of the University of Pennsylvania Law School.

universalists. As late as September, Clark was writing his friend and neighbor Bass: "I am still in hopes that we may be agreeably surprised in finding that Roberts has not completely fallen for the Streit propaganda."[10]

Significance of Dublin

The general purpose of the Dublin conference, as stated in the formal invitation, was "to explore how best to remedy the weaknesses of the United Nations Organization [and] to seek agreement upon and to formulate definite amendments to the Charter or other proposals to remedy these weaknesses." It is clear in retrospect that Clark sought a fair fight between the Atlantic unionists and the universalists, in order to publish a reasoned majority view that might unite the world government movement.

The Dublin conference was followed by the World Federalists' Cleveland convention in a week, the Federal Union Pittsburgh convention in November, the Student Federalists' Concord conference in February, and the Rollins College conference in March. None of these subsequent organizational conclaves was characterized by the presence of ideological opponents within the movement or of the unconvinced from the larger society without. (A possible exception was Rollins, which was indecisive.)

The movement, at the moment of its opportunity, was fatefully divided. Probably only Clark—outside the U.S. government but with connections to it and throughout the Eastern establishment—had the prestige and the resources to bring about so serious a conference. Ultimately 105 were invited, including senators, well-known internationalists, and veterans. Some 48 attended. Clark's spirit at Dublin, which aimed to bring antagonistic world government advocates before the bar of their peers, distinguished that conference, no less than the national prominence of its invitees or the revolutionary character of their resolutions. The Dublin conference of October 1945 was the first world government conference in the atomic age to receive national notice. It was also the last to present a united front for world federal government.

Since the original inspiration for the Dublin conference was not the atomic bomb but the San Francisco conference, Clark realized that he and others who sought a stronger world peace organization had been outpaced during the preceding year. The Charter was "as good as ratified," he wrote in August 1945, and the new United Nations Organization was "there." But he supposed that scope could still be found, while the U.N. was starting up, for "drastic" amendments to the Charter. The amendments he had in mind, analogous to recommendations he had made in previously published opinion, were to make the General Assembly popularly representative and hence to grant it real powers; to convert the Security Council into an executive organ of the Assembly; and to give the International Court of Justice compulsory jurisdiction. Clark did not propose to create in place of the U.N. a new world organization or a world government. For this there was "no prospect," he explained with an unsentimental sense of political

---

[10] Clark to Bass, 19 September 1945, ibid., 15.1; Draft Report of the Dublin Conference, 24 November 1945, ibid., 15.2.

reality, "until there is another world catastrophe."[11]

Impact of Atomic Bomb

The first use of atomic bombs seemed to be such a catastrophe. Governor Bass wrote to Clark after Hiroshima:[12]

> The discovery of the Atomic Bomb has changed many problems of international relationships. It has materially changed the relevant power of the great and the smaller nations. It has revolutionized the task of maintaining world peace.... It probably represents the most forceful and cogent reason for early change in the form and procedure of the international organization.

Clark, who still believed that the threat of war in general was reason enough to strengthen the Charter, began in September to insert phrases referring to atomic warfare in his formal invitation and program. One was that the Dumbarton Oaks–San Francisco plan was "behind the times," a phrase that appeared prominently in the Dublin conference declaration. Up to the opening day of the conference itself, Clark continued to prepare an agenda for consideration of his amendments.

Debate at Dublin

The Dublin conference opened on 11 October 1945. Justice Roberts, Clarence Streit, Emery Reves, Norman Cousins, Edgar Ansel Mowrer, Thomas K. Finletter, Thomas Mahony, Louis B. Sohn, Tom Griessemer, and younger men who would later be leaders in the federalist movement, notably Cord Meyer Jr., Alan Cranston, and Charles Bolté, were all in attendance. On the first full day Streit moved his resolution in favor of a union of "the peoples who share the atomic secret with us," achieved through the approach of a "constitutional convention." Mahony followed with a nondiscriminatory resolution simply in favor of "the consideration of specific amendments to the United Nations Charter." The conferees quickly lined up behind one or the other of these resolutions. A few stood apart.

Streit's main point was that individual freedom, in danger because the "democratic system can't go to war quickly," needed the protection of union. The atom bomb in democratic hands would not put others "in panic about us" but would "discourage aggressive elements" in Russia. Federal Union's chairman A.J.G. Priest seconded Streit's resolution, adding that Russia should have no fear of a union whose object was only to preserve its freedom "without jostling [its] neighbor." Washington publisher William B. Ziff later supported Streit with a resolution that universal federation was both "impractical" and "undesirable." What was needed for security was a union of the "Western Hemisphere," which he redrew to include North and South America, the British Isles, Australia, and

---

[11] Draft of Clark to [Invitee], 16 July 1945 (date of the atomic test at Alamogordo), Clark Papers, 15.2.

[12] Bass to Clark, 24 August 1945, Clark Papers, 15.1.

Indonesia.[13]

Streit's proposal implied a new Western union; Mahony's, since it proposed amending the existing Charter, a universal one. Clark seconded Mahony's resolution, explaining that the "democratic" test "excludes Russia" and probably also China and other countries. Russia would naturally "resent exclusion" and "build [the] bloc" that would constitute a real threat. The amendment approach would keep open the door for Russian participation and hence for the ultimate goal of world federation, he said, and he read a letter from Senator Fulbright in favor of amendments.

Debate swirled around these poles. Emery Reves, "bursting with excitement," disagreed with both Streit and Mahony. Nothing the conference resolved could weaken national sovereignty, he objected. No national government would act on a citizens' call for a world constitutional convention, nor would any government support amendments to the Charter. What was needed, argued Reves, was a massive program to "educate people to [demand] world federation."[14]

But the decisive note was struck by Princeton professor Henry DeWolf Smyth on the threat of an atomic armament race. It transformed the conference. Smyth explained in detail the atomic scientists' arguments of no secret and no defense. He alluded to "more efficient" (hydrogen) bombs of 1,000 times the force of the atomic bomb. He concluded that the only "long–range defense" was the *political* one. People must be made to realize that war between industrialized states with atomic bombs meant mutual destruction. The Charter must be modified to eliminate the veto over a system of international control of atomic energy. Federal world government, however, Smyth thought, was premature.

Clark's Advocacy of World Federation

A kind of world constitutional debate had opened. Clark introduced six prepared resolutions of his own. They called the U.N. structure "wholly inadequate" because of its one nation, one vote rule in the General Assembly and unanimity rule in the Security Council. Clark recommended weighted representation in the Assembly, popular election of representatives, majority rule, powers to abolish war, and transformation of the Council into an executive committee of the Assembly. These resolutions became the major source for the eight final resolutions of the conference. Clark explained that, while his resolutions did not say so, they did "suggest world government and modification of national sovereignty." He recognized that the problem was as much of "will" as of adequately "designed machinery." But an adequate objective could *mobilize will.* He was an advocate of world federation.[15]

Toward the final sessions the veterans drew toward Clark and the conference

---

[13] Minutes of Dublin Conference, 11–16 October 1945, pp. 3–4; Grenville Clark's Notes, 12–16 October 1945; Resolutions Offered, 12 October 1945, Clark Papers, 15.2.

[14] Minutes of Dublin Conference, pp. 4–9.

[15] Ibid.; Resolutions to Be Offered by Grenville Clark at the Third Session, n.d., c. 12 October 1945, Clark Papers, 15.2.

gravitated to his position. People were eager and excited, especially at the end of each day at the Dublin Inn, some staying until late, "plotting and arguing," drafting resolutions. Beardsley Ruml, chairman of the Federal Reserve Bank of New York, proposed that the conferees unite on a program differentiated by timing but starting with amendment of the U.N. Charter. The short–term objective, he urged, was to "relieve existing tensions." Clark agreed in large measure with Ruml. The Charter amendment step, though, would require "ninety per cent rewriting," and probably a U.S. constitutional amendment would be required, too. Streit still felt the only practical next step was a "nuclear union within the U.N. of like minded people." He admitted that his formula excluded Russia.[16]

U.N. Charter Inadequate

By the sixth session, the Dublin conference was voting on resolutions that went far beyond what Clark had originally aimed at:[17]

> First: That the implications of the atomic bomb are appalling; that upon the basis of evidence before this conference there is no presently known adequate defense against the bomb; and that there is no time to lose in creating effective international institutions to prevent war by exclusive control of the bomb and other major weapons.
>
> Second: That the United Nations Charter, despite the hopes millions of people placed in it, is inadequate and behind the times as a means to promote peace and world order.
>
> Third: That in place of the present United Nations Organization there must be substituted a world federal government with limited but definite and adequate powers to prevent war, including power to control the atomic bomb and other major weapons and to maintain world inspection and police forces.

The fourth, fifth, and sixth resolutions dealt with the legislative, executive, and judicial branches of the federal world government. The seventh called for a U.S. constitutional amendment to permit U.S. participation. The eighth appealed to the American people to support efforts to establish world government either by U.N. Charter amendment or by a world constitutional convention.

Threat of Walkout with Justice Roberts

By this point the Streitists realized the conference had quite gone against them. They proposed a ninth resolution recommending, as a matter of timing, prior establishment of a nuclear union of the democracies. Federal Union vice-president Stringfellow Barr led the counterattack. "Common ground [has] not yet [been] *struck*," he said. The Streitists threatened to walk out, taking Roberts with them. The loss of the former Supreme Court justice, the most prestigious individual there, would have been a severe blow to the majority. Then, at a cocktail party before the penultimate day of the conference, the justice made a racial

---

[16] Minutes of Dublin Conference, pp. 10–22.

[17] "Declaration of the Dublin, N.H., Conference," *New York Times,* 17 October 1945, p. 4.

remark that turned the veterans into a solid bloc behind Clark. (Roberts, *in vino veritas,* confided he had "no use for a world government with 'chinks and niggers,' and anyway we'd be fighting Russia in a few years.")[18] At the formal session next day they opposed any ninth Streitian resolution.

Why Universal World Federal Government

Clark rose to make a major speech. He said he would vote against a nuclear union of democracies, unless it should be proposed *after* world federal government. The *starting point* was world government. Russia was not to be so feared, he argued. Have we forgotten those scenes of the meeting of Russian and American soldiers on the Elbe? Russia has a vital interest in security. Her government is understandably suspicious of us, with whom she has no treaties as with other powers. The U.S. government is set in its "grooves." Stimson proposed an American–Russian–Chinese alliance as long ago as 1931. The Selective Service Act of 1940 was initiated by private citizens; so could world federation in 1945, he concluded. "Global thinking on world government [is] now necessary."

This conference, Clark argued, ought not to have an inferiority complex as to its influence. The American people have the intelligence to understand the concluding statement. They will listen to veterans especially. Now, the threat of walking out is in the air, he further stated. It must be faced. There is no harm in a majority statement and a separate minority report. "Would Justice Roberts vote against *his* convictions to stop someone from walking out? Of course not, he'd stand by his convictions come what would!" The same for the majority if it disagrees with Streit. A public statement is important. He proposed the conference issue two—a majority and a minority statement. It is the American process.[19]

This speech saved the conference. Massachusetts' Henry Cabot said it was the most remarkable handling of a tense situation he had ever seen. The ninth resolution was dropped by a vote of 26 to 5. Later 30 signed the majority "Declaration of the Dublin Conference." A dissenting minority statement, recommending exploration of a democratic union "simultaneously" with efforts to establish world federal government, was appended. A preamble, bearing Clark's stamp, was inserted before the eight resolutions:[20]

The Dublin Declaration

The application of atomic energy to warfare and impressive scientific evidence as to the consequences thereof have made the people of the world realize that the institution of war among nations must be abolished if civilization is to continue....

It is almost axiomatic that there can be no peace without order and no order without law. There can be no world peace until there is world order based

---

[18] Mrs. Grenville Clark to son Grenville Clark Jr., 17 October 1945, ibid.

[19] Minutes of Dublin Conference, pp. 30–31.

[20] Ibid., p. 33; "Declaration of the Dublin, N.H., Conference." For full text and list of signers see Appendix F.

upon principles of the limitation and the pooling of national external sovereignty by all nations for the common good of mankind. The only effective
means to create such a world order is to establish a world government....

Since the moral law applies to nations as well as to men and [since] justice dictates the necessity of seeking the greatest good for the greatest number, such a world government must be a World Federal Government providing
a minimum of centralized control ... and a maximum of self government in
the separate nations.

A Federalist Prayer

The conference ended in a flurry. The press rushed away with their first releases. A continuing "Dublin Conference Committee," Alan Cranston, chairman, was appointed to put the resolutions into effect, and Clark promised to
continue funding. Roberts led a standing vote of appreciation for Clark and his
family. Reverend Edward C. Conway, S.J., read a closing federalist prayer:[21]

> Almighty and eternal Father, under whose wise providence we Thy child-
> ren have unlocked, for weal or woe, one of the prime secrets of Thy creation,
> grant that we may summon up the moral energy we need to cope with the cri-
> sis which our discovery has wrought in the lives of men....
>
> We pray Thy all–powerful assistance that we may soon achieve that po-
> litical embodiment of the brotherhood of man, a federation of the peoples of
> the world, an objective upon which we gathered here entirely agree, despite
> our divergencies on the means of achieving it.
>
> Impelled by the driving urgency of the crisis into which our own pride and
> compromise have plunged us, we beg Thine instant aid that we may nobly
> use, not meanly lose, the last best hope of men.

Response to the Dublin Declaration

The declaration and news of the Dublin conference were immediately and
widely published. Stories appeared on the front pages of the *New York Times,
New York Herald Tribune, Boston Globe,* and *Manchester* (New Hampshire)
Union. They also appeared inside the *Christian Science Monitor, Boston Herald,
Boston Daily Record, Washington Post, Washington Star, Baltimore Sun, Chicago Sun, Chicago Daily News, St. Louis Post–Dispatch, Kansas City Star,* and
many New England local papers such as the *Peterborough* (New Hampshire)
Transcript. Clark was in direct contact with the publishers or editors of these
papers and with the Associated Press, United Press, and International News Service.

The declaration and a background report were sent to the president, his cabinet, all members of Congress, the governors of the 48 states, and the officials
and delegates to the United Nations General Assembly. By November, 3,700
copies of the declaration had been printed. They were distributed mostly in
batches of 100 by leaders like Clark, Mahony, Cranston, and Roberts. Transla-
tions were made into French (1,000 copies), Spanish (1,000), and Russian (500)

---

[21] Edward A. Conway, Closing Prayer, 16 October 1945, Clark Papers,15.2.

at a cost of $1,728.[22] Clark addressed the Harvard Faculty Club on the Dublin declaration in December.[23]

Editorial comment in the local papers was, on balance, positive; in papers of national record, negative. The *Manchester Union* editorialized that the Dublin conference had "performed an important public service" by beginning the task of "reshaping the United Nations organization ... to meet the challenge of the atomic bomb." The *Stamford* (Connecticut) *Advocate* printed a series of three editorials beginning with the "revolutionary discovery" of atomic energy and ending with the "necessity" for world government. The *Boston Globe* agreed that "something stronger than the United Nations Organization as set up at San Francisco is needed to prevent war in a world that contains the atomic bomb." The *Christian Science Monitor* asked if world government was really more "visionary" than expecting peace in a world of absolute national sovereignties or than preventing aggression by a U.N. where any great power can veto action.[24]

The *New York Times,* on the other hand, while it recognized that the Dublin conferees were "able, sincere men and women," flatly declared they had done "more harm than good." They proposed to "scrap" the U.N. They offered no practical alternative.[25]

> A true world federation, such as they contemplate, is beyond attainment at this stage of history. If the Dublin conferees doubt this assertion, let them read the day's news, or put a question to London or Moscow, not to mention Washington. The actual choice is not between the UNO and an ideal world government. It is between UNO and chaos.

Louis B. Sohn vigorously answered the charge of utopianism. "Do we have to wait," he asked in a letter to the editor, "until the bombs start falling upon us before we decide to do something about it?" The Charter was drafted before the revelation of the atomic bomb. It could hardly be harmful to seek to strengthen the Charter to cope with the new threat. Actually, only certain amendments to Chapters IV and VII were involved, said Sohn, not mentioning Clark's view that

---

[22] "World Government Is Urged To Bar Ruin in Atomic War," *New York Times,* 17 October 1945; "Super World State Urged," *New York Herald Tribune,* 16 October 1945; "World Body To Replace UNO Urged by Dublin, N.H., Parley," *Boston Globe,* 17 October 1945; "Conference Urges World Federation," *Manchester Union,* 17 October 1945; Clark to Kent Cooper, AP, et al., 6 October 1945; Clark to Blair, *New York Times,* et al., 13 October 1945; Olive G. Ricker, Exec. Sec., Am. Bar Assn., to Clark, 12 November 1945; Distribution of Document, 7 November 1945, Clark Papers, 15.2.

[23] Grenville Clark, "The Dublin Declaration," *World Affairs,* December 1945, ibid., 21.10.

[24] "The Dublin Conference," *Manchester Union,* 18 October 1945; "The Dublin Conference," "Necessity Knows No Law," "World Federation," *Stamford Advocate,* 18, 19, 20 October 1945; "For a Safer World," *Boston Globe,* 18 October 1945; "Visionary?" *Christian Science Monitor,* 19 October 1945.

[25] "UNO Under Fire," *New York Times,* 18 October 1945.

90 percent of the Charter would have to be rewritten. "Let's hope," he concluded, "we can strengthen it before a war destroys our civilization."[26]

A similar rebuff to the Dublin group came from the *New York Herald Tribune*. Major George Fielding Eliot, a conservative internationalist columnist,
member of the Council on Foreign Relations, and member of the board of
Americans United for World Organization, accused the Dublinites of "atomic
jitters." World government, he said, would require "more drastic sacrifice of sovereignty" than San Francisco would give reason to think possible. Proposing
world government "would merely be to weaken public confidence in the United
Nations Organization at the very moment when it needs the maximum of confidence and support from all the peoples of the world." Eliot followed with his
own "sensible" security program: U.N. as is, domestic control of atomic energy,
military defense, national security council, national intelligence service, and
weapons development.[27]

Thomas Mahony, in a letter to the editor of the *Boston Herald,* tried to emphasize the last resolution of the Dublin declaration, which called for amendments to the U.N. Charter. But there remained much point in Eliot's charge that
the conference aimed to "throw away" the United Nations for world federal government.[28]

Soon the prominent American Association for the United Nations issued a
counter-declaration, signed by nineteen equally prestigious Americans, calling
the Dublin declaration "shocking in its import." The association recalled that
the United States had rejected the League in 1920. What, then, would American
allies think if a high proposal came out of the U.S. to "scrap" the United Nations in 1945? The Dublin declaration sowed disillusionment and uncertainty in
the minds of the American people at the crucial moment when the U.N. was beginning to function. The "practical" course was to support the U.N. as it started
up, seek the international control of atomic energy, and develop the trusteeship
system over dependent peoples to gain strategic bases.[29]

Clark's correspondence tended to confirm the view that the Dublin conference
had gone too far. Francis E. Frothingham wrote that to say, after all the effort
that went into the Charter, that the United Nations was "all wrong and should be
scrapped," was "to disturb public sentiment and confidence so that it will be dis-
trustful of any new plan put forward." Owen Roberts wrote, "I get a good many

[26] Sohn to Editor of the *New York Times,* 24 October 1945.

[27] George Fielding Eliot, "World Government Proposal Is Traced to 'Atomic
Jitters,'" *New York Herald Tribune,* 19 October 1945.

[28] Mahony to Editor of the *Boston Herald,* 28 October 1945.

[29] "Proposal to Scrap UNO Is Denounced," *New York Times,* 27 October 1945.
Signers of the AAUN statement included Clark Eichelberger, director; Karl Compton,
president, Massachusetts Institute of Technology; Joseph E. Davies, former ambassador to Russia; Virginia C. Gildersleeve, dean, Barnard College, and U.S. delegate to
the San Francisco conference; Bishop G. Bromley Oxnam, president, Federal Council
of Churches; and George Fielding Eliot. *Time,* 29 October 1945, and *Life,* same date,
took similar views.

repercussions to the general effect that the UNO is all that we have, that we worked very hard to get it, and that to start to condemn it before the Assembly and Council have even organized causes a good deal of disappointment and disillusionment."[30]

Popular Demand Needed

A letter that took a similar view of the immediate failure of the Dublin conference to attract high leadership to the cause of world government but also showed the way to the future, came from Clark's colleague Laurence F. Peck:[31]

> Not many of our people have begun to understand the problem [of atomic war] and very few face up to its implications. The lack of appreciation of the situation is reflected in Congress and the Executive. Except for the current talks with Attlee about the atomic bomb, the energies of both branches of government have been focused for months on other problems, the solutions of which may well become futile in the mess the world is in....
>
> As Congress, in such matters as this, follows fairly closely the tempo of the country, it would seem that only an overwhelming demand for international law and all that this implies, by great numbers of our people, could prepare the United States for its proper role.

Peck saw that World Federalists, Americans United, and the like were trying to build up such a momentous popular movement for world government, but even "lumped together," their efforts were "pitifully weak." What was needed was a national, even world–wide, mass movement, motivated not by "intellectual exposition and argument" but by *"fear"* of atomic destruction. Leaders of the stature of Bernard Baruch and James B. Conant would have to be found. A treasury sponsored by the foundations or a few rich men would help make haste. About a year remained for such a movement, Peck estimated, to convince the nation "that the theory of the total sovereignty of nations has become as obsolete as tribal existence, and that we must now step into a new world order commensurate with the developments of science."

Arguments like Peck's were to lead to the founding of United World Federalists and the World Movement for World Federal Government in 1947. The year of opportunity would be lost. Clark did not shrink from world federal government, despite critics of the Dublin declaration, but he concentrated on amendments to the U.N. Charter. The alternative of a world constitutional convention he judged much less practicable. By seeking amendments, he could not be ac-

---

[30] Frothingham to Clark, 18 October 1945; Roberts to Clark, 1 November 1945, Clark Papers, 15.1.

[31] Peck to Clark, 16 November 1945, ibid., 15.1. Harvard's president Conant had written a long, confidential letter to the Dublin conference on the difficulties of international control of atomic energy in a world of sovereign states. Then he refused to sign the Dublin declaration on the grounds that it proposed "a substitution of something else for the United Nations Organization." Conant to Clark, 8 October 1945, and 25 October 1945, ibid., 15.1.

cused of trying to "scrap" the Charter. He could fit into the political movement already mobilized in favor of the U.N., and he had worked long, with Thomas H. Mahony and others, on just what amendments were needed. The question was, If the citizens at Dublin took the initiative, who would put amendments into effect to transform the United Nations into a limited, federal world government?

Notice of Dublin in the Senate

These sentiments in defense of the U.N. came to a head in the Senate debate on the U.N. Participation Act in November. Senator Glen Taylor (D., Idaho), who would later be Henry Wallace's vice–presidential running mate, had introduced, a few days after Dublin, a resolution favoring the creation of a world republic. Taylor's was the first of some 16 world federalist resolutions that were introduced in Congress (for texts, see Appendix H). His bill offered a new opportunity to fundamentally strengthen the U.N. in response to atomic weapons, if the Senate were willing.[32]

Senator Tom Connally (D., Texas), who had led the struggle for the U.N. since the Moscow declaration, took notice of the Dublin declaration, but he feared America's being outvoted by the hordes of India, China, and Russia. "We are not ready for world government," he exclaimed; "we are not ready for the consolidation of our own Nation into a conglomerate host of other nations, with their prejudices and hatreds." Connally was supported by Senator Arthur Vandenberg (R., Michigan), newly converted from isolationism and later an architect of the North Atlantic treaty. Vandenberg feared the "bedlam" of another San Francisco conference and hoped that the "continuous contacts" of the new U.N. organization would prepare the nations for an eventual closer union.[33]

So there the matter ended, at the most critical time. Taylor's resolution fell into oblivion. There would not be another Senate resolution on world federation until July 1947, when Taylor introduced a second. It and others like it then became only part of the background for the Marshall plan, the North Atlantic treaty, and in general the Cold War.[34]

U.N. Reform

The Dublin group was never able to escape the charge that it intended to "scrap" the United Nations. Hence, for the rest of his life, Grenville Clark concentrated on U.N. reform, rather than immediate creation of federal world govern-

[32] U.S. Congress, Senate, *Creation of a World Republic*, SR–183, 79th Cong., 1st sess., 24 October 1945, *Congressional Record*, 91:9987–89.

[33] U.S. Congress, Senate, *Debate on the U.N. Participation Act* [with comments by Senators Connally, Vandenberg, Taylor, Ball, and Fulbright on the Dublin declaration and Taylor's bill for a world republic], 79th Cong., 1st sess., 26 November 1945, *Congressional Record*, 91: 10,971–75.

[34] U.S. Congress, Senate, *Strengthening the United Nations*, SCR-24, 80th Cong., 1st sess., 9 July 1947, *Congressional Record*, 93: 8506; U.S. Congress, House of Representatives, Committee on Foreign Affairs, *Structure of the United Nations and the Relations of the United States to the United Nations*, hearings, 80th Cong., 2nd sess., 4–14 May 1948, House Library Vol. H1210, Tab 1, microfiche.

ment. Privately, he was doubtful that an effort to gradually *amend* the Charter would achieve anything more than a proof that amendment was impossible. But the proof was needed. Then there could be a new movement to call for a world constitutional convention.[35]

All through 1946, Clark worked indefatigably for U.N. reform. He proceeded in his usual way, forming committees of public–spirited citizens and drafting formal proposals. His first idea was that he could petition the U.N. General Assembly to adopt amendments, just as a private citizen may petition his government for a redress of grievances. He supposed, of course, that the Assembly delegates, in response to the revolutionary implications of atomic energy, might assume authority to reform the U.N. themselves. They do have the power (under Art. 108) to adopt amendments to the Charter, subject to Big Five ratification. Clark's committee drafted extensive amendments, cast the whole into the form of a petition, got the signatures of three congressmen, Albert Einstein, and 40 internationalists, and sent Alan Cranston to London for the historic first meeting of the General Assembly, where he circulated the petition.[36]

Cranston arrived not long after an important British parliamentary debate, in November 1945, on the implications of atomic energy. Foreign Secretary Ernest Bevin then made a bold speech in favor of "world law." Former foreign secretary Anthony Eden, too, spoke openly about "abating national sovereignty." Henry Usborne, a young Birmingham Labour member who would later lead the movement for a peoples' convention, addressed Parliament on the subject of world government.[37] These speeches seem to have been a trial balloon by the British government (Labour and Tory) to test American opinion. It was decidedly cold. Cranston was unable to receive introductions from U.S. ambassador John C. Winant. So he could not interview Prime Minister Attlee or Bevin, though he thought that copies of the petition got into their hands. Cranston returned to the United States convinced that "we've got to make our country take the lead."[38]

Rollins College Conference

On 11–16 March 1946, another conference of prominent Americans in favor of world government—a kind of Dublin conference without the Streit faction but with new names drawn to the cause by the passage of time—was held at Rollins College, in Winter Park, Florida. It was attended by Senators Joseph H. Ball (R., Minnesota), Carl A. Hatch (D., New Mexico), Claude Pepper (D., Florida),

[35] Clark to Fritz R. von Windegger, 22 January 1946, Clark Papers, 15.1; Clark to W. T. Holliday, 23 October 1946, ibid., 21.10.

[36] Clark to Dean Acheson, 18 December 1945, ibid., 15.1; "Proposals for Amendment of the United Nations Charter ... A Petition to the General Assembly of the United Nations," 1 February 1946, ibid., 15.2; Clark to Cranston, 13 February 1946, ibid., 15.1.

[37] Great Britain, Parliament, House of Commons, Debate on Foreign Affairs, *Hansard's Parliamentary Debates*, 22 November 1945, H.C. 416, cols. 611–13, 759–87.

[38] Clark to Robert P. Bass, 11 March 1946, Clark Papers, 15.1; Clark to Bass, 4 April 1946, ibid.; Cranston to Editor, 22 March 1946, ibid.

Charles W. Tobey (R., New Hampshire), and Representative Charles M. LaFollette (R., Indiana), implying for an instant that the United States might actually take up a world federalist policy.

The guiding spirit was Dr. Hamilton Holt, then president of Rollins. Holt had had a long internationalist career going back to his founding of the League to Enforce Peace in 1915. Since that time Holt had been associated with the League of Nations Non-Partisan Association, the Church Peace Union, and the Woodrow Wilson Foundation. His son, George C. Holt, was director of the Rollins College conference. Historian Carl Van Doren was chairman of the drafting committee. W. T. Holliday, president of Standard Oil of Ohio, made his first appearance in the movement at this Rollins conference. He shared honors with Fritz R. von Windegger, president of the Plaza Bank of St. Louis, as the greatest capitalist of the 1940s in favor of world government.[39]

Appeal to the Peoples of the World

After several days of closed–door deliberations to avoid, as at Dublin, press distraction by the differences among delegates from government, science, business, labor, religion, and the nascent world government movement, a unanimous "Appeal to the Peoples of the World" was issued. The conferees saw no hope in an appeal to governments. They specifically appealed to the people of the United States to "take the lead" in proposing measures to abolish war, atomic and general. A preamble cited the threat of the atomic bomb, the impossibility of keeping the secret, and the inconceivability of an adequate military defense against surprise atomic attack. Then there followed a statement of general principles:[40]

> There can be no absolute guarantee that peace will be maintained as long as any nation has the sovereign right to decide questions of war and peace for itself.
>
> If nations live under the permanent threat of war each sovereign state will inevitably become more and more totalitarian, thus depriving its citizens of more and more personal liberty.
>
> No nation state can today hope to be strong enough, sovereign enough, to protect its citizens from war. Twice in one generation the United States has been forced to enter a war which the people wished to avoid.
>
> Peace is not merely the absence of war but the presence of justice, of law, of order, in short of government.
>
> World peace can be created and maintained only under world law universal and strong enough to establish justice and prevent armed conflict between nations.
>
> The only way by which a people can assure its survival and preserve its

[39] Hamilton Holt, "World Government: A Burning Present Issue," n.d., c. 1947, Stephen Benedict Papers; "Drastic Change Is Advocated in U.N.O. Charter," *New York Herald Tribune*, 17 March 1946.

[40] Rollins College Conference on World Government, "An Appeal to the Peoples of the World," 16 March 1946, Stephen Benedict Papers.

liberties is to create with the other peoples a world government—a constitutional federal [world] government—to which shall be delegated the powers necessary to maintain the general peace of the world based on law and justice.

After the principles, the appeal continued with a discussion of methods. The United Nations was given credit as a "step," and world government, it was admitted, could not be achieved "overnight." "But a start must be made," it was added, with studied avoidance of just who was to make the start. There then followed an itemized list of changes necessary to transform the U.N. into a world government that was virtually identical with the Dublin declaration: the General Assembly to be made a legislature, with powers only to prohibit and control weapons of mass destruction; the Security Council to be reconstituted as the executive branch; independent judicial tribunals created; and a bill of rights provided. "Mass education" was as far as the conference would go as to means for effecting its ends. As a measure of informed opinion in favor of world federal government in early 1946, it was significant, and several of its participants later became active; as a step toward novel political action, it was disappointing.

The unanimity of the signers was purchased at the price of no commitment to a definite program of action. There was no Grenville Clark to continue the work. "The blueprints for a fine new world without wars have been drawn," one newspaper observed, "but the business of finding material contractors and priorities to carry them on to reality remains." Some 50,000 copies of the appeal were distributed, many by World Federalists, U.S.A., W. T. Holiday, and Fritz R. von Windegger. A kind of "Institute" (secretary) was maintained at Rollins for years. But Rollins' influence was mainly in providing another doctrinal statement on world government and in seconding the Dublin Conference.[41]

---

[41] "Atom Experts Agree on War–Killing Plan," *Chicago Daily News,* 15 March 1946. Von Windegger wondered how the director "kept away the people who would not have approved," like Bishop G. Bromley Oxnam. W. T. Holliday spent $25,000 to print the appeal in 75 Ohio newspapers. This was perhaps 10 times what Clark had to spend, including contributions from his conferees, on the more selectively directed Dublin declaration. Von Windegger to George C. Holt, 26 March 1946, Clark Papers, 15.3; *World Government News,* July 1946, p. 4.

9

Henry Usborne:
The Peoples' Convention

I am willing to sit with anybody, of any nation, to try to devise a franchise or a constitution—just as other great countries have done—
for a world assembly, as the right honorable Gentleman [Winston
Churchill] said, with a limited objective—the objective of peace.

—Foreign Minister, Ernest Bevin, 23 November 1945

The task before us is extremely difficult; there is little doubt of that,
but the enthusiasm of the common man is so powerful a force that if it
is harnessed for a constructive moral purpose, it can and will achieve
miracles. Indeed the birth of a supra-national federal parliament, or
even the prospect for it in our children's time, might well release the
repressed emotions of progressive peoples all over the world to a degree unknown and unsuspected by the plodding politicians of our day.

—Henry Usborne, M.P., *If They Won't—We Will*, October 1946

Roots of the Idea of a Peoples' Convention

Historically, two broad approaches to world federal government have been
tried—United Nations reform, of the sort that Grenville Clark and his associates
pursued, and the peoples' convention, which was conceived by Rosika Schwimmer at the start of World War I, revived at the start of World War II by her and
Lola Maverick Lloyd in a group called the Campaign for World Government, and
passed on, at what looked like the start of World War III, by campaign workers
Edith Wynner and Georgia Lloyd to British Member of Parliament (M.P.) Henry
Usborne.[1] The idea was picked up by U.S. radical veterans and students Jack
Whitehouse, David McCoy, and Paul Sauer at Northwestern University and then
their group, World Republic. (A third, parliamentary approach, also begun by
Usborne, briefly flowered until 1952, declined during the Cold War, then revived

---

[1] Usborne to Schwimmer and Wynner, 29 August 1945, New York Public Library,
Schwimmer–Lloyd Collection, T60.

during the 1980s.)[2]

In principle, U.N. reform was *official;* and the peoples' convention, *unofficial.* The basic idea was that, if the governments of the world should fail to protect their citizens from war, the people in all lands should send representatives to a new constitutional convention to draft a working world constitution. Grenville Clark had originally thought in terms of a world constitutional convention, and he always was tolerant of the political activism in campaigns for a peoples' convention. A little reflection upon the history of the United States and other federal systems shows that, at the founding, the lines between official and unofficial action become very much blurred. A revolutionary modern situation calls for a revolutionary response, advocates argued. A peoples' convention would be a revolutionary exercise of the sovereignty of the people for the establishment of a higher government above the national states.

Rosika Schwimmer was a Hungarian feminist and guiding spirit of the Ford Peace Ship of 1915. Its purpose was to arrange a "Neutral Conference for Continuous Mediation," which would negotiate with the belligerents to end the Great War and prepare a plan for permanent peace. Stung by ridicule in press and government circles, she continued to guide pacifism toward world government. Lola Maverick Lloyd, of the prominent Lloyd family in Chicago, heard Schwimmer speak during her first U.S. trip in 1914, and the two formed a fruitful friendship lasting 30 years. Four of her children were active in continuing campaigns, including William Bross Lloyd Jr. and Georgia Lloyd. Edith Wynner was a bright, multilingual assistant taken on as Schwimmer's lobbyist and campaign manager in 1934. She proved an apt pupil of her mentor's moral fervor and political iconoclasm. She became an effective speaker, and we will often have occasion to quote her in this history. U.S. proposals on the U.N. Charter she passed off as the "Dumbarton Hoax."

In the 1930s, in response to the plight of other stateless persons, Schwimmer drafted a plan for their international recognition as world citizens. In response to Mussolini's invasion of Ethiopia, she wrote another international appeal to have the *Duce* interned in an insane asylum. Both measures, she realized—world citizenship and the apprehension of individual war criminals—required world government.[3] It was at a gala celebration in New York's Waldorf Astoria in honor of her 60th birthday on 4 December 1937, that a group of about 200 of her friends and colleagues from 18 countries presented her with a world

---

[2] The Parliamentary Group for World Government, Gilbert McAllister, ed., *The Report of the First London Parliamentary Conference,* 24–29 September 1951 (London: John Roberts, 1952); World Association of Parliamentarians for World Government, Gilbert McAllister, ed., *The Report of the Third World Parliamentary Conference on World Government,* 22–29 August 1953 (Coatbridge, Scotland: Pettigrew, 1953). In 1978, the defunct Parliamentary Group within the World Association of World Federalists was revived by New Zealand's Nick Dunlop as Parliamentarians for World Order (now Parliamentarians for Global Action).

[3] Gobat, "Schwimmer," p. 7; Edith Wynner, "Schwimmer–Lloyd Papers Open for Research," *World Peace News,* February 1974, p. 6.

peace award of $8,300. There Mme Schwimmer and Mrs. Lloyd announced the formation of the Campaign for World Government.[4] This close–knit group of workers—and the 200 friends and colleagues—constituted the Campaign for World Government. It was not a mass–membership organization.[5]

The Peoples' Convention

In May 1938, the campaign published a short plan for bringing about a "World Convention to draft the best possible constitution for an all–inclusive, non-military, democratic Federation of Nations." This plan narrowly antedated Clarence Streit's more influential proposal. The plan provided for both official or unofficial action. A "committee of experts" was to be appointed to communicate to the people and supervise elections of representatives to the convention. The constitutional convention was charged only to produce a "federal ... superstructure where the states are free to develop independently, their national sovereignty being unlimited except where their interdependence requires federal regulation." A world parliament, executive, and legal system were proposed for consideration by the convention. Also proposed were what would later be called maximal powers to regulate demilitarization, economic life, decolonization, trade, transportation, communication, world finance, arbitration of international disputes, migration, world citizenship, health, and education. Cooperation of the national governments was to be invited three times: before appointment of the committee of experts, after the committee had prepared its plans for the world constitutional convention, and after the convention had promulgated its world constitution. If governments still refused to accept the constitution, the authors concluded daringly, "unofficial steps must be taken by the people" to put into operation the first world government.[6]

Campaign Activities

This was the basic idea of the peoples' convention (PC).[7] It was the idea behind the campaign's state and U.S. legislative initiatives of 1938–42. For example, on 5 June 1939, U.S. Congressman Jerry Voorhis (D., California) intro-

---

[4] Gobat, "Schwimmer," pp. 8–11; *Encyclopedia Britannica,* 15th ed.,s.v. "Hungary, History of," by Carlile Aylmer Macartney.

[5] Gobat, "Schwimmer," p. 10; Harold R. Peat, "Edith Wynner," speakers bureau circular, n.d., c. 1944, Schwimmer–Lloyd Collection; Edith Wynner and Georgia Lloyd, *Searchlight on Peace Plans* (New York: E. P. Dutton, 1944; 2nd ed., 1949).

[6] Rosika Schwimmer and Lola Maverick Lloyd, *Chaos, War, or a New World Order,* enlarged ed., fourth printing (Chicago: Authors, November 1942), Schwimmer–Lloyd Collection. The antimilitarism of this pamphlet was most immediately inspired by the resistance to disarmament of the naval delegates to the Disarmament Conference of 1932.

[7] Also called the Peoples' World Convention (PWC), Peoples' World Constitutional Convention (PWCC), World Constituent Assembly (WCA), and the like. In this history peoples' convention (PC) will be used for all these terms except when quoting.

duced House Concurrent Resolution 27 favoring their plan.[8] In the summer of 1940, William Bross Lloyd Jr. appeared before the resolutions committees of the Republican and Democratic national conventions and urged neutral mediation and inclusion of a world government plank in their platforms.[9] Similar private appeals were made through 1940 to Congress, the Canadian Parliament, the Inter–Parliamentary Union, and the Havana Pan American Conference, but to little effect.[10]

Loss of Opportunity

Mediation with Hitler was a lost cause after Munich. By the time of the Democratic and Republican conventions of mid–1940, France was a conquered country, and by October Britain was fighting for its life against the Luftwaffe. By May 1941, the United States was virtually at war in the Atlantic, and the sequence of events had begun in the Pacific that was to lead to Pearl Harbor. From the perspective of a history of the idea of world federal government, such measures as those of the Campaign for World Government have to be placed historically into the opposition, though not the isolationist opposition, to U.S. entry into World War II. The strict pacifist character of their measures, indicated by the keyword "non-military," could hardly have recommended the campaign's federalist alternative to national leaders faced with the overwhelming reality of Japanese, Italian, and German aggression. The campaign's thinking had reached the point of Einstein's at the same time in favor of "sound pacifism" (support for world government, however it might be achieved).[11] It had yet to find someone to organize a neutral conference.

Henry Usborne

In England by 1945, the most remarkable development from a world government perspective was the rise of Henry Usborne. Usborne was a 37–year–old Member of Parliament (M.P.) from Acocks Green, Birmingham, who had been elected in the Labour landslide of July 1945. Educated at Bradfield and Cambridge, he had founded and directed Nu–Way Heating Plants, Ltd., capitalized at £250,000. What was "new" about the firm was its being run on cooperative principles: the workers owned shares and elected a representative to the board,

---

    [8] Ibid.; *World Federation—Now*, June, 1939, p. 1, Georgia Lloyd Papers; U.S. Congress, House, *Calling a World Convention of the Nonmilitary Federation of Nations*, HCR–27, 76th Cong., 1st sess., 5 June 1939.

    [9] Schwimmer, *New World Order*, p. 8; William Bross Lloyd Jr., "Statement ... before the Resolutions Committee of the Republican Party, Philadelphia," 19 June 1940; Lloyd, "Statement before the Resolutions Committee of the Democratic National Convention," Chicago, 12 July 1940, Georgia Lloyd Papers.

    [10] Ibid. The earliest use of the term "waging peace," later much used in the Cold War period and ridiculed as Newspeak by George Orwell, occurred in these pacifist statements of 1940. Lloyd meant simply joint mediation by neutral countries.

    [11] Reply to a conscientious objector, summer 1941. Otto Nathan and Heinz Norden, eds., *Einstein on Peace* (New York: Schocken, 1960), 319.

for Usborne was a convinced socialist. He was deeply excited by the "social revolution" then taking place in Great Britain, and he agreed with his party that
uplifting the working class out of poverty was the primary task of his generation.

He had been a vice–president of Britain's Federal Union since 1939. Usborne
was interested originally in a European federation of socialist states in order to
coordinate their several planned economies, especially bulk state purchase of imports and state control of exports, in turn to provide full employment. He became interested in world federation, even including "capitalist America," after the
atomic bomb presented a greater threat than capitalism to the social revolution in
Britain.[12]

Usborne's attitude toward political problems owed something to his engi-
neering experience. He had seen so many "impossible" things accomplished during the war that he imagined anything could still be done once the necessity for
it was demonstrated. After two years of preparations, which included initiating
the organizational conference of the World Movement for World Federal Government in Luxembourg in October 1946, and introducing a "world federation" motion, with 72 co-signers, in the House of Commons in January 1947, this pragmatic, untraditional young M.P. launched, in July 1947, the Crusade for World
Government. Its object was the *election* of delegates to a peoples' convention.[13]

Usborne's Visit to New York in 1945

In April 1945, while British troops were still fighting in Germany, the young
Birmingham manufacturer sailed to New York partly for business and partly to
consult with Noel and Violet Rawnsley, parents of Derek, a founder of Federal
Union. The Rawnsleys were religious pacifists, but of the "sound" variety (in
Einstein's sense), who saw the necessity for world law. Their personal gentle-
ness and kindness has become a legend in federalist circles to this day. In 1945
their apartment was one of several centers in New York for the nascent federalist
movement. They naturally attracted the English.[14]

Usborne was unusual among the Rawnsleys' visitors in that he foresaw, at
the climax of Churchill's triumph, a Labour Party sweep in the elections that

[12] Harry Hopkins, "Crank or Crusader?" *John Bull,* 24 January 1948, p. 12,
Schwimmer–Lloyd Collection, T60; Usborne to the Rawnsleys, 26 November 1945,
ibid.

[13] Tom O. Griessemer, Report on the International Conference of Federalists in
Luxembourg, 14–16 October 1946, Lilly Library, UWF Papers, 42.Lux. Conf.;
"British M.P.'s Urge World Federation," *New York Times,* 1 February 1947; Henry
Usborne et al., The British Parliamentary Committee of the Crusade for World Gover-
nment, "The Plan in Outline (for World Government by 1955)," n.d., c. July 1947,
Schwimmer–Lloyd Collection.

[14] Noel and Violet Rawnsley, "Calling All People: Strike Down the Barriers," *The
Churchman,* 15 September 1943, Schwimmer–Lloyd Collection, N305; Noel and
Violet Rawnsley, "Spark Wanted! Union as a World System," *The Churchman,* 15
September 1944, ibid., N306; "Quotes," *World Government News,* February–March
1945, p. 7; Edith Wynner, Interview, 26 August 1980.

year. He planned to stand for Parliament. The beginning of socialism in Great Britain was the order of political change made possible by the war. Usborne met Robert Lee Humber at the Rawnsleys' and lectured him on socialism, which "shocked" the propertied English couple. Usborne was concerned that internationally the Labour Party was not much advanced over the Tories; only he and a few others were federalists, that is, *European* federalists. (The atomic bomb was still shrouded in the future.) During his New York visit, in addition to the Rawnsleys and Humber, Usborne met Streit, Utah's Paul Thatcher, Tennessee's Fyke Farmer, the League of Nations lawyer Max Habicht, Rosika Schwimmer, and Edith Wynner. The latter two seem to have given him the federalist advice he sought by coming across the sea.[15]

Schwimmer and Wynner argued effectively for universal federation achieved by a direct appeal to the people. They were soon confirmed by events. After Hiroshima, Usborne ceased to advocate European federation and began lobbying for *world* federal government. Then, after disappointment with official British initiatives, he proposed the desperate approach of the peoples' convention.[16]

Response of British Government to the Bomb

There was a period from about August 1945 to November 1946 when the British Government had to formulate a new foreign policy in response to the United Nations, the atomic bomb, and the breakdown in relations with the Soviet Union. The fundamental alternatives were transforming the U.N. into something like a world state or developing a new alliance with the United States and democratic European allies. Henry Usborne was used by the Labour Party to sound out public opinion about federal union, moving acceptance of the king's speech from the throne in November 1946. Soon thereafter, Foreign Secretary Ernest Bevin found it prudent, in the absence of massive support for world government, to turn to what by 1949 would be the North Atlantic treaty, which itself was a wrench for the English people.

Rather typical of the inchoate British policy were brief but profound exchanges on world government between Clement Attlee and Ernest Bevin for the new Labour Government and Anthony Eden and Winston Churchill of the loyal opposition. Prime Minister Attlee said a week after Nagasaki, "We shall have to make a revaluation of the whole situation, especially in the sphere of interna-

---

[15] After the war the Rawnsleys retired to the Isle of Capri, off Italy. They kept in touch with a widespread group of friends—like the Campaign for World Government—who called themselves "the Federalists." "The Companionship grows naturally without pressure, because it meets a need of the human heart: the need to be actively helpful to others in a common cause." Bower Aly, ed., *World Government: The Twenty–Second Annual Debate Handbook,* 2 vols. (Columbia, MO: Artcraft Press, 1948), 2: 33.

[16] Telephone Diary, 3–14 April 1945, Schwimmer–Lloyd Collection, A548; Usborne to Schwimmer and Wynner, 29 August 1945, ibid., T60.

tional relations."[17] In the debate on ratification of the U.N. Charter a week after Attlee's remarks on the atomic bomb, Bevin said:[18]

> The point has been raised in the course of the Debate that everything would be all right if only we had a world State now. In theory I do not disagree, but ... [another speaker remembered] the length of time it had taken to make Great Britain. The only way we could make Great Britain was by handing ourselves over to the Welsh and the Scots....

Bevin explained that no world organization in 1945 could function without the "unanimity of the Great Powers in great matters." If a great power was going to undertake a course of aggression or exercise its veto to permit a small power to commit aggression, "we may as well shut up shop." No U.N. could prevent it without a major war. Peace could be maintained only if the great powers were "reasonably true to the promises which they have made in the Charter." International popular support for the rule of world law was not yet existent. Nevertheless, Usborne, an advocate of a "world State," spoke to Bevin in August and asked him "point blank whether he had thought in terms of political federation." Bevin replied, Usborne reported to the Rawnsleys, "that he believed the troubles in Europe could and should be solved on the economic level and by functional cooperation."[19]

The Charter was ratified, but the new fact of atomic energy was in the air. In November, during the debate over the Truman–Attlee–King declaration calling for the international control of atomic energy, the prime minister explained that the declaration applied not only to atomic weapons but to all weapons of mass destruction. "No one of these weapons has any legitimate place in the armaments which are necessary for ordinary purposes of internal security, or for the protection of the Government against lawlessness," said Attlee.[20]

That aroused Winston Churchill: "Against what?"

"Against lawlessness," the prime minister repeated.

Attlee was followed by Anthony Eden, who explicitly argued that, to control atomic energy, Britain should "abate" her national sovereignty:[21]

> Every succeeding scientific discovery makes greater nonsense of old–time conceptions of sovereignty.... There was the Briand plan after the last war

---

[17] "British Federalists in Parliament," *World Government News*, August 1945, p. 2; Great Britain, Parliament, House of Commons, *Hansard's Parliamentary Debates*, 16 August 1945, H.C. 413, col. 100.

[18] Great Britain, Parliament, House of Commons, *Debate on Ratification of the United Nations Charter*, August 22–23, 1945. *Hansard's Parliamentary Debates*, H.C. 413, cols. 659–755, 861–950; ibid., cols. 947–48, 941–42.

[19] Usborne to the Rawnsleys, 26 November 1945, Schwimmer–Lloyd Collection, T60.

[20] Great Britain, Parliament, House of Commons, *Debate on Foreign Affairs*, 22–23 November 1945, *Hansard's Parliamentary Debates*, H.C. 416, col. 608.

[21] Ibid., cols. 611–13.

for the Federation of Europe.... In the darkest hour of 1940 there was the offer made to France.... I have thought much on this question of atomic energy both before and since that bomb burst on Nagasaki, and for the life of me I have been unable to see, and am still unable to see, any final solution which will make the world safe for atomic power save that we abate our present ideas of sovereignty.

At the conclusion of these words, a voice called out that there was no applause from Eden's Conservative benches.

Usborne's Maiden Speech

The rest of the day was taken up with the maiden speeches of the many new and predominantly young M.P.s. Henry Usborne made his first speech. He had found about 15 fellow M.P.s who agreed with the substance of what he intended to say. The substance was more specific than anything else heard that day on abating national sovereignty:[22]

> I believe that there is only one hope of permanent peace, and that it lies in world government....
> I want to suggest that His Majesty's Government should signify its readiness to form an organic political union with any other country which will accept in principle these conditions:
> A. The Constitution of the Union shall contain a Bill of human rights and thus guarantee political liberty and democracy;
> B. The powers of the federal government of the union shall enable it to coordinate a full employment policy for all the constituent States;
> C. The union shall be disarmed down to the level of its policing commitments, but will at the same time subscribe to the United Nations Organization a sum of money to be agreed by the Security Council as its quota of the cost of the Organization's armed force, and recruit and supply to this armed force a similarly agreed quota of manpower;
> D. The union government will directly own and control all research stations in its area devoted to the development of atomic energy, and undertake to make all the information it discovers, with all laboratories, records and plant, constantly open to inspection by accredited representatives of all other Governments. It has been suggested that the union might be called "The United Commonwealth of Nations."
> Is the proposal fantastic? Is it Utopian? Yes, it is both fantastic and Utopian. It is just as fantastic as the atomic age in which we now live; it is just as Utopian as the hope for world peace. I have suggested in one of the clauses that we should put our armed forces at the disposal of the Security Council, even in spite of the fact that Russia and America now have a veto. Some people will say that is ludicrous. I do not believe that it is ludicrous to expect to break down the suspicion of Russia by doing directly what we believe is right, without waiting for anyone else to do it likewise.

It was natural for a British subject to think in terms of a "United *Common-*

[22] Ibid., cols. 678–81, paragraphing added.

wealth." An echo could be heard here of Lionel Curtis and Philip Kerr's imperial federation. What Usborne proposed was a liberal, democratic union with one economic power to provide for full employment—a Labour Party goal, not incompatible with the domestic policy of the Soviet Union. Point D was very like the emerging Baruch plan in the United States. But point C did not come to grips with the problem of armed states remaining outside the union. Disarmament cannot lead to peace if powerful armed states remain outside, nor can international control of atomic energy eliminate the threat of atomic destruction if some atomic powers do not participate. There is no record of a response to this speech, but in the next year the Labour Government would use Usborne to launch a trial balloon in hopes of avoiding the Cold War.[23]

Bevin's Great Speech for "World Law"

On the next day, 23 November 1945, Bevin returned to the House of Commons to make a speech that went as far as the British Government ever went in favor of "world law." The significance of this speech must be judged with respect to the Dublin conference amendments to the U.N. Charter that Alan Cranston would bring to London in February 1946. It is evident that Bevin for the government and Eden for the opposition clearly saw the world government implications of the international control of atomic energy.

Bevin began with hope for the international control of atomic energy. He tried to allay "suspicions" of Great Britain and announced his purpose to "stretch [the U.N.] to the limit of its capacity from the security point of view." He reviewed the postwar situation in France, Poland, Greece, Persia, and the Netherlands East Indies. Then, about a quarter from the end of his speech, he considered the "question of sovereignty" introduced the day before by Eden. Bevin recalled that he had advocated a "Federation of Europe" as early as 1927, when he succeeded in carrying a favorable resolution at the Trade Union congress of that year. The purpose then was "to prevent any one country dominating another, and to confer the benefit of a great free trade area, with common services in railways, shipping, and all kinds of transport, posts, and customs." He thought now that such a "United States of Europe" would have saved the Weimar Republic. That "regional" idea was still being heard.

But the atomic bomb had rendered European union obsolete. Bevin warned, "The coming of the atomic bomb and other devastating instruments has caused offensive action to jump ahead both of defense and of the machinery of diplomacy." He agreed with Eden that "there must be established a rule of law." He asked how such world law could be established, by governments or by peoples?

[23]Edith Wynner later analyzed the speech: "A. is a slam at Soviet Russia; B. is so phrased as to scare the pants off the USA; C. reminds me of Streit's nuclear Union within the UN confederacy; D. doesn't make any sense at all." Wynner to Usborne, 6 December 1945, Schwimmer–Lloyd Collection, T60. Usborne in this period was trying to find funds to bring Wynner to England to help him, as she put it, "to bring about the miracle of world federation." Wynner to Usborne, 5 October 1945, ibid., T60.

"Will the people feel that the law is their law if it is derived and enforced by the adoption of past methods, whether League of Nations, or Concert of Europe, or anything of that kind? ... Where does the power to make law actually rest? It is not even in this House, it is certainly not in the Executive, it is in the votes of the people. They are sovereign authority."

But the people were not ready, Bevin claimed. Yet he acknowledged the precedents of the federal government of the United States, the federal parliaments in South Africa and in Australia, and Churchill's offer of union to France in 1940. "The fact is, no one ever surrenders sovereignty," he explained, trying to divert opposition; "they merge it into a greater sovereignty."[24]

> I feel we are driven relentlessly along this road: we need a new study for the purpose of creating a world assembly elected directly from the people of the world, as a whole, to whom the Governments who form the United Nations are responsible and who, in fact, make the world law which they, the people, will then accept and be morally bound and willing to carry out. For it will be from their votes that the power will have been derived, and it will be for their direct representatives to carry it out. You may invent all sorts of devices to decide who is the aggressor but, after all the thought you can give to it, the only repository of faith I have ever been able to find to determine that is the common people.
>
> There has never been a war yet which, if the facts had been put calmly before the ordinary folk, could not have been prevented. The fact is they are kept separated from one another. How did Hitler do that? He enslaved Germany with a law as bad as our Vagabond Act of centuries ago, and did not allow anybody to move hither or thither.... The supreme act of Government is the horrible duty of deciding matters which affect the life or death of the people. That power rests in this House as far as this country is concerned. I would merge that power into the greater power of a directly elected world assembly....

Then he made an historic statement:

> I am willing to sit with anybody, of any nation, to try to devise a franchise or a constitution—just as other great countries have done—for a world assembly, as the right hon. Gentleman [Churchill] said, with a limited objective—the objective of peace. ... In the meantime, there must be no weakening of the institution which my right hon. Friends built in San Francisco.... This must not be considered a substitute for it, but rather a completion or development of it, so that the benefit of experience and administration derived in that institution may be carried to its final end. From the moment you accept that, one phrase goes, and that is "international law." That phrase presupposes conflict between nations. It would be replaced by "world law," with a moral force behind it, rather than a law built upon case–made law and agreements. It would be a world law with a world judiciary to interpret it, with a world police to enforce it, with the decision of the people with their own

---

[24] Ibid., cols. 759–87.

votes resting in their own hands, irrespective of race or creed, as the great world sovereign elected authority which would hold in its care the destinies of the people of the world.

Response to Bevin's Speech

But even this speech failed to rouse the Parliament to undertake fundamental new world leadership. Britain was no longer a first–ranking world power, as M.P.s would tell Alan Cranston when he brought the Dublin proposals to London early next year.[25] Usborne reported two months later that "the opinion in the House has been crystallizing on the intention to take the next step through the U.N.O.... I myself have very little hope indeed that U.N.O. will do anything about it, even if the British delegation do propose it." The Dublin proposals Usborne thought futile: "We are not likely to be able to amend the Charter piecemeal. All we can do is to build up pressure to that end until one day the steam blows the lid off and we call a new convention to write an entirely new constitution."[26]

Churchill's Iron Curtain Speech

It was after Bevin's speech, hinting at Britain's willingness to federate with other nations, and after a speech by Stalin warning of war with the capitalist West, that Winston Churchill delivered his historic "iron curtain" address. Speaking on 5 March 1946 at Westminster College, in Fulton, Missouri, with President Truman beside him, Churchill described the challenge of Soviet "tyranny" to the democracies of the West: "From Stettin in the Baltic to Trieste in the Adriatic, an iron curtain has descended across the Continent."[27] In a year's time this speech came to be seen as one of the opening rounds of the Cold War. But from a world government perspective, the solution Churchill proposed, easily overlooked by realist historians, was "common citizenship," growing out of a military alliance of the United States and Britain. This was reminiscent of his proposed union with France on the eve of her destruction.

If They Won't—We Will

Within six months Bevin could not be made to admit he had ever said he would be willing to sit with anybody to devise a world assembly. The realistic policy alternatives were what Bevin was calling *Western union,* in contrast to his rival Churchill's *European union.* (The former became the North Atlantic

[25] "Britain Will Seek Security Congress Not Bound by Veto," *New York Times,* 14 January 1946; Cranston to Clark, 10 March 1946, Clark Papers, 15.1.

[26] Usborne to Wynner, 31 January 1946, Schwimmer–Lloyd Collection, T60. Wynner thought the Dublin proposals were "well stressed," but of course she thought only a peoples' convention was adequate to the task. Wynner to Usborne, 19 February 1946, ibid.

[27] Winston Churchill, "Address Calling for United Effort for World Peace," *New York Times,* 6 March 1946, p. 4. It was in this address that Churchill said, "There is nothing [the Russians] admire so much as strength, and there is nothing they have less respect for than weakness, especially military weakness."

treaty; the latter, the Council of Europe.) Statesmen could not get too far ahead of the people. But Usborne continued to plug for supporters of his ideas, which were becoming clarified. He had virtually taken over the direction of Federal Union. He invited M.P.s to allow their names to be printed on the crusade letterhead. By March 1946, he had almost 40. The slow work of aligning co-workers for so revolutionary an object as world government took most of the year. His activity was not visible again till the Baruch plan negotiations were manifestly failing in the fall of 1946.[28] By October, he made up his mind in a daring little pamphlet calling for an unofficial peoples' convention entitled, *If They Won't—We Will!*[29]

Radical Veterans and Students in America

The scene now shifts to the United States. About the time in 1946 that Henry Usborne was forming a dissident group in Parliament in favor of world government, a radical veteran and student movement formed at Northwestern University north of Chicago. It was first known as Students for Federal World Government (SFFWG); then in 1947 it took the name of World Republic (WR). "Radical" is meant not in the European sense of left–socialist, though there was a tinge of that, but in the American sense of *direct–democratic*.

Students for Federal World Government was a grassroots organization. Its members united spontaneously, very little influenced by the world government movement of the times. One of their most striking innovations—and a secret of their enormous energy—was a requirement that members contribute not *dues* but *one hour's work per week*. At least for one period, a male dormitory was part of headquarters, so the staff actually devoted their *lives* to the organization. They understood outreach; they acquired a printing press and even a radio station, and they were masters of the public rally on a shoestring. They had a sense of symbolism; they acquired a World Republic *flag*—Boris Artzybasheff's rainbow flag, a runner–up in the 1946 contest for a United Nations flag. They tried to raise an independent income from the sale of sponges and the like, though in the end these schemes failed.

The original leaders were World War II veterans who were not about to take a complaisant view of what seemed to them like preparations for World War III. They immediately saw that world government was the goal, if war were to be abolished, and that a peoples' world constitutional convention was the means to get it, since national governments showed hardly any signs of taking the initiative. They were in no position, like Grenville Clark, to engage the Eastern establishment in serious discussion, so the peoples' convention offered them a way to engage ordinary Americans.

Students for Federal World Government then began a kind of inspired, angry

[28] Usborne to Wynner, 5 March 1946, Schwimmer–Lloyd Collection, T60.

[29] "If They Won't, We Will!" n.d., c. October 1946, excerpted in Wynner to Farmer, von Windegger, Gerber, and Rust, 12 October 1946, AORES Papers, 9.3; The Organizational Pattern of the Crusade (privately circulated), 12 January,1947, Stephen Benedict Papers.

mass speaking and letter–writing campaign that first covered Northwestern, then contacted many colleges and universities in the United States and selected ones abroad, and finally tried to reach all strata of society, beginning in a few cities mostly in the Midwest. In their short life (1946–47, though an office lingered on until 1953), Students for Federal World Government or World Republic were the greatest champions, since Rosika Schwimmer, of the peoples' convention approach to world government, as opposed to government–initiated U.N. reform. Theirs was the revolutionary approach, not the evolutionary.

They had two significant achievements. First, their audacity broke the inter-organizational jealousies between Americans United and World Federalists to bring about the merger of five world government mass organizations into United World Federalists in early 1947. Second, their recklessness moved them to send one of their members, Fred Carney, to England in late 1946, where he organized the Student Movement for World Government, precursor to World Student Federalists of late 1947, which repeatedly, despite many name changes, kept the world movement alive down to the 1990s.

Historically, the "World Republic boys," as they came to be affectionately known by their opponents in the mainstream of the movement, represented a stage of a slowly forming, briefly strong popular *will* to take the sovereign power from national governments and redistribute it between a federal world government and the federated national governments. The next stage of this popular movement would be Henry Usborne's Crusade for World Government, whose object was the holding of an actual peoples' convention in Geneva in 1950.[30]

Organizing against *In Loco Parentis*

One of the veterans was Rempfer Lee ("Jack") Whitehouse, a senior and chairman of Anchor and Eagle, who had been seriously wounded in France. Another was David McCoy, sophomore, a navy corpsman. A third was Paul W. Sauer, graduate student, who had had two ships torpedoed under him while serving in the merchant marine. Something of their state of mind is indicated by an editorial McCoy wrote in mid–1946 for the university paper:[31]

> Northwestern veterans are plenty disgusted! They're disgusted with the appalling mental slothfulness of American citizens concerning life–and–death issues before them! ...
>
> The Egyptians order the British out. The Javanese revolt at dominion. The Russo–Turk non-aggression pact has lapsed. Russia wants the Dardanelles. The United States have pledged aid to Turkey. China is locked in Civil War. Russia and the United States are involved in delicate international relations as a result of mutual commitments to the Chinese.
>
> Does all that look like peace?

[30] Their records very nearly perished, but we found them in an attic of former activist Frances Fenner in upstate Afton, New York; they have since been deposited in the University of Chicago's Regenstein Library.

[31] History of Students for Federal World Government, n.d., ante 8 July 1946, p. 1, Regenstein Library, World Republic, Minutes, 1946.

The young men were reading Emery Reves' *The Anatomy of Peace,* as reprinted in the *Reader's Digest,* Robert Lee Humber's Declaration on the Federation of the World, and proposals for a peoples' convention by Georgia Lloyd of the Campaign for World Government.[32] They defined federal world government as follows; with some editorial rearranging, it would become the platform of Students for Federal World Government and World Republic throughout its existence:[33]

1. Universal membership;
2. Transfer of national sovereignty to world sovereignty;
3. A supreme code of world laws based on human rights;
4. One world guard to maintain world laws;
5. Call a constitutional convention—
    Now! It's later than you think!

Campus organizing was not then what it has since become, and before exams that spring the radicals got themselves thrown off campus. The traditions of *In loco parentis* could not accommodate the thousands of mature men and women then flocking to colleges and universities after the war. Whitehouse, Sauer, McCoy, Robert Halverson (former navy flyer), James Andrews, and co-eds Heidi Buchler and Carolyn Karp (married to a former army air force captain) found office space in a garage at 626 ¹/₂ Library Place, one block off campus. There they formally set up Students for Federal World Government. A placard next to the clock said, "It's later than you think." Another sign on the wall of the garage repeated a Chinese proverb: "To see what is right and to fail to do it is the mark of a coward."[34]

Teams of speakers (eight teams of one professor and one student each) went about the campus speaking on world government to some 31 student groups. Thousands of letters describing their program, asking for contributions, and announcing their activities went out. Some 10,000 copies of the U.N. Charter (obtained free from the U.S. State Department) were distributed. Also, 50,000 copies of Representative Jennings Randolph's pre-atomic bomb "Department of Peace" resolution ($138 from the Government Printing Office) were distributed. A very large part of such paperwork must have been wasted effort, but the stud-

[32] Umberto Reinthal, "World Republic" (M.S. thesis, Northwestern University, 1953), pp. 8–9, ibid.; "Veterans Hope Hutchins Will Arouse Sleeping NU," *Daily Northwestern,* n.d., ante March 1946; Reves and Humber reprints in file; Lloyd to John and Charlotte Davenport, 25 February 1946, 23 March 1946, ibid., SFFWG, 1946.

[33] Whitehouse to Ray Allen Billington, 18 March 1946, World Republic Papers, SFFWG, 1946. The leading American historian went no further than to return the letter with approval. He hoped to make a contribution to their cause through his own historical writing.

[34] History, p. 3; "NU Students Organize for World Federation," *Daily Northwestern,* 3 May 1946, ibid., SFFWG, 1946; "300 at N.U. Join Fight for a World Government," *Chicago Sun,* 15 May 1946.

ents addressed their appeals to everybody, and they could hardly be blamed, as the world began to divide between East and West, for sending them out broadside.

By May, membership had grown to about 300. Three pairs of students visited 60 schools in the East and Midwest through May, including Oberlin (Ohio), Vassar (New York), Syracuse (New York), and Wesleyan (Connecticut). The student president of the Vassar Student Federalist chapter wrote a typical positive acceptance: "I've seen enough of the small interest stirred up by some of our best speakers not to be too optimistic, but if your speakers are willing to come under these circumstances, we should be happy to have them." A typical negative reply came from the president of the International Relations club of the Illinois Institute of Technology: "Judging from ... the nature of your organization, we wish to inform you that our interest in your project has ended."[35]

Lining Up Einstein to Speak at First Mass Rally

Then, carried away by their enthusiasm, the board of SFFWG decided at the beginning of May 1946 to hold a mass rally in the Chicago Stadium (capacity 20,000) for Memorial Day at the end of the month. Businessmen told them they were "crazy" to try to do in four weeks what normally took six months. The rental was $9,500. The students characteristically decided that to draw a crowd, the rally should be open to the public for *free*. Attractive speakers would also be necessary. So Whitehouse and Sauer got in a fellow member's car, drove to New York, and knocked on the doors of prominent Americans who in the students' judgment were likely to be sympathetic.

They secured promises to speak from Socialist party leader Norman Thomas, quota force advocate Ely Culbertson, and popular master of ceremonies Clifton Fadiman. Then they drove to Washington, D.C., spoke to about 20 congressmen about federal world government, and secured a promise from Senator Glen Taylor. Still not satisfied, they drove to Princeton, knocked without introduction on the door of Albert Einstein, found the great scientist in bed with a dictionary open to the Qs, and coolly asked him to speak, too, if not in person, then by radio. "Well," Einstein replied, the bed lamp shining on his long white hair, "I am not a very good speaker, but if you think it will do any good for me to speak, I'll do it."[36]

Meanwhile, members back at the garage were busy with all the complicated arrangements to smoothly bring off a mass rally. The mail operation went into high gear. A souvenir program was prepared. A federal world government essay contest, with prizes totaling $1,000, open only to high school and college stud-

---

[35] History, pp. 7–8, 10; Susan Ervin to Sauer, 16 May 1946; Mercedes E. Hurley to Sauer, 4 May 1946, ibid., SFFWG, 1946.

[36] History, pp. 9–11; "Top Speakers for Peace Rally 'Won' by Students' Confidence," *Christian Science Monitor*, 13 June 1946; "Three Youths and an Idea Enlist Einstein to Speak to Rally Here," *Chicago Sun*, 20 May 1946. SFFWG also had rejections from Harlow Shapley, Harold Urey, Fiorello Laguardia, Sumner Welles, Charles Lindbergh, Raymond Swing, Helen Hayes, Harold Stassen, Trygve Lie, and Harry Truman.

ents attending the rally, was announced. Radio hookups with ABC for Chicago broadcast were made to carry Einstein's message from Princeton. When funds became absolutely critical, members dug into their own pockets; Whitehouse himself cashed his war bonds of $1,100 and closed out his bank account of $346 for the cause. Bob Halverson got permission from the mayor's office to fly over the Loop and drop thousands of leaflets advertising the rally. A parade of students, bearing signs saying "Chicago Stadium Peace Rally" and "Tomorrow's World Today," marched from State and Randolph Streets on the day of the rally.[37]

At the rally, Ely Culbertson in person effectively explained how anarchy is the "one cause" of wars. But he concluded with his current "indispensable" amendments to the U.N. Charter, which fell short of creating a world government to end the anarchy. Norman Thomas warned against army opinion still being heard that after atomic attack the United States would still have the "will to win." He urged that advocates of world government not neglect the racial discriminations, social injustices, economic inequalities, and rival imperialisms that would undo the best–laid "formula" of arms control. Senator Taylor urged the audience to "do something," as had the "exuberant" youths who organized the rally. Where there is a will, he affirmed, "mountains can be moved." Clifton Fadiman spoke, probably too optimistically, of a coming political struggle between a "pre-Hiroshima" party and a "post-Hiroshima" party.

Einstein spoke (by radio link–up) briefly and realistically on the political situation and the nature of the federal solution. "Real power" since the end of the war, he observed, remained in the hands of only the United States and the Soviet Union. A general agreement between those two would "cause the other nations to give up their sovereignty to the degree necessary for the establishment of military security for all." But the United States shared the blame, Einstein charged, for the antagonism of the Soviet Union. "There was no need to manufacture new atomic bombs without letup and to appropriate $12 billion for defense in a year [fiscal 1946] in which no military threat was to be expected for the nearest future." The work for young people was to alleviate the mistrust caused by such policy errors in order to make agreement on a federal world order possible.[38]

The rally drew about 5,000. SFFWG leaders were privately disappointed, though publicly they maintained the rally had been a "giant" success. Considering how far the World Republic boys had come, this public attitude had some

[37] History, pp. 10–11; "Want 'One World' Now," *Chicago Times,* 29 May 1946; "Stadium Rally Tonight Will Hear Einstein," *Chicago Sun,* 29 May 1946; Program, Tomorrow's World Today, n.d, c. 29 May 1946, World Republic Papers, SFFWG, 1946; "Ex-Sergeant Gives Life Savings to Peace Cause," *San Francisco News,* 22 July 1946.

[38] Addresses, World Republic Papers, SFFWG, 1946. Supportive messages were also sent by Robert Lee Humber, Emery Reves, and Robert M. Hutchins. Culbertson had just published another small book along his usual lines, *Must We Fight Russia?* (Philadelphia: John C. Winston, [May] 1946).

merit. The historical significance of the Chicago Stadium rally of 29 May 1946 was that a new active spirit began to stir in the world government movement.

Spirit of Students for Federal World Government

As the History of SFFWG truly said, "THEY WERE DOING SOMETHING." Had Federal Union or World Federalists or Americans United or Student Federalists ever had a rally on this order, reaching out to the unconverted and bringing 5,000 of the general population to a rally for peace? Had demonstrators carrying signs for federal world government or airplanes dropping flyers for a world government rally ever been seen before? Where else had hundreds of students, even if inefficiently, worked 18 hours a day, sacrificed their life savings, and dropped out of school (as Whitehouse and the other leaders did in May) for the abolition of war?[39]

The spirit of Students for Federal World Government seems to have burst forth full–blown. Perhaps the experience of the war was the strongest immediate factor, but Christian nonviolence was also at work. Whitehouse had lost a brother in action. He returned to Northwestern to study for the Episcopal ministry and soon grew impatient. He replied to an older man who had criticized him for seeking some easier way for eliminating greed, hatred, envy, and jealousy from the human heart than spiritualizing:[40]

> I myself ... feel at this moment that the true philosophy of the Master has
> been so perverted that it is almost unrecognizable. The church has been
> "spiritualizing" for almost twenty centuries now and each war is getting
> worse.

World government was the only means he could find now to reach the "universal brotherhood of man and permanent peace." "The idea is simple," said McCoy; "only the work is hard." "It isn't easy ... but we must be prepared to make sacrifices if we are to live at all. We must now think until it hurts. We must act wisely and swiftly."[41]

Principles of a Progressive Movement

Later in 1946, during one of the several times when Students for Federal World Government were considering merger with Harris Wofford's Student Federalists, the former students explained that they were reluctant to join forces with existing federalist organizations "because it seemed to us that their programs were not making the swift progress which had to be made if we were to avert a war." The radicals then laid down their principles for a progressive world gov-

---

[39] Sauer to John O. Levinson, 31 May 1946; Whitehouse to James N. Wright, 20 June 1946; History, p. 13, World Republic Papers, SFFWG, 1946.

[40] Whitehouse to Charles S. La Berge, 17 June 1946, ibid., SFFWG, 1946.

[41] "Center of Youth Drive for Peace," *Roosevelt College Torch*, 6 June 1946; Irving Pflaum, "Later Than You Think," *Chicago Times*, 18 May 1946.

ernment movement:[42]

    1. That emphasis be placed solely on the movement—the idea—rather than the organization. Our goals can not be accomplished through the development of an organization, but only through the development of a movement among the people.
    2. That the movement plan a maximum program—as the urgency of the times demands—and depend upon the people to respond to the need, rather than bind itself to a rigid budget based upon fixed income which results in an inflexible program.
    3. The program of the movement must have no restrictions imposed externally. Spontaneity must not be sacrificed to the regulations of a university or the inertia of influential financial contributors. Thus the dynamic quality of a movement will be maintained.
    4. That the basic membership requirement of the movement be that each member work one hour per week (at least) if he is to retain his membership. We consider this more important in terms of individual interest as well as community action than the payment of dues.
    5. That the movement derive its strength from the people themselves—the grassroots of society—and not from the mastheads of prominent citizens.

They went on to propose a "federation of the federalists," loss of their name, even loss of their identity, so long as an effective movement could be set going to achieve federal world government.
On 9 July 1946, the first issue appeared of SFFWG's irregular little journal, *The Planet*. It was given that title because on 6 August 1945, separate national sovereignties were "blown out" of existence. The lead article was a reprinting of Bernard Baruch's speech before the U.N. AEC.[43]

---

    [42] McCoy to Dorothy Nessler, 10 July 1946, World Republic Papers, Minutes, 1946.
    [43] *The Planet,* 9 July 1946, ibid., Envelope Vol. 2, No. 1.

10

The Baruch Plan for the International Control of Atomic Energy

> It went boom and it killed millions of people and I thought it
> was an ethical and political problem and I would proceed on
> that theory.
>
> —Bernard Baruch to Herbert B. Swope, 16 June 1947

Significance of the Plan

In mid–1946, prompted by the atomic scientists and motivated by a realistic concern to prevent an atomic arms race and possibly a nuclear third world war, the United States proposed to surrender its ultimate weapon to an authority representative of all the nations in the world. The U.S. plan for the international control of atomic energy was introduced in the U.N. Atomic Energy Commission by financier and "advisor to presidents" Bernard Baruch; hence it is known as the Baruch plan. This extraordinary plan, in which a modern sovereign state renounced nuclear war, was plainly conceived at the time as a step toward ultimate world federal government. In retrospect many historians have tried to understand why the plan failed. A third world war has not yet come, but in another year what would be called the Cold War definitely did. Why did the plan fail? What are the lessons for the future?

A current consensus holds that Americans were as insincere in their proposal as the Russians were obdurate in rejecting it. Larry Gerber, who has surveyed the sources and literature, concludes that Baruch's "realism" about U.S. national security as a world power, combined with his "Wilsonian internationalism" aimed at a liberal capitalist world order and supported by similar attitudes and assumptions of other American policy makers, "prevented them from considering the possibility of agreement on anything but American terms."[1] Gregg Herken has found that belief in the atomic bomb as the "winning weapon" in the war with Japan and then in the diplomatic conflict with the Soviet Union undermined the reluctant conviction among American policy makers, including Baruch, that control of atomic energy should be surrendered to an impartial international au-

---

[1] Larry G. Gerber, "The Baruch Plan and the Origins of the Cold War," *Diplomatic History*, 6 (Winter 1982): 95.

thority. But reliance on the bomb, because it ushered in the nuclear arms race, produced not victory but the "illusion of security."[2]

Joseph Lieberman called the Baruch plan "a disastrous failure in statecraft" —the guilt and responsibility for which he saw shared by both the United States and the Soviet Union, though he particularly blamed American ignorance of Russian history and postwar defense interests. Failure was consequence and cause of the Cold War; the two powers seemed to have cast themselves adrift toward the latter of Baruch's two alternatives in 1946 "between the quick and the dead."[3] Barton Bernstein similarly has concluded that "neither the United States nor the Soviet Union was prepared in 1945 or 1946 to take the risks that the other power required for agreement," such as sharing atomic secrets or destroying the bomb stockpile as the Russians demanded, or submitting to controls and inspections that would interfere in economic affairs as the Americans did.[4] Lloyd Gardner saw Baruch as an "architect of illusion," a founder of the Cold War, whose plan functioned merely to "free Americans of any uneasy feelings about going ahead with the arms race."[5] Daniel Yergin passed over the Baruch plan in just a few pages—so transparently "impossible," during the conflict over Germany, did he think was agreement on the international control of atomic energy.[6]

The Nearest U.S. Approach to World Government

In our view of the record, recent historians have overlooked the idealistic influences of the time, the most extreme of which was the diffuse, but vocal, movement for world federal government. Their histories tend to be trenchant critiques of the "realist" conduct of foreign policy, without leaving the reader with a clear sense of a better alternative for the future. If the history of the Baruch plan is "the story of a disastrous failure in statecraft," what might have been a success? If the national security state has given us only "the illusion of security," what could give us real security and permanent peace?

A thesis of this book is that the Baruch plan was the nearest approach to a world government proposal offered by the United States; that such a proposal could have been more "fair" to the Russians, who in the circumstances of 1946 probably would still have rejected it but would at least not have been alarmed by the deceptiveness of the plan actually offered; and that the story of the failure to make the plan a complete world government proposal casts a sidelight on the or-

---

[2] Gregg Herken, *The Winning Weapon: The Atomic Bomb in the Cold War, 1945–1950* (New York: Knopf, 1980), 171–91, 342.

[3] Joseph I. Lieberman, *The Scorpion and the Tarantula: The Struggle to Control Atomic Weapons, 1945–1949* (Boston: Houghton Mifflin, 1970), ix, 399, 411–12.

[4] Barton J. Bernstein, "The Quest for Security: American Foreign Policy and International Control of Atomic Energy, 1942–1946," *Journal of American History*, 60 (March 1974): 1044.

[5] Lloyd C. Gardner, *Architects of Illusion: Men and Ideas in American Foreign Policy, 1941–1949* (Chicago: Quadrangle, 1970), 192–201, 318.

[6] Daniel Yergin, *Shattered Peace: The Origins of the Cold War and the National Security State* (Boston: Houghton Mifflin, 1977), 237–42.

igins of the Cold War and offers some guidance for a way out of the present arms race.

Long study of great power politics may incline us to forget the hope and willingness to create new international institutions that characterized the last year of World War II and at least a year thereafter. The war had been a "people's war" not only in the Soviet Union but also in the United States, Great Britain, and the other United Nations. About 125 million people had been put into uniform on all sides during the war. Soldiers and people on the home front throughout the world were determined that never again would there be another general war. "Practically every soldier has asked for the elimination of war," Baruch noted in an early policy draft.[7] Statesmen were willing to bring their nations into closer relations within a general security organization, the exact structure of which was somewhat undecided. Secretary of State Cordell Hull said after the Moscow declaration of 1943 that "there will no longer be need for spheres of influence, for alliances, for balance of power."[8] Former ambassador to Russia William C. Bullitt declared about the same time to a world federalist convention: "After a great war like this there comes a brief moment when world affairs are in a period of flux, ... or as Tom Paine would have put it, when 'we have it in our power to begin the world over again.'"[9] David E. Lilienthal recalled as late as March 1946, when his board was drafting the first U.S. proposal on the international control of atomic energy: "This was a rare period which led to an elevation of feeling in the country that impossible things can be done."[10] Between these years the United Nations Organization was established without a rejection by the U.S. Senate nor an exclusion of the U.S.S.R. under the Communist party. The organization was still a league of sovereign states, however, like the discredited League of Nations, and some veterans were dissatisfied that all the sacrifices in the war had achieved so little.[11]

The Acheson–Lilienthal Report

How did the Baruch plan arise? In the same month that the atomic scientists' *One World or None* came out, March 1946, the Acheson–Lilienthal "Report on the International Control of Atomic Energy" was released by the U.S. State Department. The report was more specific and coherent than anything written by the scientists on exactly what was meant by the international control of atomic energy. President Truman, Prime Minister Clement Attlee, and Mackenzie King

---

[7] Memo, 31 May, 1946, Bernard Baruch Papers, 52.4 [Seeley Mudd Library, Princeton University].

[8] "Secretary Hull's Report on Moscow Conference to Meeting of Senate and House," *New York Times,* 19 November 1943.

[9] William C. Bullitt, Address to third annual convention of Federal Union, November 1943, quoted by Harris Wofford, Address to first convention of Student Federalists, 1 April 1944, private Wofford papers.

[10] Quoted in Herken, *Winning Weapon,* 156 n.

[11] Cord Meyer Jr., "A Serviceman Looks at the Peace," *Atlantic Monthly,* September 1945, pp. 43–48.

of Canada issued a declaration on 15 November 1945 that made international control a goal of Western foreign policy. Then Foreign Ministers V. M. Molotov, Ernest Bevin, and James F. Byrnes issued a declaration on 27 December 1945 that proposed formation of the United Nations Atomic Energy Commission (U.N. AEC) in order to bring such control into reality.

The atomic scientists had a background influence, but Vannevar Bush, chief civilian administrator of the atomic bomb project, was the one who most immediately suggested a study committee to Secretary of State Byrnes. On 7 January 1946, he appointed a Committee on Atomic Energy "to study the subject of controls and safeguards necessary to protect this Government." It consisted of Dean Acheson, undersecretary of State, chairman; David E. Lilienthal, chairman of the Tennessee Valley Authority; and eight other members and consultants, most notably J. Robert Oppenheimer. The board worked full–time for about seven weeks, visiting Oak Ridge and Los Alamos and consulting with numerous scientists, industrial experts, and geologists. Discouraged at the beginning, they ended in a spirit of "hopefulness." As Lilienthal reported: "That hopefulness grew not out of any preconceived "solution" but out of a patient and time–consuming analysis and understanding of the facts that throw light on the various alternatives that we explored."[12]

International Control of Atomic Energy to Acheson–Lilienthal

The Acheson–Lilienthal report, which was the direct precursor of the Baruch plan, was written in the scientists' spirit that looked beyond even the international control of atomic energy to the "end of all war." Lilienthal, Oppenheimer, and the other main authors recognized the revolutionary nature of atomic weapons, the inadequacy of conventional defense, the lack of scientific secrets that would prevent other nations from developing similar weapons, and hence the necessity for international control. The United States had a monopoly of atomic weapons in 1946, but the situation would be changed "profoundly," they wrote, in "five to twenty years."

Repeatedly, the authors returned to a broader theme. They found "hope and some reason to believe that in solving [the problem of atomic energy by international means], new patterns of cooperative effort could be established which would be capable of extension to other fields, and which might make a contribution toward the gradual achievement of a greater degree of community among the peoples of the world." The Truman–Attlee–King declaration of the previous November had asserted that "the only complete protection for the civilized world from the destructive use of scientific knowledge lies in the prevention of war." Cooperative effort among nations offered hope of "solving the problem of war

---

[12] U.S. Department of State, [Dean Acheson, David E. Lilienthal, et al.,] "A Report on the International Control of Atomic Energy," Pub. 2498, 16 March 1946; Raymond Dennett and Robert K. Turner, eds., *Documents on American Foreign Relations, July 1, 1945 – December 31, 1946,* vol. 8 (Princeton: Princeton University Press for World Peace Foundation, 1948), 547–50 (abridged); Smith, *A Peril,* 451–54.

itself."[13]

The actual proposals of the Acheson–Lilienthal group—particularly an international atomic development authority instead of a prohibitory convention or "police–like" inspection system—were cautious, it is true, but it could not be said that they were motivated by a desire to preserve American atomic superiority, as some historians now say of the Baruch plan.[14] The report's authors were convinced that "our monopoly cannot last." They explicitly set out the transition steps to international control: transfer to the authority of U.S. theoretical information, then raw materials, then production plants at Oak Ridge and Hanford, then stockpiles of fissionable materials and atomic bombs, and finally the Los Alamos bomb plant (though they left the timing of the transition to negotiation). Most boldly, they candidly discussed the great political problem of the authority to establish a "strategic balance" among the nations.[15]

On the other hand, it could not be said that Acheson and Lilienthal proposed world government. They placed the authority under the U.N. Security Council, never mentioning the veto, since they assumed that enforcement among great powers was impossible without war. All that could be immediately hoped for was an *early warning system*, which would be in the interest of every nation to maintain. No constitutional or legal enforcement system was proposed. Deliberate seizure, by a national government (or even a revolutionary group), of atomic energy plants in its territory would be a warning of aggressive intent; other nations would respond by seizing their own plants, converting them to weapons production (3 to 12 months was thought to be the likely lead time), and preparing for nuclear war.[16] This last concept was the one that Baruch challenged.

Bernard Baruch

On the day when the Acheson–Lilienthal group completed their report, President Truman and Secretary Byrnes agreed to nominate public servant Bernard M. Baruch to be U.S. delegate to the U.N. Atomic Energy Commission. His vanity may have been "enormous," as Lilienthal said, but, at 75, Baruch was conscious of the honor and of his historic opportunity. He was accorded the greatest respect in Washington (the Senate confirmed his appointment without requiring his appearance). He insisted upon, and received, a part in determining policy.[17]

---

[13] [Dean Acheson, David E. Lilienthal, et al.,] "A Report on the International Control of Atomic Energy" (Washington, DC: U.S. Department of State Publication No. 2498, 16 March 1946), 2–3, 27, 46–47.

[14] Herken, *Winning Weapon*, 166–67 ("Pax Atomica"); Yergin, *Shattered Peace*, 240 (U.S. "advantage"); Gardner, *Architects*, 200 (U.S. atomic "peacemaking"); John W. Spanier and Joseph L. Nogee, *The Politics of Disarmament: A Study in Soviet–American Gamesmanship* (New York: Praeger, 1962), 58 ("psychological warfare").

[15] Acheson–Lilienthal "Report," 46–48, 50, 42.

[16] Ibid., 40, 42, 47.

[17] Baruch to Truman, 26 March 1946, U.S. Department of State, *Foreign Relations of the United States*, 1946, 1: 767–68; Byrnes to Baruch, 19 April 1946, ibid., 1: 777–78.

Through March and April 1946, he was busy assembling his team of associates, reading the Acheson–Lilienthal report, and considering various alternatives, including world government. The State Department policy toward the U.N. at this time still professed to favor "the rule of law among nations" in order to "banish the scourge of war from the earth."[18] Even the joint chiefs of staff, when they were exploring activation of the U.N.'s military staff committee (Articles 46–47), were on record in favor of an educational program to hurry "establishment of the regime of world law and order."[19] The objective was called an Atomic Development Authority (ADA).

Bernard Baruch was somewhat notorious in American annals as a Wall Street speculator who rose to the widely accorded stature of "elder statesman." In the 1890s, starting as an office boy in a linen business, he came to associate with such figures as Thomas Fortune Ryan, John ("Bet a Million") Gates, railroad baron E. W. Harriman, oil king John D. Rockefeller, steel magnate J. Pierpont Morgan, and mining monopolists Meyer and Daniel Guggenheim. By the turn of the century, Baruch, at age 30, had risen to partnership in a brokerage firm and made his first million dollars. Over the years he continued to amass a fortune from the stock market.

In 1916 President Wilson appointed him to the Advisory Commission of the Council of National Defense. In early 1918 Baruch became chairman of the War Industries Board, which he soon developed into an exemplary agency for military–industrial cooperation in time of war. In 1919 he served on the Supreme Economic Council at Versailles and advised President Wilson on the terms of peace. Later, Baruch, a Democrat, supported the president on his League fight in the Senate. Twenty years later the elder statesman was again brought to Washington to advise President Roosevelt on mobilization, especially in setting up the War Production Board under Sears, Roebuck executive Donald Nelson (not Baruch's nominee). Baruch himself held no administrative position. An industrialist who worked with Baruch in this period later recalled his "simplicity and judicial reasonableness." Baruch's appointment by President Truman as American representative to the U.N. AEC at age 75 was his last major public responsibility, though he continued to make himself available as advisor to presidents until Eisenhower's administration.[20]

Baruch's hand–picked delegation to the U.N. AEC had more to recommend them than association with him on Wall Street. They were: Herbert B. Swope, reporter and editor for the *New York World* and member of the War Industries

---

[18] Department of State, Foreign Policy of the United States, 1 December 1945, ibid., 1: 712–14.

[19] Joint Chiefs of Staff to State–War–Navy Coordinating Committee, Guidance as to the Military Implications of a United Nations Commission on Atomic Energy, 23 January 1946, ibid., 1: 748–49.

[20] *Encyclopedia Britannica*, 15th ed. (1979), s.v. "Baruch, Bernard (Mannes)," 1: 847; Bernard M. Baruch, *Baruch: The Public Years* (New York: Holt, Rinehart & Winston, 1960), 1–2, 293–94, 357–82; Holliday to Clark, 12 October 1946, Clark Papers, 21.10.

Board; John Hancock, investment banker and assistant to Baruch at the Office of War Mobilization; Ferdinand Eberstadt, member of the War Production Board; and Fred Searls, president of Newmont Mining Corp. and assistant to Byrnes in the Office of War Mobilization.

Goal of the Abolition of War

Baruch's original idea for discussion with the State Department was that the U.N. should be "strengthened." His aide John Hancock asked Undersecretary Acheson, "What if the Russians or someone else should ... want to strengthen the United Nations—then what would be the answer?" Acheson squelched the idea: "There would be no power in the United Nations to pass legislation along those lines." The foundation of the atomic development authority "had to be a *Treaty.*"[21] This effectively meant no U.N. Charter revision, since that would require a new grant of sovereignty. Within such a constraint, the team nevertheless pressed for the abolition of war. Baruch's second aide, Ferdinand Eberstadt, suggested that goal:[22]

> One thing is certain. The release of atomic energy will revolutionize the world. The great uncertainty is whether this revolution will be for the betterment of mankind or for its destruction. There is one power on earth greater even than the release of atomic energy. That is the determination of all peoples that war shall end. The true measure of our success will be the nearness of our approach to this goal.

Baruch himself on 7 May, in the earliest record of his thought, set the goal as the "elimination of war." He had in mind stopping the manufacture of atomic bombs, *subsequent* establishment of an international atomic control agency, enlargement of its functions to include control of conventional weapons, elimination of the veto power, world command of all armed forces, reduction of national forces to police levels, constitutional prohibitions in all countries against resort to war analogous to the clause General MacArthur had inserted into the Japanese constitution, and enlarged courts "to decide all ... questions by arbitrament of reason rather than by arbitrament of force." "This may seem like an ambitious program," Baruch commented, "but here is the opportunity to go towards the light at the end of the tunnel—eternal peace."[23]

Reports by the Carnegie Endowment for International Peace in Baruch's files indicate a lively debate at the time between atomic scientists who advocated "speedy adoption of World Government" and cautious political scientists who thought "international controls of fissionable materials should lie within the

---

[21] Memo of Conversation by John Hancock, 1 May 1946, Baruch Papers, 52.4; also in *Foreign Relations,* 1946, 1: 782.

[22] Ferdinand Eberstadt to Boss, 6 May 1946, Baruch Papers, 52.4.

[23] Draft [for Discussion], 7 May 1946, ibid. "Eternal" crossed out in typescript.

field of the United Nations."[24] A study by the prominent professor of international law Quincy Wright provided for an atomic energy commission to "make
recommendations to the Security Council or the General Assembly by majority
vote" and, like the Russians later, provided for *national* criminal prosecution of
offenders.[25] The highly articulate Marine Corps veteran Cord Meyer Jr., on
whom many eyes were focused as an able spokesman for peace and who would
become the first president of United World Federalists, submitted a first–rate
world government critique of the Acheson–Lilienthal proposal. He concentrated
on the ambiguities in the transfer stages and the need for fundamental U.N. reform to end the international anarchy. Baruch did not reply, but actually Meyer
seems to have been articulating the older man's looser thought.[26] J. Robert Oppenheimer gave Baruch a clear briefing on the world government implications of
the international control of atomic energy. There could be "no prevention of war
unless international law could apply to the citizens of nations, as federal law does
to those of states." What was needed, he wrote, was "an appropriate delegation
of national sovereignty," a "world government in the field of atomic energy."[27]

The Problem of Enforcement

Talk of world government like this in the U.S. delegation, amidst the many
technical concerns about uranium ores, ownership or dominion over potentially
dangerous activities, and other matters implied in the Acheson–Lilienthal report,
produced an "explosion," to use the word of the official historians, at the Blair–
Lee house in mid–May. The plan purported to provide "controls and safeguards,"
said H. B. Swope, Baruch's third in line. What would happen if a "definite violation" occurred? Hancock recommended "penalties for infringement." The truth
is, added Eberstadt, the plan does not "abolish atomic warfare." The public
should be so informed.

To this outburst by Baruch's chief aides, Acheson retorted that there were
only two ways to go further than the Lilienthal board—collective security, in
which all nations would bind themselves by treaty to go to war against a viola-

---

[24] James T. Shotwell, Report of Progress, 5 April 1946, Baruch Papers, 56. One of
the atomic scientists was Columbia's I. I. Rabi, who advocated "effective international government." Shotwell replied: "Mr. Rabi might have logic on his side but in politics logic is seldom the guide. The policies adopted by the peoples of the world are
more often creatures of history than of reason.... If we try for too high stakes, if we
were to be misled by the mirage of world government, we might fail in our task and
bring the whole structure down. We cannot gamble with the future of humanity."
Minutes of Committee on Atomic Energy, 11 May 1946, ibid. Both Baruch and State
rejected a Carnegie draft treaty because it provided for virtually no international control.

[25] Quincy Wright, Draft for a Convention on Development and Control of Atomic
Energy, 1 May 1946, ibid. Wright's proposal was first published in *Bulletin of the
Atomic Scientists,* 1 April 1946, pp. 11–13. It was probably the most legally strict
and politically neutral of all proposals for the international control of atomic energy.

[26] Cord Meyer Jr., Hope or Illusion, 29 May 1946, Baruch Papers, 52.4.

[27] Oppenheimer, Atomic Explosives, pp. 7–8.

tor, and "world government," which would treat all wars as civil wars. The first meant little, and the second not a "damned thing."[28] Later, Acheson explained his contempt for world government. "He said that any organization, any government, is based on the emotional, spiritual acceptance of it by 95% of the people. When you have 20% of the people who are not going along, the government just does not work.... This is true in our own country with our strikes and labor difficulties.... It has been true with the British in Ireland, and [in] Palestine, [and] in India."[29] The upshot was that Baruch found State extremely reluctant to reconsider its Acheson–Lilienthal proposal. This fact would have disastrous consequences on the subsequent negotiations.

For the next three weeks until Truman's 7 June decision on policy, Baruch and his aides chafed against the restrictions of the State Department. They seem to have been swept up in honest enthusiasm for their task, if not intellectually prepared for its full implications. Control of all weapons of mass destruction, intervention in domestic affairs by either an inspecting or owning control agency, supremacy or subordination of the international authority to national authorities, conflicts of obedience of military officers to the authority or to heads of states, reliable finances not dependent on national contributions, penalties for violators, the necessity to prevent—not win—the next war: these political implications of an international atomic development authority had begun to puzzle the Baruch team. Perusal of the record indicates not that Baruch was devising some Machiavellian scheme to dominate Russia but that he sincerely wished to establish an international atomic energy control system, while carefully guarding American security. Later, during the negotiations, his American concerns got the better of his internationalism. But in this formative period, he and his team took internationalism seriously, including the alternative of world government, such as it was presented at the time.[30]

---

[28] [J. P. Davis,] Notes on Conference at Blair–Lee House, 17 May 1946, ibid.; Richard G. Hewlett and Oscar E. Anderson Jr., *A History of the United States Atomic Energy Commission*, vol. 1: *The New World, 1939–1946* (University Park, PA, 1962), 563–66.

[29] Memo of Conversation [between Acheson and Baruch] by John C. Ross, 2 November 1946, *Foreign Relations*, 1946, 1: 985.

[30] It was in *this* period that Hancock began to hedge on ownership of uranium and thorium ores, production plants, fissionable materials, and power stations, in favor of "dominion," since a number of capitalists had expressed fear that the Acheson–Lilienthal plan would be "the first step to an international socialized State." Hancock thought ownership of the ores in the ground, in addition to inspection, would be sufficient, without owning the plants, materials, and stations. Even so, there would be much interference with local economies. That was necessary "for national safety." Hancock certainly did not have world government in mind. He seems to have imagined the ADA as a sort of international war industries board. Still, he saw the necessity for personal responsibility to the authority and for amending national constitutions accordingly. Memo of Conversation by John M. Hancock, 1 June 1946, *Foreign Relations*, 1946, 1: 817–24. Cf. Gardner, *Architects*, 193–94; Lieberman, *Scorpion*, 276.

Baruch continued his thinking on "outlawing war." To prohibitions against the atomic bomb, he suggested adding others against bombers, rockets, and biological warfare. He brought in the precedent of the Nuremberg trials for individual responsibility. An "agency" would supervise the courts and an international police force, after standing armies were eliminated. He imagined:[31]

> There would be turned loose the energies of mankind and these would be used to look forward with hope to the development of their bodies and spirit, and the comforts of education for themselves and their children. It would release more energy than atomic energy could develop.

He perceived that "automatic penalization" or enforcement was essential to a workable plan. "Unless teeth are put into action, [the] public (the American and the World) will dismiss [the] plan as merely a pious wish."[32] In an interview with Byrnes on 30 May, Baruch fully developed his ideas—especially inclusion of "all other major weapons adaptable to mass destruction," to conform to the terms of reference of the U.N. AEC, and enlargement of the "International Court or Tribunal," in order to provide sure enforcement on individuals as at Nuremberg. "Why not try to do the thing which must be done," Baruch concluded, "rather than do something piecemeal [like the Acheson–Lilienthal proposal] which would raise hopes for peace, but never quiet the fears of war?"[33]

In the next few days, a deep policy dispute developed between Baruch and Acheson on the issue of penalties. As so often in the 1940s, the dispute was over nascent conceptions of world government versus the traditions of nationalism.[34] Hancock explained that, in the Baruch team's conception, the international control of atomic energy implied limitations of national sovereignty: "Any international control is going to involve some surrender of jurisdiction." No great power could be allowed to defy the judgments of the international authority. But that ran straight against the veto provision in the U.N. Charter. Hancock struggled to find a way to limit the veto power without opening the question of

---

[31] War hurries things that are in the making, 22 May 1946, Baruch Papers, 52.4.

[32] BMB Agenda, 23 May 1946, ibid.

[33] Draft of Mr. Baruch's talk to JFB, 26 May 1946, ibid.; B.M.B. Memo, 31 May 1946, ibid. Hancock attended this interview and found that State was giving very little thought to the international control of atomic energy. When Baruch asked Byrnes what his policies were, Byrnes replied, "Oh, hell, I have none. What are your views?" Memo of Conversation [between Baruch, Byrnes, Hancock, and Acheson] by John M. Hancock, 30 May 1946, *Foreign Relations,* 1946, 1: 802–06.

[34] The historian D. F. Fleming, who was a trusted consultant to Baruch at this time, urged him to seek "the elimination of war itself." He should avoid "the method of simple renunciation, unsupported by effective guarantees of security and armament limitation," as had been tried without success in the 1920s. "This time we must take the hard road of setting up controls and establishing institutions to make them work. ... We cannot admit that man is gaining the infinite secrets of the universe itself only as a means for his own destruction." D. F. Fleming, 27 May 1946, Baruch Papers, 52.4.

U.N. revision. It was an impossible task, but he thought he had it in specific penalties for crimes relating to atomic energy, in which cases the veto would be disallowed. "The essence of our suggestions regarding penalties is that this may be a way of getting around the veto. There isn't any use in blinking that fact. Otherwise, penalty for violation will not be immediate and certain."[35] He elaborated the "crimes" (e.g., seizure of an ADA plant) but he did not define the legal recourse.[36] On whom were the punishments to be inflicted? States or individuals? What would be the nature of the punishments? War or police action?

Baruch never gave clear answers to these questions, except to hint that he had in mind strengthening the U.N., enlarging the World Court, and creating an international police force.[37] Acheson was contemptuous. In the world of 1946, "The only sanction is war." He advised leaving out any mention of penalties for violations, since they amounted to war, and no useful purpose would be served by so stating. He gave no support to notions of strengthening the U.N. into a world government with legal powers reaching to individuals.[38]

Baruch's Enlargement of U.S. Policy

Baruch, however, carried the fight to the top in a meeting with the president, and in the final policy statement he prevailed. Now his full eloquence and sense for the historic moment were brought to bear as he said to President Truman: "I am deeply convinced that any expression which falls short of bringing a sense of security and a sense of truth to the public would be a gigantic error.... I want to go farther than the text of that document [Acheson–Lilienthal report]." He clearly saw the necessity for "punishments" and even for "eliminating war." He left for the future, however, "an outline of the mechanism whereby punishment is to come." He doubted that in a matter so great as the establishment of international control over atomic energy, and hence over war itself, the way to proceed to an agreement was by "the ordinary processes of diplomacy." He recommended a method "that strikes to the very heart of public thinking and feeling"—"a proclamation of not merely a basis of negotiations but a formula of lasting peace."[39] Truman apparently was impressed. He approved what was in effect a limitation of U.S. sovereignty in the policy provision that any national atomic energy authority would be "subordinate to direction and absolute dominion" of an interna-

---

[35] Hancock to Byrnes, 1 June 1946, ibid.; *Foreign Relations*, 1946, 1: 824–26.

[36] Hancock, Draft [of U.S. Policy], 4 June 1946, Baruch Papers, 52.4; *Foreign Relations*, 1946, 1: 827–33.

[37] B.M.B. Memo, 31 May 1946, Baruch Papers, 52.4; Hancock to Baruch, 4 June 1946, ibid.

[38] Meeting in State Department, 30 May 1946, ibid.; Acheson to Byrnes, 6 June 1946, *Foreign Relations*, 1946, 1: 836–37. Byrnes actually thought that "there is now in being adequate international law to cover the matter of personal responsibility." Hancock, Memo of Meeting, 1 June 1946, Baruch Papers, 52.4.

[39] Baruch to Truman, 6 June 1946, *Foreign Relations*, 1946, 1: 838–40.

tional atomic authority.[40] Baruch had won.

But what had he won? He had won a commitment from the president, against the advice of the State Department, to support a proposal for the international control of atomic energy that went beyond an early warning system, preparatory to an atomic arms race and probable nuclear war. He had not been allowed to enlarge his terms of reference to include conventional weapons. Nor had the substance of the Acheson–Lilienthal proposal, notably the ownership functions and the untimed transition stages, been discarded. Still, Baruch was encouraged. Speaking to five highly placed military officers, he said a warning system alone was not "worth a damn." The alternative was reliable international control, which implied "an immediate and drastic transformation of our form of government." It meant *"effective world control of war (counterpart of our own Federal Government)."*[41] In principle, then, though he himself rarely used the term, Baruch was authorized to make a world government proposal. Success would largely depend on favorable Soviet response and on American flexibility in negotiations.

The Baruch Plan before the United Nations

"My Fellow Members of the United Nations Atomic Energy Commission and my Fellow Citizens of the World," Bernard Baruch began in his historic address to the U.N. AEC on 14 June 1946: "We are here to make a choice between the quick and the dead." A reader looking for the world government implications of this speech cannot fail to be impressed. Baruch accepted the atomic scientists' view that ultimately there were no secret and no defense. He acknowledged the "will of mankind" to find a "mechanism to assure that atomic energy is used for peaceful purposes and preclude its use in war." He referred to the fundamental concept of enforcement by law—"individual responsibility and punishment on the principles applied at Nuremberg." He reminded the members of the commission that they represented not only their governments but also the peoples of the world, who are sovereign: "Governments belong to the peoples."[42] "They are not afraid of an internationalism that protects; they are unwilling to be fobbed off by mouthings about narrow sovereignty, which is today's phrase for yester-

[40] Truman to Baruch [with enclosed policy statement], 7 June 1946, ibid., 1: 846–51.

[41] Memo by the United States Representatives on the Military Staff Committee to the Joint Chiefs of Staff, 7 June 1946, ibid., 1: 845, emphasis added. The Joint Chiefs were skeptical, even of international control. "We can yield much, even certain points of our sovereignty, to reach this solution [of the control of atomic energy]," wrote General Eisenhower. "Whether our people could be brought to see this necessity at present is a question." Eisenhower to Baruch, 14 June 1946, ibid., 1: 854–56. Admirals Turner, Leahy, and Nimitz doubted that world government could be established in time to obviate a program of national defense. Ibid., 1: 843–54.

[42] "United States Atomic Energy Proposals: Statement of the United States Policy on Control of Atomic Energy as Presented by Bernard M. Baruch, Esq., to the United Nations Atomic Energy Commission, June 14, 1946" (Washington, DC: Department of State Publication No. 2560, 1946).

day's isolation." He outlined the control system in some detail; sketched the U.S. view on stages of transfer, beginning with agreement on the charter of the atomic authority, then full transfer of secret information, and so on; and argued forcefully for abolition of the veto in atomic energy matters: "There must be no veto to protect those who violate their solemn agreements not to develop or use atomic energy for destructive purposes." Early warning was no basis for atomic security. "In the elimination of war lies our solution."

The People's Response

Public response to Baruch's initiative was about two to one in favor.[43] The *New York Times* opined that the United States had made a first step toward a "world government over split atoms."[44] The Russian press, however, was critical of any proposal from the capitalist West to convert the United Nations into a "world state" whose "mission it will be to save the world from atomic war." The intention was U.S. domination of the world. "The florid talk about a 'world state' is actually a frank plea for American imperialism," said Moscow.[45]

Grenville Clark congratulated Baruch but explained that partial abolition of the veto, leaving the league structure of the U.N. intact, was not enough. Transforming the General Assembly into a world legislature, according to a plan of weighted representation, was necessary to make abolition of the veto acceptable to the Russians. Under the current structure, the Russians were "hopelessly outvoted" in the Assembly, where the Latin American countries had voting power (20 votes of 51) far out of proportion to their population (7 percent). In the Security Council, where six members were elected by the Assembly, the Russians were also consistently outvoted. "As long as this condition prevails," Clark argued, "one can see why they hang on grimly to the veto."

Under Clark's plan, however, where voting would be more proportional to population, economic strength, and political power, the Russians would still be in a minority, but world legislators could *vote as individuals*. Presumably, Russian representatives and those from the Soviet sphere of influence would vote solidly, while those from other countries would split, depending on the issue. Such a reform would make voting by majority rule on international disputes possible and acceptable. "After all, isn't having a fair chance to carry a vote on

---

[43] "Bull's Eye," wired James Forrestal. "Every citizen of our one world owes you his profoundest gratitude for your revolutionary and historic statement," telegrammed James H. Cox, president of Washington and Jefferson College. Baruch Papers, 59. "I refuse to become a citizen of the world. I owe allegiance to 1 flag. If you like Russia, go there," one Anna Armstrong scrawled on a postcard. "I did not suggest for anybody to become a citizen of the world," Baruch defended himself, "but, as American representative, I was addressing ... the peoples of the world." Ibid.

[44] "The Atom Knows No Nations," *New York Times,* 16 June 1946.

[45] Modest Rubenstein, "The Atomic Age as American Scientists Picture It," *New Times* (Moscow), 15 June 1946, quoted in Joseph L. Nogee, *Soviet Policy towards International Control of Atomic Energy* (Notre Dame, 1961), 31. Rubenstein was reviewing the atomic scientists' manifesto, *One World or None.*

the merits the essence of any governmental plan where 'sovereignty' and the veto are waived?"[46] Clark amplified these views in a long letter to the *Times*. The Baruch plan was the "entering wedge" for "world government," he wrote.[47] Baruch did not reply.[48]

Remaining Historical Opportunity

Many historians, orthodox and revisionist, have recounted the disastrous failure of the subsequent negotiations.[49] It would be a mistake, we think, to regard Baruch's proposal and the one by Andrei Gromyko that followed in five days as mere great power propaganda ploys. That did develop, but not for several months when the fears, distrust, and misunderstandings that had been accumulating since the end of the war produced paralysis in the U.N. AEC at New York and in the peace conference at Paris. The problem is to see why relations between the United States and the Soviet Union were not as cordial as they had been at Yalta 16 months before. Soviet political expansion into Eastern Europe, exclusive American occupation of Japan, British intervention in Greece, Russian intervention in Iran, U.S. intervention in China, American objections to extension of a Russian sphere of influence toward Turkey and the Dardanelles, Russian fears of new American strategic bases from Iceland to the Pacific islands, the vague threat to civilization by the atomic bomb, and the inadequacy of the United Nations to resolve such issues were key events in the decline of friendly relations.[50]

Nevertheless, the opportunity in mid–1946 was not entirely closed. The world knew nothing yet of the containment doctrine, the Marshall plan, the Czechoslovakian coup, the Berlin blockade, NATO, the Russian A–bomb, the American H–bomb, and the Korean War. There was genuine support, world–wide, for Baruch's proposal to abolish the veto, though its full implications for limiting national sovereignty and reforming the U.N. may not have been as viv-

---

[46] Clark to Baruch, 20 June 1946, Baruch Papers, 59.

[47] Clark to Editor, "An Atomic Energy Authority and World Government," *New York Times,* 23 June 1946.

[48] Baruch never replied to implications of "world government" that correspondents pointed out in his speech. See Bishop Henry Hobsen to Baruch, 3 July 1946, and reply, Baruch Papers, 59. He seems to have feared being linked to "One Worlders," though his ideas inclined with theirs. After State squelched his idea of "strengthening the U.N.," his mind apparently did not advance beyond increasing the jurisdiction of the World Court.

[49] U.S. Department of State, "Growth of a Policy: The International Control of Atomic Energy, August 6, 1945 – October 15, 1946" (Washington, DC: Department of State Publication No. 2702, n.d., c. February 1947); U.S. Department of State, "Policy at the Crossroads: The International Control of Atomic Energy, October 15, 1946 – May 17, 1948" (Washington, DC: Department of State Publication No. 3161, June 1948); Hewlett and Anderson, *New World,* 531–619; Lieberman, *Scorpion,* 303–412; Gardner, *Architects,* 195–201; Herken, *Winning Weapon,* 171–91; Nogee, *Soviet Policy,* 33–67, 81–89.

[50] Clyde Eagleton, "The Beam in Our Own Eye," *Harper's,* June 1946, pp. 481–86.

idly perceived as its usefulness for getting tough with the Russians.[51] Nor was Russia's use of the veto as "frequent" as is often recalled today; by 14 June 1946, Russia had used the veto *once,* in the Syria–Lebanon case, and then on 25 and 26 June, four times, all in reference to the Spanish case.[52] Gromyko's proposal of a convention to "outlaw" atomic weapons (not by world law but by *nationally* enforced international law), before establishment of the international authority, had occurred first to the Lilienthal board itself about six months before.[53] Generally, on the complex and novel questions of atomic energy control, the Russians simply remained several months behind the Americans. Despite the atmosphere of a U.S. ultimatum that developed, the Russians actually made significant concessions to the American plan, reaching *unanimity* on scientific and technical questions by September,[54] and acceptance of inspection by November.[55] When the crucial vote on the Baruch plan was called on 30 December 1946, only *four* sentences (all about the veto) were in dispute.[56]

Andrei A. Gromyko

Baruch's counterpart was Andrei Gromyko, whose service to his country spanned the Stalin and Gorbachev eras. Gromyko was trained as an agricultural economist. He was senior research associate at the Institute of Economics of the Academy of Sciences, 1936–39, when, in the wake of Stalin's great purge of the Communist party, he was elevated to the U.S. division of the People's Commissariat of Foreign Affairs in 1939. He was then appointed counselor at the Soviet embassy in Washington, where he learned English. In 1943 he was made ambassador to the United States, after Maxim Litvinov, who had struggled for collective security at the League. Throughout the war Gromyko represented Russia in the capital of her leading ally. In 1946 he became Soviet representative to the U.N. Security Council.

Gromyko had responsibility for bringing the Soviet Union into relation to the new world security organization during the epochal breakup of wartime unanimity, when Russia's great interests were reconstruction and security against a revival of German militarism. He was often photographed in the Security Council staring off into space. Gromyko's immediate superior was Vice–Foreign Commissar Andrei Vishinsky, chief prosecutor at the Stalin purge trials. The

[51] Great Britain, Canada, Brazil, China, and Mexico seconded the U.S. plan on the 19th, followed in time by Australia, Egypt, and France.

[52] Sidney D. Bailey, *Voting in the Security Council* (Bloomington, 1969), 28. Cf. Lieberman, *Scorpion,* 306.

[53] Acheson–Lilienthal "Report," p. 4.

[54] "The Scientific and Technical Aspects of Atomic Energy Control, A First Report by the Scientific and Technical Committee of the UN Atomic Energy Commission," 27 September 1946, *Bulletin of the Atomic Scientists,* October 1946, pp. 6–12.

[55] "Disarmament Debate in the United Nations General Assembly" and "Principles Governing the General Regulation and Reduction of Armaments," *Bulletin of the Atomic Scientists,* January 1947, pp. 8–9.

[56] "First Report of the Atomic Energy Commission to the Security Council," 30 December 1946, *Bulletin of the Atomic Scientists,* January 1947, pp. 16–27.

witnessing of the purge and his long absence from Russia during her battle for life seems to have left their mark on the dutiful, obdurate, but yet not humorless Russian representative in the United States. Bernard Baruch told a story that revealed something of Gromyko's character as well as of the atmosphere of the U.N. AEC negotiations. One evening Baruch took Gromyko to the second Joe Louis–Billy Conn fight. The champion made a poor showing in the first round, but in the second he pounded poor Conn from pillar to post. At that point Gromyko leaned over to the distinguished white–haired American and said, "Conn must wish he had the veto."[57]

The Gromyko Plan

Gromyko's counterproposal came on 19 June. He proposed, first, an "exchange of scientific information" on fission and "technological processes," then, second, a "convention" for the "outlawing of weapons based upon the use of atomic energy," like the Hague convention and Geneva protocol against the use of poisonous gases and bacteriological weapons. The "high contracting parties" would "solemnly declare" that they forbid the production and use of atomic weapons, will destroy within three months their existing stockpiles of atomic bombs (this was the provision that so alarmed the Americans), will regard a violation of the agreement as a crime against humanity, and will pass national legislation within six months to punish violators. After such a convention was put into effect, Gromyko proposed (without timetable) the establishment of a "system of control" and "supervision" to "insure the observance" of the convention. Lastly, a "system of sanctions for the unlawful use of atomic energy" was to be provided. He hinted at further possible agreements following from the "immense moral and political significance" of the convention. But he made no reference to an international authority and absolutely rejected the proposal to abolish the veto:[58] "Efforts made ... to undermine the unanimity of the Members of the Security Council, upon questions of substance, are incompatible with the interests of the United Nations ... for the preservation of peace and security." In short, only *national* control of atomic energy would be countenanced.

Gromyko's proposal was a disappointment—perhaps a deliberate delaying tactic, since it was largely aimed at the Acheson–Lilienthal report available since March—but it seems now *not* to have been completely intractable for negotiation, since it differed primarily in the *sequence* of control and abolition. Further signs of good faith from both sides were surely needed. These, however, were not forthcoming.

---

[57] *Encyclopedia Britannica*, 15th ed. (1979), s.v. "Gromyko, Andrei A(ndreyovich)," 4: 749; Baruch, *The Public Years*, 378–79. In 1957, Mr. Gromyko became foreign commissar, and in 1985 he approved the appointment of Mikhail Gorbachev as general secretary of the Communist Party of the Soviet Union.

[58] State, "Growth of a Policy," Appendix No. 22, pp. 209–16.

Atomic Tests at Bikini Atoll

The U.N. AEC had hardly divided into committees to reconcile the proposals when the United States began atomic tests at Bikini atoll in the Pacific. On 1 July, a B–29 dropped another 20–kiloton bomb of the Hiroshima type on a test fleet of 73 ships anchored in the lagoon. Why President Truman could have permitted the navy to conduct such a provocative test—at such a delicate moment in negotiations to rid the world of war, or at least to provide for the security of the United States by some means other than leadership in an atomic arms race—can only be guessed. There is no doubt that the test, in *Pravda's* words, "fundamentally undermined the belief in the seriousness of American talk about atomic disarmament."[59]

Hedging on Abolition of the Veto

After the test, the U.S. submitted three key memos in the U.N. AEC clarifying the Baruch plan. The third, of July 12th, dealt with the most critical problem of the relation of the authority to the United Nations. Abolition of the veto was to apply *only* to cases involving atomic weapons. But then atomic weapons might play only an "incidental" part in a general case of aggression, when the powers, authority, and responsibility of the Security Council would be "unaffected" (that is, the veto would apply in full). And to underscore the meaning of such a situation, reference was made to Article 51, which provides for "individual and collective self–defense" in cases when the Security Council cannot act. This memo, apparently State's doing, hedged Baruch's proposal until it was emptied of meaning.[60]

The second Bikini test, on 25 July, provoked a complete Russian rejection of the Baruch plan. Referring specifically to Memo No. 3, Gromyko stated on the 24th: "The American proposals, as they are presented now, cannot be accepted by the Soviet Union either as a whole or in parts." He took a very strict constructionist view of the U.N. Charter. There could be no artificial distinction between the atomic bomb and other weapons used by a potential aggressor (this was Baruch's original view, now coming back to haunt him). The Charter gave responsibility to the Security Council (not some new authority) to prevent aggression. There could be no tampering with national sovereignty, one of the "cornerstones" of the U.N. To abandon the principle of the unanimity of the

---

[59] Boris Izakov, "Bikini," *Pravda,* 3 July 1946, quoted in Nogee, *Soviet Policy,* 62. Nevertheless, the test failed to convey the full threat of atomic weapons. Only two ships went down immediately; even the battleship *Nevada,* at target zero, remained afloat. The Russian observer Professor Simon Alexandrov, who served on the Russian delegation to the U.N. AEC, merely shrugged his shoulders. "Atom Bomb Exploded over Bikini Fleet; 2 Ships Are Sunk, 19 Damaged out of 73; Blast Force Seems Less than Expected," *New York Times,* 1 July 1946.

[60] United States Memorandum No. 3, Dealing with the Relations between the Atomic Development Authority and the Organs of the United Nations, Submitted to Subcommittee No. 1 of the United Nations Atomic Energy Commission, New York, 12 July 1946, "Growth of a Policy," pp. 160–63.

permanent members of the Security Council would be "fatal" (an attack on the independence of the Soviet Union).[61]

The Russian Rejection

On the 26th, Gromyko defended the Russian alternative. A convention, he implied, would eliminate the American bomb stockpile so that the United States and the Soviet Union could proceed to "practical steps toward control" on a basis of equality. There could be no "guarantees" other than "international cooperation." National legislation would punish individuals. Security Council action would apply sanctions against nations. When the Brazilian and American delegates both pressed him with references to the seriousness of atomic weapons as demonstrated by the recent Bikini tests, Gromyko angrily burst out: "I don't see how one can ask other states blindly to believe in the good intentions of the United States and to accept the U.S. proposal as regards atomic weapons and at the same time to doubt the good intentions of others." In this heated atmosphere, political negotiations broke off.[62]

Could the proposals have been reconciled? We now know that the Russians were actively pursuing their own atomic energy program. Indeed, they achieved a sustained nuclear reaction five days before the critical vote on the Baruch plan on 30 December,[63] and there is even evidence that they began mining uranium in Saxony in May 1945, well before Potsdam.[64] Their convention would not have hindered this program except for the final production of bombs. Nor would it have interfered with the American program except to require the destruction of existing bomb stockpiles. The ores, piles, plants, labs, and fissionable materials were technically exempt. The international authority proposed by the Americans, however, would have terminated the Russian program, as a small army of controllers, inspectors, licensers, and researchers fanned out across the country, while the Americans would have been allowed to retain and even add to their bomb stockpile until the last stage. "In time in America," Gromyko remarked

---

[61] Ibid., pp. 81–85. The second test also had a disastrous effect on public opinion. The battleship *Arkansas* and carrier *Saratoga* were sunk, but only because the atomic bomb was exploded in water beneath them, and the water column rose only a mile, not the two to five predicted by the press. The *Times's* science reporter William L. Lawrence, who witnessed the tests, was "amazed" on his return to the States. "Before Bikini the world stood in awe of this new cosmic force.... Since Bikini this feeling of awe has largely evaporated and has been supplemented by a sense of relief that the atomic bomb is, after all, just another weapon." "Atomic Bomb Sinks Battleship and Carrier; Four Submarines Are Lost in Mounting Toll; Soviet Flatly Rejects Baruch Control Plan," *New York Times*, 25 July 1946; "The Bikini Tests and Public Opinion," *Bulletin of the Atomic Scientists*, September 1946, p. 2.

[62] "Growth of a Policy," pp. 81–85.

[63] I. N. Golovin, William H. Doughterty, trans., *I. V. Kurchatov: A Socialist–Realist Biography of the Soviet Nuclear Scientist* (Selbstverlag Press, P.O. Drawer 606, Bloomington, IN 47401, 1968), 48–49, 55, 64. The Russian atomic bomb program began in Kazan in May 1942. Ibid., 40.

[64] Herken, *Winning Weapon*, 394, n. 29. Cf. Golovin, 47.

in August 1946, "your plan will be seen to be unfair."[65]

World Federalist Analysis

The proposal immediately to exchange scientific information could have been a maneuver to acquire U.S. atomic secrets. Yet virtually all atomic scientists denied there were any scientific secrets, and technical secrets had been generally released in the published Smyth report.[66] In fact, scientific and technical matters were the least of the problems of the negotiators, on which they soon reached unanimity.

The destruction of the American stockpile of atomic bombs was a sticking point. Judging by the Bikini experience, this was one point on which the United States might have budged. Destroying the bombs or postponing the tests might have been enough of an extra good–faith gesture to move the Russians to more serious consideration of the authority. The scientists were quick to observe that the danger was not in the *bombs* but in the plants and materials[67]—a point that the Russians themselves emphasized.[68] We now know that the number of bombs in the American "stockpile" was *12*.[69] Could not 12 bombs have been sacrificed for the elimination of war?

On the other hand, the United States had already made a major good–faith gesture in the offer itself to surrender its atomic power to an international authority, on condition of adequate safeguards. A like offer could not be found in all of national history. Even the timing of the Americans' stages was privately planned to be only four to six years.[70] Could not six years of American atomic diplomacy have been endured to place atomic energy in the service of humanity? If the Russians had dared, they could have been more receptive to an international control scheme, as they had been in the 1920s.[71]

Russian refusal to countenance the abolition of the veto was as understandable as American refusal to destroy the stockpile. Both were shaky props of national defense. The veto was one point on which the U.S.S.R. could have budged. By upholding so rigidly the principle of great power sovereignty, the Russians were really defending the founding principle of the League of Nations, which had failed them so disastrously in 1938, and they were blocking reform of the United Nations, whose league structure had been proved inadequate by 1946.

---

[65] Quoted in Herken, *Winning Weapon,* 178.

[66] Henry Dewolf Smyth, *Atomic Energy for Military Purposes: The Official Report on the Development of the Atomic Bomb under the Auspices of the United States Government, 1940–1945* (Princeton, [12 August] 1945).

[67] Eugene Rabinowitch, Editorial, *Bulletin of the Atomic Scientists,* July 1946, p. 24.

[68] Memo [on Meeting with A. A. Sobolev] by Franklin A. Lindsay, 21 October 1946, *Foreign Relations,* 1946, 1: 956.

[69] Herken, *Winning Weapon,* 197.

[70] Groves to Hancock, 16 August 1946, *Foreign Relations,* 1946, 1: 880.

[71] U.S. Department of State, The U.S.S.R. and Disarmament, 1921–1932, August 1946, Baruch Papers, 56.

On the other hand, the American proposal to abolish the veto only in cases of national violation of international atomic energy rules—leaving the veto intact for larger questions of aggression—was certainly unfair and unwise. Without a veto, the Soviet Union would have been exposed to the "majority" in the Security Council then effectively within the sphere of influence of the United States. Council action according to the confederal rules of the U.N. would mean *war*. Acheson understood this, and so did Gromyko. Yet retaining a veto over general questions was no solution, for any atomic dispute could hardly not escalate into a general one, and then the U.N. would be paralyzed as before.

The proposal of national enforcement versus that of U.N. sanctions without protection of veto was a real impasse. Without organs of world law to reach individual violators, how could international control of atomic energy really work? Only national leaders were apt to be guilty of clandestine atomic armament. The Russian proposal would have national law enforcement agents arrest national executives (Stalin, Truman) whose chief duty was enforcement of the law. The American would have the U.N. apply sanctions, ultimately including war, against a whole nation whose leaders were arming it with atomic weapons. Baruch said little more in the months to come about "punishment on the principles applied at Nuremberg," and Gromyko never elaborated on how the "system of sanctions" he contemplated would apply in a case of "crime against humanity." Actually, the Baruch plan was the more dangerous for the security of the U.S., for it would have allowed a combination in the Security Council to decide to make *war on the United States*. This was hardly a "formula of lasting peace." Neither proposal went far enough toward world law.

The Cold War

The remainder of the negotiations followed the familiar pattern of the developing Cold War. Grenville Clark predicted that the "impasse" held "the elements of a great tragedy." The issue over sovereignty, "the modification of which is of the essence of the American proposal," was the cause, he said. Clark urged understanding of Russian history, an end to the "shocking mutual recriminations" in the press, avoidance of the appearance of atomic coercion, and a new spirit of "mutual toleration."[72] Baruch during negotiations remained tolerant, but he was glum. In case of failure, he muttered, all must be prepared to say, "Good Morning, Death."[73] Most Western diplomats, including George Kennan, were convinced the Russians were engaged in a program of delay rather than natural hesitation over the revolutionary proposals put before them.[74] When the Soviets formally objected to Western air and naval bases maintained outside of occupied Germany and Japan, the reaction in the State Department was: "Obviously pro-

---

[72] Clark et al. to Editor, *New York Times*, 18 August 1946.

[73] Notes on Meeting, 20 August 1946, *Foreign Relations*, 1946, 1: 884.

[74] Frederick H. Osborn, "The Russians Delay Action on Atomic Control," *Washington Post*, 3 August 1947; reprinted in the *Bulletin of the Atomic Scientists*, October 1947, pp. 299–300.

paganda."[75]

Soon the Soviets introduced a general conventional *and* atomic disarmament proposal in the U.N. General Assembly that fairly matched whatever propaganda value there may have been in the Americans' proposal in the U.N. AEC to surrender their atomic monopoly to an international atomic authority. Baruch complained bitterly that his advice to include the whole scope of war in the U.S. plan had not been followed, for now the Russians had seized the initiative.[76] The Soviet proposal called for disclosure of all Allied forces still abroad, apparently to prove the extent of Western imperialism; this formula was deceptive, since Russia's extended troops could technically be said to be within the home territory or in that of former belligerents. Disclosure of the size of the American stockpile was also threatened.[77] For months, the State Department was intensely preoccupied with meeting this Soviet challenge.[78]

A Showdown with the Soviets

By September 1946, the U.N. AEC negotiations were only a "sideshow" compared to State's maneuverings,[79] and Baruch decided to seek a "showdown" vote with the Soviets.[80] No compromise was possible because the U.S. plan represented the "minimum" for effective control.[81] At this moment there occurred the dispute between Baruch and Secretary of Commerce Henry Wallace over the plan, which resulted in Wallace's dismissal from the cabinet. The old New Dealer raised fundamental criticism of American foreign policy. Apart from

[75] Johnson to Byrnes, 29 August 1946, ibid., 1: 893; Position Paper, ... with Regard to Regulation of Armaments, 5 September 1946, ibid., 1: 899–902.

[76] Baruch to Byrnes, 8 December 1946, ibid., 1: 1089–90.

[77] Notes of Informal Meeting, 24 July 1946, ibid., 1: 869; Hiss to Acheson, 19 November 1946, ibid., 1: 1019.

[78] British Embassy to State, 23 October 1946, ibid., 1: 962–63; Acheson to Byrnes, 26 October 1946, ibid., 1: 966–69.

[79] Notes of Meeting, 10 September 1946, ibid., 1: 907. Acheson became openly opposed: "Talk of enforcement is really paper talk.... The peace forces envisaged in the Charter would be no good against a major power.... Baruch, by his emphasis on enforcement, had gotten us into an insoluble problem." Memo of Conversation [between Acheson and Baruch] by John C. Ross, 2 November 1946, ibid., 1: 984.

[80] Baruch to Truman, 17 September 1946, ibid., 1: 924; Memo of Conversation [between Acheson and Baruch] by John C. Ross, 2 November 1946, ibid., 1: 987–88. Strange new arguments began to be heard about why the U.S. could not cease manufacturing atomic bombs. Cessation would adversely affect U.S. security at a time of demobilization, would erode the Allies' sense of security, would make the U.S. appear belligerent if manufacture had to be resumed, and would weaken the U.S. bargaining position for international control. The gesture would be "utterly ineffective." This seems to have been the first appearance of the argument, in strategic arms limitation talks, that we must build up in order to build down. Tolman to Hancock, 4 October 1946, ibid., 1: 952; Memo by Hancock, 21 November 1946, ibid., 1: 1034.

[81] Notes of a Meeting between the United States Delegates to the Atomic Energy Commission and the United States Representatives on the Military Staff Committee, 22 August 1946, ibid., 1: 889.

some errors of detail (he put the stage of atomic secret disclosure last instead of first), Wallace vividly showed that continuing the atomic buildup, developing the 10,000–mile–range B–36, and acquiring strategic bases all around the globe were undermining Russian trust. Moreover, the American stand on the veto was "completely irrelevant" because enforcement by the Security Council could only mean war.[82] But such were the fear and fixity of mind at the time that all that such opinions earned Wallace was the charge of "Red."[83]

National action, especially national military action, was so ingrained a mental framework that there was rarely a thought, East or West, of supranational peacekeeping. There were a few hopeful signs—the Russian A. A. Sobolev, on Gromyko's team, recognized the Baruch plan as a proposal of "world government,"[84] John Foster Dulles briefly advocated an "international law that operated on individuals,"[85] and Foreign Minister Molotov was "conciliatory" in December about the veto issue (the Security Council veto would apply only to the rules of the ADA, not to its day–to–day operations).[86] But when the U.S. plan came to a vote on 30 December 1946, even Baruch expressly admitted that enforcement under the plan meant "war": "Let all nations that willingly set their pens to the terms of this treaty realize that its willful breech means punishment and, if necessary, war. Then we will not lightly have breeches and evasions." The vote was 10–2–0, the Russians and Poles abstaining. Although this was not an absolute rejection, and though negotiations continued until May 1948, the spirit of good faith had gone out of the talks.[87]

---

[82] Henry A. Wallace, Madison Square Garden Speech, 12 September 1946, reprinted in idem, *The Fight for Peace* (New York, 1946), 17–22; Wallace to Truman, 24 July 1946, *New York Times,* 18 September 1946; Bernard Baruch, "Memorandum to the President," 24 September 1946, *Bulletin of the Atomic Scientists,* October 1946, pp. 4–5, 31.

[83] Memo by Hancock, 19 September 1946, *Foreign Relations,* 1946, 1: 933.

[84] Memo [on Meeting with A. A. Sobolev] by Franklin A. Lindsay, 21 October 1946, ibid., 1: 956, 960.

[85] Minutes of the United States Delegation [to the United Nations], 15 November 1946, ibid., 1: 541–43.

[86] Memo of Conversation [with the Turkish ambassador] by Robert McClintock, 4 December 1946, ibid., 1: 1084; Memo by Naval Representative to Army and Air Force Representatives on the Military Staff Committee, 5 December 1946, ibid., 1: 1087–88.

[87] "Proceedings of the UN Atomic Energy Commission," *Bulletin of the Atomic Scientists,* January 1947, pp. 12–13; State, "Policy at the Crossroads," 54–55. Later it was admitted that Baruch hurried the vote to avoid the "census of armaments" required under the General Assembly's disarmament resolution of 14 December. Edward A. Shils, "The Failure of the UNAEC: An Interpretation," *Bulletin of the Atomic Scientists,* July 1948, p. 206.

11

U.N. Reform as the Baruch Plan Failed

We sit here and feel the United Nations tremble. We watch it fail
to meet forcefully the great issues of our time. We know in our
hearts that its structure is faulty. We know that therefore no
nation—yes, *no nation, great or small*—trusts the United Nations
to provide its security and peace.

—Carlos P. Romulo, Philippines Delegate, Speech in the U.N.
General Assembly, 13 December 1946

Clark's Continued U.N. Reform Effort

Meanwhile, Grenville Clark was trying to follow up the opening of the U.N.
AEC negotiations with further approaches to the General Assembly in order to
open debate on "radical amendment of the Charter." He was still circulating the
Dublin petition. Clark thought it would soon be evident that the Baruch proposals could not be carried out without such amendment. He hoped that the question on the Baruch proposal would not be called quickly since Russia's fear and
suspicion for some time were sure to end in a *No* vote. Clark wrote to Washington columnist and foreign policy commentator Edgar Ansel Mowrer, who
was in touch with Australia's Herbert Evatt and some of the other U.N. delegates, to discuss tactics. Clark suggested the calling of a "joint conference committee" of the Atomic Energy Commission, General Assembly, and Security
Council. Mowrer thought the idea should be passed to the sympathetic delegations *"just as a suggestion,"* so it would seem to be *"their* idea." Their idea was
to lead to the Assembly debate in November and December 1946.[1]

Visit to Byrnes

Clark wrote twice to Secretary of State James Byrnes, explaining that the
U.S. proposal of 14 June 1946 implied "limited world government," and he suggested that *amendment* was preferable to treaty to relate the Atomic Development
Authority to the United Nations. Clark added: "It will be wise not to permit acceptance of the American plan to come to a Yes or No issue at an early date. If
this were done, it is likely that Russia will refuse, precipitating a breach that it
is vitally important to avoid." Then on 24 July, Boston's Henry B. Cabot, Alan

---

[1] Clark to Mowrer, 6 July 1946, Baker Library, Clark Papers, 15.3.

Cranston, T. K. Finletter, and California representative Jerry Voorhis went to see Byrnes. They urged him to support the Charter amendments. They came away with the grim impression that there was already a "very bad impasse on the atomic energy matter," and that "our Government has not got any good constructive plan for solving it."[2]

A Fair Chance

Clark then prepared a letter for the *Times* over the signatures of seven members of the Dublin committee, which appeared a few days after the U.N. AEC decision to suspend meetings. "The present impasse in the Atomic Energy Commission holds, it seems clear, the elements of a great tragedy," he began. He rehearsed the main points in the American and Russian plans that culminated in the issue over sovereignty, "the modification of which is of the essence of the American proposals." Then he warned:[3]

> Unless, therefore, this impasse is broken, nothing less than a great armament race, not only in atomic bombs, but in all other weapons, is impending. Experience shows that such a race would, at best, involve almost intolerable tension, and, at the worst, war.

Clark himself proposed a constructive alternative policy for the government —his Charter amendment plan. He went over the recent history of Russia's being outvoted in Assembly and Council (admission of Argentina, failed censure of Franco, ouster from Iran), which explained why she held on to the veto as a protection. However, a popularly representative Assembly, reformed on the "fair" principle of weighted representation and of voting by individuals, would give Russia a fair chance. A representative General Assembly would permit the United Nations to begin to function as a limited world government, Clark argued. He proposed a U.N. committee along the lines of his letter to Mowrer. He closed with a plea for a "cessation of the shocking mutual recriminations between Russia and the United States, as reflected in the press of both countries."

---

[2] Clark to Byrnes, 23 July 1946, Clark Papers, 15.1; Clark to Stimson, 30 July 1946, ibid., 21.10. Finletter was still having his differences with Clark and coming off the worse for them. The Americans United director thought that the administration intended to reject the Baruch proposal on the veto and go back to the veto–safe Acheson–Lilienthal Report. Hence, the movement should fight for the Baruch plan without "diverting attention" by proposals to develop it with reforms of the General Assembly on the principle of weighted representation. Finletter added, too, strangely, that the movement should de-emphasize "institutional elements in world government" and make the principle of disarmament "part of the law." Who was the greater realist? Finletter to Clark, 1 August 1946, ibid., 21.10.

[3] Clark et al. to Editor, *New York Times*, 18 August 1946, p. E8. The letter was signed by Douglas Arant, Henry B. Cabot, Clark, Alan Cranston, and F. R. von Windegger, dated 13 August 1946.

Federalists' Aloofness to Clark's Effort

The world government movement in the summer of 1946 never generally appreciated the opportunity presented by the Baruch plan for beginning the practical political approach to world government. World Federalists heard of Clark, Mowrer, and Cranston's approach to Cuba, whose delegate took the initiative to place on the agenda for the upcoming session of the U.N. General Assembly a conference to eliminate the veto privilege. Tom Griessemer thought the move "useless" and "senseless." What was needed, he wrote, was a "Majority Rule World Legislature," which was exactly what Clark was proposing. Two months later, when the thoroughgoing nature of the Clark proposals behind the Cuban initiative had become evident, Griessemer at last urged support. Americans United fell back on their laurels after winning U.S. qualified adherence to the World Court on 1 August. They began gearing up for a 13–week radio series on the ABC Network entitled *The World Security Workshop*, to start in November. The first installment, "Citizen Delevan," was about an atomic scientist whose conscience conflicted with security regulations. Scripts, documentary or dramatic, were invited from the public for a $250 prize. Student Federalists were preparing for their big Chicago institute and convention.[4]

Climax of U.N. Reform Efforts

Meanwhile, the private efforts of Grenville Clark and others to bring about a general conference of the United Nations to amend the Charter were reaching a climax. There were three resolutions on the agenda of the General Assembly pointing the way. The most "drastic" was the first of two introduced by the delegate from Cuba, Dr. Guillermo Belt (drafted by Clark):

[Resolved:] To convene in conformity with Article 109 of the Charter a General Conference of the Members of the United Nations for the purpose of reviewing the present Charter of the Organization. The said Conference should be held at the same place as the second session of the General Assembly in 1947 and should begin work immediately after the conclusion of the Assembly.

This clear resolution, worded to make evasion impossible and to transform the second session of the Assembly into a great preparatory conference, at no time had "a chance of winning more than a handful of votes," observed Alan Cranston, who managed the campaign. It was too drastic a step for the "very first" Assembly to take. Later, delegates said, this step might be taken, "if the

⁴ "Slay That Dragon: Veto," *World Government News*, August 1946, pp. 2–4; "The Conference No One Can Veto," ibid., October 1946, p. 1; "World Security Workshop," ibid., September 1946, p. 6; Gehman to Balderston, 16 September 1946; ABC Press Release, 14 November 1946, Regenstein Library, AORES Papers, 8.9. ABC donated all but $8,000 of the $450,000 air time.

workings of the Security Council are not soon improved."[5]
The second Cuban resolution (also drafted by Clark) was:

> [Resolved:] To appoint a special committee composed of representatives of
> all Members of the United Nations which, before 1 February 1947, express
> their desire to serve on the committee ... to consider and report to the General
> Assembly what amendments would make the United Nations a more effective
> instrument to maintain world peace and security, and to invite the organs and
> agencies of the United Nations and interested official and private organiza-
> tions to submit to the committee their observations and proposals.

This fall–back resolution, more than a mere "study" resolution, won "substan-
tially more support" in the ensuing debate. At one time, when the disarmament
debate was bogged down, it seemed to have a chance for approval.[6]
The third resolution was a very "mild" one, introduced by Australia, around
which most of the discontent of the small nations with the veto revolved. Delegates of over 30 nations criticized the veto as exercised to date in the Security
Council, but in the end they dared to approve the Australian resolution, only
"much amended" and "much watered down." At the last moment, even the clause
to use the word "veto" in this mild censure was excised (here enclosed in
brackets):

> THE GENERAL ASSEMBLY,
> MINDFUL of the purposes and principles of the Charter of the United Na-
> tions, and having taken notice of the divergencies which have arisen in re-
> gard to the application and interpretation of Article 27 of the Charter,
> [CONSIDERS that, in some instances, the use and the threatened use of
> such power of veto have not been in keeping either with the general purposes
> and principles of the Charter or with the understanding of the United Nations
> Conference on International Organization held at San Francisco, and]
> THEREFORE, EARNESTLY REQUESTS the permanent members of the
> Security Council to make every effort, in consultation with one another and
> with fellow members of the Security Council, to ensure that the use of the
> special voting privilege of its permanent members does not impede the Se-
> curity Council in reaching decisions promptly.

The campaign for votes for either this Australian censure or the Cuban review committee, Cranston remarked, was exactly like that to get a bill through a
state legislature or Congress. "Votes were won or lost, traded and traded in, for
important and relevant or unimportant and irrelevant reasons."[7]

---

[5] Alan Cranston, The Campaign for World Government at the General Assembly,
23 October, 15 December 1946, pp. 1–2, Clark Papers, 15.3; Clark to Holliday, 19
September 1946, ibid., 21.10. Eight nations (of 36 needed) in the end voted *Yes*.

[6] Ibid. Twelve nations eventually approved the committee.

[7] Campaign for World Government, pp. 2–3, 5.

Carlos P. Romulo

The debate brought out the important and relevant reasons. Three speeches by the Philippine delegate, General Carlos P. Romulo, were generally accorded to have been the strongest for the three resolutions and indeed for world government. The speeches deserve to be remembered, for they marked a historical turning point in the fate of the United Nations and still show a way into the future.

Carlos Romulo was educated at the University of the Philippines and at Columbia in New York. He rapidly rose in newspaper publishing in Manila during the 1930s, earning his first honorary doctor of laws degree (from Notre Dame) in 1935 and Pulitzer Prize in 1941. During the war, he served as General MacArthur's aide–de–camp on Bataan, Corregidor, and Australia, rising rapidly to the rank in the U.S. Army of colonel (later brigadier general). In 1944 he became secretary of information in President Quezon's exile Philippine government in Washington. Romulo rejoined MacArthur for the liberation of Leyte and Manila, represented his country at the San Francisco conference, and headed the Philippine delegation to the United Nations thereafter.[8]

U.N. General Assembly Debate on Atomic Energy

The General Assembly reopened at Flushing Meadows, New York. President Truman appeared the first day, 23 October 1946, and set forth two great goals for the second session—the international control of atomic energy and general disarmament. He declared that success would require "setting fundamental precedents in the law of nations."[9] As atomic energy was the province of the U.N. AEC, which was then holding its informal discussions, the Assembly took up the question of regulation and reduction of armaments *other* than atomic. Another question, not raised by the United States but being discussed in the aisles and lounges, was review of the entire Charter, especially the veto, as occasioned by the Cuban and Australian initiatives on the agenda.

Molotov's Speech on the Atomic Bomb

Six days into the session, V. M. Molotov appeared to initiate debate on general disarmament. His speech was not limited to weapons of mass destruction other than atomic, and it expressed the full range of Russian political objections to the U.S. plan. The "monopolistic possession of the atomic bomb" was said to be a "threat to the peace." The Baruch plan for control gave only "an appearance of international character" while it really protected "in a veiled form the monopolistic position of the United States." Its provisions, said Molotov, were based on "a narrow conception of the interests of one country." Abolition of the veto was "an inadmissible denial of the equality of states and their legitimate interests." To "upset the United Nations Charter" (abolish the veto) was "to give a free hand to the worshipers of the atomic bomb" (leave Russia to the mercy of

[8] Philippine Mission to the United Nations, Ambassador Carlos P. Romulo, n.d., c. June 1949, Lilly Library, UWF Papers, 32.

[9] "The Discussion in the UN Assembly," *Bulletin of the Atomic Scientists*, November 1946, p. 18.

the U.S.–dominated "majority"). There could be no diminution of sovereignty, as Baruch was proposing. Molotov left an unmistakable impression of how the Russian people regarded the threat of atomic bombs, which had first been used by the Americans on Japanese civilians.[10]

U.S. Response to Molotov's Speech

In the United States, this speech caused much offense. Even the atomic scientists called it "vicious" and "wildly exaggerated." Indeed, it takes much close reading of the U.S. proposals and of Baruch's eloquent speeches to see, as Clark and others pointed out, that nothing was proposed there except abolition of the veto in cases involving atomic energy—and that little made effectively nugatory by State Department qualifications. The U.S. did not propose effective atomic control, let alone the abolition of war.

Shortly before the Molotov speech, the National Council of Soviet–American Friendship had endorsed, as a sign of good faith, U.S. cessation of stockpiling atomic bombs (adding that they hoped the Soviets would be more responsive on the issue of controls). On the 29th it was reported in the press that former Public Works Administration head Harold L. Ickes had promptly resigned from the council in protest. American labor split. The Congress of Industrial Organizations at its Atlantic City convention also resolved to end the stockpiling. The American Federation of Labor in Chicago approved the Baruch plan, "condemning Communists at home and abroad."[11] Even the informed public were uncertain where to turn.

Romulo: Representative Assembly Needed

Shortly after the Cuban resolutions were first presented to the Assembly's full Political and Security Committee, Romulo made a major address on 16 November 1946. He took the floor to answer a charge by Russia's Andrei Vishinsky (who had joined Molotov for the Assembly debate on disarmament) that the small nations supporting the resolutions were "ungrateful" for the World War II victory "handed them by the Big Five." Romulo defended the part played by the Philippine people, recalled that at San Francisco *both* the U.S. and the U.S.S.R. had demanded the veto, and argued that, because of the veto, the Security Council "can do virtually nothing in moments of real crisis." What, Vishinsky had asked, could replace the veto? Romulo then sketched several proposals, which included

---

[10] Ibid., pp. 18–19.

[11] "Baruch and Hancock Defend the American Plan," ibid., pp. 20–23; Ickes, *New York Times*, 29 October 1946; CIO, *New York Times*, 20 November 1946; AFL, *PM*, 17 October 1946. On the day of Molotov's speech, Baruch team member Ferdinand Eberstadt went as far as any of them toward world government. He answered a reporter: "World government may be the only final solution to the problems of international relations…. [But] the goal is a long way off." "Baruch and Hancock Defend the American Plan," p. 23.

Clark's:[12]

> There are many who believe the General Assembly must be turned into a legislative body with limited powers before peace can be assured. There are others who propose the creation of a world bicameral legislature. Some feel that representation should be based upon population, others that there must be a system called "functional representation." More and more people the world over are coming to support what is known as "weighted representation."

Romulo gave a small–nation slant on the "fundamental weakness" of the Charter, which was not the veto ("the power *not* to do anything") but the one nation, one vote rule. Such a rule may be "pleasing" to small states like the Philippines, Romulo joked, but it "prevents the Great Powers from according the Assembly any power to enact binding world law." The United States, with a population of 140 million, was not going to submit to the enactments of an Assembly in which she was represented equally with the Philippines, whose population was 18 million! "As a spokesman for a small nation," he concluded, "my nation would be very happy indeed to trade the fiction of equality in a powerless Assembly for the reality of a vote equal to our actual position in the world in an Assembly endowed with real power.... What is needed is a narrowly limited World Federal Government."[13]

Romulo: Turning from the U.N. back to Power Politics

While the Assembly's Political and Security Committee was debating disarmament, which it did from 28 November to 13 December 1946, Romulo made a second speech in the subcommittee, which was getting itself tied up in knots over the Cuban and Australian resolutions. He spoke plainly of the indecision and impotence then becoming manifest in the United Nations. What was happening, Romulo asserted, was that nations were turning from the U.N., as common protector of their peoples from war, to "those obsolete methods that have never, never, in the long run, succeeded in keeping the peace: power politics, and powerful arms and armies." Again he rehearsed the reforms necessary to give "real authority" to the U.N.

The one nation, one vote rule makes it possible for the vote of the Soviet Union to be "neutralized" by the vote of Iceland; the vote of the United States to be "overwhelmed" by the vote of Iceland and Luxembourg. The Soviet Union uses the veto openly because in the Assembly it is in a minority position "out of all proportion to its actual power and prestige in the world." The United States uses the veto covertly, as in its "present monopoly position with relation

---

[12] Carlos P. Romulo, "Statement ... before Committee I—Political and Security Committee," 16 November 1946, Regenstein Library, World Republic Papers.

[13] Cranston claimed that "Romulo delivered our address word for word exactly as I typed it," except for increasing the population of the Philippines from 16 million (a figure Cranston got from the *World Almanac*) to 18 million! Romulo's second and third speeches, however, seem to be from his own hand. Cranston to Clark, 17 November 1946, Clark Papers, 15.1.

to the atom bomb." The Philippine delegation, Romulo repeated, would vote for the Cuban proposals.[14]

The first Cuban proposal—to call a General Conference under Article 109—would have required a two–thirds vote of the Assembly plus any 7 of the then 11 members of the Security Council; the second—to set up a study committee—a simple majority in the Assembly. In the Security Council, the alignment originally seemed to be as follows. *Pro:* Holland, Australia, Mexico, Brazil; *con:* U.S., U.S.S.R., Poland, France; *uncertain:* England, Egypt, China. Cranston observed that most delegates felt that England and hence Egypt would end up in the *con* group, and that the U.S. would pull Mexico and Brazil into the opposition, too. Moscow was firmly opposed, seeing an "occult power" behind the initiative of a state presumably so close within the American sphere of interest.[15]

Politicking in the Assembly

In the Assembly the votes were more uncertain. That was where the most "trading" was done, as Cranston put it, with the second Cuban proposal in view. The Dutch delegate, J. H. Van Roijen, recognized the special rights of the Big Five because of "their greater contributions to the common cause," but he thought the veto went beyond "reasonable bounds." A system of weighted voting would be more reasonable to him. M. F. Van Langenhove of Belgium spoke out in favor of majority rule, "this majority being in good time calculated in relation to the relative importance of states." Alexandre Parodi of France, though opposed, reminded delegates of France's constitutional provision for entering a supranational organization. China's Wellington Koo echoed his country's view at San Francisco that sovereignty must be diminished. Sir Hartley Shawcross of Britain in another debate mentioned his hope that the U.N. might become a "World Parliament." But he then went on to oppose U.N. intervention in Southwest Africa on the grounds that the U.N. was *not* a world government. Even Warren Austin of the United States let slip a remark, during discussion of a site for the permanent U.N. headquarters, that he hoped the site would be that of an eventual world government.[16]

Final Vote on Resolutions to Call a Review Conference

But in general the United States and Great Britain were, "paradoxically," as

[14] Carlos P. Romulo, Speech No. 2 ... before Sub-committee II of Committee I, 4 December 1946, ibid., 15.3. The record of the Soviet Union on its use of the veto to the end of 1946 was as follows: veto of U.S. resolution on withdrawal of foreign troops in Syria–Lebanon case, 16 February 1946; four vetoes in Spanish case, 25–26 June 1946; three vetoes on memberships of Trans-Jordan, Portugal, and Ireland, 29 August 1946; veto of resolution to appoint commission to investigate Greek border situation, 20 September 1946. Use of the Veto by the U.S.S.R. in Public Meetings of the Security Council, UWF Reference and Research Branch Memo, 14 August 1950, UWF Papers, 68.US–Russian Relations.

[15] Cranston to Clark, 17 October 1946; Clark to Cranston, 30 October 1946, Clark papers, 15.1.

[16] Campaign for World Government, pp. 2–4.

many observed, as hostile to abolition of the veto in the debates on the Cuban proposals as they were violent in attacking it in those on disarmament and atomic energy. The small nations, generally favorable in private, would not vote against the great powers for revision of the Charter—"not now." The final vote on the study committee in the Political and Security Committee was as follows:

YES	ABSTENTIONS	NOT PRESENT	NO
1. Argentina*	1. Afghanistan	N 1. Costa Rica	1. Byelorussia
2. Australia	2. Belgium	N 2. Czech.	2. Denmark
3. Bolivia*	3. Chile	N 3. Ecuador	3. France
4. Brazil	4. China	? 4. Ethiopia	4. Canada
5. Colombia	5. Iran	? 5. Guatemala	5. Greece
6. Cuba*	6. Luxembourg	Y 6. Haiti	6. India
7. Dominican R.*	7. Mexico	? 7. Iceland	7. Netherlands
8. Egypt	8. Turkey	Y 8. Iraq	8. Nicaragua
9. El Salvador*	9. Venezuela	Y 9. Lebanon	9. Norway
10. Honduras*		Y 10. Liberia	10. Panama
11. New Zealand*		Y 11. Paraguay	11. Peru
12. Philippines*		? 12. Uruguay	12. Poland
		N 13. S. Africa	13. S. Arabia
			14. Sweden
			15. Syria
			16. Ukraine
* Also voted for General Conference			17. U.K
N Probable no vote if present			18. U.S.A
Y Probable yes vote if present			19. U.S.S.R
			20. Yugoslavia

The vote came at a hastily called Sunday meeting (8 December 1946). Some not present were caught unawares, others deliberately stayed away, not to go on record. Note that China abstained. Also that Mexico and Brazil resisted the Colossus of the North. Egypt bucked England, but Holland went over to the opposition. Only Argentina's vote was understood to be anti–Soviet. As there was no majority, Ambassador Belt did not request a vote in plenary session of the Assembly. For the future, Cranston thought the key was the attitude of the United States toward revision, since "nation after nation looked to us for leadership."[17]

First Disarmament Debate

Meanwhile, the debate on disarmament in the Political and Security Committee had reached a seemingly opposite conclusion. Both the Soviet Union and the United States made concessions to one another. Molotov for the first time used the code word "inspection" in his proposals. He clarified the Russian posi-

[17] Ibid., pp. 5–6. The press took little note of this historic effort to revise the Charter, overshadowed by the general disarmament debate. Without great power leadership, the vote on the abolition of the veto was a "non-event."

tion that the general disarmament and atomic control commissions (finally united in his resolution) should function under the Security Council, which was subject to the unanimity rule or veto. Unanimity, Molotov explained, would be required only for the "decision on the reduction of armaments, including the prohi-
bition of atomic weapons and the establishment of control commissions"—not
for the day–to–day "work" of the commissions.

The United States also made a significant concession when the American delegate agreed to the Soviet proposal that the control commission should not derive its authority from a treaty or convention outside the U.N. but from the
Charter. A final compromise provided, rather strangely if suggestively, for an
"international system ... within the framework of the Security Council," whose
legal instrument would be a "convention" between nations.[18]

Carlos Romulo's Speech on Doing the U.N. to Death

Then, on 13 December 1946, the day before the final vote on the disarmament resolution, Carlos Romulo rose before all the principal delegates and before
packed galleries of the plenary session of the General Assembly to make his
third speech. "I rub my eyes, and wonder where I am," he said on recounting
U.N. debates on disarmament and voting rules; "I listen, and cannot believe my
ears." Romulo began by recalling the presumption that they were all there "to
create conditions of everlasting peace." He referred back to the San Francisco
conference, where "at the insistence of the United States, the Soviet Union, and
the United Kingdom, a provision virtually disfranchising well over sixty per cent
of the people of the world was written into the Charter." But the small nations
were told, Take the veto, or there will be no Charter.

Then, after use of the atomic bomb, the United States proposed that the veto
should be abolished for the control of atomic energy. Senator Connally later
came to the Assembly to urge abolition of the veto also for control of all weapons of mass destruction. "How many people," the senator asked, "would be in
jail if they had the right of veto over the sheriff or the judge?" Yet the United
States voted against both Cuban proposals for immediate or *eventual* Charter revision. Senator Austin, also of the American delegation, stated, "The United
States is opposed to amendment of Article 27 at this time." Said Romulo: "I
cannot understand this. How can the United States denounce the veto one day,
and defend the veto the next day? Does the United States know what it wants?"

The United Kingdom, by comparison, Romulo added, was caught in the same
contradiction, judging by statements of Shawcross and Bevin. The Soviet Union,
too, agreed to abolition of the veto in the *operation* of the general disarmament
control commission but voted against proposals to amend the Charter to do away
with the veto. Why this inconsistency? Romulo found two answers. The Big
Three were beginning to see that the veto was a "monstrosity," preventing all
practical action in the United Nations for the control of modern weapons, but
they were "afraid to admit that they made an unforgivable mistake when they in-

---

[18] "Disarmament Debate in United Nations General Assembly," 28 November – 13
December 1946, *Bulletin of the Atomic Scientists*, January 1947, pp. 6–8.

sisted upon a Charter containing a veto clause." Or they covered up their mistake with talk of "realism," since an attempt to really eliminate the veto "might offend somebody." He asked, "Is this fair to the United Nations? Is this fair to the *people of the world?*"

The new organs proposed for peacekeeping were effectively outside the United Nations, he plainly stated.[19]

> If we adopt this policy, we shall be *doing the United Nations to death.* If we do this, we shall leave only a shell, a shell to deal with mere trivia. This shell will bear a marked resemblance to the League of Nations, famed for its achievements in such matters as the prevention of international narcotic smuggling, notorious for its failure to prevent world war.

Once more Romulo went over the arguments for strengthening the United Nations by replacing the unanimity rule in the Security Council with a majority rule in the General Assembly, reformed to make it representative of peoples. He saw no great obstacle in the competing eco-political systems of communism, socialism, and capitalism to a federal structure of world government. But what made this speech so significant was his plain statement of the breakup of any effective superior government over the nation–states and their consequent turn to national programs of military defense. Romulo was recording the historic end of the brief hope of basing peace on government. Henceforth the attempt would be made again to base it on fear.

> We sit here and feel the United Nations tremble. We watch it fail to meet forcefully the great issues of our time. We know in our hearts that its structure is faulty. We know that therefore no nation—yes, *no nation, great or small*—trusts the United Nations to provide its security and peace.

He made one last appeal for the Cuban proposals.[20]

Climax of U.N. AEC Negotiations, 30 December 1946

Events now moved to a parallel climax in the U.N. Atomic Energy Commission, which we have already sketched in Chapter 10. The General Assembly passed, unanimously, its disarmament resolution—"Principles Governing General Regulation and Reduction of Armaments"—on 14 December 1946. The reso-

---

[19] Carlos P. Romulo, Speech No. 3 ... before the General Assembly, 13 December 1946, his emphases, Clark Papers, 15.3.

[20] Ambassador Romulo was honored for his speeches by being presented with the first World Government News Award Medal at a dinner attended by Carl Van Doren, Justice William O. Douglas, Senator Carl A. Hatch, and Lin Yu-tang on 12 March 1947. "By this powerful call," the award citation read, "the Ambassador lifted into practical international politics an idea to which lesser statesmen have given lip service but small public support." (Also honored with the medals were Emery Reves and E. B. White of the *New Yorker.*) Carl Van Doren, "The World Government News Award," *World Government News,* 1 March 1947.

lution contained language urging dispatch in the U.N. AEC. The latter, as an organ of the Security Council, was not bound to regard the Assembly resolution as more than a recommendation, of course, but the resolution clearly expressed the hope of the nations that international control of atomic and all other weapons of mass destruction (now at last united in one control proposal) would be realized, and Bernard Baruch for the United States at least regarded it as a sign of a "new spirit" urging the AEC "to proceed expeditiously to the development of a formula of action."[21]

Baruch pressed impatiently for a vote on the American plan in the form of the "General Findings and Recommendations" dated 5 December 1946. Only three "political" clauses were in dispute:[22]

> The treaty shall provide that the rule of unanimity of the permanent Members, which in certain circumstances exists in the Security Council, shall have no relation to the work of the international agency. No government shall possess any right of veto over the fulfillment by the international control agency of the obligations imposed upon it by the treaty nor shall any government have the power, through exercise of veto or otherwise, to obstruct the course of control or inspection.
>
> Once the violations constituting international crimes have been defined and the measures of enforcement and punishment therefore agreed to in the treaty or convention, there shall be no legal right, by veto or otherwise, whereby a willful violator of the terms of the treaty or convention shall be protected from the consequences of violation of its terms.
>
> The enforcement and punishment provisions of the treaty or convention would be ineffectual if, in any such situations, they could be rendered nugatory by the veto of a State which had voluntarily signed the treaty.

Baruch: A Breach Means War

Baruch urged haste, in retrospect in order to reveal Soviet dilatoriness as all states began to realign themselves in the emerging Cold War. The proposals he claimed were "generous and just." They aimed to erect an "international authority which shall effectively prevent the manufacture and use of atomic bombs for war purposes and which shall develop the use of atomic energy for social gain." They required "full and free international inspection." They provided "deterrents" and "punishments."[23]

> The time for action is here. Each of us perceives clearly what must be done. We may differ as to detail. We are in accord as to purpose. To the achieve-

---

[21] "Proceedings of the UN Atomic Energy Commission," *Bulletin of the Atomic Scientists*, January 1947, p. 11. The United States drafted the clause urging dispatch in the U.N. AEC. *Policy at the Crossroads*, 60–63.

[22] *Policy of the Crossroads*, 48–51; "First Report of the Atomic Energy Commission to the Security Council," 30 December 1946, *Bulletin of the Atomic Scientists*, January 1947, pp. 16–27.

[23] *Policy at the Crossroads*, 52–53; "Proceedings," p. 10.

ment of that purpose, I present a programme in the form of a resolution, which has been placed before you.

Except for the American delegation, there was general reluctance to bring matters quickly to a vote. The U.S.S.R.'s Gromyko pointed out that the Assembly's disarmament resolution, which was being cited to precipitate matters, was silent on the veto question. He urged that no decision be taken until they could reach "unanimous agreement." Other diplomatic representatives foresaw a nuclear arms race even as they saw immediately a threat of war. Baruch agreed to a postponement of a few days before the Christmas holidays.[24] Meetings of Committee 2 (political) were held on the 18th and 19th. The Soviet delegate refused to participate. On the 20th the full AEC met again, and Gromyko formally asked for six or seven days to study the Baruch resolutions in the light of the Assembly resolution of the 14th. This was rejected.

On the 27th, Baruch attacked the remaining ambiguity of the Russian position on the veto, if it should be necessary for the control commission "to enforce the obligations of the treaty." He admitted that enforcement as envisaged in the American proposal meant "war." He even urged that the treaty terms make punishment by war explicit:

Let all nations that willingly set their pens to the terms of this treaty realize that its willful breech means punishment and, if necessary, war. Then we will not lightly have breaches and evasions.

He could not recommend to the people or the Senate of the United States that they "surrender this potent weapon" and transfer their atomic secrets to a U.N. body—"in the belief that they are outlawing the use of this weapon for war and opening the gates for the uses of atomic energy for the good of all mankind—under any system which is open to nullification of punishment by what can be called a subterfuge."[25]

Gromyko on Violation of Charter

Then on 30 December 1946, at the plenary meeting to vote the Baruch resolutions, Andrei Gromyko answered in effect that the atomic energy proposals were not in accord with international realities. The U.S. proposals, said the Soviet delegate, were "in contradiction with the principles of the United Nations Organization." The Charter had given supreme responsibility for the maintenance of peace and security to the Security Council, while now the United States proposed to set up a new atomic energy control authority in competition with the Council. The proposals were dangerous to the peace, Gromyko stated. The new authority was not granted "real ... powers," yet the Security Council was to be enabled to apply sanctions, including war, even if not unanimous. The United States was actually proposing "revision of the Charter" yet had rejected the recent

[24] "Proceedings," pp. 10–12; *Policy at the Crossroads,* 53–55.
[25] "Proceedings," pp. 12–13; *Policy at the Crossroads,* 54–55.

proposals in the Assembly to do so openly. He resented remarks that "only those nations want to protect the principle of unanimity in connection with atomic energy control which have an intention of breaking the treaty on the control." Gromyko pointed out the specific clauses on the veto in the Baruch resolutions that he rejected. He added that the Soviet government was willing to continue discussions. He returned to the basis of his 19 June proposals, providing for prior destruction of American atomic weapons as a precondition for establishing "control and inspection" organs in which "decisions by a majority" should apply "in appropriate cases."[26]

The Vote on 30 December 1946

Gromyko's reply was in principle constitutional, but it was perceived as evasive—pious references to the Charter already being seen as code for inaction. Baruch moved to adopt the report finalized by the working committees. Other delegates seem to have lost patience or to have come to regard the Russians as did the Americans.

The vote was as follows:[27]

YES	ABSTENTIONS	NO
1. Australia	1. Poland	
2. Brazil	2. U.S.S.R	
3. Canada		
4. China		
5. Egypt		
6. France		
7. Mexico		
8. Netherlands		
9. U.K.		
10. U.S.A		

Analysis: Inadequate Proposals for Effective International Control

It was not clear immediately just what had happened. The Soviets and Poles had not voted *against* the U.S. plan; they had abstained, which seemed to indicate continued willingness to negotiate. But within days Baruch and his whole team resigned, convinced of "one central fact"—"The Russians would not countenance an effective system of international control of nuclear energy."

Nevertheless, in the months to come, the Russians would continue to make major concessions. They had already conceded at least "limited" inspection. On 18 February 1947, Gromyko submitted 12 amendments, in one of which the code word "management" occurred. On 5 March, in an otherwise violent attack

---

[26] "Proceedings," pp. 13–14.

[27] "Proceedings," pp. 14–15; *Policy of the Crossroads*, 55. Canada, not in 1946 a member of the Security Council, had been brought into the U.N. AEC by special arrangement in recognition of her association with the U.S. and U.K. on the atomic bomb project.

on the American plan, he elaborated the new Russian attitude on inspection and management. On 11 June, he accepted the principle of an international cooperative research organization. But by then even the atomic scientists had run out of patience. One of them wrote in the summer of 1947: "It is difficult to believe that it took the Soviet leaders a whole year to begin to understand the first things about atomic energy and the elementary requirement for its effective control."[28]

What had happened? The end had come for the political effort, inspired by the atomic scientists, initiated by the United States, to bring about the international control of atomic energy. The opportunity to establish limited world government by peaceful means, implicit in the proposal to abolish the sovereign veto in cases of enforcement of decisions of the atomic control agency, was lost. The Cold War would follow very soon. Within years all nations would be embarked on programs of national defense, having learned, as Romulo said, that the United Nations could not be trusted to provide peace and security. The peoples of the world have been living in the aftermath of the failure of the Baruch plan ever since.

Americans Overextended

Was six months or one year too long to wait to accomplish what Baruch himself called "some diminution of absolute national sovereignty"? Why, then, the rush? Because delays were thought to give the Russians, otherwise so intransigent over Eastern Europe, the Dardanelles, Iran, and China, opportunity to develop atomic weapons for themselves. On a rereading of the record, the American plan *does* seem to have been, both in the minds of its proponents and in truth, "generous and just." In the history of modern nations, the offer to surrender control of the greatest of weapons to a common sovereign was unparalleled. Baruch sensed this, going beyond the State Department to advocate abolition of the veto, but he could bear to risk the security of the United States only for so long, without signs of greater appreciation of the positive elements of his courageous proposal from the Soviet Union.

Russians Slow

What about the Russians? The Russians, for their part, were slow to be impressed with the problem of atomic energy. They began, much as the Lilienthal board had six months before, with the idea that not even international inspection

---

[28] Baruch to Truman, 4 January 1947; Truman to Baruch, 12 January 1947, quoted in *Policy at the Crossroads*, 56; Baruch, *The Public Years*, 374; "The Soviet Amendments and Mr. Gromyko's Speech," *Bulletin of the Atomic Scientists*, March 1947, pp. 69, 100; Andrei A. Gromyko, "Soviet Proposals for Atomic Energy Control," ibid., August 1947, pp. 219–20; Eugene Rabinowitch, "The Soviet Plan for Atomic Energy Control," ibid., August 1947, p. 201. Baruch's place was taken by the regular U.S. delegate to the U.N., Warren Austin. There were two more major reports to the Security Council, neither unanimously agreed to. On 17 May 1948, the U.N. AEC reported that it had reached an impasse in its work beyond its competence to overcome. In September 1949, the Russians tested their first atomic bomb.

was necessary but that another Geneva convention could "outlaw" such a mass weapon. Their scientists, however, within three months of the June opening of negotiations, saw the scientific and technical problem exactly as the Americans did. Their political representatives, in an atmosphere of ultimatum, slowly saw the need for inspection by December and later for management and research to solve the problem of control.

But there was an element of truth in Molotov's charge that the American plan was characterized by a certain degree of "selfishness." It was natural for the Russians to be suspicious of the stages for the transfer of U.S. atomic secrets, materials, plants, and weapons to the international control agency and for the agency's "strategic" redevelopment, which stages, indeed, were never spelled out. What they thought of the Bikini tests immediately after the introduction of the Baruch plan and of the Americans' refusal to enter into a convention to stop adding to, and to destroy, the atomic bomb stockpile—leaving the critical materials and plants quite untouched—may be imagined by the reader. Lastly, the Russians had no use at all for the notion of abolishing the Security Council veto, as if it would be possible to enforce a plan like the Americans' by a kind of U.N. *war*.

World Government Necessary

In fact, the Baruch plan was so seriously flawed that only major modifications—never forthcoming—would have made it workable. It is, perhaps, natural for an American reading the record to suppose that Russians would be the violators, but the language of the plan was universal. Imagine the effect if the United States should ever have been adjudged a violator. Would it be right to apply sanctions, ultimately including war, on the whole American people in order to "enforce" the control agency's decisions?

Never, after one obscure reference in Baruch's first speech, was there any argument in the U.N. AEC for establishing a rule of law reaching to individuals. Never was there argument, as Grenville Clark suggested, for taking dissatisfaction with the veto as an opportunity for fundamentally revising the Charter, making the Assembly a world legislature under a system of weighted representation, the Council an executive branch, and the Court a judiciary. It was world federal government like this that was necessary, in our historical judgment, to make the international control of atomic energy a reality.

12

Formation of
United World Federalists

Rep. Jacob Javits: "I will say that I consider World Federal-
ists the men and women of the future."
Chairman Charles Eaton: "How about the present?"
Rep. Javits: "I think we are of the present, Mr. Chairman."
—House hearings on revision of the U.N. Charter, 11 May 1948

Toward Asheville

By November 1946, the movement for world federal government in the
United States was rising to the climax of its organizers' hopes—the union of all
mass membership federalist groups. (Nonmembership groups were kept out.)
This union, United World Federalists, would be effectively accomplished at the
Asheville (North Carolina) congress of 21–23 February 1947. Historically, it is
puzzling why the federalists took so long. Their principal motivation was to
meet the threat of the atomic bomb, one and a half years before. In the interim,
the United Nations Organization began to meet, the United States proposed the
international control of atomic energy, and the Allies at Paris sat down to negotiate a peace treaty with Germany and her Axis partners in Europe. Most world
federalists, like their fellow citizens, seem to have trusted their governments,
which had brought them to victory in the war. "Roosevelt would take care of
the peace," Millie Blake had said of federalist expectations.

But Roosevelt was no more; Harry Truman was in the White House. His
cabinet, except for Henry Wallace, was made up of advisors schooled in the war.
The U.N. proved no match for Western–Soviet controversy over the treatment of
Poland, the Baruch plan was headed for failure, and the peace conference was
marred by insults and accusations of Hitlerite ambitions. (A peace treaty with
Germany was never negotiated, though years later in 1975 the Helsinki Accords
served an equivalent function.) It was in response to the breakup of friendly relations in 1946 that the federalists turned seriously to union. The trouble was that
there were different conceptions of the desired form of a government of the world
(universal or democratic, minimal or maximal) and particularly of the means of
attainment (U.N. reform or peoples' convention). Money was at stake, and so

were reputations. High principles had to be defended.

Why unite? Because to do so was a demonstration of the principle of federation, because it was an application of the people's power in democracy. Tom Griessemer of World Federalists looked forward to *"one strong, consolidated movement"* that would have roots *"across the country"* rather than in one national headquarters. Broadcaster Raymond Gram Swing foresaw an evangelical movement that would sweep the country with a *"fire of fervor"* provided by *50 million* adherents. Corporation lawyer Thomas Finletter of Americans United aimed to establish a "new corporation" in which would be vested "all of the property, personnel and interests of the constituent groups," a united citizens' organization to lobby and influence the government. Jack Whitehouse wanted the strongest possible grassroots organization to stop the drift toward a third world war.[1]

It was reflective of the caution and principled divisions of the movement that the initiative to unite it should have come from impassioned youth in Students for Federal World Government.

A Divided and Dispirited Movement

Grenville Clark thought the strategy of pressing for U.N. Charter amendments was still the right one. Time would make it apparent that atomic control made amending the Charter a "necessity." Within the year he would, in fact, lead another effort in the General Assembly, through the Argentines, to introduce the necessary amendments. But he was convinced the movement could not expect "strong leadership for world government" from U.S. officials. General Marshall, who was replacing Byrnes as secretary of state, probably could not "grasp the concept." He wrote to his Dublin follow–up group:

> I am impressed with how slowly the thing develops. For example, they just now seem to be getting down to a real discussion of what "weapons adaptable to mass destruction" (other than the atomic bomb) consist of. That is something that we were all debating and forming pretty clear ideas about nearly a year ago. The moral is, I think, that the advocates of world government ought to be prepared to go through with their efforts over quite a long period and not strike so fast a pace that they get tired and can't put on a spurt at the critical moment.

Through 1947, Clark was surprisingly silent. Not that he had given up. He was filling notebooks with observations of the perplexing course of American foreign policy. This business of moving the government, through citizens' initiatives, toward a policy of world government was much harder than moving it

---

[1] Griessemer to Friend, "Extra!" n.d., ante 21 February 1947, his emphases; UWF Papers, 57.Asheville Convention Reports; Swing to von Windegger, 6 February 1947, Schwimmer–Lloyd Collection, T65, my emphases; Finletter to Griessemer, 17 December 1946, UWF Papers, 42.Asheville; "World Government Peace Conference," *Planet*, 28 August 1946, Regenstein Library, World Republic Papers, Envelope Vol. 2, No. 4.

toward a policy of traditional defense, as in his old Plattsburg and Selective Service Act days.[2]

World Federalists, U.S.A., were "bee–busy" with Millie Blake's advertising campaign, claiming that its effects were "impressive" in the U.N. fight against the veto. Evidence was also cited of the advertising's political impact in a congressional candidate's view with alarm of World Federalists' "communist" tendencies; a similar effect was seen in Moscow's *Izvestia*, which saw a "capitalist plot."[3]

Americans United for World Government were recovering from their disappointment at not getting former secretary of state Stettinius—chief defender of the "adequacy" of the U.N.—to speak at their big dinner for the élite of American internationalists. The organization's pretensions were being punctured at many points by World Federalists, whose interest in merger was just about spent. Americans United were concealing their financial situation; their membership claims were down to 10,000; they admitted they never had an explicitly stated policy; their suggestions for a joint board were such as to give them dominant control, even though it was apparent that most of their strength was in New York City while World Federalists were nation–wide. Talks of merger were suspended in an atmosphere of maneuver and mistrust.[4]

Student Federalists had just put out a new number of their paper after a three–month lapse in the summer. A series of "monthly forums on questions of current interest" were planned. St. John's graduate Charles Nelson's list of books on world government was recommended for self–education.[5]

The Massachusetts Committee for World Federation was marshaling its resources after its referendum success to introduce an action resolution in the State House on Beacon Hill.[6]

The Oak Ridge World Government Committee, at a moment when the atomic scientists' movement seemed to be in a state of arrested disintegration due to public apathy, official slurs, member resignations, and U.N. AEC tension, was asking what issue could "whip up enthusiasm" like that of a year before. Cuthbert Daniel for the committee proclaimed his well–known belief that world government was the response of an order sufficient to meet the challenge of atomic war. He was opposed by W. Arnold for the majority in the Association of Oak

[2] Cranston to Douglas Arant et al., 24 January 1947; Grenville Clark, Memorandum, 17 February 1947, Baker Library, Clark Papers, 15.3.

[3] "The Pay Off," *World Government News*, November 1946, p. 2.

[4] Blake to Leo Cherne, 28 October 1946, Lilly Library, UWF Papers, 42.Cleveland Convention [sic]. Ulric Bell had recently left Americans United. His place was taken effectively by Thomas K. Finletter, who brought a somewhat more realistic spirit to merger negotiations.

[5] Student Federalist Headquarters Bulletin, 25 September 1946; Chapter Bulletin, 1 October 1946, UWF Papers, 57.Asheville Convention Reports.

[6] Commonwealth of Massachusetts, Senate, Resolutions Providing for Request for Amendments to the Charter of the United Nations Resulting in a Limited World Federal Government, S204, 14 January 1947.

Ridge Engineers and Scientists: "Our members are out to save [the] world. Piffle and Epworth League! We should be more concerned about secrecy in science, and [the] Army and Navy taking over science."[7]

The one new ray of light from the atomic scientists' movement—and one of the last of their original spirit—was Norbert Wiener's open letter refusing to cooperate with the military rocket program of December 1946. Wiener was the distinguished Massachusetts Institute of Technology professor of mathematics who had founded the branch of science he called "cybernetics," dealing with feedback control systems; it found some application during the war in antiaircraft systems and later in automation, economics, and psychology. He replied to an unnamed research scientist working on the new ballistic missiles who had asked for a paper of his written for Vannevar Bush's National Defense Research Committee. Wiener refused on moral grounds:[8]

> In the past, the comity of scholars has made it a custom to furnish scientific information to any person seriously seeking it. However, we must face these facts: The policy of the government itself during and after the war, say in the bombing of Hiroshima and Nagasaki, has made it clear that to provide scientific information is not a necessarily innocent act, and may entail the gravest consequences....
>
> The practical use of guided missiles can only be to kill foreign civilians indiscriminately, and it furnishes no protection whatsoever to civilians in this country. I cannot conceive a situation in which such weapons can produce any effect other than extending the kamikaze way of fighting to whole nations. Their possession can do nothing but endanger us by encouraging the tragic insolence of the military mind.

Wiener's moving letter was in effect a call for scientists to *strike* the national defense program. But with the failure of the effort to establish the international control of atomic weapons and other weapons of mass destruction—that is, to establish a limited world government, which Wiener apparently never advocated —what choice was there for scientists who still wished to defend the United States? Wiener's was, in Einstein's phrase, "unsound pacifism."

The University of Chicago's Committee to Frame a World Constitution, under Robert M. Hutchins, had formed soon after Hiroshima but conducted its deliberations in secret, virtually unknown to the larger movement. Participants reached working consensus on their model world legislature, grant of powers, and executive during the summer, then recessed for three months after its 10th meeting on 24 October 1946. Time was needed, said secretary G. A. Borgese blithely, for "softening up" remaining issues and waiting for opportunities presented by the "deterioration of other hopes" in the U.N. George Peck, assistant professor of history on leave from Lehigh University, had just been hired as editor of a projected "heavy" journal of the committee. The first issue was planned for

---

[7] AORES Log, 30 October 1946, p. 89, Regenstein Library, AORES Papers, 8.1.

[8] Norbert Wiener, "A Scientist Rebels," *Atlantic,* December 1946, p. 46; reprinted in *Bulletin of the Atomic Scientists,* January 1947, p. 31.

January 1947.[9] True to academic pattern, the new journal, *Common Cause*, did not appear until July 1947. Precious time was being lost.

The Campaign for World Government was licking its wounds after an unfortunate split in 1945, after Lola Maverick Lloyd's death and certain disagreements between the younger Lloyds and the aging Rosika Schwimmer. The group divided into the Campaign for World Government, based in Chicago, and the *International* Campaign for World Government, based in New York. Georgia Lloyd became effective leader of the former; Edith Wynner, of the latter.[10] The Campaign was not a membership organization, but splits in movements to unite the world were a bad sign.

Lastly, in November 1946, the deceptive Ely Culbertson was winning new tricks. During the summer and fall a quite spontaneous citizens' endorsement of his Quota Force plan developed in Middletown, Ohio, which was all the more remarkable in that it was led by World War II veterans in the American Legion. They were alarmed by the drift toward war, the return of power politics, the prospects of an armament race, and the talk of preventive war. The alternative, they saw, was to strengthen the United Nations. Culbertson's plan seemed to the veterans most "concrete and workable" (there was hardly another in 1946 of similar published scope). It required the United States to give up only the "sovereign right" to wage war, and it would abolish the veto, strengthen the World Court, and establish an "international police [military] force."[11]

Critics pointed out, however, that the "three reforms" of the plan provided only for the same old abolition of the veto in a Security Council representative of sovereign states, the Baruch plan with artificial quota strictures, and an international police force to enforce U.N. decisions by *war*. An ultimatum was even provided to Russia: join within three months or the rest of the nations will unite under the plan without you. The deceptiveness of this revived Culbertson plan was a serious obstacle to the movement. His group, the Citizens Committee for United Nations Reform (CCUNR), became strong enough to support national legislation, but its popular following seems never to have been as influential as the force of Culbertson's personality. The American Legion officially adopted the Quota Force plan as its foreign policy recommendation on 23 November 1946, before Asheville.[12]

European Federalists

Abroad, in October 1946, the first meeting of what would become the World Movement for World Federal Government and the European Union of Federalists

---

[9] "Brief History of the Committee," *Common Cause*, 1 (July 1947): 18–19; "Constitution Drafting," *World Government News*, December 1946, pp. 2–3.

[10] International Campaign for World Government, 19 July 1947, New York Public Library, Schwimmer–Lloyd Collection; Georgia Lloyd, Interview, 30 May 1981.

[11] "Crossroads Middletown," n.d., post 2 September 1946, pp. 2, 3, 5, 10, 12, 14, 15, UWF Papers, 9.CCUNR.

[12] Culbertson to Friend, 9 December 1946; CCUNR, "Our Purpose and Program," n.d., c. December 1946, UWF Papers, 9.CCUNR.

was held in Luxembourg. So great a matter as the unification of Europe and of the world could not be left to the Americans. Britain's Federal Union, in which Henry Usborne was more and more being named as a rising star, issued the invitation to the conference. World Federalists, U.S.A., had set the goals of both a national merger and an international conference as far back as their Cleveland convention in April 1946, but the English group was first to take the initiative internationally.[13]

Seventy–five representatives from 37 organizations in 14 countries assembled. There was vigorous debate at Luxembourg about the priorities of European versus world federation—England's Frances L. Josephy and Holland's H. R. Nord viewed the former as all that was then practical; the United States' Edward Clark and Tom Griessemer regarded the latter as alone able to prevent war among states or regions. The upshot, under the guidance of international lawyer Max Habicht, was the creation of *two* organizations: the Movement for World Federal Government and the European Union of Federalists. It began a split that would last until the 1980s. Permanent headquarters was to be on the European continent; temporary, at World Government House in New York. Griessemer was to be temporary secretary. The conference to formally organize the two organizations would be held in Montreux in Switzerland the next summer.[14]

In November, Henry Usborne was still trying to raise the money in sterling amid the many financial restrictions of postwar England to bring Edith Wynner over as peoples' convention advisor. During the year, she had been working mostly with Nashville attorney Fyke Farmer on a "popular initiative" for world government. Financing—always one of the greatest problems of popular approaches—was then being considered by Missouri banker F. R. von Windegger and mechanical cotton picker inventor John D. Rust. When Usborne's radical pamphlet *If They Won't, We Will!* came her way, she immediately wrote her associates of his "parallel efforts." Usborne in turn was quick to credit her "persistent influence" for the idea of world government established by a direct appeal to the sovereignty of the people.[15]

At the end of 1946, Usborne was asked by the Labour Party to move the acceptance of the king's annual speech from the throne, a traditional occasion for the governing party to state its future policy. Apparently with Labour party approval, Usborne used the occasion to make his second speech to Parliament on world government. The trial balloon was deflated, and British policy soon turned

---

[13] "Luxembourg Declaration," 16 October 1946, World Republic Papers, WMWFG, 1946.

[14] Proceedings, Luxembourg Conference, pp. 9–16; Report by Tom Griessemer of the International Conference of Federalists in Luxembourg, 14–16 October 1946, UWF Papers, 42.Luxembourg Conference. Foster Parmelee of Student Federalists came to the conference from a trip behind the "Iron Curtain." He reported there "great enthusiasm for federation."

[15] Wynner to Usborne, 29 September 1945, Schwimmer–Lloyd Collection, T60; Wynner to Farmer, von Windegger, Gerber, and Rust, 12 October 1946; Usborne to Wynner, 12 October 1946, AORES Papers, 9.3.

to support for an Atlantic alliance with the United States.[16]

Prospects for a Mass, Popular, Grassroots Movement

In contrast to this disarray was the enthusiasm of Students for Federal World Government in Chicago. The youth group toyed briefly with the idea of a "student march on Washington" to support the Baruch plan, but that was beyond their financial resources then being developed. Instead, their student teams on the road distributed 10,000 copies of Baruch's speech, which the State Department gave them. Several SFFWG members wrote letters to correspondents in Poland and Eastern Europe. In response to a *Saturday Evening Post* article of 13 July, "Your Flesh *Should* Creep" (on lack of defense against atomic and other new weapons of modern war), David McCoy of the "off–campus unrecognized student organization" got himself received before the Northwestern international relations club. McCoy spoke on the political defense—world government—"An Antidote to Gooseflesh."[17]

Ronald Reagan Gives $200

Talk like this raised money for the radical student group. In early July 1946, Paul Sauer went to Los Angeles to start up another garage operation at 4967 ½ North Figueroa Street. One contributor he found, who gave $200, was the film star Ronald Reagan. Hardly had Sauer started ringing doorbells, however, when Jack Whitehouse called for him to come to New York. A meeting with Mrs. John Alden Carpenter of Beverly, Massachusetts, who had given them $1,000 for an essay contest, and other potential big contributors had been arranged, including Orson Welles. Sauer instantly flew to New York. "History will be in your hands Wednesday night," McCoy wrote them both. It is not clear from the records just what history was made there, but apparently Sauer got a lead to Charles Henry Davis, prominent civil engineer (designer of the first railroad tunnel under the Hudson River), Quaker, pacifist, and friend of youth.

It is said that Sauer *walked* from Boston to Cape Cod to meet Davis, who was so taken that he advised the boys until after Asheville (February 1947). He gave them $5,000, which paid for many of their trips, and seems to have lent them another $5,000. It was Davis who secured the large building in downtown Evanston into which SFFWG moved before Asheville, changing their name to

---

[16] Great Britain, Parliament, House of Commons, 12 November 1946, *Hansard's Parliamentary Debates*, cols. 9–12, 25–28. The Associated Press excerpted Usborne's speech at length. The fullest accounts came in the *New York Herald Tribune* the day after. No notice in the *New York Times* nor in the "liberal" *PM*. Wynner to Usborne, 12 and 13 November 1946, Schwimmer–Lloyd Collection, T60.

[17] Sauer to McCoy, 6 July 1946; Francis H. Russell, Chief, Division of Public Liaison, to Whitehouse, 28 August 1946; Press Release on Warsaw Exhibit, n.d., c. 7 July 1946; John Huebner to Jire Kalaja and Wojciech Goralczyk, 1 August 1946; Kalaja to SFFWG, 10 December 1946; Press Release to *Daily Northwestern,* 19 July 1946, World Republic Papers, SFFWG, July–August 1946; David McCoy, "An Antidote to Gooseflesh," *Planet,* 24 July 1946, p. 2.

World Republic. The World Republic headquarters, for the six months the boys could afford to pay the rent, was in its time the largest building in the world dedicated to world government.[18]

At the end of July 1946, Paul Hoffman, president of Studebaker Corp. and future administrator of the European Cooperation Administration (Marshall plan), and his wife Edith gave SFFWG a new Studebaker Champion for one of their 14 teams. The boys explained to the Hoffmans that Clarence Streit's movement, by contrast, would promote "gigantic power blocks, *ergo* war." Another group, the World Citizens of Oberlin, was too "dusty and timidly academic." "We are deeply impressed," the Hoffmans wrote, "by the sacrifices you have made, which shows us your great sincerity and integrity."[19]

World Republic on Breakup of Paris Peace Conference

By early August, Whitehouse appointed himself temporary chairman of a coordinating committee to bring about a national conference to unite all world government groups on Thanksgiving Day in November. "This action," he wrote the invitees, "is long overdue. There often appears to be a duplication of efforts and a waste of time, energy and finances because of the lack of correlated activities of all groups concerned." This was the initiative that would lead to the formation of United World Federalists.[20]

Whitehouse was alarmed by the breakup of the Paris peace conference, held to draft the peace treaties with Italy and the Balkan countries preparatory to the peace treaty with Germany, in early August 1946. Molotov and Byrnes exchanged accusations: the former that the United States was building a Western "bloc" against the Soviet Union, the latter that the Soviet Union was directing its "satellites" to oppose the United States. In the debate over Italy, the United States and Great Britain were charged with seeking alliances with "Fascists," attempting to "enslave" Italy through "foreign trusts and cartels." In turn the Soviet Union was accused of claiming that ex-enemy states were more democratic than Italy because "they have harmonized their views with the Soviet Union." Serious differences arose over Trieste, reparations obligations, and control of the Danube. The conference almost broke up when an American transport plane strayed over Yugoslav territory and was shot down on 9 August, followed by a second on the 19th, with the loss of five American lives. A satisfactory apology came only after Byrnes threatened to call upon the Security Council to take "appropriate action." Although the conference lingered on until October 15, it

---

[18] Contributions of $10.00 or More, March '46 to September '47, World Republic Papers, Minutes, 1946; McCoy to Sauer and Whitehouse, 8 July 1946, ibid., SFFWG, July–August 1946; Davis to Harold Bock, 31 July 1946; Davis to Whitehouse, 12 December 1946; Davis to Whitehouse, 15 January 1947, ibid., Davis.

[19] Hoffman to Whitehouse, 22 July 1946; L. S. Morrin, Assistant Regional Manager for Studebaker, to Sauer, 30 July 1946.

[20] Minutes, 3 August, 1946, ibid., Minutes, 1946; "World Government Peace Conference," *Planet*, 28 August 1946, ibid., Envelope Vol. 2, No. 4.

was clear in August that there would be no peace treaties.[21]

Whitehouse's Speech against a New War

Whitehouse's reaction was extreme. He went to speak before rival Student Federalists, who happened to be holding their annual convention in Chicago during the first week of September. His raw, angry speech revealed a slow, deep popular will in opposition to another war.[22]

> We have been betrayed! We have been betrayed! Some of us are the veterans of this war, and others are the veterans of heartache....
>
> The first great betrayal ... is in fact that you and I went all around the world and slaughtered Japs and Germans because our Government said we were fighting on the cross of nationalism ... for the rights of democracies.... Today there is more chaos and destruction in the world. Today you and I have come back and we are not sitting at the peace tables. The old men are there [and took from us our victory and remade it in the likeness of the former world they knew]....
>
> That is the second and greatest betrayal. They have left us with $275 billions in debt, and expect us to pay it off. And yet they go on spending $12 billion a year for armaments. That should tell you that we are heading for war.
>
> A third great betrayal is the United Nations.... These are not the things that you went to war for. If the United Nations had the law and the power they could step into China and stop [the civil war].
>
> The fourth great betrayal is our present Government.... They are building atomic bombs, they have their Navy set in places all over the world. We maintain a heavy patrol in the skies over Yugoslavia until shot down as a protest by the Yugoslav Government. What is the Navy doing all around the world? What are we doing building 500 atomic bombs a year? What are we doing drafting 185,000 men in peace time?

Embedded in this speech was Whitehouse's solution: "If you want world government, give up school, and live on your savings, and devote twenty-four hours a day to getting world government.... Peace is attainable. You can't wage it like war...."

The Issue of Merger

The Thanksgiving Day conference, after rather heroic efforts, did take place, and a planning committee, entitled the U.S. Council of the Movement for World Federal Government (by reference to the recent Luxembourg conference), was formed for the legal merger. The committee, usually consisting of Stewart Ogil-

---

[21] James F. Byrnes, *Speaking Frankly* (New York: Harper & Bros., 1947), 140–49.

[22] [Sauer?] to Nelson, 9 September 1946, ibid., SFFWG, September–October 1946; Jack Whitehouse, Speech before Student Federalist Convention, n.d., c. 5 September 1946, UWF Papers, 57.Chicago Convention Reports. This is the only speech by the founder of SFFWG to come down in the records.

vy for World Federalists, Thomas Finletter for Americans United, Helen Ball for Student Federalists, Thomas Mahony for the Massachusetts Committee, and Phillips Ruopp for Students for Federal World Government, began meeting at World Government House in New York to lay the groundwork for the unification "congress." They decided to hold the congress in the popular Blue Ridge mountain resort town of Asheville, North Carolina.

World Federalists had active chapters in the state under the general leadership of attorney R. Mayne Albright of Raleigh. Americans United also had a strong chapter at the University of North Carolina at Chapel Hill, led by President Frank P. Graham and Dean of the Law School Henry Brandis. The idea of world government was thought to be "politically accepted" in the state (it was the first to pass Humber's resolution), so hopes were high for a "good showing." The committee also quickly decided to invite to *merge* only "real membership organizations" whose aim was to establish world government through "propaganda, education, and political action."

Finletter's Design for UWF

Merger was a serious step. It was not setting up a mere coordinating council but rather the "establishment of a New Corporation in which would be vested all of the property, personnel and interests of the constituent groups, the latter to disappear from the scene," as Thomas Finletter proposed. Voting on merger was to be proportional to proven membership. The intent was to create what we would call a *political lobby*. Finletter designed it on the model of a *public corporation*. A board of directors of 30 would be elected, who would have the power to co-opt an additional 20 and appoint an executive committee of 12. Policy, other than the general one to "engage in activities looking to a federal world government," would be decided by an annual convention of the membership and in the interim by the executive committee. Dues were to be $3 per year, of which $1 was to go for a subscription to *World Government News,* $1 to the local chapter, 50¢ to the state branch, and 50¢ to the national corporation.[23]

In addition to merger sessions, there were to be parallel "general" sessions at which nonmembership organizations could be brought into "the same cooperative spirit and closer affiliation." These latter organizations, in a list of invitees that exhausted the field of the world government movement at the beginning of 1947, included:

Action Committee for a World Constitutional Convention	(Philip Isely),
American Lawyers Committee for World Government	(Fyke Farmer),
Campaign for World Government	(Georgia Lloyd),

---

[23] Minutes of ... Committee ... Making Plans for a Joint Convention of All World Federalist Groups ..., 7 December 1946, UWF Papers, 57.Asheville; Finletter to Griessemer, 17 December 1946, ibid., 42.Asheville; Minutes of Meeting of Movement for World Federal Government, U.S. Council, 4–5 January 1947; Convention Announcement, 10 January 1947; Minutes of Meeting Preliminary to Asheville Convention, 1 February 1947, ibid., 57.Asheville.

Committee to Frame a World Constitution	(G. A. Borgese),
Citizens Committee for United Nations Reform	(Ely Culbertson),
Federal Union	(Clarence Streit),
Institute for World Government	(George C. Holt of Rollins College),
International Campaign for World Government	(Edith Wynner),
Missouri State Committee for World Government	(Fritz von Windegger),
World Citizenship Movement	(Col. M. Thomas Tchou), and the
World Government Committee of the Association of Oak Ridge Engineers and Scientists	(Norton Gerber).

Position Statements before Asheville: 50,000,000 World Federalists

Major position statements preceded the congress. The great issue was peoples' convention versus U.N. reform. Generally, the older, adult, and more established groups preferred to work through the United Nations, while the younger, student, and more independent groups urged radical action. Grenville Clark, who was not planning to go to Asheville, was frankly doubtful that amalgamation would be possible without "diluting" the new organization's platform to get everyone in. He preferred mere affiliation so that at least some organizations could take vigorous action without internal conflicts. Effective merger would be a "miracle."[24]

World Federalists—Tom Griessemer especially—tried to resolve the issue over methods by bringing as democratically representative a voting delegation from all over the country as possible. He hoped that the desire to create *"one strong, consolidated movement"* for world government in the United States would overcome all differences, especially if it were drawn from *across the country*—not just from New York or Chicago.[25]

Raymond Swing of Americans United warned the planners against distraction by the "ideological problem" from the "evangelical." They should develop a general will, a *fire of fervor*, for world federation, drawing as many as *50 million* people to the cause, leaving constitutional details to the governments. This was to be a "great grassroots movement," Swing argued, analogous to the one that made the Republican Party accept a United Nations policy at its Mackinac Island (Michigan) conference in late 1943:[26]

> Once again the politicians must be made to realize that the people insist on peace. But this time they must know it can only be achieved through the introduction of law in the present vacuum of anarchy in world relations.

Student Federalists (SF), always pressing their elders, were divided over policy. It had taken most of the year to organize now over 100 chapters, and the

---

[24] Grenville Clark, Memorandum, 17 February 1947, Clark Papers, 15.3.

[25] Griessemer to Friend, "Extra!" n.d., ante 21 February 1947, his emphases; Griessemer to Accreditations Committee, 12 February 1947, UWF Papers, 57.Asheville Convention Reports.

[26] Swing to von Windegger, 6 February 1947, Schwimmer–Lloyd Collection, T65, my emphases.

problem facing their leaders was, Whatever were the members going to *do?* The educational program was hard to sustain after the summer institutes. A political program had yet to be undertaken. Even "adults" privately urged SF to become political. The pollster Elmo Roper recommended the students abolish their adult advisory board lest they "add to [their] own mistakes those of an older generation who had already made many." The students should "go it alone."[27]

Founder Harris Wofford wanted Student Federalists to get into the politics of the 1948 elections, propagating world federation as a great national issue, supporting the nomination of federalists for office and the inclusion of federalist planks in the party platforms, then campaigning and "taking stands." College representative Tom Hughes objected that if SF became "militant," the high schools would drop their chapters "like hot potatoes." John Logue thought a middle position was to agitate for world government as a single issue that could unite swing blocs of voters in both parties, as in the women's suffrage movement in 1920 or in the Negro desegregation movement that won bipartisan Fair Employment Practices Commission planks in 1944. Chapter secretary Virginia Lastayo and public information director Eleanor Schneider disagreed about whether to portray the U.N. as "no good."

Helen Ball, national chairman [sic], surveyed these views and urged adherence to the "majority" in the new merged organization in order to present a "united front to the public." The high school chapters would have to be sacrificed or become mere clubs. The college chapters, having many veterans, were determined to become political. The balance of wisdom on the U.N. seemed to be that Student Federalists should not *seem* to advocate its destruction, while agitating for world federal government. A large delegation (half the size of that of World Federalists') was being elected by the chapters. Most of the board was going.[28]

The "Peace Palace" at 807 Davis Street

On the eve of Asheville, in February 1947, Students for Federal World Government were moving into what the *Chicago Sun* called a "Peace Palace" at 807 Davis Street in the heart of the Evanston business district. The three-story building with showroom windows on the sidewalk level had space for receptions and small assemblies, a score of private offices, a library, printing shop, radio studio, darkroom, and, on the top floor, a dormitory for 30 men, employed full-time at "no salaries." (Volunteer women were to cook in a basement kitchen.) There was a little fleet of two jeeps, eight cars, a motor scooter, and 16 bicycles. Numbers of available volunteer workers "coast-to-coast" had climbed, it was

---

[27] Ball to Board Members, 10 December 1946, UWF Papers, 57.Asheville Convention Reports.

[28] Minutes, SF Board Meeting, 17–18 November 1946, UWF Papers, 57.Student Council; John Logue, "Target—1948," *Student Federalist,* November 1946, p. 2, Riorden Papers; Virginia Lastayo, "If This Be Treason... ," *Student Federalists,* December–January 1947, p. 2, ibid.; Schneider to Ball, 6 February 1947, UWF Papers, 57.Student Council; Ball to Delegates and Board, Memorandum on Asheville Convention, n.d., c. 15 February 1947, ibid., 57.Asheville.

claimed, to 7,000.[29]

"We're going to put peace on every main street in the world," said White-house to the press, "and we're starting right here in Evanston." Announcement was soon made of a name change to World Republic. "It is more descriptive and easier to understand," said McCoy; "our aim is an international republic." An 18–month budget of $2 million was also announced. Plans were to have 50 men on the road by summer, promoting the peoples' convention and soliciting funds. Businessmen were usually incredulous. "They can't believe we really operate the way we do," observed Whitehouse, "on a shoestring and a prayer." An oil com-pany executive was heard repeating to himself, "It's a regular children's crusade." A veteran reporter of many crusades was frightened: "They're too young to be afraid. They just don't know." He continued, "They're so sure they can pull it off that—well, somehow, they almost make you believe it." A columnist won-dered if someday the old garage might be as famous as Constitution Hall in Phil-adelphia.[30]

World Republic's Position before Asheville

The position paper for World Republic on the eve of Asheville was written by Phillips Ruopp, just released by the U.S. Army. Ruopp began with the goal of federal world government as the *"minimal* framework" for a "dynamic peace," then passed directly to the impending split over means. His whole paper was an argument that the two means of government–initiated U.N. reform and the peo-ples' convention were not contradictory but complementary. It was only too likely that both means would fail and the world would be united by atomic con-quest and tyranny, Ruopp argued. The older movement had been working for years for governmental action and become fairly well recognized; but the newer one aiming at a direct appeal to the people had recently gained in popularity. What was needed was "a program which keeps world government squarely in the public eye. This means world government is an issue in the 1948 elections," Ruopp argued. A direct appeal to the people was consistent with American Rev-olutionary traditions. "We are working against *time."*[31]

Ruopp was immediately answered by Vernon Nash of World Federalists. Nash came straight to the threat of revolution: "In my judgment, no enemy of the effort for world government could possibly do us as much harm as spokes-men on our side urging a kind of direct action which would try to bypass gov-

---

[29] Whitehouse to Byron, 13 December 1946, World Republic Papers, SFFWG, No-vember–December 1946; "The Federalist Manual: How to Organize a World Govern-ment Movement... ," [2 September] 1946, Regenstein Library, Committee to Frame a World Constitution Papers, 24.2. "Federalists Plan to Unify," *Christian Science Monitor,* 5 December 1946.

[30] "How 7 War Vets Fired a Shot for Peace Now Heard around the World," *Chicago Sun,* 23 February 1947; "SFFWG Gets New Name: Becomes 'World Republic,'" *Daily Northwestern,* 20 February 1947.

[31] Phillips Ruopp, An Open Letter to My Friends Who Are Working for a Warless World and a Positive Peace, 10 January 1947, UWF Papers, 57.Asheville.

ernments." His shrinking from the peoples' convention was not just fear, said Nash. It might be possible to bypass governments to draft a world constitution, but to ratify the constitution and put it into effect, activists would run into *"exactly the same handicap"* that made them turn from governments in the first place.[32]

> There is thus no escaping the necessity of persuading our governments to act, unless one is prepared to espouse revolutionary tactics at some stage in the process. Since we must win over our political leaders (or change them) sooner or later, why not stay on the ball from the beginning?

Two Attitudes toward the People

The controversy between the advocates of a peoples' convention or U.N. reform went to the depths of the world government movement. The issue was not revolution, for both approaches were in principle revolutionary, in the sense of aiming to establish a new sovereign authority above those of the nation–states for at least minimal common purposes. Grenville Clark cited the same precedent of the U.S. Constitution for his proposals to amend the U.N. Charter as did Georgia Lloyd for a peoples' convention. Even Vernon Nash, who threw up fear of violent revolution to oppose the most radical popular approach, did not doubt that world government was something new in human history, which needed popular backing. A year later Harris Wofford would be saying:[33]

> What is proposed is that federalists wake up to the fact that they have stumbled into man's greatest peaceful revolution, and that they are its vanguard. It is the revolution to establish the brotherhood of man.

No one, apparently, openly cited the precedents of the French Revolution or the Russian Revolution, though terms like "constituent assembly" or "provisional world government" would seem to be drawn from those historic cases. Deep down, everybody realized, with greater or lesser degrees of reasonableness, that federal world government was *untried.*

Who could tell what would happen if vast numbers of people loosened their loyalties to their established governments? What new birth of freedom or decline into chaos might develop in a world constitutional convention? How could even a minimal world government, granted power only to prevent war, be established peacefully? There were the precedents of all the other federal systems, but never one over such a "bedlam" of peoples, to use Senator Vandenberg's word, as the whole world.

On the other hand, there was also a long history of war, and the next war, if atomic, threatened to destroy all civilization. To the people excitedly gathering in Asheville, the historical experiment was *necessary.* Their differences came down to a difference in temperament, in attitude, in courage, manifested in the

[32] Nash to Ruopp, 20 January 1947, his emphasis, ibid.
[33] Harris Wofford, "Dead End: Federalism Limited," *Common Cause,* 1 (May 1948): 388.

two attitudes toward the people. One side feared them, the other trusted them. One side preferred a "top–level" approach as the safest course; the other, an active field program as the only effective political one.

One would work cautiously through governments, giving the people little to do but register their opinions (Nash was especially fond at this time of World Federalists' "call–for–action" postcards), in order to provide for the most orderly transition to world government. The other, convinced that national governments were the great obstacle to peace, would seek to exercise the theoretical sovereignty of the people, in order to establish world government at all. The one, *in nuce*,[34] was the party of Hamilton, Lafayette, and Plekhanov. The other, that of Jefferson, Robespierre, and Lenin. At Asheville, the little world government movement decided to take the side of caution.

Foundation of United World Federalists

The World Government Congress opened at Asheville, North Carolina, on Friday, 21 February 1947. Two hundred seven delegates arrived on a snowy day for the merger session, the largest of which was from World Federalists; perhaps 50 came from other sections of the movement. Mildred Blake, Tom Griessemer, Max Habicht, George Holt, Vernon Nash, Stewart Ogilvy, the Rawnsleys, Mark Van Doren, Fritz R. von Windegger, and Robert Wheelwright were among the World Federalists.

The Americans United contingent included Cass Canfield, publisher of Harpers, who after Asheville would play an increasing important background role; Norman Cousins, editor of the *Saturday Review;* Thomas K. Finletter, later Truman's secretary of the air force; Mrs. J. Borden Harriman, former U.S. ambassador to Norway; Cord Meyer Jr., veteran assistant to Harold Stassen at San Francisco; J. A. Migel, Rhode Island industrialist; and A.J.G. Priest, New York lawyer and well–regarded convention chairman.

Of Student Federalists, Helen Ball, Laurence Fuchs, Virginia Lastayo, Clare Lindgren, Colgate Prentice, Joseph Wheeler, and Harris Wofford were in attendance.

Thomas H. Mahony and Conrad Hobbs came from Massachusetts.

World Republic was represented by Fred Carney, Charles H. Davis, Frances Duncan, Phillips Ruopp, Paul Sauer, and Jack Whitehouse.[35]

Strength of Organizations Uniting

The true strength of the various organizations in the movement was revealed by the credentials committee. Most striking was Americans United, now down to fewer than 5,500:

---

[34] L., "in its core"—an expression favored by G. A. Borgese.

[35] List of Delegates and Observers, Asheville Convention, 21–23 February 1947, UWF Papers, 42.Asheville.

GROUP	MEMBERS	DELEGATES	VOTES	STATES
World Federalists	6,033	84	135	24
Americans United	5,498	34	107	13
Student Federalists	4,380	69	107	19
Massachusetts Committee	713	7	16	1
World Republic	1,366	11	52	3
Georgia World Citizens[36]	37	2	2	1
Totals	18,027	207	419	31

Advocates of a peoples' convention, Fyke Farmer and Fred Carney, were allowed to give the keynote speeches on the morning of the first day. Then the congress got down to business, with the merger session at the Hotel George Vanderbilt and the general session at the Battery Park Hotel. At the public meeting on the evening of the first day, all the speakers were advocates of U.N. reform: Norman Cousins, Frank P. Graham, Cord Meyer, and Mark Van Doren. Carl Sandburg, whose home was in Asheville, also spoke, but he seems not to made any memorable poetic contribution to the immediate cause of world federation. In 1936, however, Sandburg had written:[37]

Man will never write,
they said before the alphabet came
and man at last began to write
Man will never fly,
they said before the planes and blimps
zoomed and purred in arcs
winding their circles around the globe

Man will never make the United States of Europe
nor later yet the United States of the World
No, you are going too far when you talk about one
world flag for the great Family of Nations,
they say that now.

Statement of Beliefs
The next day, Saturday, was taken up with the split sessions, and, when merger proved not quite so easy to effect as planned, the merger session ran over into Sunday. Mahony on Saturday presented the policy committee's resolution, which was adroitly worded to exclude any notion of a peoples' convention:[38]

[36] The Georgia World Citizens were a small group who appeared by surprise and took no more leading part after merger.

[37] Carl Sandburg, *The People, Yes* (New York: Harcourt, Brace, 1936; renewed 1964), 240–41; (cf. 221–24). Used by permission.

[38] Program, Asheville Congress, 21–23 February 1947, UWF Papers, 42.Asheville; Asheville—General Time Table, 21–23 February, 1947, ibid., 57.Student Division.

Statement of Beliefs:

We believe that peace is not merely the absence of war, but the presence of justice, of law, of order—in short of government and the institutions of government; that world peace can be created and maintained only under world law, universal and strong enough to prevent armed conflict between nations.

Statement of Purposes:

Therefore, while endorsing the efforts of the United Nations to bring about a world community favorable to peace, we will work to strengthen the United Nations into a world government of limited powers adequate to prevent war and having a direct jurisdiction over individuals.

The committee also proposed the name "United World Federalists," with the subtitle "for World Government with Limited Powers Adequate to Prevent War."

U.N. Reform or Peoples' Convention

Within minutes it was moved and seconded by members of World Republic that the words "strengthen the United Nations into a world government" be changed to "create a world government." Never in public controversy did more hang on one word.

"The proposed amendment would indicate bypassing and working outside of the UN," responded Mahony. "The committee felt that it was necessary to work through the instrument already at hand in order to avoid dangerous delay in establishing world government."

Edgar Ansel Mowrer, formerly one of the bitterest critics of the U.N., added, "Not to support the UN while it is the organization in the public eye and while it has a chance of going ahead to the goal in view would be the sheerest folly."

"World Republic," Fred Carney defiantly replied, "cannot join the merger if the proposed statement passes."

Whitehouse spoke sharply: "The issue is not the United Nations but how to get peace. Governments and men appointed by governments to the UN do not represent the people directly but represent various interests and are not qualified to make a constitution for the people of the world."

"There is the right of revolution," exclaimed Finletter, "but we haven't come to that yet."

Whitehouse, unable any longer to contain his antipathy for the corporation lawyer, answered, "This is not revolution but a democratic method!"

Student Federalists at this point acted as the peacemakers. Younger and more idealistic, they were amenable to a dual approach. Both Colgate Prentice and Harris Wofford urged that the group not split on the issue.[39]

At the afternoon session, after all sides had caucused in great heat, Mahony proposed a compromise. The word "primarily" would be inserted into the statement, to read, "primarily to strengthen the United Nations."

There was a moment of drama when Norman Cousins of Americans United said, "That will be acceptable...."

[39] Minutes of Congress, Second Day; World Republic Group Troubles [Helen Ball Notes?], 22 February 1947, UWF Papers, 57.Student Division.

The World Republic boys were still caucusing outside the room and asked for a 10–minute delay on the vote. In the interim Mahony reread the amended statement. Finally the group returned. Carney spoke. "World Republic agrees to the amendment ['primarily'] and will merge organically, subject to approval of their members in Chicago and of the general public. But we are committed to a program of working for a peoples' world constitutional convention and have funds earmarked for that purpose. We will forgo the peoples' convention program for six months. However, we should be allowed to carry on publicity for it within the movement. We want a review convention held in six months to decide the effectiveness of the present policy."

Mahony wanted no conditions, no six–month policy.

Cord Meyer objected to earmarked funds and to propaganda for a peoples' convention within the merged movement.

Cousins and Wofford urged compromise. The members were being asked only to "keep their minds open on the subject." A six–month policy review convention was not unreasonable. On this understanding the policy, amended with the word "primarily," was voted unanimously.[40]

After that, agreement was reached quickly on the constitution. United World Federalists (UWF) was constitutionally not a federal organization, with strong state and local divisions, but a *unitary organization*, with decisive power concentrated in the executive council and committee, meeting between annual general assemblies, as in Finletter's original design. This design was to prove an obstacle to popular initiatives within United World Federalists in the years to come.

A Mistake

Years later Mildred Blake, one of the founders of World Federalists in 1941, looked back on the formation of United World Federalists in 1947 as a "mistake." Merger meant domination of the popular forces of World Federalists by the prominent men in Americans United:

> They were men who already knew people in government, and who felt that they had some influence, and that that was the way to go about it.... And there were others of us who thought that it didn't pay to lobby around in Washington when ... there was no constituent pressure to do anything about it at all. We felt that the workout in the country was more important than Washington.

"I'm not sure that it would have been at all harmful if we had all gone ahead hoeing our own row," she added.[41]

---

[40] Ibid. Carney's speech reconstructed.

[41] Minutes of Congress, Second Day; Mildred R. Blake, Reminiscences, pp. 27, 20, Columbia University, Oral History Research Office.

UWF Action Program

On Sunday, the merger, in the end *without* World Republic, was accomplished. A resolution was accepted stating that a peoples' convention was a "possible step" toward world government, but, when A.J.G. Priest invited some member of World Republic to make the formal motion for merger, Whitehouse refused, Carney was willing, and Ruopp was undecided. So Finletter made the motion. In the afternoon, the action committee finally made its report, largely based on Swing's recommendations:

> The aim of the new organization must be to mobilize popular opinion and action toward world government so that the local and national representatives of the people will be impelled to world federalism by an irresistible force.

Town meetings, resolutions of civic organizations, statements by local leaders, mass petitions, area conventions, referenda, state legislation, polling of congressmen, pressure on congressmen, world government party planks, nomination of candidates for national offices favorable to federal world government, and national legislation were the kinds of activities recommended. The national organization of United World Federalists would work through the media of communication, contact high officials, build up the membership, and in general promote the "dramatizing of the idea of world government."

United World Federalists

At last the time came for merger resolutions from the separate organizations. Dramatically, the constituent organizations ceased their existence. Harris Wofford led off for Student Federalists:

> Resolved, that Student Federalists, Inc., is dissolved and merges organically into UNITED WORLD FEDERALISTS, Inc., in accordance with the bylaws as passed by the Asheville Convention.

Arthur Goldsmith declared that the board of directors of Americans United for World Government had decided to merge. Tom Griessemer said that the membership of World Federalists had voted to merge. Tom Mahony announced that the Massachusetts Committee for World Federation would merge. The new executive council was elected. A motion was made that a telegram be sent to E. B. White of the *New Yorker* declaring that his exhortation after Dumbarton Oaks had been fulfilled: "Federalists of the World, Unite!"[42]

The outside world was slow to notice the formation of a united federalist organization in the mountains of North Carolina. Initial reports were somewhat confused about whether World Republic had merged, which it had not. One of the first editors to comment on the event, in nearby Charlotte, wrote:

> It is ironic that this little band of intellectuals should now hold virtually uncontested title to the internationalism that has always been a part of the

---

[42] Minutes of Congress, Final Day; World Republic Group Troubles.

American ideal. This is a time when only "visionaries" hold out hope of one world in which men can lay aside their weapons and live in peace; "practical" men still cling to the expensive—and historically unsound—idea that the best way to avoid war is to prepare for it. ...The flame tended by the United World Federalists is weak and flickering, but it is one of the few lights in the spreading darkness. We wish them Godspeed.[43]

Weeks now were to elapse while the incorporation proceedings were completed. United World Federalists did not even have a president until May. There were inevitable delays while the new national organization set up its offices, hired its staff, brought chapters into relation with it, prepared its plans, estimated its budget, met the press, and made its contacts.[44]

---

[43] "Six Groups Project Federalist World," *New York Times*, 23 February 1947; "Federalists Join in a World Body," *New York Times*, 24 February 1947; "Light in the Spreading Darkness," *Charlotte* (North Carolina) *News*, 25 February 1947.

[44] Minutes, Executive Council of UWF, 17 May 1947, UWF Papers, 43.

13

The Truman Doctrine: Containment

It was expected that the early postwar [period] would witness a degree of unity and good-will in international relations among the victorious allies never before reached in peace time. It was expected that the world would move rapidly ... toward "One World." ... No influential persons, as far as I remember, expressed the expectation or the fear that international relations would worsen during those years.

—Harry Dexter White, Draft of statement on amendment of the Articles of Agreement establishing the International Monetary Fund, 19 May 1948. Quoted by Richard N. Gardner, *Sterling–Dollar Diplomacy* (1980), p. 7

The Truman Doctrine

"We have considered how the United Nations might assist in this crisis," President Truman remarked in his historic address to Congress on the Greek and Turkish crisis in March 1947. "But the situation is an urgent one requiring immediate action, and the United Nations and its related organizations are not in a position to extend help of the kind that is required." Henceforth the United States, Truman announced, would undertake the responsibility of resisting aggression anywhere in the world. This speech was the first open repudiation by a sovereign great power of Chapters V and VII of the U.N. Charter that gave to the Security Council joint responsibility for resistance to aggression.[1]

"Yesterday, March 12, 1947," said Roosevelt's former vice–president and Truman's dissident secretary of commerce, Henry A. Wallace, in a broadcast to the nation, "marked a turning point in American history. Fellow Americans, it is not a Greek crisis that we face, it is an American crisis. It is a crisis in the American spirit." The president, said Wallace, proposed a policy of "imperialism and power politics." To resist Communist party expansion, the United States would give dollars, tanks, and guns to unpopular but anticommunist regimes like the Greek monarchy, rather than channel reconstruction aid, trucks, and plows through impartial U.N. agencies to desperate peoples or so practice democracy that communism would lose its attractiveness to them. America was assuming the role of world policeman. Wallace feared for the consequences of this unilateral step:

[1] "The Truman Doctrine," 12 March 1947, Henry Steel Commager, ed., *Documents of American History* (Englewood Cliffs, NJ: Prentice–Hall, 9th ed., 1973), 2: 526.

When President Truman proclaims the world–wide conflict between East and
West, he is telling the Soviet leaders that we are preparing for eventual war.
They will reply by measures to strengthen their position in the event of war.

Military control, he warned, will pass into the hands of élites. In the interests of national security, the people's civil liberties will be restricted. Defense
budgets will hold down standards of living. A constant war footing will divide
families. Ultimately, reliance on military solutions will sacrifice freedom at
home and abroad.[2]

The Cold War

Something like a state of war, characterized by preparations for total war, did
follow the Truman doctrine. Ideological campaigns, economic competition, narrow pursuit of national interests, rivalry for spheres of interest, alignment of allies, a nuclear and conventional arms race—all the traditional practices, and some
new ones, of national power politics returned to take the place of the hesitant experiment in keeping international peace under the United Nations. Only the lack
of direct military hostilities between the two surviving sovereign great powers
has justified for the postwar period the term "Cold War."[3]

But Truman was not simply to blame. The alternative was lacking. Later,
in the debate on the first $400 million appropriations bill for Greece and Turkey
under the new policy, senator after senator, representative after representative,
stated that the United Nations was inadequate. Senator Vandenberg, who two
years before had opposed Senator Taylor's World Republic bill on the ground
that the U.N.'s continuous contacts ought to be allowed to develop, now admitted that the U.N. "cannot accept this responsibility" of meeting aggression.
Thirty–four others expressed at least a pious wish to strengthen the U.N., but
only a few knew specifically how, and none thought the reforms could be accomplished in time to meet the crisis.

Representative Walter H. Judd (R., Minnesota), who would later take a leading part with the United World Federalist resolutions, mentioned the need for enforceable world laws. Representative Brooks Hays (D., Arkansas), who would
later join Judd, argued for adequate international force. Senator J. William Fulbright (D., Arkansas) explained that, until powerful nations subject themselves

---

[2] Henry A. Wallace, Address on American Foreign Policy, NBC, 13 March 1947,
UWF Papers, 26.

[3] Bernard Baruch, who had led the U.S. initiative to establish the international
control of atomic energy in 1946, coined this term in an address to the South Caroli-
na legislature a month after Truman enunciated his doctrine. *Baruch: The Public Years*
(New York: Holt, Rinehart & Winston, 1960), 388. It was popularized by Walter
Lippmann in a slim, critical study of George Kennan's "X" article on "The Sources of
Soviet Conduct" in July 1947, which publicized his earlier cable that had become the
inspiration for the new containment policy. *The Cold War: A Study in U.S. Foreign
Policy* (New York: Harper & Bros., 1947), 29, 58–59.

to definite rules of law, there would be no other power to constrain them.[4]

The State Department, too, in answer to a series of penetrating questions from Senator Charles W. Tobey (R., New Hampshire) that ranged all the way to whether the department would take the lead in proposing amendments to the Charter making the U.N. a federal world government, explained that the U.N. provided for "the greatest degree of international cooperation now attainable." The United States had to act alone, Assistant Secretary Acheson said, since "time would have been lost."[5]

No Time for World Federation

There was no longer any time to make the United Nations Organization adequate to keep the peace. Had there ever been time? At San Francisco in June 1945, China and the small nations expressed willingness to limit national sovereignty in the U.N. Charter, but the United States and the Soviet Union would not accept the Charter without vetoes for themselves. Then atomic weapons were first used in war. About the time of Grenville Clark's Dublin conference in October 1945, critics warned that a league of sovereign states could never be relied on for national security, but they were silenced by charges of "scrapping" the U.N. before it was even tried. When the U.S. plan for the international control of atomic energy was actually introduced in the U.N. in 1946, formal proposals to reform the U.N. in the direction of limited, federal world government were in hand, but they were ignored.

By 1947, disputes between the United States and the Soviet Union about the independence of Poland and Eastern Europe, the peace treaties with Germany, Italy, and the Balkans, the future of Greece, the outlet from the Black Sea, Iran, and China had produced such a crisis of international security that there was hardly a thought of strengthening the common organization. Leadership was unprepared —"uneducated," in W. T. Holliday's view[6]—to undertake the novel work of abolishing war by extending government over the whole world, especially in 1945. The significance of the Truman doctrine from a perspective of world federal government is that it marked the end of what potential there ever may have been to strengthen the U.N. Charter along the lines of voluntary limitations of national sovereignty by creation of new world legal institutions.

For the next few years, there would still be occasional opportunities for U.N. reform, such as the continued negotiations over the American plan for control of atomic energy in the U.N. AEC, Secretary of State Marshall's proposal to create an interim committee of the General Assembly between sessions to evade Russian vetoes (the "Little Assembly"), or the Security Council decision to take military action in Korea when the Soviet Union happened to be boycotting the Council and Assembly because of the U.N.'s refusal to seat Communist China.

[4] U.S. Congress, Senate, Senator Glen H. Taylor, *Strengthening the United Nations,* SCR–24, 80th Cong., 1st sess., 9 July 1947, *Congressional Record,* 93: 8508–9.

[5] Dean Acheson to Tobey, 31 March 1947, UWF Papers, 43.

[6] Holliday to Clark, 23 September 1946, Clark Papers, 21.10.

But the spirit in these departures from traditional diplomacy was rather that of power politics using the forms of the empty United Nations. Once the United States began a policy of what was called "containment," and the Soviet Union its policy of "anti-imperialism" (they were both strictly policies of defense, though offensive in capability), there was never any going back to international control.

It was in response to the Truman doctrine that United World Federalists, only weeks after Asheville, issued their first public statement. UWF protested Truman's omission of reliance on the U.N. and urged his administration "to strengthen the United Nations by Charter alteration into a world government with limited powers adequate to prevent war." Nothing was added about just how such an ideal could still be realized. Such a statement must have had a hollow sound to responsible American officials who were grasping for a response to Britain's decision to withdraw from Greece at the end of March 1947.[7]

Origins of the Cold War after 1945

Many historians have traced the origins of the Cold War, including John Lewis Gaddis.[8] Our purpose here is only to cast a sidelight from the world federalist perspective. That perspective is indicated by a UWF study on the origins of the Cold War prepared in about 1950.[9] Trouble first arose over Poland, then extended to occupied Germany. Britain and France had gone to war over the independence of Poland, while Russia, for the second time in the 20th century, had been invaded by the Germans through Poland. Stalin demanded "friendly governments" on a defensive frontier from Estonia to Yugoslavia (and Greece if he could get it), while the Western Allies were determined not to lose the independent and "democratic" governments in Eastern Europe that they had fought for.

Between the United States and the Soviet Union through 1945 and 1946, there were fundamental disagreements about the peace treaty with Germany, occupation policy, and restoration of a sovereign German national government. The latter was the most difficult issue. The U.S.S.R. wanted a centralized, socialist Germany, based on the landholding peasantry and the industrial trade unions. The U.S. and Britain preferred a looser federalized union, like the Weimar Republic, that would guarantee political freedoms and safeguard against renewed state control of German industry. France proposed a thoroughly decentralized agrarian state, with the Ruhr industries under U.N. control.

The Russians, judging by their radio broadcasts, were extremely angry over the amnesties granted to German industrialists, "backbone of Nazism and its war

---

[7] "Object Lesson," *World Government News,* April 1947, pp. 1–2. Statement signed by Grenville Clark, T. K. Finletter, Cord Meyer, Raymond Gram Swing, Mark Van Doren, and F. R. von Windegger.

[8] John L. Gaddis, *The United States and the Origins of the Cold War* (New York: Columbia University Press, 1972); Gaddis, *The Long Peace: Inquiries into the History of the Cold War* (New York: Oxford University Press, 1987).

[9] UWF Research Staff, Early Notes on Origin of the Cold War, n.d., c. 1950, UWF Papers, 68.

of aggrandizement." A centralized Germany would be able to "wipe out the Nazi party," Russians argued, and to prevent turning the industrialized areas "into a colony of Anglo–U.S. monopoly capital." The Americans, on the other hand, publicized the view that a centralized Germany had been the cause of the last war, while greater power in the states of a federation would ensure that "politically Germany will remain weak and will never again be able to threaten the peace of Europe and the world."[10]

All sides seemed to agree that a revival of German industry, without its former political manifestations, was essential to a reconstructed Europe. But they could not agree on the democratic model for industrial Germany. The Americans preferred a political democracy like what they were accustomed to, which implied free enterprise. They were quite indifferent to Communist doctrine that private capital dominates a free democracy, leading it inevitably to war, and they were willing to tolerate the return to positions of power and influence in a reformed German republic of a large fraction of former Nazis.[11]

The Russians, for their part, demanded an economic democracy closely allied with the Soviet Union. They quite clearly intended that their centralized state would socialize all German industry, and they were indifferent to Western objections that a revolutionary vanguard of the working class, without having to face competing parties in free elections, will suffer the corruptions of power, will destroy the liberties on which economic prosperity depends, and ultimately will end in a worse tyranny than Nazism. Since the ideological differences seemed irreconcilable, the issue of how best to reorganize Germany—and by implication how to unite the world—came down to a contest of power.

Implications of the Cold War for World Federalism

The problem of Germany's future was fundamental to the Cold War. Questions of occupation policy, the Oder–Neisse border, protocols governing reparations to Russia, freedom of speech and press and latitude for German criticism of the Allies, exchange of information between the Allied commanders, Ruhr and Saar administration, the fate of the defeated country's heavy industry, and, above all, political guarantees for any central German government were deeply disputed. These disputes appeared to the Russians to be grounded in secret Western sympathy for revived German militarism; to the Americans, in Communist expansionism like that in Eastern Europe.

There were also, in the years after World War II, many world–wide disputes that cannot be understood as rooted so directly in differing conceptions of political and economic democracy, but rather must be understood, within an international "system" lacking a common organization to keep the peace, as traditional rivalries between sovereign great powers for spheres of influence, even though Americans especially tried to deny that they had any such ambitions. An international political scientist who was guardedly sympathetic to the movement for

---

[10] UWF Notes on Origin of the Cold War.

[11] John H. Herz, "The Fiasco of Denazification in Germany," *Political Science Quarterly,* 63, 4 (December 1948): 569-94.

world government, Clyde Eagleton, early in the Cold War set out the comparable deeds of Russia and America with magisterial impartiality, as follows.

U.S. protests against Soviet influence in Eastern Europe were answered by ironical Soviet protests against U.S. influence in Japan. Objections to the continued presence of Russian troops in Manchuria were matched by complaints about American troops in China and about U.S. efforts to get strategic bases in Iceland and Greenland. Russian protests against British military action in Greece and Indonesia were countermanded by Western opposition to use of Russian forces in Iran; in 1946 the Soviet Union actually withdrew, leaving a power vacuum in that strategic country on the Indian Ocean. Talk of internationalizing the Dardanelles and the Danube River was met by suggestions that the Panama Canal also be put under international administration. When the United States proposed before the U.N. Security Council to create its own trust territory for the Pacific islands captured from Japan, the Soviet Union did not exercise its veto, apparently regarding those islands as within the acceptable American sphere of influence, analogous to its own claimed sphere in Eastern Europe and the Dardanelles.[12]

Lastly, the atomic threat, which originally was possessed only by the United States but potentially by the Soviet Union too, was not brought under international control in the U.N. Atomic Energy Commission through 1946. In general, the failure of the great powers to entrust the United Nations—or a stronger world government—with powers of compulsory jurisdiction or majority rule under some system of popular representation meant the return of power politics, national armament programs, and the settlement of international disputes by the threat or use of force. So weak was the U.N. that, after its first year, most of which was spent organizing its agencies and secretariat, its budget was cut from $30 million to $27.7 million—about one–fourth of what the U.S. State Department spent each day, or less than what New York City spent each year on its sanitation services.[13]

U.N. Internationalism between Nationalism and World Government
Another source of federalist analysis in this early period was *United Nations World,* edited by Louis Dolivet. In his lead editorial, Dolivet took a stand between traditional nationalists and advocates of world government:[14]

In our opinion, the first group does not take into account the deep anxiety of peoples everywhere, their dissatisfaction with the miseries of the world,

---

[12] Clyde Eagleton, Address at the Institute on World Understanding, Bradley University, 9 May 1947, UWF Papers, 33. Eagleton was the author of *International Government* (1932, 1947, 1957).

[13] "State of World Organization," *United Nations World,* March 1947, p. 50.

[14] Louis Dolivet, "Hopeful Atmosphere," *United Nations World,* February 1947, p. 39. *United Nations World* was a merger of *Asia, The Inter–American,* and *Free World* and began with a circulation of 65,000. This compared with 36,600 for *World Government News* and 12,000 for *Common Cause* at their height in 1949.

their sense of insecurity, their indifference to world organization, and, above all, the truly alarming disaffection among the peoples of the world with government in general. On the other hand, the second group eliminates itself, through advocacy of world government and nothing else, from the day–to–day struggle for the improvement of the present world organization. It eliminates itself, for instance, from the fight for international relief, disarmament, freedom of speech, and the international bill of rights.

This criticism was near the mark, though nationalists did make some concessions, in the U.N., to popular demand for peace, and world governmentalists, to the extent they could do so without surrender of their principles, did support the U.N. and comment on the events of the day from the perspective of their ultimate goal. *United Nations World* bridged these two extremes in its coverage of world politics and hence became a valuable source for the history of the world government movement. "The goal is the federation of free peoples of the world —the instrument, the U.N.," concluded Dolivet.

The Coming of the Cold War by 1947
By 1947, "immense historical changes," in the language of the new watchdog journal *United Nations World,* were under way. The world was awaiting a redefinition of American foreign policy under the new secretary of state, General George C. Marshall, who had just returned to the U.S. after his unsuccessful mission to Chiang Kai–shek's China. The Chinese economy, following withdrawal of American aid on Marshall's negative report, collapsed to that stage where the National government ordered all wealthy Chinese to transfer their money from overseas banks to Chinese banks or to exchange it for Chinese paper. Inflation had reduced the value of the Chinese dollar to 1/12,000 of the American dollar. Civil war with the Chinese Communists over unification of the country entered its final stage.

In Indochina, a war of liberation between the French and the Annamese was expected. Malaya and Burma were in ferment over negotiations with Britain to end colonial rule. In India, Jawaharlal Nehru's Congress Party was losing ground to the leftists and Muslims, but independence from Britain seemed approaching. In the Middle East, the Arab League had not succeeded in forming an Arabian federation. Palestine was again a crossroads of history—this time of awakening Arab nationalism and the exodus of Jews fleeing the Nazi holocaust toward a Jewish national homeland. Great Britain, bankrupt by the Second World War, as Churchill admitted, could no longer maintain its mandate over Palestine. The British Empire was slipping away and with it Britain's historic role of "balancer" of national states competing for world power. Into this vacuum of world "responsibilities" the United States would move, while relinquishing its own claimed protectorate over China.

We have already seen that, in Europe, Britain was being forced by the financial drain of its military operations to withdraw from Greece. In Eastern Europe, 1946–47 was the period of what historians call "alleged" coalitions, though in

Hungary and Czechoslovakia "genuine" coalitions of Communists and Socialists still were functioning. In Italy, Prime Minister Alcide De Gasperi of the Christian Democratic Party failed to obtain from the United States more than half of a loan he needed to stave off starvation in his country. In France, inflation, with 15 times more francs in circulation than before the war, was wiping out every wage gain for the workers and reducing the peasants to black market or barter transactions. Loans from the United States and one for $250 million from the World Bank were inadequate to restore the balance of payments, which were upset by imports of machinery for reconstruction, coal, and wheat. The Communists and Socialists had split, while Free France's hero Charles de Gaulle's movement of "anti-political parties," the *Rassemblement Populaire Français*, was making gains on the right. The constitutional elections, scheduled for 1948, promised to be a test of whether the Communists or the Gaullist rightists would join the Socialists in a coalition government. In Germany, "renascent Nazi tendencies ... particularly in the form of anti-Semitism" appeared. There was much anticipation of the Allied Foreign Ministers' conference in Moscow in March 1947 to decide Germany's fate.

In Britain, the shaky Labour government decided to tell the people the "full truth of the economic situation." Imports of tobacco, newsprint, and even movies from hard–currency countries like the United States and Sweden had to be curtailed and exports to these countries increased. The government was not even able to provide sufficient coal for its people during the hard winter of early 1947. For once, "heroic" Britons "queued up for the dole." The Attlee government expected world financial trouble when its current American loan was exhausted. Some even outside the U.S.S.R. feared a postwar depression beginning in the United States and spreading over the world.[15]

It was while Secretary of State Marshall was discussing Germany's fate at the Moscow conference of March 1947 that President Truman announced his doctrine of aid to Greece and Turkey and, by implication, to all "free peoples who are resisting attempted subjugation by armed minorities or by outside pressures." The conference, undercut by the president's belligerent speech, broke up without producing any peace treaty. The United States had officially changed its foreign policy from cooperation with the Soviet Union, through the war and most recently in the founding of the U.N., to containment of Communist expansion.

End of the Period of Flux

Thereafter, events followed clearly and rapidly in an acknowledged Cold War. Whatever "period of flux," in Ambassador William Bullett's words, there had been at the close of the Second World War, when Americans and Russians had not yet made up their minds about what they thought of each other or where they would turn for safety, had surely passed. Throughout 1947, negotiations over the international control of atomic energy in the U.N. AEC became obviously

---

[15] "Roundup," *United Nations World*, February 1947, p. 17; "Immense Historical Changes," ibid., March 1947, p. 17; Louis Dolivet, "Inside Report on Europe," ibid., July 1947, pp. 12–13, 54.

perfunctory.

In 1947, the United States put itself on a new institutional footing for renewed total war. Truman's loyalty order curtailed traditional freedoms of speech
and assembly.[16] The Marshall plan for the reconstruction of Europe was, like
the Truman doctrine, conceived outside the United Nations and was expressly opposed to "governments, political parties, or groups which seek to perpetuate human misery in order to profit therefrom politically."[17] The National Security
Act, which created the modern Departments of Defense, Army, Navy, and Air
Force, put American forces on a footing for total war.[18] The Central Intelligence
Agency was formed.

In turn, the Soviet Union began its first ideological campaign in April 1947
to "correct" the thinking of the Russian and Soviet peoples about their wartime
American ally.[19] The Soviet bloc at Paris duly rejected the Marshall plan, partly
because its economic clauses required opening the books of Eastern European and
Soviet industries to American accountants, thus revealing the true state of postwar Communist economies.[20] The Cominform, which replaced the Comintern
(abolished in 1943 as a goodwill gesture to the West), was established in September 1947. The Cominform, as its name implied, was a propaganda organization aiming to coordinate Communist Parties, especially in Italy and France, in
opposition to the Truman doctrine and Marshall plan. By the autumn of 1947,
the coalition governments of Poland, Bulgaria, and Romania had been definitely
replaced by "monolithic" Communist governments; Hungary and Czechoslovakia followed in early 1948.[21]

One of the casualties of the emerging Cold War was the international project
on behalf of world federal government. Cominform director A. A. Zhdanov made
uncompromising speeches against world federalism:[22]

One of the directions of the ideological campaign, which accompany the
plans of enslaving Europe, is the attack against the principles of national

---

[16] "Truman Loyalty Order," Commager, *Documents of American History,* 2:
529–32.

[17] "The Marshal Plan," ibid., 2: 532–34.

[18] "National Security Act of 1947," ibid., 2: 541–43.

[19] The All–Union Society for the Dissemination of Political and Scientific Knowledge (a body of 70 Soviet scientists, writers, and artists) was formed on 30 April
1947. "Let not our hatred of our foes grow cold ... while, like profligates, they spend
billions of dollars in the making of atom bombs and for the preparation of monstrous
war." Mikhail Sholokhov (author of *And Quiet Flows the Don), Pravda,* 23 January
1948, quoted by Robert S. Bird, *New York Times,* 1 March 1948. It was this society
that condemned the "incorrect" music of Dmitri Shostakovich and Sergei Prokofiev.

[20] UWF Notes on Origin of Cold War.

[21] *Encyclopedia Britannica,* 15th ed. (1979), s.v. "Communism," by L. B. Scha-
piro, 4: 1022.

[22] Quoted by Vera Sandomirsky, World Government without Russia, draft of article,
n.d., c. 1951, Committee to Frame a World Constitution Papers, 10.7; "The Politburo
Speaks," *World Government News,* January 1948, p. 1–2.

sovereignty, an appeal to peoples to abrogate their sovereign rights, and the setting against them of the ideas of "world government." The meaning of this campaign consists in covering up the unbridled expansion of American imperialism which unceremoniously interferes with sovereign rights of peoples.

Zhdanov expressly identified the idea of world government as the ideological spearhead of American expansion directed against the Soviet Union:

> The idea of "world government," which some bourgeois intellectuals of the dreamer and pacifist type have taken up, is being used not only as a means of pressure for the purpose of an ideological disarmament of peoples who defend their independence from the encroachment of American imperialism, but also as a slogan especially directed against the Soviet Union, which indefatigably and consistently defends the principles of genuine equality and of safeguarding the sovereign rights of all peoples, great and small.

Nothing was said about the sovereign rights of Poland, where this congress was held.

In newspapers, magazines, and books through 1947, a palpable reversal of public sentiments from wartime amity to hostility as if in preparation for a new war is evident. A month after Truman's speech, the independent *United Nations World* printed a "probable lineup" of countries in case of general war. The Western bloc outnumbered the Soviet bloc by 414 million to 293 million in population. But there were many neutral states, mostly the continental European countries and India (435 million), uncertain states (259 million), and states on the verge of civil war, China, France, Italy, and Spain (570 million).[23]

The North Atlantic Treaty

In April 1949, with astonishing speed considering the revolutionary character of the act, the United States entered into a defensive military alliance with Great Britain and 10 other Western democracies. The North Atlantic treaty is usually considered a watershed in American history, dividing the past from the future, for it ended the traditional foreign policy of the United States, memorably expressed in George Washington's Farewell Address, of entering "no entangling alliances with Europe." Isolationism was not completely dead, nor had internationalism been unreservedly accepted, but the United States took up a place in crowded Europe and, hence, in the shrinking interdependent modern world.

A resolution by Senator Arthur S. Vandenberg of 19 May 1948 preceded the North Atlantic Treaty. Vandenberg was one of the architects of the bipartisan foreign policy who had hitherto opposed as premature any reform or strengthening of the United Nations. His resolution was now expressed in the highest terms of "international cooperation through more effective use of the United Nations." The president was explicitly advised that the sense of the Senate approved such objectives as eliminating the Security Council veto from questions

---

[23] *United Nations World*, April 1947, p. 15.

involving pacific settlement of disputes, providing armed forces to the U.N., reaching agreement on disarmament, and even holding a general conference for reform of the U.N. Charter under Article 109. These were the sort of things Grenville Clark and others struggled for in 1946 and 1947.

However, so far had the Cold War advanced by 1948 that such objectives were evidently presented as a cover (they were all conditional on "agreement") for the operative objective of establishing "regional and other collective arrangements for individual and collective self-defense" under Article 51, which had been provided for just such military alliances as the North Atlantic treaty in case the United Nations should fail.[24] United World Federalists' state and congressional legislative initiatives of 1948 and 1949 would be made in this ambiguous political atmosphere.

After the Czech coup followed the Berlin blockade, the establishment of West and East Germany, the Russian A–bomb, the victory of the Chinese Communist revolution, and the Korean War. President Truman had to relieve General Douglas MacArthur from his command in Japan and Korea when the general pressed too hard for "victory." Truman explained to the American people, "In the simplest terms, what we are doing in Korea is this: We are trying to prevent a third world war." It was actually the determination on both the Soviet Union's and the United States' parts to avoid direct military confrontation, which could so easily expand into total war—despite manifest preparations for it—that fixed the term "Cold War" in the public mind for the state of relations between the two superpowers.[25]

[24] "The Vandenberg Resolution," Commager, *Documents,* 2: 543. See Appendix H.

[25] Walter Lippmann, *The Cold War: A Study in U.S. Foreign Policy* (New York: Harper & Bros., 1947).

Conclusion to Volume 1

Politics is the art of making possible that which is necessary.

—Paul Valéry, 1945

Too Late and Too Few

The Truman doctrine marks a divide because it inaugurated the policy of containment of international communism, which endured for over 40 years of the Cold War and represented a rejection of the proposed policy of world federation. Still, until the Korean War, the new U.S. and Western policy was subject to vigorous debate, which the federalists entered warmly. But United World Federalists were not effectively organized until two weeks before President Truman announced the new policy, so they were too late to have a major effect on events.

Others—some not professedly federalist—had more influence from the coming of World War II in 1939 to the Cold War in 1947. These included Clarence Streit with his proposal of a union of democracies to overawe Hitler and Mussolini; the British Federal Unionists struggling bravely during the *Drôle de Guerre;* Winston Churchill, who made a historic offer of British union with France on the eve of her capitulation to Nazi Germany on 16 June 1940; planners in the U.S. State Department, who explored the logic of federation no less than international organization until by 1943 it was evident that neither the Soviet Union nor the United States would accept anything that was not expressly based on "sovereign equality"; Grenville Clark, who was highly placed and thought through the issues methodically before anybody; and the atomic scientists, whose "international control of atomic energy" meant an atomic development authority that would have had many of the attributes of a world government.

That the United States actually made an *offer* of international control in the Baruch plan of 1946 is surely an event that shows how far sovereign states would go toward political union in modern times. The nearest analogy is Churchill's offer of union. It is true that the British prime minister's offer has to be ranked with the series of historic events that is leading to European Union, while the Baruch plan has led at best to the series of arms control treaties from the Antarctica treaty of 1959 to the latest START treaty of 2002, which are very far in conception from a world political union. But the beginning has been made.

The deeper achievement historically in this early period is not that the world federalist movement, little organized as it was, can exhibit a beginning like the Philadelphia convention of 1787, but that thousands of people all over the globe began to reflect seriously about what would be necessary to establish peace, and they began to write a large literature to show the way (see Appendix J). The analogy is rather with James Madison's study of republican constitutions in 1786 and with the letters and dinner conversations of the Founding Fathers in the years before Philadelphia. The United Nations was established by a kind of grudging, cautious state compromise with the larger current of popular thought by 1945. Vital to the U.N. was that the United States led in establishing it, that the U.N. provided for two-thirds majority rule in every organ (qualified only by Big Five unanimity or veto in the Security Council), that national sovereignty was constitutionally limited by such a two–thirds rule, and that the Senate consented to the U.N. Charter *without reservations.* The Charter was all the soldiers and the bereaved had won from the war, but in the history of international organization, it was a greater achievement than is commonly remembered today as its inadequacies are only too evident. Probably, Roosevelt could have dared more than Wilson by the end of the Second World War.

The peoples of the earth demanded changes in diplomacy so that never again would there be another general war. Statesmen and politicians sensed the public will and declared that they were creating an international organization to maintain international peace and security. Things then became unraveled from 1945 to 1947. The breakup of wartime amity with the victorious Allies came more quickly than most responsible people, like Bernard Baruch or Harry Dexter White, ever imagined. G. A. Borgese of the Chicago Committee to Frame a World Constitution, which began its deliberations immediately after Hiroshima and Nagasaki, was astonished at the sudden reversal. Borgese wrote in March 1947 that the committee could no longer base its deliberations on the assumption that "the Big Three hand in hand" would progress toward a world state. Without this assumption, it is very doubtful that the Chicago committee would have ever undertaken the project of drafting a world constitution.

Atomic fear was a principal motivation in the West—and there were those who argued that only *fear* would produce the size of a public to unite sovereignties—but in the East and what we now call the South, the demand for social and economic justice was far more important. The world federation of the future would have to be based not merely on fear, but on solidarity with world citizens everywhere. Grenville Clark and Louis B. Sohn, for their part, continued to work after the start of the Korean War in 1950, which they did not look upon as a terminal event, but they knew they were writing for posterity. The lesson would seem to be that historic opportunities for fundamental revision of international relations are not likely to last more than a few years. The next comparable opportunity would come at the end of the Cold War, after 1990.

Appendix A

Abbreviations and Acronyms

AAUN	American Association for the United Nations
ABM	Anti-Ballistic Missile
ACLU	American Civil Liberties Union
ADA	Americans for Democratic Action
ADA	Atomic Development Authority
AEC	Atomic Energy Commission [U.S. or U.N.]
AEOR	Atomic Engineers of Oak Ridge
AFL	American Federation of Labor
AFSC	American Friends Service Committee
ALAS	Association of Los Alamos Scientists
AO	Associated Organization
AORES	Association of Oak Ridge Engineers and Scientists
AORS	Association of Oak Ridge Scientists
AORSCL	Association of Oak Ridge Scientists at Clinton Labs
AP	Associated Press
APSOR	Association of Production Scientists at Oak Ridge
ASAE	Association of Scientists for Atomic Education
ASC	Atomic Scientists of Chicago
AU	Americans United [for World Organization or Government]
AUC	Atlantic Union Committee
AUWG	Americans United for World Government
AUWO	Americans United for World Organization
AVC	American Veterans Committee
c.	About (L., *circa*)
CCUNR	Citizens Committee for United Nations Reform
CE	Council of Europe
CEIP	Carnegie Endowment for International Peace

CFWC	Committee to Frame a World Constitution
CIA	Central Intelligence Agency
CIO	Congress of Industrial Organizations
CO	Conscientious Objector
comp.	Compiler
CP	Communist Party
CPSU	Communist Party of the Soviet Union
CSOP	Commission to Study the Organization of Peace
CWG	Campaign for World Government
DAR	Daughters of the American Revolution
EC	European Community [Communities]
ECA	European Cooperation Administration [Marshall Plan]
ECAS	Emergency Committee of the Atomic Scientists
Ecosoc	Economic and Social Council [of the U.N.—not an acronym]
ECSC	European Coal and Steel Community
ed.	Editor or edited.
EDC	European Defense Community [proposed in 1952]
EEC	European Economic Community
EPC	European Political Community [proposed in 1952]
ERP	European Recovery Plan
EU	European Union
ff.	Following pages
FAmS	Federation of American Scientists
FAO	Food and Agricultural Organization
FAS	Federation of American Scientists
FAtS	Federation of Atomic Scientists
FBI	Federal Bureau of Investigation
FDR	Franklin Delano Roosevelt
FU	Federal Union
FURI	Federal Union Research Institute
FWG	Foundation for World Government
GATT	General Agreement on Tariffs and Trade
HCR	House Concurrent Resolution
HMSO	His (or Her) Majesty's Stationery Office
HQ	Headquarters
ibid.	In the same place (L., *ibidem*)
idem	The same person (L.)
ICBM	Intercontinental Ballistic Missile
ICJ	International Court of Justice
ILO	International Labour Organisation
INGO	International Nongovernmental Organization
IO	International Organization
IR	International Relations
ITO	International Trade Organization (1948)

ITU	International Telecommunications Union
JFK	John Fitzgerald Kennedy
LNA	League of Nations Association
LNU	League of Nations Union
MCWF	Massachusetts Committee for World Federation
MIRV	Multiple Independently–targetable Reentry Vehicle
MIT	Massachusetts Institute of Technology
MNC	Multinational Corporation
M.P.	Member of Parliament
NASA	National Aeronautics and Space Administration
NATO	North Atlantic Treaty Organization
NCAI	National Committee for Atomic Information
n.	Note
n.d.	No date
NGO	Nongovernmental Organization
NO	National Organization
OECD	Organization for Economic Cooperation and Development
OEEC	Organization for European Economic Cooperation [Marshall Plan] [continued as OECD]
OPEC	Organization of Petroleum Exporting Countries
ORES	Oak Ridge Engineers and Scientists
OSCE	Organization for Security and Cooperation in Europe
passim	Here and there (L.)
PC	Peoples' Convention
PCIJ	Permanent Court of International Justice
PGA	Parliamentarians for Global Action
PWC	Peoples' World Convention [PC]
PWCC	Peoples' World Constitutional Convention [PC]
RAF	Royal Air Force
SAC	Strategic Air Command
SANE	Committee for a Sane Nuclear Policy
SCR	Senate Concurrent Resolution
SF	Student Federalists [later Student Division, UWF]
SFFWG	Students for Federal World Government [World Republic]
SDI	Strategic Defense Initiative
TNCs	Transnational Corporations
UAW	United Auto Workers
UEF	*Union Européenne des Fédéralistes* [became Union of European Federalists; same acronym]
U.N.	United Nations [Alliance or Organization]
UNA	United Nations Association
UNCTAD	U.N. Conference on Trade and Development
UNCTC	United Nations Center on Transnational Corporations
UNESCO	United Nations Educational, Scientific, and Cultural Organization

UNO   United Nations Organization
UNRRWA U.N. Relief and Rehabilitation Administration
UPU   Universal Postal Union
USAF   United States Air Force
UWF   United World Federalists
VE   Victory in Europe [Day]
VFW   Veterans of Foreign Wars
VIP   Very Important Person
VJ   Victory in Japan [Day]
WAWF   World Association of World Federalists [successor to WMWFG]
WBWG   Writers Board for World Government
WCA   World Constituent Assembly [PC]
WCC   World Constituional Convention [PC]
WCM   World Citizenship Movement
WF   World Federalists and World Federalists, U.S.A.
WFA   World Federalist Association
WFG   World Federal Government
WFM   World Federalist Movement [continues WMWFG and WAWF]
WFUSA   World Federalists, U.S.A. [same as UWF after 1969]
WG   World Government
WGN   *World Government News*
WM   World Movement [for World Federal Government, WMWFG]
WMWFG World Movement for World Federal Government [later WAWF]
WOMP   World Order Models Project
WR   World Republic
WSF   World Student Federalists
WTO   World Trade Organization
WWS   Workers for World Security

Appendix B

Historic Federal Unions

United States of America	(1787)
United Provinces of Central America	(1821–38)
Gran Colombia	(1822–30)
Mexico	(1824, 1857, 1917)
Switzerland	(1848, 1874)
Argentina	(1853)
Venezuela	(1864, 1947, 1961)
Canada	(1867, 1982)
Austria–Hungary	(1867, 1919)
Germany	(1871, 1919, 1949)
Brazil	(1891)
Australia	(1901)
Austria	(1920, 1945)
Czechoslovakia	(1920, 1948, 1960)
Russia (R.S.F.S.R.)	(1922, 1993)
U.S.S.R.	(1924, 1936, 1977–91)
Yugoslavia	(1946, 1953, 1963, 1974)
India	(1949)
Ethiopia	(1952, 1995)
Central African Federation of Rhodesia and Nyasaland	(1953–63)
Pakistan	(1956, 1962, 1973)
West Indies Federation	(1956–62)
Malaya, Malaysia	(1957, 1963)
Mali Federation	(1959–60)
Nigeria	(1960, 1963)
Micronesia	(1986)
St. Kitts and Nevis	(1983)
Cormoros	(1992)
Bosnia and Herzegovina	(1995)
United Arab Emirates	(1996)

Sources: Albert P. Blaustein and Gisbert H. Flanz, eds., *Constitutions of the Countries of the World,* 18 binders (Dobbs Ferry, NY: Oceana, 1971–), passim; Ann L. Griffiths, ed., *Handbook of Federal Countries, 2002* (Montreal: McGill–Queens University Press, 2002).

FORMER FEDERAL UNIONS

United Provinces of Central America	(1838)
Gran Colombia	(1830)
Central African Federation	(1963)
West Indies Federation	(1962)
Mali Federation	(1960)
U.S.S.R.	(1991)
Czechoslovakia	(1992)

FEDERALIST EXPERIMENTS

South Africa	(1910)
Burma	(1948)
Libya	(1951)
Peoples Republic of China	(1954)
United Arab Republic	(1958–61)
Jordan–Iraq Federation	(1958)
Cyprus	(1960)
Yugoslavia	(1991)

"Federalist Experiments" does not include proposed federations, like Sukarno's Malphindo (Malaysia, Philippines, Indonesia). Ireland and Puerto Rico were never incorporated into a federation, though the idea was discussed.

DECENTRALIZATIONS AND DEVOLUTIONS

Italy	(1948)
Belgium	(1980)
Spain	(1982)
France	(1982)
Great Britain	(1997)

Source: Joseph E. Schwartzberg, "The U.S. Constitution: A Model for Global Government," *Journal of Geography,* 86 (November–December 1987): 246–52.

Appendix C

Clauses in National Constitutions Limiting Sovereignty

EUROPE

1. Austria

Art 9(1). The generally recognized rules of International Law are valid parts of Federal Law.

(2). By Law or by a State Treaty which must be ratified in accordance with Art. 50(1), specific sovereign rights of the Bund can be transferred to intergovernmental institutions and their organs, and the activity of organs of foreign states in Austria as well as the activity of Austrian organs abroad can be regulated within the framework of International Law.

—(Constitution of 1929, as amended on 1 July 1981.)

2. Belgium

Art. 25 bis. The exercise of given powers may be conferred by a pact or law on institutions coming under international civil law.

—(Constitution of 1831, as amended on 29 September 1971.)

3. Denmark

Art. 20(1). Powers vested in the authorities of the Realm under this Constitution may, to such extent as shall be provided by Statute, be delegated to international authorities set up by mutual agreement with other states for the promotion of international rules of law and cooperation.

(2). For the passing of a Bill dealing with the above a majority of five–sixths of the Members of the Folketing shall be required. If this majority is not obtained, and if the Government maintains it, the Bill shall be submitted to the Electorate for approval or rejection in accordance with the rules for Referenda laid down in section 42.

—(Constitution of 5 June 1953.)

4. Finland
Chapter 4a. Consideration of the Affairs of the European Union....

Section 54b. The Council of State shall without delay send to the Speaker a communication on any proposal which has come to its notice for an act, agreement, or other measure to be decided by the Council of the European Union and which otherwise pursuant to the constitution would fall within the competence of Parliament.

—(Constitution of 1919; Parliament Act of 1928;
amendment of 31 December 1994.)

5. France
Preamble. On condition of reciprocity, France accepts the limitations of sovereignty necessary for the organization and defense of peace.

—(Constitution of the Fourth Republic, 1946.)

Preamble. The French people hereby solemnly proclaims its attachment to the Rights of Man and the principles of national sovereignty as defined by the Declaration of 1789, reaffirmed and complemented by the Preamble of the Constitution of 1946.

Art. 54. If the Constitutional Council, the matter having been referred to it by the President of the Republic, by the Premier, or by the President of one or the other assembly, shall declare that an international commitment contains a clause contrary to the Constitution, the authorization to ratify or approve this commitment may be given only after amendment of the Constitution.

Art. 55. Treaties or agreements duly ratified and approved shall, upon their publication, have an authority superior to that of laws, subject, for each agreement or treaty, to its application by the other party.

—(Constitution of the Fifth Republic, 4 October 1958.)

6. Germany
Art. 24. Entry into a collective security system:

(1). The Federation may by legislation transfer sovereign powers to intergovernmental institutions.

(2). For the maintenance of peace, the Federation may enter a system of mutual collective security; in doing so, it will consent to such limitations upon its rights of sovereignty as will bring about and secure peaceful and lasting order in Europe and among the nations of the world.

(3). For the settlement of disputes between states, the Federation will accede to agreements concerning international arbitration of a general comprehensive, and obligatory nature.

—(Constitution of 1949, confirmed by
Unification Treaty of 31 August 1990.)

7. Greece

Art. 28(2). To serve an important national interest and promote cooperation with other states, authorities may be vested by a convention or agreement in agencies of an international organization. A majority of three–fifths of the total number of members of Parliament shall be necessary to vote the law sanctioning the treaty or agreement.

(3). Greece shall freely proceed by law voted by the absolute majority of the total number of members of Parliament, to limit the exercise of national sovereignty, insofar as this is dictated by an important national interest, does not infringe upon the rights of man and the foundations of democratic government, and is effected on the basis of the principles of equality and under condition of reciprocity.

—(Constitution of 7 June 1975.)

8. Ireland

Art. 29(1). Ireland affirms its devotion to the ideal of peace and friendly cooperation amongst nations founded on international justice and morality.

(4). For the purpose of the exercise of any executive function of the State in or in connection with its external relations, the Government may to such extent and subject to such conditions, if any, as may be determined by law, avail of or adopt any organ, instrument, or method of procedure used or adopted for the like purpose by the members of any group or league of nations with which the State is or becomes associated for the purpose of international cooperation in matters of common concern.

The State may become a member of the European Coal and Steel Community ... the European Economic Community ... the European Atomic Energy Community.... The State may ratify the Single European Act..... No provision of this Constitution invalidates laws enacted, acts done or measures adopted by the State necessitated by the obligations of membership in the Communities, or prevents laws enacted, acts done or measures adopted by the Communities, or instruments thereof, from having the force of law in the State.

—(Constitution of 1937, as amended by 1972.)

9. Italy

Art. 11. Italy renounces war as an instrument of offense to the liberty of other peoples or as a means of settlement of international disputes, and, on conditions of equality with other states, agrees to the limitations of her sovereignty necessary to an organization which will ensure peace and justice among nations, and promotes and encourages international organizations constituted for this purpose.   —(Constitution of 1 January 1948.)

10. Luxembourg

Art. 49(A). The exercise of the powers reserved by the Constitution to the legislative, executive, and judiciary may be temporarily vested by treaty in institutions governed by international law.

—(Constitution of 1868, as amended on 10 July 1973.)

11. Netherlands

Art. 195(a). For the maintenance of external or internal security, in extraordinary circumstances, it may be decreed by, or in the name of, the King, for any part of the territory of the Kingdom, that the constitutional powers of organs of civil authority in respect of public order and the police are transferred in whole or in part to other organs of civil authority.

—(Constitution of 1815, as amended on 3 September 1948.)

Art. 92. Legislative, executive, and judicial powers may be conferred on international institutions by or pursuant to a treaty, subject, where necessary, to the provisions of Article 91, paragraph 3.

—(Constitution of 13 February 1983.)

12. Norway

Art. 93. In order to secure international peace and security, or in order to promote international law and order and cooperation between nations, the Storting may, by a three–fourths majority, consent that an international organization, of which Norway is or becomes a member, shall have the right, within a functionally limited field, to exercise powers which in accordance with this Constitution are normally vested in the Norwegian authorities, exclusive of the power to alter this Constitution. For such consent as provided above at least two–thirds of the members of the Storting— the same quorum as is required for changes in or amendments to this Constitution—shall be present and voting.

—(Constitution of 1814, as amended in 1952.)

13. Poland

Art. 9. The Republic of Poland shall respect international law binding upon it.

Art. 89(1). Ratification of an international agreement by the Republic of Poland, as well as denunciation thereof, shall require prior consent granted by statute, if such agreement concerns:

1)   Peace, alliances, political or military treaties;

2)   Freedoms, rights or obligations of citizens, as specified in the Constitution;

3)   The Republic of Poland's membership in an international organization.

—(Constitution of 1997)

14. Portugal

Art. 7(2). Portugal commends the abolition of all forms of imperialism, colonialism, and aggression; general, simultaneous, and controlled disarmament; the dissolution of politico–military blocs; and the establishment of a system of collective security, in order to create an international order capable of assuring peace and justice in relations among peoples.

Art. 8(3). The standards issuing from the qualified international organizations to which Portugal belongs shall directly be enforced domestically, since that is expressly stipulated in the respective constituent agreements.

—(Constitution of 25 April 1976.)

15. Spain

Art. 93. By means of an organic law, authorization may be established for the conclusion of treaties which attribute to an international organization or institution the exercise of competence derived from the constitution. It is the responsibility of the Cortes Generals or the Government, depending on the cases, to guarantee compliance with these treaties and the resolutions emanating from the international or supranational organization who have been entitled by this cession.   —(Constitution of 29 December 1978.)

16. Sweden

Chap. 10, Art. 5. The right to make decisions which under the present Instrument of Government devolves on the Riksdag, on the Government, or on any other organ referred to in the Instrument of Government, may be entrusted, to a limited extent, to an international organization for peaceful cooperation of which Sweden is to become a member, or to an International Tribunal. No right to make decisions in matters regarding the enactment, amendment, or repeal of a fundamental law or [to restrict] any of the freedoms and rights referred to in Chapter 2 may thus be transferred. The Riksdag shall decide on a transfer of the right to make decisions in the manner prescribed for the fundamental laws or, if a decision in accordance with such procedure cannot be abided, by way of a decision agreed upon by not less than five–sixths of those present and voting and by not less than three–fourths of the Riksdag members.

—(Constitution of 1809, as amended in 1976.)

17. Switzerland

Art. 89(5). The entry into organizations of collective security or supranational entities is subject to a vote by the people and the Cantons.

—(Constitution of 1874, as amended in 1982.)

LATIN AMERICA

18. Argentina

Art. 27. The Federal government is bound to strengthen its relations of peace and commerce with foreign powers, by means of treaties that are in conformity with the principles of public law laid down in this constitution.

—(Constitution of 1953.)

19. Brazil

Art. 4, Sole Paragraph. The Federative Republic of Brazil shall seek the economic, political, social, and cultural integration of the peoples of Latin America, with a view to the formation of a Latin American community of nations.

—(Constitution of 1891, as amended on 5 October 1988.)

20. Colombia

Art. 9. The external relations of the state are based on national sovereignty, on respect for the self-determination of peoples, and on the recognition of international law approved by Colombia.

In the same manner, the foreign policy of Colombia will be oriented toward the integration of Latin America and the Caribbean.

—(Constitution of 5 July 1991.)

21. Costa Rica

Art. 121(4). Public treaties and international conventions extending or transferring jurisdictional powers to a communitarian juridical order for the purpose of realizing common regional objectives shall require the approval of the Legislative Assembly by a vote of not less than two thirds of its entire membership.

—(Constitution of 1949, as amended on 31 May 1968.)

22. Cuba

Art. 12. The Republic of Cuba espouses the principles of proletarian internationalism and of the combative solidarity of the peoples and ... (g) aspires to establish along with the other countries of Latin America and of the Caribbean—freed from foreign domination and internal oppression— one large community of nations joined by the fraternal ties of historical tradition and the common struggle against colonialism, neocolonialism, and imperialism, and in the desire to foster national and social progress.

—(Constitution of 24 February 1976, as amended to 1989.)

23. El Salvador

Art. 89. El Salvador shall encourage and promote the human, economic, social, and cultural integration of the American republics, and especially those of the Central American isthmus. The realization of this [objective] shall be carried out through treaties or agreements among the interested republics, which treaties may contemplate the creation of organizations with supranational functions.

El Salvador shall also promote the total or partial reestablishment of the Republic of Central America, in either unitary, federal, or confederated form, provided that democratic and republican principles are respected in the new state, and the essential rights of individuals and of associations are fully guaranteed.

The project and bases of union shall be submitted to popular opinion (conference). —(Constitution of 1983.)

24. Guatemala

Art. 150. Guatemala, as part of the Central American community, will maintain and cultivate relations of cooperation and solidarity with the other states making up the Central American Federation; will adopt adequate means to put into practice, in part or entirely, the political and economic unity of Central America. The competent authorities are obligated to strengthen Central American integration on the basis of equity. —(Constitution of 1986.)

25. Nicaragua

Art. 9. Nicaragua firmly defends Central American unity, and supports and promotes all efforts to achieve political and economic integration and cooperation in the region. It also supports the efforts to establish and preserve peace in Central America.

Nicaragua desires the unity of the people of Latin America and the Caribbean, inspired by the ideals of Bolívar and Sandino.

Therefore, Nicaragua will participate with other Central American and Latin American countries in the creation and election of the bodies necessary to achieve such goals. This principle shall be regulated by the appropriate legislation and treaties.   —(Constitution of 1986.)

26. Peru

Art. 103. When an international treaty contains a stipulation that affects a constitutional provision, it must be approved by the same procedure that governs amendments to the Constitution before being ratified by the President of the Republic.

Art. 106. Integration treaties with Latin American countries prevail over other multilateral treaties concluded among the same parties.
                                 —(Constitution of 1979, as amended by 1988.)

27. Venezuela

Preamble. The Congress of the Republic of Venezuela ... cooperating with all other nations and especially with the sister Republics of the Hemisphere, in the aims of the international community, on the basis of mutual respect for sovereignties, the self-determination of peoples, the universal guarantee of the individual and social rights of the human person, and the repudiation of war, conquest, and economic predominance as instruments of international policy.

Art. 129. In international treaties, conventions, and agreements concluded by the Republic, there shall be inserted a clause by which the parties bind themselves to decide by peaceful means recognized by international law or previously agreed to by them, if such is the case, all controversies that may arise between the parties....   —(Constitution of 23 January 1961.)

AFRICA

28. Congo

Art. 39. The People's Republic of the Congo subscribes to the fundamental principles and objectives contained in the Charters of the United Nations and the Organization of African Unity.

Art. 120. The People's Republic of the Congo may conclude agreements of cooperation or association with other states. It is willing to create with them international organizations for joint management, coordination, and open cooperation.   —(Constitution of 8 July 1979, as amended to 1989.)

29. Egypt

Preamble. We, the Egyptian people, in the name of God and by his assistance, pledge indefinitely and unconditionally to exert every effort to realize: ... Union: the hope of our Arab nation, being convinced that Arab unity is a call of history and of the future, and a demand of destiny; and that it cannot materialize except through an Arab nation, capable of warding off any threat, whatever the sources or the pretexts for such a threat.   —(Constitution of 22 May 1980.)

30. Guinea

Preamble.... The people of Guinea ... reaffirm ... its willingness to establish amicable relations and cooperation with all peoples of the world on a foundation of principles of equality, respect for national sovereignty, territorial integrity, and reciprocal interests; its attachment to the cause of African Unity, [and] of the sub-regional integration of the continent.   —(Constitution of 1990.)

31. Mali

Preamble.... The Malian people, aware of the historical and material obligations which unite the States of Africa, and anxious to achieve the liberation and the political, economic, and social unity indispensable to the assertion of the African personality, affirm their determination to continue working for the total realization of this liberation and this unity.

—(Constitution of 1974, amended through 1988.)

32. Rwanda

Preamble. The people of Rwanda ... resolved to contribute to peaceful coexistence between nations, to strengthened cooperation between peoples, and to the construction of African unity....

Art. 44(8). The federation of the Republic of Rwanda with one or several other democratic nations must be approved by popular referendum.

—(Constitution of 20 December 1978.)

33. Zaire

Art. 110. In order to promote African Unity, the Republic may conclude treaties and agreements of association which involve partial abandonment of its sovereignty.   —(Constitution of 1978, as amended on 5 July 1990.)

ASIA, AUSTRALASIA

34. India

Art. 51. The State shall endeavor to—

  (a) Promote international peace and security;
  (b) Maintain just and honorable relations between nations;
  (c) Foster respect for international law and treaty obligations in the
      dealings of organized people with one another;

(d) Encourage settlement of international disputes by arbitration....

Art. 246. Parliament has exclusive power to make laws with respect to:

(13) Participation in international conferences, associations, and other bodies and implementing of decisions made thereat.

—(Constitution of 1949, as amended to 1989.)

35. Japan

Art. 9. Aspiring sincerely to an international peace based on justice and order, the Japanese people forever renounce war as a sovereign right of the nation and the threat or use of force as a means of settling international disputes.

In order to accomplish the aim of the preceding paragraph, land, sea and air forces, as well as other war potential will never be maintained.

The right of the belligerency of the State will not be recognized.

—(Constitution of 3 May 1947.)

36. Philippines

Art. 2(3). The Philippines renounces war as an instrument of national policy, adopts the generally accepted principles of international law as part of the law of the land, and adheres to the policy of peace, equality, justice, freedom, cooperation, and amity with all nations.

—(Constitution of 1935, as amended in 1946 and 1973.)

37. Singapore

Art. 7. Without in any way derogating from the force and effect of Article 6, nothing in that article shall be construed as precluding Singapore or any association, body, or organization therein from ... (b) Entering into a treaty, agreement, contract, pact, or other arrangement with any other sovereign state or with any Federation, Confederation, country or countries, or any association, body, or organization therein, where such treaty, agreement, contract, pact, or arrangement provides for mutual or collective security or any other object or purpose whatsoever which is, or appears to be, beneficial or advantageous to Singapore in any way.   —(Constitution of 31 March 1980.)

WORLD

United States of America (proposed)

Whereas, war is now a threat to the very existence of our civilization, because modern science has produced weapons of war which are overwhelmingly destructive and against which there is no sure defense; and

Whereas, the effective maintenance of world peace is the proper concern and responsibility of every American citizen; and

Whereas, the people of the State of California, while now enjoying domestic peace and security under the laws of their local, state, and federal governments, deeply desire the guarantee ow world peace; and

Whereas, all history shows that peace is the product of law and order, and that law and order are the product of government; and

Whereas, the United Nations, as presently constituted, although accomplishing great good in many fields, lacks authority to enact, interpret or enforce world law, and under its present Charter is incapable of restraining any major nations which may foster or foment war; and

Whereas, the Charter of the United Nations expressly provides in Articles 108 and 109, a procedure for reviewing and altering the Charter; and

Whereas, the necessity for endowing the United Nations with limited powers rendering it capable of enacting, interpreting or enforcing world law adequate to prevent war, and guaranteeing the inalienable rights of freedom for every human being on earth and the dignity of the individual as exemplified by the American Bill of Rights, has been recognized in the California State conventions and platforms of both the Republican and Democratic parties; and

Whereas, many states have memorialized Congress, through resolutions by their state legislatures or in referenda by their voters, to initiate steps toward the creation of a world federal government reserving to the nations and to the people those rights not specifically granted as necessary to the establishment of the maintenance of world law and order; and

Whereas, several nations (Italy, India, France) have recently adopted constitutional provisions to facilitate their entry into a world federal government by authorizing a delegation to such a world federal government of a portion of their sovereignty to endow it with powers adequate to prevent war;

Now, therefore, be it:

Resolved, By the Assembly and Senate of the State of California, jointly, that application is hereby made to the Congress of the United States, pursuant to Article V of the Constitution of the United States, to call a convention for the sole purpose of proposing amendment of the Constitution to expedite and insure the participation of the United States in a world federal government, open to all nations, with powers which, while defined and limited, shall be adequate to preserve peace, whether the proposed charter or constitution of such world federal government be presented in the form of amendments to the Charter of the United Nations, or by a world constitutional convention, or otherwise; and be it further:

Resolved, That the Chief Clerk of the Assembly is hereby directed to transmit copies of this application to the Senate and the House of Representatives from this state, and to the presiding officers of each of the legislatures in the several states, requesting their cooperation.

—(Draft U.S. Constitutional Amendment, California Plan, 1949)

(Passed in California, Maine, North Carolina, Connecticut, and New Jersey.)

United Nations

Art. 2(2). All Members, in order to ensure to all of them the rights and benefits resulting from membership, shall fulfill in good faith the obligations assumed by them in accordance with the present Charter.

Art. 25. The Members of the United Nations agree to accept and carry out the decisions of the Security Council in accordance with the present Charter.

Art. 43(1). All Members of the United Nations, in order to contribute to the maintenance of international peace and security, undertake to make available to the Security Council, on its call and in accordance with a special agreement or agreements, armed forces, assistance, and facilities, including rights of passage, necessary for the purpose of maintaining international peace and security.

Art. 49. The Members of the United Nations shall join in affording mutual assistance in carrying out the measures decided upon by the Security Council.

Art. 56. All Members pledge themselves to take joint and separate action in cooperation with the Organization for the achievement of the [economic and social] purposes set forth in Article 55.

—(Charter of the United Nations, 1945)

Sources: Amos Peaslee, ed. *Constitutions of Nations*. Rumford, NH: 1950; The Hague: M. Nijhoff, 2nd ed., 1956, 3 vols.; 3rd ed., 1965–70, 6 vols.

Albert P. Blaustein and Gisbert H. Flanz, eds. *Constitutions of the Countries of the World*. Dobbs Ferry, NY: Oceana, 1971– , 18 binders.

The Constitution Society: www.constitution.org/cons/natlcons.htm

Notes: The recent constitution of Honduras seems to have elided earlier clauses providing for a return to the Central American Republic. The constitutions of Zimbabwe, Zambia, and Malawi no longer contain traces of their aspirations in the Central African Federation. Ghana and Senegal, though once members of the Mali Federation, have lost provisions for union in a West African federation. Tanzania, once the seat of the East African Community (1967–77) and the font of the ideal of an East African federation, also no longer provides for union. Neither does Uganda nor Kenya.

Appendix D

Archives and Collections

NORTH AMERICAN COLLECTIONS

Americans United for World Organization (later Americans United for World Government).
  No known archives but some records in United World Federalists Papers, Cousins Papers, Eichelberger Papers, and Hoover Institution on War, Revolution, and Peace. Americans United were a major component of United World Federalists on formation in 1947.

Atlantic Union Papers. Butler Library, Columbia University.
  Papers of a project under Britain's Federal Union, supported by its secretary, Douglas Robinson, and directed by American Walden Moore, 1952–65. Project had some influence on formation of NATO's North Atlantic Assembly (1955) and the Organization for Economic Cooperation and Development (1960).

Atomic Scientists Papers. Regenstein Library, University of Chicago:
  Association of Cambridge Scientists;
  Association of Los Alamos Scientists;
  Association of Oak Ridge Engineers and Scientists;
  Association of Pasadena Scientists;
  Association of Scientists for Atomic Education;
  Atomic Scientists of Chicago (and *Bulletin*);
  Emergency Committee of the Atomic Scientists;
  Federation of Atomic Scientists;
  Federation of American Scientists;
  Washington Association of Scientists.

Papers of atomic scientists as they organized politically, after Hiroshima, for the international control of atomic energy.

Barr, Stringfellow, Papers. University of Virginia, Charlottesville (?).
Papers of historian, co-founder of St. John's College's New Program (great books), member of the Committee to Frame a World Constitution, and director of the Foundation for World Government.

Baruch, Bernard, Papers. Seeley Mudd Library, Princeton University.
Background of the United States plan for the international control of atomic energy in the United Nations Atomic Energy Commission, 1946.

Blaine, Anita McCormick, Papers. State Historical Society of Wisconsin.
Foundation for World Government records, correspondence with Stringfellow Barr, Henry Wallace, and others in world government movement and Progressive Party; World Citizenship Association records.

Blake, Mildred Riorden, Reminiscences. Oral History Research Office, Butler Library, Columbia University.
Reminiscences of formation of World Federalists after split with Streit in 1941. World Federalists became the second major component of United World Federalists in 1947.

Buchanan, Scott, Papers. Widenor Library, Harvard University.
Papers of liberal educator, co-founder of St. John's College's New Program (great books), leading advocate of world government, and supporter of Henry Wallace in 1948 Progressive Party campaign.

Canadian Peace Research Institute Papers, 1945–77. Archives of Canada, Toronto, Ontario.
Papers of Norman Alcock, founder of the Canadian Peace Research Institute (1961), William Eckhardt, Jerome Laulicht, and Alan and Hanna Newcombe, who began publishing *Peace Research Abstracts* in 1964. Includes correspondence, office files, books, files of abstracts, records of Canadian Peace Research and Educational Association (1968–76; Anatol Rapaport last president), records of World Federalists of Canada (1948–77), and peace movement ephemera.

Carnegie Endowment for International Peace Archives. Butler Library, Columbia University.
Extensive holdings on private groups favoring international organization, notably the Commission to Study the Organization of Peace.

Clark, Grenville, Papers. Baker Library, Dartmouth College.
Papers of the New York lawyer, associate of Elihu Root Sr. and Henry L. Stimson, who became the "elder statesman" of the world government movement after 1944. Clark was the leading proponent of minimal or limited world government.

Clayton, William, L., Papers. Rice University.
Papers of architect of North Atlantic Treaty and leading member of the Atlantic Union Committee. See also selected papers in edition by Frederick Dobner.

Committee to Frame a World Constitution Papers. Regenstein Library, University of Chicago.
Records of the Committee under Robert M. Hutchins and G. A. Borgese that issued the "Preliminary Draft of a World Constitution," a maximalist document. "Peace and justice stand or fall together."

Cousins, Norman, Papers. Brooklyn College Library, Brooklyn, New York.
Papers on the *Saturday Review of Literature,* Americans United, and United World Federalists.

Culbertson, Ely, Papers. Yale University Library, New Haven, Connecticut; Syracuse University Library, Syracuse, New York.
Papers of the famous bridge expert, who devoted the last years of his life to what he called "world federalism."

Eichelberger, Clark, Papers. New York Public Library.
Papers of Eichelberger's directorship of the League of Nations Association, Commission to Study the Organization of Peace, and American Association for the United Nations.

Finletter, Thomas K., Papers. State Historical Society of Wisconsin, Madison.
Papers of brains of Americans United for World Government, occasional antagonist of Grenville Clark, and secretary of the air force in Truman's administration.

Griessimer, Tom Otto, Papers. Tulane University, New Orleans, Louisiana.
Includes his partially completed manuscript, "Force and Peace," which contains his most matured thought on the use of force to maintain peace, that is, on the problem of government.

Holt, Hamilton, Papers. Mills Library, Rollins College, Winter Park, Florida.
Papers of the founder of the League to Enforce Peace, who in 1946 organized the Rollins College conference on world government. Records of the Institute for World Government, which came out of the conference, are also here.

Hudson, Manley O., Papers. Harvard Law Library (Langdell Building). Harvard University.
Personal and professional papers of law professor, judge, international mediator, and legal scholar whom the public reguarded as "Mr. World Court."

Hutchins, Robert M., Papers. Regenstein Library, University of Chicago.
Correspondence with prominent citizens and leaders of the movement.

Lippmann, Walter, Papers. Sterling Library, Yale University.
This sophisticated and shrewd political commentator saw the necessity for world government as early as the First World War.

Mansfield, Connecticut, chapter of United World Federalists. University of Connecticut Library, Storrs, Connecticut.
This was a prominent chapter with links throughout New England, 1948–88. Led by George C. Holt. (Lawrence Abbott's papers went to Indiana University.)

Morgenthau, Hans J., Papers. Alderman Library, University of Virginia, Charlottesville.
Morgenthau, like other teachers of "realism" in America, including Carl J. Fredrich and Frederick L. Schuman, explained the transitory practice of power politics by reference to the eventually necessary world state. In 1978, he admitted to Francis A. Boyle that, in the nuclear age, continued avoidance of departures like the Clark–Sohn plan were leading inexorably toward a nuclear Third World War. [See Boyle, *World Politics and International Law* (1985); and *The Future of International Law and American Foreign Policy* (1989).]

Mowrer, Edgar Ansel, Papers. Library of Congress, Washington, D.C.
Papers of journalist who worked particularly with Grenville Clark at the United Nations.

Niebuhr, Reinhold, Papers. Library of Congress, Washington, DC.
Includes records of his brief participation in the Chicago Committee to Frame a World Constitution, followed by influential resistance to it.

Notter, Harley A., Papers. U.S. National Archives, Washington, DC.
Records of several State Department planning committees, including the Advisory Committee on Postwar Foreign Relations and the Subcommittee on International Organization. In Notter's formal report, *Postwar Foreign Policy Preparation, 1939–1945* (Washington, DC: Dept. of State, Pub. No. 3580, General Foreign Policy Series 15, 1949 [released February 1950]), it is revealed that the Advisory Committee briefly considered in the fall of 1942 a "federalized international organization—or government." See also *Foreign*

Relations of the United States, general volumes.

Patterson, Robert P., Papers. Library of Congress.
Associate of Grenville Clark, secretary of war, and member of the Atlantic Union Committee.

Roberts, Owen, Papers. Library of Congress.
Papers of Supreme Court Justice and prominent advocate of Atlantic Union.

Schmidt, Adolph, Papers. University of Pittsburgh.
Patent attorney and co-author of *The New Federalist.*

Schwimmer–Lloyd Collection. New York Public Library.
Extensive collection on the Ford Peace Ship, pacifism, and world government organizations. Rosika Schwimmer was the radical forebear of the peoples' convention approach to world government.

Shotwell, James T., Papers. Carnegie Endowment Archive, Butler Library, Columbia University.
Papers of the distinguished defender of the League of Nations and leading proponent of the "realist" concept of international organization.

Sohn, Louis B., Papers. Harvard Law Library (Langdell Building), Harvard University.
Manuscripts, writings, correspondence (as with Grenville Clark) of law professor, international organizer, and legal scholar.

State Historical Society of Wisconsin Library, Madison.
Like the Swarthmore Peace Collection, this archive is a major repository on the peace movement, especially in opposition to the Vietnam War. Contains Anita McCormick Blaine Papers and those of her World Citizens Association, which led to the Foundation for World Government.

Stimson, Henry L., Papers. Yale University Library. Microfilm, 1973.
For Stimson's "unguarded" views on world government to succeed the U.N., see letter to George Wharton Pepper, 27 October 1947 (118).

Streit, Clarence K., Papers. Library of Congress.
New York Times Geneva correspondent, author of *Union Now,* editor of *Freedom and Union,* founder of Federal Union in the United States, and inspiring genius of World Federalists. Papers include records of Atlantic Union Committee.

Swarthmore Peace Collection. Swarthmore College, Pennsylvania.
Major collection in eastern United States, mostly pacifism, especially in opposition to the Vietnam War. Includes Donald Keys' U.N. papers.

Szilard, Leo, Papers. Special Collections, University of California, San Diego.
Papers of one of the most radical of the atomic scientists, who vigorously advocated some form of world government to control atomic energy.

United World Federalists Archive. Lilly Library, Indiana University.
Organizational files, including much correspondence, of the mainstream mass membership world government organization in the United States. Additional material on all branches of the movement.

Vandenberg, Arthur H. Jr., ed. *The Private Papers of Senator Vandenberg.* Boston: Houghton Mifflin, 1952.
Relevant to United Nations, world government, North Atlantic Treaty (see especially p. 479).

Warburg, James P., Papers. John F. Kennedy Library, Boston, Mass.
Papers of prominent New York banker and critic of U.S. foreign policy.

Weik, Mary Hays, Papers, 1921–79. University of Michigan at Ann Arbor.

Wells, Herbert George, Papers. University of Illinois at Urbana.
Manuscripts and typescripts of Wells' books, letters to him, copies of letters from him, press clippings, etc.

World Citizens Association Papers. Regenstein Library, University of Chicago.
Files of an organization that during the war supported the Commission to Study the Organization of Peace. Some additional records in Blaine Papers.

World Federalists of Canada Papers, 1958–75. Archives of Canada, Toronto, Ontario.
Correspondence of William M. Sheehan (president, 1958–61), general correspondence (1961–74), national secretary's files, financial records, conferences, ephemera, Canadian World Federalists (1961–68, complete), Arnold Simoni's book, *Beyond Repair: The Urgent Need for a New World Organization* (1972), and one audio tape of addresses by Ross Smyth and Andrew Clarke.

World Knowledge Bank. Academy of World Studies, 2820 Van Ness Avenue, San Francisco, CA 94109.
80,000–item research file on world historical, political, economic, and social issues. Collected by Bennet Skewes–Cox, who took a broad view of the trends, since the advent of nuclear weapons, toward federal world government. An invaluable repository of primary sources for world history.

World Movement for World Federal Government Papers. Regenstein Library, University of Chicago.
Records especially valuable for European branches of the movement.

World Republic Papers. Regenstein Library, University of Chicago.
Papers of radical veteran and student group, which for a time threatened to rival United World Federalists with a grassroots popular movement for world government.

World without War Council Records, Bancroft Library, University of California, Berkeley.
Records of Robert Woito's group (formerly Turn toward Peace), which occasionally gave a little notice to the world federalist movement.

Wright, Quincy, Papers. Regenstein Library, University of Chicago.
Papers of distinguished professor of international law and leading political theorist, whose thought provides a connective between United Nations and world government supporters.

EUROPEAN COLLECTIONS

Borgese, Giuseppe Antonio, Papers. University of Milan (?).
Papers of humanist, critic, professor of literature, anti-Fascist, and leading spirit of the Committee to Frame a World Constitution at the University of Chicago.

Curtis, Lionel, Papers. Bodleian Library, Oxford University.
Papers of the founder of the Round Table Movement (imperial federation), its journal *The Round Table,* the Royal Institute of International Affairs (Chatham House), and the Institute of Pacific Relations. Author of *The Commonwealth of Nations* (1916) and *Civitas Dei* (1934–37). Prophet of a world commonwealth.

European Movement. Collège d'Europe Bibliothèque, B–8000 Bruges, Dyver 11, Les Pays–Bas.

Federal Union Archives. London School of Economics and Political Science Library.
Papers and reports of Federal Union (1938–63) and the Federal Union Research Institute (1940–43). Federal Union was a leading British public organization aiming to establish European, Atlantic, or world federation as a war aim in World War II. It had demonstrable influence on Churchill's offer of Anglo–French union to France on 16 June 1940. It was followed by the Federal Trust for Education and Research (1945–   ) and Wyndham Place

Trust (1963–   ).

Frances L. ("Jo") Josephy Papers. London School of Economics and Political Science.
Papers of a founder and long–term leader of Federal Union, particularly in favor of European federation. Active in the European Union of Federalists and in the European Movement. Liberal Party member.

Lothian Papers. Scottish Record Office, Edinburgh.
Records of Philip Kerr (Lord Lothian by 1930), the Round Table Movement, and Lothian's lectures, notably *Pacifism Is Not Enough—Nor Patriotism Either* (1935).

R.W.G. Mackay, M.P., Papers. London School of Economics and Political Science.
Personal papers of Australian–born M.P. and leader of Federal Union, the All-Party Parliamentary Group for European Federation, and the Parliamentary Group for the European Movement (1947–62). Especially active at the Congress of Europe (1948) and with the Constituent Assembly of the Council of Europe (European Political Community) (to 1951).

Union Européenne des Fédéralistes Archives.
c/o Movimento Federalista Europeo
Via Schina 26
I–10128 Torino, Italia;
Mr. Sergio Pistone, 39-11-472843.

World Federalist Youth Collection, 1946–68 (Copenhagen, Amsterdam) in personal possession of Dr. Finn Laursen, Odense.

World Movement for World Federal Government/World Association of World Federalists Archives, 1947–96.
These apparently have been lost, but the record can be pieced together from materials in American repositories (like the Regenstein Library at the University of Chicago), Canada, and the organization's journals, especially *World Federalist*.

See also those of Abbé Pierre (Henri Groués–Pierre, Paris), Guy Marchand (Paris), Hendrik Brugmans (Bruges), Per Haekkerup (Copenhagen), Hjalmar Riiser–Larsen (Oslo), Lord Boyd–Orr (Glasgow), Monica Wingate (London), Patrick Armstrong (London), Walter Lipgens (books and articles), and the Bahá'í World Center (Haifa, Israel).

Appendix E

Interviews

Richard A. Falk, Letter, June 1976; Boston, March 1994; March 1997
Elisabeth Mann Borgese, Greenwich Village, NY, 8 July 1977
Louis B. Sohn, Harvard, 26 August 1977; Washington, DC 19 June 1997
Arnold A. Offner, Boston, September 1977
Edith Wynner, New York, 26 August 1980, 6 January 1982
Stewart Ogilvy, Yonkers, NY, 21 October 1980
Steven Benedict, Annapolis, September 1980; New York, 25 November 1980
Harris Wofford, New York, 24 November 1980
Frances Fenner, Afton, NY, 30 November 1980
Max Habicht, Columbia Oral History, 1980
Virginia Lastayo Riorden, Williamstown, MA, 17 January 1981
Mildred ("Milly") Riorden Blake, Williamstown, MA, 18 January 1981
Shane Riorden, Williamstown, MA, 18 January 1981
Garry Davis, Letters, April 1981
Georgia Lloyd, Glencoe, IL, 3 May 1981
Charles A. Nelson, Annapolis, September 1981
Alan K. Henrikson, Medford, MA June 1983
Warren Kuehl, Washington, DC, 3 August 1983
Lawrence Wittner, Washington, DC, 3 August 1983
Charles DeBenedetti, Washington, DC, 3 August 1983
J. Malcomb ("Jock") Forbes, Cambridge, MA, April 1983, 1987–99
Winston Langley, Cambridge, MA, April 1983, 1987–99
Remfer Lee ("Jack") Whitehouse, Chicago, 27 December 1984
Cord Meyer Jr., Washington, DC, 10 April 1985
John Logue, Cambridge, MA, May 1985
Walter Hoffman, Washington, DC, 1985–90
Eric Cox, Washington, DC, 1985–88

Bennett Skewes–Cox, New York, May 1985
Ervin Laszlo, New York, 1985
Ira Straus, Washington, DC, 1985; Oxford, March 1990; Washington, June 1997
Ronald J. Glossop, Washington, DC, 1985–99
Lawrence Abbott, Northfield, MA, 1985
Finn Laursen, Woods Hole, MA, June 1985
Barbara Walker, New York, 1985, 1997
Shunsaku Kato, London, 1985; Washington, DC, 19 June 1997
Jean Francis Billion, London, 1985
Charlotte Waterlow, London, 1985
Lucy Law Webster, New York, 1985–87
Edward Rawson, Amsterdam, 1986
Donald Harrington, New York, 1986
Maurice Bertrand, New York, 1986
Hermod Lannung, New York, 1986
René Wadlow, Aosta, Italy, 1986
Philip Isely, Philadelphia, 1986
Stillman P. Williams, Northfield, MA, 1986
Donald Keys, New York, 1987
Andrea Bosco, New York, 1987
Norman Cousins, New York, December 1987
Jeanne Defrance (Mrs. Clarence Streit), Washington, DC, June 1988
Hanna Newcombe, Dundas, Ontario, September 1988
Ralph Levering, Manhattan College, New York, 19 October 1988
Kenneth Boulding, New York, 19 October 1988
Elizabeth Cady Fenn, Arlington, VA, January 1989
Lincoln Bloomfield, Washington, DC, 1989
Gary Ostrower, Williamsburg, VA, 15 June 1989
Lucio Levi, Oxford, 27 March 1990
Archibald A. Evans, Oxford, 27 March 1990
Alexandre Marc, Oxford, 27 March 1990
Guy Marchand, Oxford, 27 March 1990
Henry Usborne, Oxford, 27 March 1990
John Pinder, Oxford, 27 March 1990
John Roberts, Oxford, April 1990
Philip Morrison, Cambridge, MA, 1990
Saul Mendlovitz, Washington, DC, 1993
Francis S. Bourne, Washington, DC, 1993
E. Charles Chatfield, Boston, 1994
Erskine Childers, Boston, November 1995
Wesley T. Wooley, Washington, DC, 19–20 June 1997
Rolf P. Haegler, Washington, DC, 19 June 1997
Tiziana Stella, Washington, DC, 19–20 June 1997
Alan Cranston, San Francisco, 5 October 1999

Index to Volume 1